AUSTRALIAN

Signpost

MATHS

NSW

STAGE 2

4

Alan McSeveny Rachel McSeveny Diane McSeveny-Foster

Pearson Australia
(a division of Pearson Australia Group Pty Ltd)
459–471 Church St, Level 1, Building B, Richmond, Victoria, 3121
PO Box 23360, Melbourne, Victoria 8012
www.pearson.com.au

Publishers: Sophie Matta and Kerry Nagle
Project Manager: Michelle Thomas
Production Editor: Laura Rentsch
Development Editor: Rachel Elliott
Designer: Anne Donald
Proofreaders: Laura Rentsch and Ann M. Philpott
Rights & Permissions Editor: Alice McBroom
Cover Design: Jennifer Johnston
Cover Art: Michael Barter
Illustrator: Michael Barter
Publishing Services: Jit-Pin Chong
Printed in Singapore by Markono/02 (2025)

ISBN 978 0 6557 0905 3
Pearson Australia Group Pty Ltd ABN 40 004 245 943

Attributions
We would like to thank the following for permission to reproduce copyright material.

123rf.com: Mastak80, p. 145 (bricks); Shootingtheworld, p. 55 (stamps).

Shutterstock: Cattlaya Art, p. 94 (measuring vessels); Eastimages, p. 99 (scales); Tatiana Foxy, p. 156 (ruler); Gtranquillity, p. 98 (scale apple); Peter Gudella, p. 96 (bucket); Wu Hsoung, p. 113 (analogue stopwatch); Andrey Lobachev, p. 154 (coin); Nayoka, p. 26 (toy car); Ohukas, p. 96 (juice box); Mega Pixel, p. 153 (dice); Reji, p. 96 (spoon); Manfred Ruckszio, p. 91 (tree); Sandsun, p. 120 (pool); Sunnypicsoz/Geoff Childs, pp. 149, 153 (penny); Hong Vo, p. 09 (cheese); Ziviani, p. 113 (digital stopwatch).

Acknowledgement of Country
Pearson respects and honours Aboriginal and Torres Strait Islander Elders past, present and future. We acknowledge the stories, traditions and living cultures of the Traditional Custodians of the lands on which our company is located and where we conduct our business. Pearson is committed to honouring Australian Aboriginal and Torres Strait Islander peoples' unique cultural and spiritual relationships to the land, waters and seas and their rich contribution to society.

Aboriginal and Torres Strait Islander peoples are advised that this text may contain images, voices and names of deceased persons.

What is Australian Signpost Maths NSW?

Australian Signpost Maths NSW is a mathematics program providing direction and support for teaching and learning. The series covers the content and skills presented in the NSW Mathematics Syllabus K–6, 2024.

A Student Book and an online Teacher Resource are provided for Kindergarten (Early Stage 1).

For Years 1 to 6, a Student Book, an online Teacher Resource and a Mentals Book are provided for each year level. The online Teacher Resources provide a wealth of support for teachers.

The content has been carefully sequenced within each year level and across the K–6 series to take into account students' expected mathematical development. However, from the rich and varied material provided, teachers can develop individual learning programs to meet the needs of each student.

The Student Books are designed to support explicit teaching methods. Many group activities are provided in Activity, Investigation and Fun spots within the Student Books and the online Teacher Resource.

To maximise the benefits of the program, the Student Book, the online Teacher Resource and the Mentals Book should be used together.

Student Books

Mentals Books

Teacher Resource

Structure of Australian Signpost Maths NSW

In the Year 3 to 6 books, the worksheet pages cover all three elements: Number sense and algebra, Measurement and geometry, and Statistics and probability.

These are presented in five chapters:

- Number and algebra
- Operations and algebra
- Measurement
- Space
- Statistics and probability.

This gives teachers flexibility in programming that is more appropriate to Years 3 to 6.

The contents cross-reference allows teachers to quickly find the pages where each concept has been covered.

Within the program, explicit teaching, critical and creative thinking, language development and identification and treatment of weaknesses are given high priority.

Identification and addressing areas of need

Five progress tests are designed to identify each student's areas of need, and the follow-up program after each of the tests is designed to address these needs. A reference to the relevant worksheet page is given for each test question. A remediation record page is used to track the student's progress.

Parallel progress retests are provided for further testing after remediation has taken place.

These testing resources can be found in the online Teacher Resource.

Special features of Australian Signpost Maths NSW

- **The traffic light icons**
  These are found on the top right of each worksheet page in the Student Books. They allow students to assess their own progress and give feedback to the teacher.
  - ☐ **Green:** I found this work easy.
  - ☐ **Orange:** I found some work on the page difficult.
  - ☐ **Red:** I don't understand the work on this page.

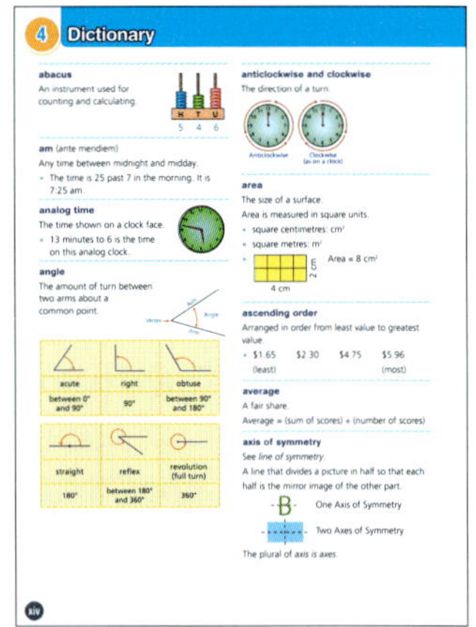

- **Dictionary**
  Terms used in the Student Book and terms that should be understood at this level are recorded here to provide a reference for students and teachers. This is found on pages xiv–xxiv of this book.

- **ID cards (Years 1 to 6)**
  These cards review the language of Mathematics by asking students to identify common terms, shapes and symbols. They are designed to be reused and are found in the online Teacher Resource and in the front of the Mentals Books.

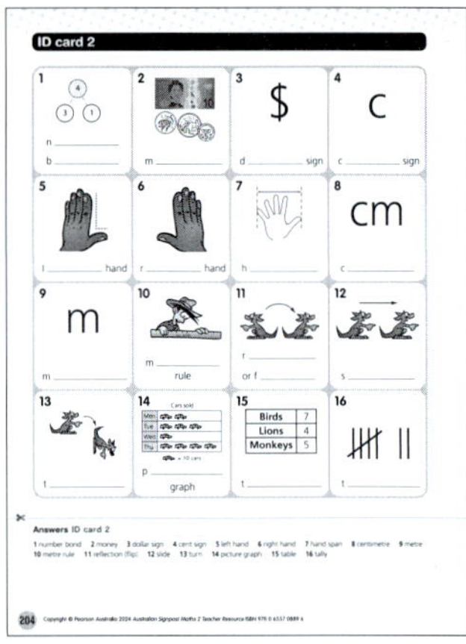

- **Progress tests**
  These allow the teacher to identify each student's strengths and needs. Cross-references for each question direct teachers and students to the pages where that work is introduced. Tables are provided to record the follow-up that takes place and parallel tests are provided for retesting. These tests can be found in the online Teacher Resource.

- **Year 3 Consolidation booklet**
  This booklet is found in the online Teacher Resource. It is designed to reinforce work completed in class and provides practice of important skills and addition and subtraction facts. The booklet can be used when there is limited supervision or when a student finishes classwork early.

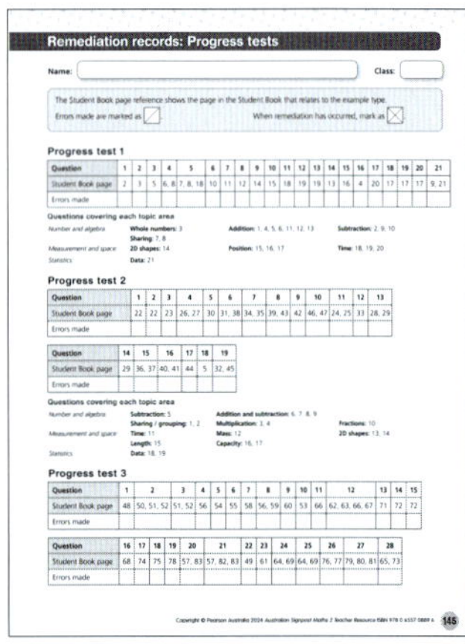

- **Answers**
  These are supplied in the Student Book and online Teacher Resource.

- **Blackline masters (BLM)**
  References are made to the blackline masters in the teaching suggestions provided for each student work page in the online Teacher Resource.

- **Differentiation**
  Each student work page has a Teacher Resource page to support it. Cross-references direct the teacher to pages where the concept is introduced and developed. These references may be from the Student Book for the previous year, the current year or the next year.

  The Teacher Resource support pages provide additional learning activities for students who need remediation or extension activities. The Blackline Masters provide activities to support students of various learning abilities.

- **Cartoons**
  Cartoons are used to motivate and instruct.

- **Extra support pages**
  Addition and subtraction facts, addition strategies, algorithms, measurement and space are reinforced.

Australian Signpost Maths NSW icons

Signpost icons are used throughout the book as cues to the essential nature of exercises and activities, and as a guide to ways of engaging with them. These icons often indicate alternative or more concrete approaches to dealing with concepts.

This icon highlights **important rules and concepts** occurring throughout the book. It often appears with worked examples.

Activities provide **applications and enrichment**. These activities usually involve the use of concrete materials and partner or group work.

These enjoyable activities are used to **motivate and involve** students in mathematical pursuits. They usually involve games and puzzles.

Investigations allow students to **explore and discover** maths concepts.

These activities involve the use of computers or other technology.

Structure of the New South Wales Mathematics K-6

The NSW Mathematics Syllabus content is presented in three strands:

1 Number and algebra   2 Measurement and space   3 Statistics and probability
Working mathematically pervades each of these strands.

Textbook structure
Within the Year 3 **Contents** (pages vi to xi), we show related pages using these categories:

Chapter 1: Number and algebra
- Counting number • Place value • Rounding • Fractions • Patterns

Chapter 2: Operations and algebra
- Addition • Subtraction • Multiplication • Division • Mental strategies • Money • Problem solving

Chapter 3: Measurement
- Length • Area • Volume • Capacity • Mass • Telling the time • Duration • Problem solving

Chapter 4: Space
- 2D space • Angles, lines • Symmetry, turning • 3D space • Position, directions

Chapter 5: Statistics and Probability
- Collecting data • Surveys • Creating data displays • Analysing data displays
- Chance language • Chance experiments

The **Cross-reference** (pages xii and xiii) give a clear indication of where syllabus content is addressed.
The **Suggested program** is provided in the Contents pages and aligns with the Mentals Book, and Progress tests and Retests.
Each Mentals unit reviews the previous 2 weeks' content from the Student Book suggested program.

Contents and syllabus overview

Contents cross-reference xii
Dictionary xiv
Chapter 1 Number and algebra 1
Chapter 2 Operations and algebra 24
Chapter 3 Measurement 83
Chapter 4 Space 121
Chapter 5 Statistics and probability 148
Extra support 164
Answers 183

Suggested program: The Teacher Resource has a program that aligns with the Mentals Book, e.g. Mentals Book, Unit 9 covers work taught in Weeks 7 and 8 of this book

Number and algebra			Content							Suggested program	
Page	Unit	Title		Counting, number	Place value	Rounding	Fractions	Decimals	Patterns, algebra		
1	1:01	Numbers to 10 000		●	●					Week 3	Term 1
2	1:02	Numbers to 100 000		●	●						
3	1:03	Rounding off			●	●					
4	1:04	Partitioning large numbers		●	●						
5	1:05	Fractions					●			Week 4	
6	1:06	Comparing fractions					●				
7	1:07	Fractions beyond 1					●			Week 6	
8	1:08	Fractions beyond 1					●				
9	1:09	Numbers to 1 000 000		●	●					Week 8	
10	1:10	Numbers to 1 000 000		●	●						
11	1:11	Rounding off				●				Week 9	
12	1:12	Equivalent fractions					●				
13	1:13	Equivalent fractions					●				
14	1:14	Comparing fractions					●		●	Week 11	Term 2
15	1:15	Tenths and fifths			●		●	●			
16	1:16	Place value using tenths					●	●			
17	1:17	Decimals					●	●		Week 12	
18	1:18	Decimals			●		●	●			
19	1:19	Decimals and place value			●		●	●			
20	1:20	Comparing decimals						●		Week 13	
21	1:21	Place value to hundredths			●			●			
22	1:22	Place value to hundredths			●			●		Week 14	
23	1:23	Reading and writing decimals			●			●			

- The teacher will decide when testing occurs. The Progress Tests are found in the online Teacher Resource.
- The first two units of the Mentals Book review the previous year and could be completed in Weeks 1 and 2.

Operations and algebra

Page	Unit	Title	Addition	Subtraction	Multiplication	Division	Mental strategies	Number patterns	Money	Problem solving	Suggested program	Term
24	2:01	Number patterns						●			Week 2	Term 1
25	2:02	Multiplication tables revision			●						Week 3	
26	2:03	× 4 tables			●						Week 5	
27	2:04	Times tables review			●							
28	2:05	Addition, no trading	●						●		Week 7	
29	2:06	Addition and subtraction, no trading	●						●	●		
30	2:07	Addition to 99 with trading	●						●	●	Week 8	
31	2:08	Addition to 99 with trading	●						●	●		
32	2:09	Jump strategy, +	●				●				Week 11	Term 2
33	2:10	Jump strategy, –		●			●					
34	2:11	× 8 tables			●						Week 12	
35	2:12	× 8 tables			●							
36	2:13	Addition, trading 2 tens	●								Week 15	
37	2:14	Addition involving hundreds	●							●		
38	2:15	Addition problems to 99	●							●		
39	2:16	× 3, × 6 tables			●		●				Week 16	
40	2:17	× 3 and × 6 tables			●							
41	2:18	Subtraction with trading		●						●	Week 17	
42	2:19	Subtracting from tens		●					●	●		
43	2:20	Subtracting with trading		●					●			
44	2:21	× 9 tables			●		●				Week 18	
45	2:22	× 9 tables			●							
46	2:23	Addition to 999	●								Week 19	
47	2:24	Addition to 999	●									
48	2:25	Writing algorithms	●							●		
49	2:26	What's the rule?						●			Week 21	Term 3
50	2:27	Number patterns						●				
51	2:28	× 7 tables			●						Week 22	
52	2:29	× 7 tables			●							
53	2:30	Multiplication tables review			●							
54	2:31	Subtraction without trading to 999		●							Week 23	
55	2:32	Subtraction with trading to 999		●								
56	2:33	Subtraction with trading to 999		●							Week 24	
57	2:34	Subtraction with 2 trades to 999		●								
58	2:35	Mental strategies, +	●				●				Week 25	
59	2:36	Mental strategies, + and –	●	●			●					
60	2:37	Subtraction from hundreds		●						●	Week 26	
61	2:38	Subtraction from hundreds strategy		●					●	●		
62	2:39	Division as repeated subtraction				●				●	Week 27	
63	2:40	Understanding division				●						
64	2:41	Division facts				●				●	Week 28	
65	2:42	Division facts				●						
66	2:43	Odd and even numbers	●	●							Week 29	
67	2:44	Odd and even	●	●	●	●						
68	2:45	Division using a grid				●					Week 30	
69	2:46	× and ÷ (by 2, 4, 8)				●	●					

Content

Suggested program The Teacher Resource has a program that aligns with the Mentals Book, e.g. Mentals Book, Unit 9 covers work taught in Weeks 7 and 8 of this book.

- The teacher will decide when testing occurs. The Progress Tests and Retests are found in the online Teacher Resource.

Operations and algebra

Suggested program

The Teacher Resource has a program that aligns with the Mentals Book, e.g. Mentals Book, Unit 9 covers work taught in Weeks 7 and 8 of this book.

Page	Unit	Title	Content	Addition	Subtraction	Multiplication	Division	Mental strategies	Number patterns	Money	Problem solving	Suggested program (Term 4)
70	2:47	Mental strategies, × and ÷				●	●	●				Week 31
71	2:48	Working with numbers				●	●	●			●	
72	2:49	× and ÷ tables (by 3, 6, 9)				●	●					Week 32
73	2:50	Division facts				●	●					
74	2:51	Money		●						●		Week 33
75	2:52	Rounding off money		●						●		
76	2:53	Counting change		●						●		
77	2:54	Multiplying by 10, 100, 1000				●		●				Week 34
78	2:55	Dividing by 10, 100, 1000					●	●				
79	2:56	Linking ÷ and ×				●	●	●				Week 35
80	2:57	Missing number strategies		●	●	●	●	●				
81	2:58	Partitioning, + and –		●	●			●				Week 36
82	2:59	Mental strategies, + and –		●	●			●				

Suggested program

The Teacher Resource has a program that aligns with the Mentals Book, e.g. Mentals Book, Unit 9 covers work taught in Weeks 7 and 8 of this book.

Measurement			Content									Suggested program	
Page	Unit	Title		Length	Area	Volume	Capacity	Mass	Telling the time	Duration	Problem solving		
83	3:01	Analog time							●	●		Week 2	Term 1
84	3:02	Analog and digital time							●			Week 4	
85	3:03	Analog and digital time							●	●			
86	3:04	Analog and digital time							●	●	●		
87	3:05	Perimeter							●			Week 5	
88	3:06	Centimetres and millimetres		●									
89	3:07	Using millimetres		●									
90	3:08	The square centimetre			●							Week 6	
91	3:09	The square centimetre			●								
92	3:10	The square centimetre			●								
93	3:11	Using measurement scales		●				●				Week 10	
94	3:12	The millilitre					●					Week 16	Term 2
95	3:13	Using millilitres					●						
96	3:14	Using millilitres					●						
97	3:15	Using L and mL					●					Week 20	
98	3:16	Using grams						●				Week 22	Term 3
99	3:17	Measuring mass						●					
100	3:18	Telling the time							●			Week 23	
101	3:19	Time							●	●	●		
102	3:20	am and pm time							●	●	●		
103	3:21	Converting lengths		●								Week 24	
104	3:22	Length		●									
105	3:23	Length		●									
106	3:24	The square metre			●							Week 25	
107	3:25	The area of a triangle			●								
108	3:26	The area of a triangle			●						●		
109	3:27	Using grams						●				Week 28	
110	3:28	Measuring mass						●			●		
111	3:29	Using am and pm time								●		Week 29	
112	3:30	Seconds							●	●			
113	3:31	The stopwatch							●	●			
114	3:32	Comparing lengths		●								Week 31	Term 4
115	3:33	Using mm when building		●									
116	3:34	Length on a map		●									
117	3:35	Problem solving		●			●	●		●	●	Week 36	
118	3:36	Problem solving		●	●		●	●		●	●		
119	3:37	Calculating volume				●						Week 37	
120	3:38	Personal benchmarks		●	●	●	●	●					

• The teacher will decide when testing occurs. The Progress Tests and Retests are found in the online Teacher Resource.

Space

Page	Unit	Title	Content	2D space	Angles, lines	Symmetry, turning	3D objects	Position, directions	Suggested program See the Teacher Resource for more information. This program aligns with the Mentals Book, e.g. Mentals Book, Unit 9 covers work taught in Weeks 7 and 8 of this book.	
121	4:01	Flip, slide and turn				●			Week 7	Term 1
122	4:02	Angles and 2D shapes		●	●					
123	4:03	Comparing angles			●					
124	4:04	3D objects					●		Week 13	Term 2
125	4:05	Prisms and pyramids					●			
126	4:06	Faces of prisms and pyramids					●		Week 14	
127	4:07	Prisms and pyramids					●			
128	4:08	Drawing angles			●				Week 17	
129	4:09	Angles as quarter and half turns			●	●				
130	4:10	Investigating polygons		●		●			Week 18	
131	4:11	Visualising shapes		●						
132	4:12	Maps						●	Week 19	
133	4:13	Creating a map						●		
134	4:14	Cones, cylinders and spheres					●		Week 21	Term 3
135	4:15	Views of 3D objects					●			
136	4:16	Compass directions						●	Week 26	
137	4:17	Compass directions						●		
138	4:18	Describing position						●	Week 27	
139	4:19	Using position in maps						●		
140	4:20	Visualising shapes		●		●			Week 32	Term 4
141	4:21	Acute and obtuse angles			●					
142	4:22	Angles of any size			●					
143	4:23	Horizontal and vertical			●				Week 34	
144	4:24	Tessellating designs		●		●				
145	4:25	Tessellations		●						
146	4:26	Spreadsheets						●	Week 35	
147	4:27	Drawing views of objects					●		Week 36	

- The teacher will decide when testing occurs. The Progress Tests are found in the online Teacher Resource.

Statistics and probability

Page	Unit	Title	Content	Collecting data	Surveys	Creating data displays	Analysing data displays	Chance language	Chance experiments	Suggested program	
148	5:01	Drawing tables		●		●				Week 8	Term 1
149	5:02	Chance						●	●	Week 9	
150	5:03	Chance						●	●		
151	5:04	Using graphs				●	●			Week 15	Term 2
152	5:05	Reading graphs					●				
153	5:06	Ordering events						●	●	Week 20	
154	5:07	Chance used in games						●	●		
155	5:08	Tally marks		●	●	●	●			Week 26	Term 3
156	5:09	Collecting information		●		●	●			Week 27	
157	5:10	Using spinners						●	●	Week 33	Term 4
158	5:11	Unequal outcomes						●	●		
159	5:12	Surveys		●	●	●				Week 35	
160	5:13	Graphing data		●		●	●			Week 36	
161	5:14	Chance experiments						●	●	Week 37	
162	5:15	Carry out your own survey						●	●		
163	5:16	Chance experiments						●			

Suggested program
See the Teacher Resource for more information. This program aligns with the Mentals Book, e.g. Mentals Book, Unit 9 covers work taught in Weeks 7 and 8 of this book.

Extra support pages

164	1 Addition and subtraction facts	2 Building to the next 10	3 Tangrams
167	4 Flip, slide turn	5 Addition of money	6 Addition to 9999
170	7 Addition to 9999	8 Addition to 999 999	9 Subtraction of money
173	10 Subtraction with trading to 9999	11 Four-digit subtraction from 1000s	12 Subtraction to 999 999
176	13 The calendar	14 The calendar	15 Timelines
179	16 Comparing decimal measurements	17 Temperature	18 Recording temperature
182	19 Fraction patterns		

- The teacher will decide when testing occurs. The Progress Tests and Retests are found in the online Teacher Resource.

Suggested Program	Term 1	Term 2	Term 3	Term 4
Number and algebra	1:01 - 1:13	1:14 - 1:23	-	-
Operations and algebra	2:01 - 2:08	2:09 - 2:25	2:26 - 2:46	2:47 - 2:59
Measurement	3:01 - 3:11	3:12 - 3:15	3:16 - 3:31	3:32 - 3:38
Space	4:01 - 4:03	4:04 - 4:13	4:14 - 4:19	4:20 - 4:27
Statistics and probability	5:01 - 5:03	5:04 - 5:07	5:08 - 5:09	5:10 - 5:16
Total number of pages:	39	46	45	34

- See the Teacher Resource for a more detailed suggested program.
- The suggested program aligns with the Mentals book, Progress Tests and Retests.

Contents cross-reference

Number and algebra

1	Whole numbers	Pages
	Counting, ordering numbers	1, 4, 9, 10, 11, 66, 67
	Place value	1, 2, 3, 4, 9, 10, 11, 16, 19, 21, 22, 23, 77, 78
	Fractions	5, 6, 7, 8, 12, 13, 14, 15, 16, 17, 18, 19, 20, 50, 182
	Decimals	15, 16, 17, 18, 19, 20, 21, 22, 23, 179
	Rounding numbers	3, 11, 37, 46, 75
2	**Addition and subtraction**	**Pages**
	Addition	28, 29, 30, 31, 32, 36, 37, 38, 46, 47, 48, 58, 59, 67, 74, 75, 76, 80, 81, 82, 164, 165, 168, 169, 170, 171
	Subtraction / difference	29, 33, 41, 42, 43, 54, 55, 56, 57, 59, 60, 61, 63, 67, 80, 81, 82, 164, 172, 173, 174, 175
	Mental strategies (+ and –)	32, 33, 58, 59, 62, 80, 81, 82, 165
	Algorithm strategy (+ and –)	28, 29, 31, 36, 35, 41, 42, 43, 46, 47, 48, 54, 55, 56, 57, 60, 61, 168, 169, 170, 171, 173, 174, 175
	Problem solving (+ and –)	29, 30, 31, 38, 41, 42, 48, 54, 60, 61, 168, 170, 173, 174, 175
	Money	28, 29, 30, 31, 36, 42, 43, 74, 75, 76, 168, 169, 170, 172, 173
3	**Multiplication and division**	**Pages**
	Multiplication	25, 26, 27, 34, 35, 39, 40, 44, 45, 51, 52, 53, 67, 69, 70, 71, 72, 76, 80
	Division (sharing and grouping)	62, 63, 64, 65, 67, 68, 69, 70, 72, 73, 78, 79, 80
	Multiplication and division (linking)	64, 65, 69, 72, 73, 78, 79, 80
	Doubling and halving	26, 27, 34, 35, 40, 70, 71
	Mental strategies (× and ÷)	64, 65, 69, 70, 71
	Problem solving (× and ÷)	62, 63, 64, 71
4	**Algebra**	**Pages**
	Patterns	7, 8, 12, 13, 14, 15, 24, 34, 39, 44, 49, 50, 182
	Addition and subtraction facts to 20	164
	Multiplication and division facts (× 2, × 10, 2 ×, ÷ 2)	25, 26, 27, 34, 35, 39, 40, 44, 45, 51, 52, 53, 68, 72
5	**Tools used in problems**	**Pages**
	Number lines (and bead strings)	6, 7, 11, 12, 14, 15, 16, 17, 20, 21, 28, 31, 33, 35, 40, 45, 52, 63, 65, 82

Measurement and space

1	Measurement	Pages
	Length	87, 88, 89, 93, 103, 104, 105, 114, 115, 116, 117, 118, 120
	Area	90, 91, 92, 106, 107, 108, 118, 120
	Capacity and volume	94, 95, 96, 97, 117, 118, 119, 120
	Mass (weight)	93, 98, 99, 109, 110, 117, 120
	Temperature	180, 181, 117, 120
	Time (duration)	83, 85, 86, 101, 102, 111, 112, 113, 117, 118, 176, 177, 179,
	Clocks	83, 84, 85, 86, 100, 101, 102, 112, 113
	Problem solving with measurement	117, 118
	Estimation of measurements	87, 88, 89, 90, 91, 92, 104, 106, 113
2	**Space**	**Pages**
	2D shapes	121, 122, 130, 131, 138, 140, 143, 166
	Angles, parallel and perpendicular lines	122, 123, 128, 129, 130, 141, 142, 143
	Symmetry, flip, slide, turn, tessellations	121, 122, 129, 130, 140, 144, 145, 167
	3D objects	124, 125, 126, 127, 134, 135, 138, 147
	Position, maps	132, 133, 136, 137, 138, 139, 146
	Directions, giving directions	132, 136, 137

Statistics and probability

1	Data	Pages
	Collecting data and recording data	148, 151, 155, 156, 159, 160, 162, 180
	Analysing data displays	151, 152, 155, 156, 160, 162, 171
2	**Chance**	**Pages**
	Chance and the language of chance	149, 150, 153, 154, 157, 158, 161, 163
	Chance experiments	149, 150, 153, 154, 157, 158, 161, 163

4 Dictionary

abacus

An instrument used for counting and calculating.

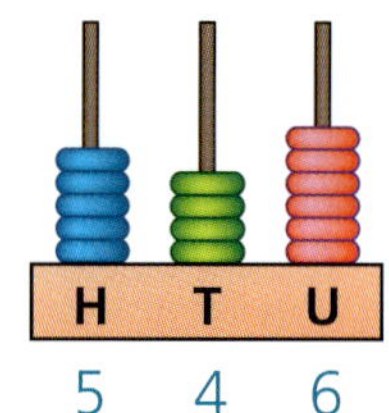

am (ante meridiem)

Any time between midnight and midday.

- The time is 25 past 7 in the morning. It is 7:25 am.

analog time

The time shown on a clock face.

- 13 minutes to 6 is the time on this analog clock.

angle

The amount of turn between two arms about a common point.

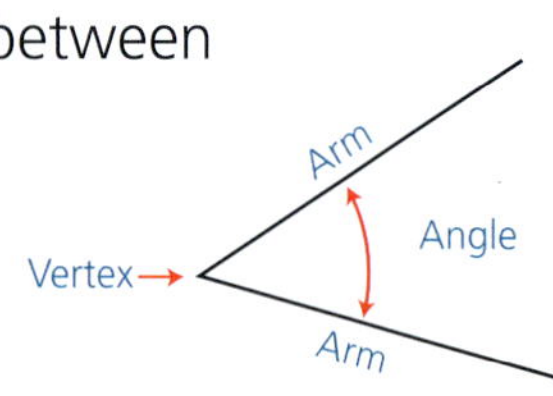

acute	right	obtuse
between 0° and 90°	90°	between 90° and 180°

straight	reflex	revolution (full turn)
180°	between 180° and 360°	360°

anticlockwise and clockwise

The direction of a turn.

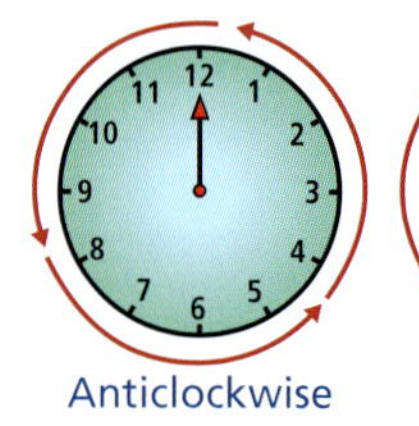
Anticlockwise

Clockwise (as on a clock)

area

The size of a surface.

Area is measured in square units.

- square centimetres: cm^2
- square metres: m^2

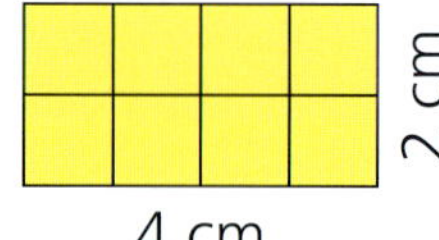

Area = 8 cm^2

ascending order

Arranged in order from least value to greatest value.

- $1.65 (least) $2.30 $4.75 $5.96 (most)

average

A fair share.

Average = (sum of scores) ÷ (number of scores)

axis of symmetry

A line that divides a picture in half so that each half is the mirror image of the other part.

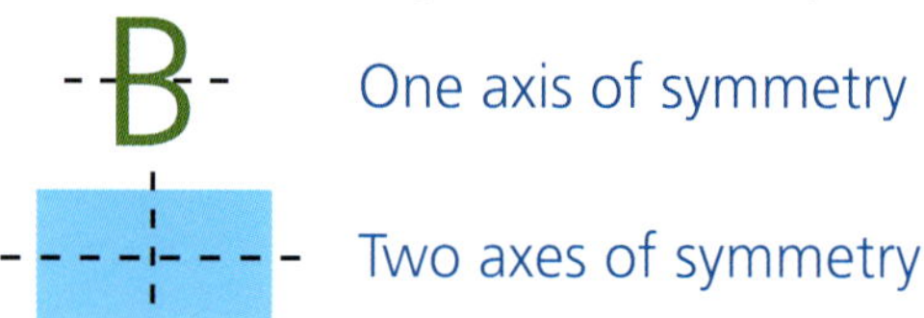

The plural of *axis* is *axes*.

See also *line of symmetry*.

billion

A thousand millions.

- 1 000 000 000

capacity

The amount that a container can hold.

- The capacity of this juice bottle is 250 ml.

centimetre (cm)

A unit of length equal to one hundredth of a metre.

- 100 cm = 1 m, 1 cm = 10 mm

chance

The chance (or probability) of something happening is its likelihood of happening.

- If you toss a coin, there is an even chance of tossing a head.

See also *probability*.

compass directions

The needle of a compass points north (N) .

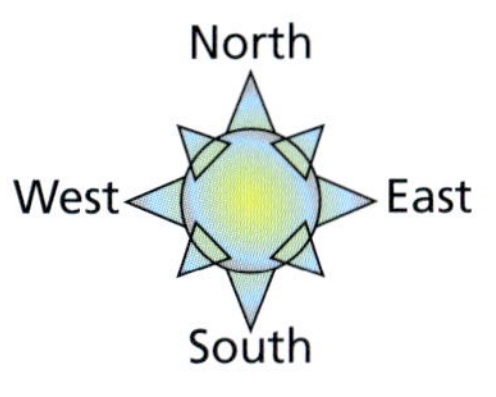

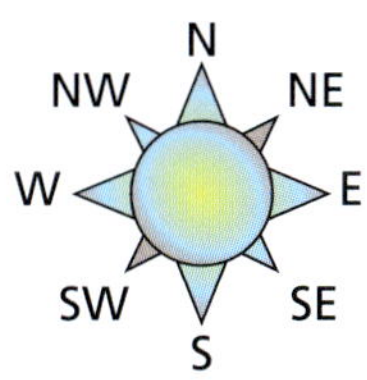

cone

A three-dimensional object with a circular base that tapers to a point.

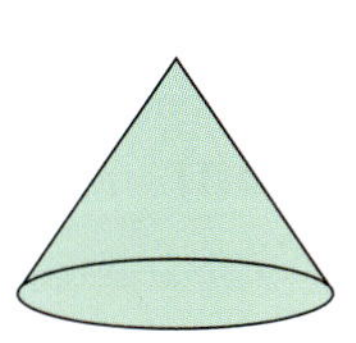

coordinates

Pairs of letters or numbers used to show position on a grid.

- This position is D3 or (D, 3).

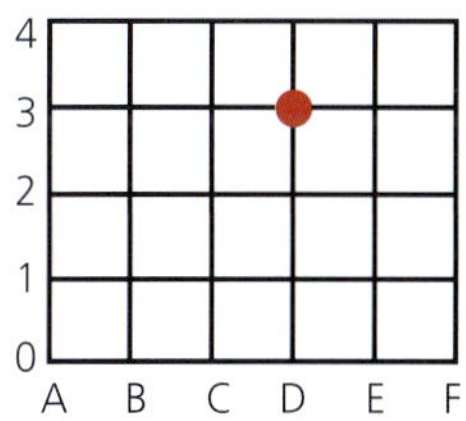

cross-section

A face that is exposed when a 3D object is cut through.

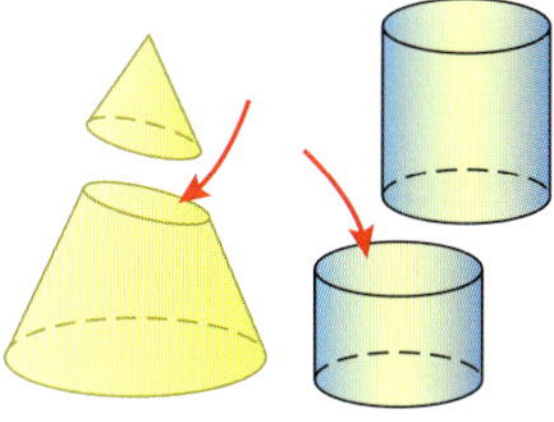

cube

A three-dimensional object that has six equal square faces, eight vertices and twelve equal edges.

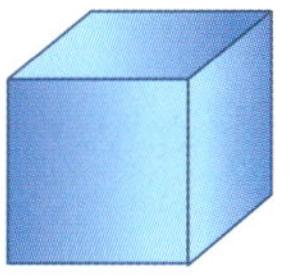
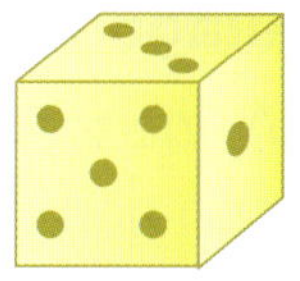

cubic centimetre (cm³)

A unit of volume equal to the volume of a cube of side length 1 cm.

cubic metre (m³)

A unit of volume equal to the volume of a cube of side length 1 m.

cylinder

A three-dimensional object with two equal circular faces and one curved surface.

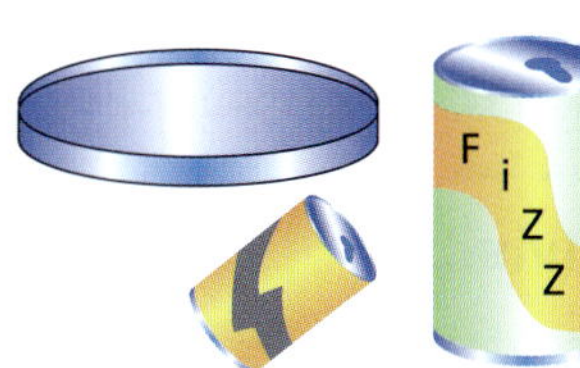

decimal notation

The decimal point separates the whole number part from the fraction part.

7·5

↑ decimal point

0·7 means 7 tenths.

6·5 means 6 ones and 5 tenths.

3·07 means 3 ones and 7 hundredths.

denominator

The bottom number of a fraction. It tells the number of equal parts there are in the whole.

Numerator ⟶ 7
Denominator ⟶ 8

$\frac{7}{8}$

descending order

Arranged in order from greatest value to least value.

$5.96 (most)	$4.75	$2.30	$1.65 (least)

diagonal

A line that joins any two non-adjacent corners of a polygon.

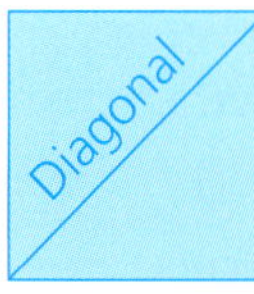

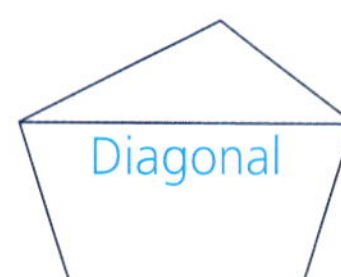

digital time

Time expressed using digits.

- This digital clock shows 24 minutes past 10.

digits

Symbols used to write a number.

- 6 Six is a 1-digit number.
- 47 Forty-seven is a 2-digit number.

divisible

To have no remainder when divided.

- 30 is divisible by 3.

division (÷)

Breaking up groups into equal parts.

- 10 ÷ 5

  - How much will each receive if you share between 2?
  - How many groups of 2 can be made?

edge

Two faces of a 3D object meet at an edge.

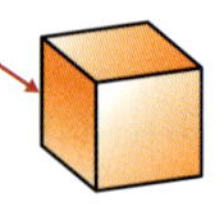

equivalent fractions

These are equal. They refer to the same part of the whole.

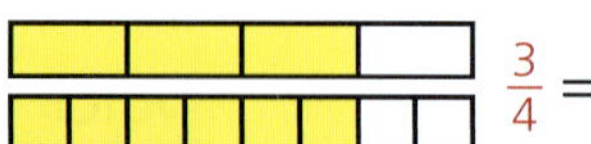

$\frac{3}{4} = \frac{6}{8}$

estimate (estimation)

A good guess.

even number

Any number that is a multiple of two and can be grouped in twos. They end in 0, 2, 4, 6 or 8.

- 16, 300, 4394

The other counting numbers are **odd**.

expanded notation

A way of writing numerals to show the place value of each digit.

- 137 = (1 × 100) + (3 × 10) + 7

face

A flat surface of a three-dimensional object that is bounded by only straight sides.

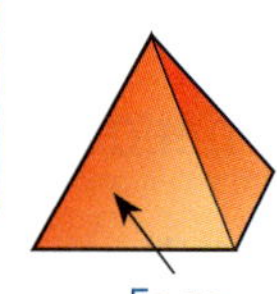

factor

A factor of a number divides the number exactly, leaving no remainder.

- The factors of 12 are 1, 12, 2, 6, 3 and 4 .

flip (reflection)

To turn over.

- A mirror image is made.

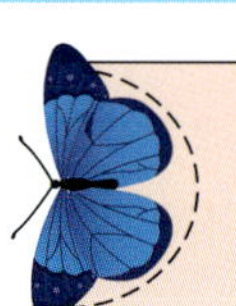

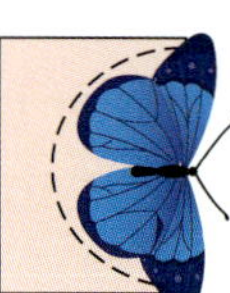

fraction

A part of a whole or group.

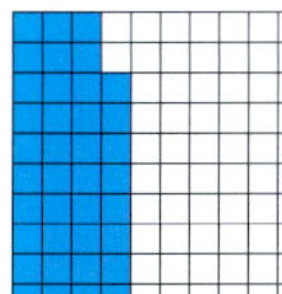

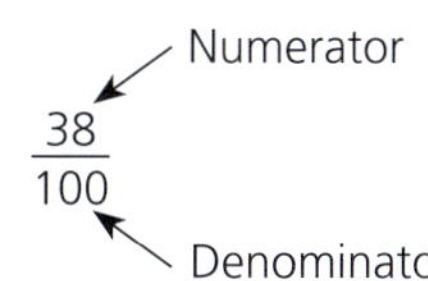

Fractions can be shown on a number line.

Equivalent fractions

Fractions of equal size.

- $\frac{1}{2} = \frac{5}{10} = \frac{7}{14} = \ldots$

Improper fraction

A fraction which has a numerator that is bigger than the denominator.

- $\frac{9}{8}$

Mixed numerals

A numeral that has a whole number part and a fraction part.

- $1\frac{2}{3}$

gram (g)

A unit of mass.

- 1 kilogram = 1000 grams, 1 kg = 1000 g

graphs

- Bar graph

  A graph which uses horizontal bars to compare the size of groups.

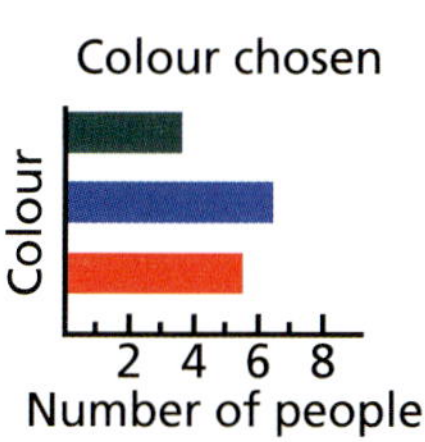

- Column graph

  Groups are compared using the lengths of columns or bars.
  The graph can be vertical or horizontal.
  A bar graph is a type of column graph.

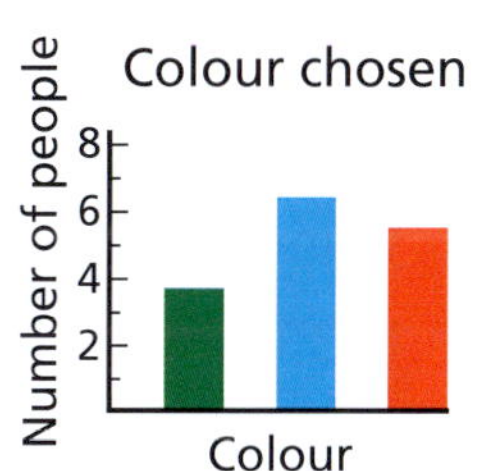

- Divided bar graph

  A bar is divided to show the make-up of the data.

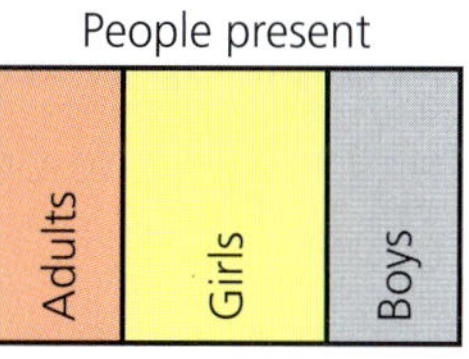

- Dot plot

  A graph which uses dots to compare the size of groups.

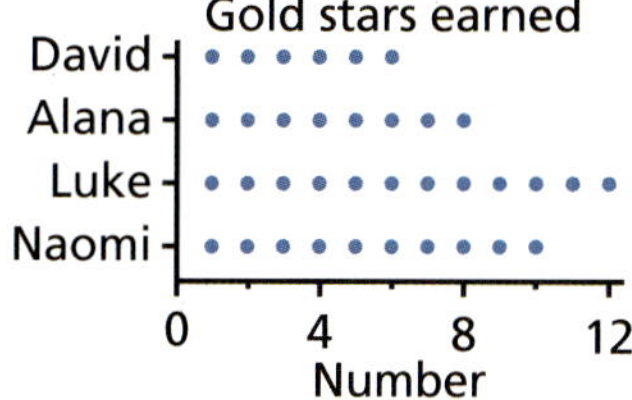

- Line graph

  A continuous line shows the connection between variables.

- Picture graph

  A picture is used as a unit to show how many.

- Sector graph

  A circle is cut into sectors to show the parts of a whole.

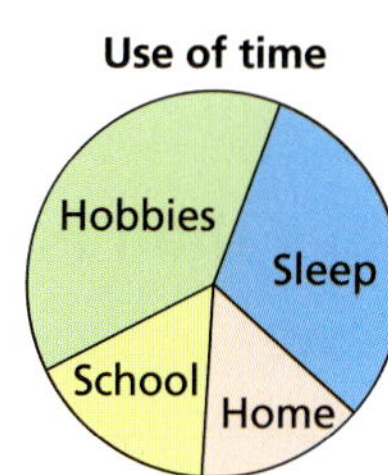

greater than (>)

A way of showing that a number is larger than another number.

- 7 > 3 means '7 is greater than 3'.

See also *less than* (<).

horizontal

- Parallel to the horizon
- Level or flat.
- Any direction at right angles to the vertical.

inverse operations

Adding 8 is the opposite (the inverse) of subtracting 8.

- 100 + 8 – 8 = 100

Multiplying by 2 is the opposite (the inverse) of dividing by 2.

- 4 × 2 ÷ 2 = 4

jump strategy

Adding or subtracting numbers, jumping by hundreds, tens and ones.

- 52 – 14 = 38

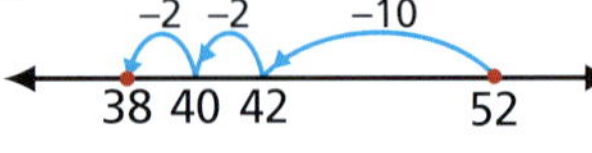

kilo (k)

Kilo means 1000.

kilogram (kg)

The basic unit of mass, equal to 1000 grams.

- 1 kg = 1000 g

kilometre (km)

A unit of length equal to one thousand metres.

- 1 km = 1000 m

less than (<)

A way of showing that a number is smaller than another number.

- 3 < 7 means '3 is less than 7'.

See also *greater than* (>).

line of symmetry

A line that divides something in half so that each half is a mirror image of the other part.

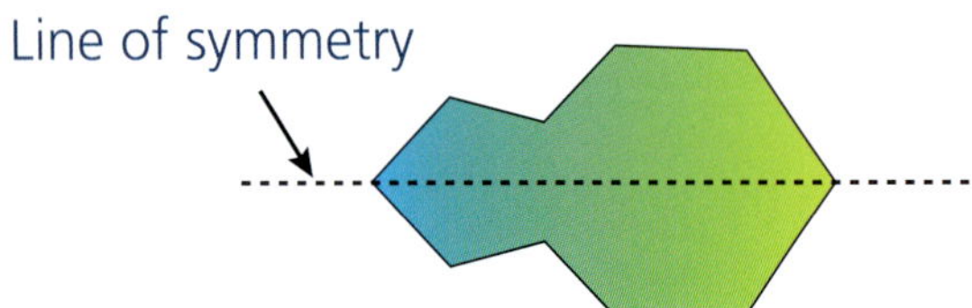

litre (L)

A unit of capacity (or volume) used for the measurement of liquids.

- 1 L = 1000 mL

map or plan

A picture of an area viewed from above.

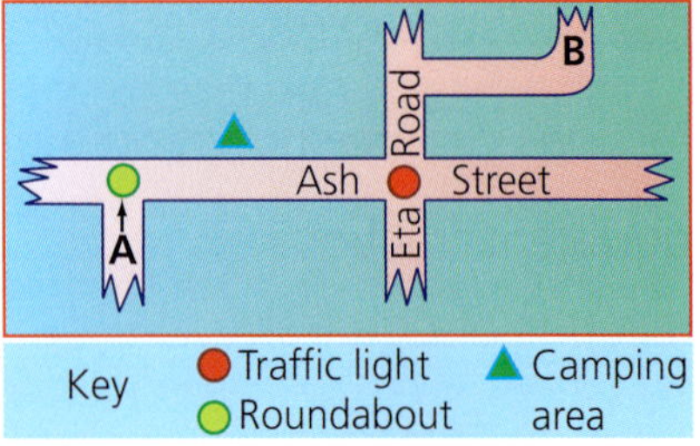

mass

The amount of matter in an object, a measure of how heavy something is.

mean

The arithmetic average.

- $\text{mean} = \dfrac{\text{sum of scores}}{\text{number of scores}}$

See also *average*.

metre (m)

The basic unit of length, equal to 100 centimetres.

- 1 m = 100 cm

millilitre (mL)

A unit of capacity (or volume) equal to one thousandth of a litre.

- 1000 mL = 1 L

millimetre (mm)

A unit of length equal to one tenth of a centimetre, or one thousandth of a metre.

- 10 mm = 1 cm
- 1000 mm = 1 m

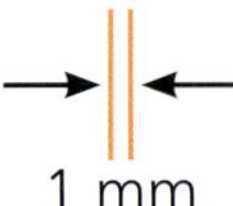

million

A thousand thousands

- 1 000 000

mixed number (or mixed numeral)

A numeral that has a whole number part and a fraction part.

- $4\frac{1}{8}$

net

A flat shape that can be folded to make a three-dimensional object.

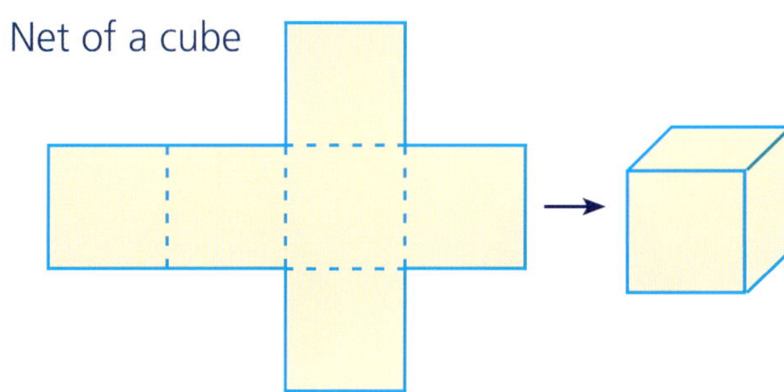

object

The term used to describe a three-dimensional shape.

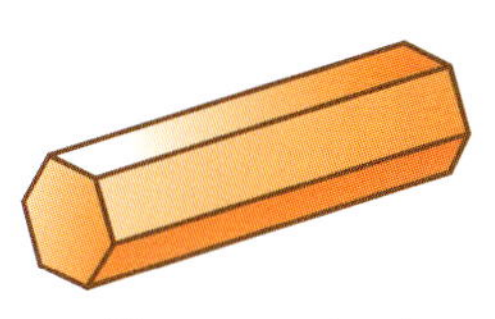

Hexagonal prism

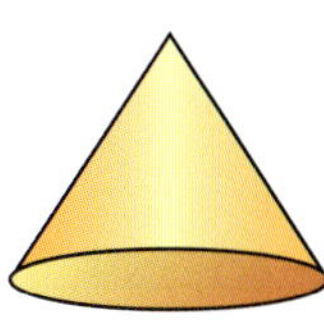

Cone

octagon

A polygon with eight sides.

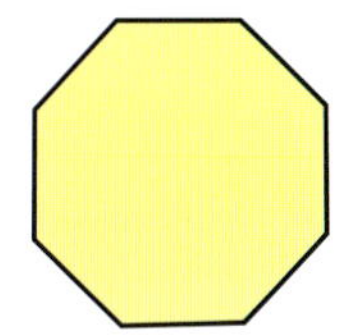

Regular octagon

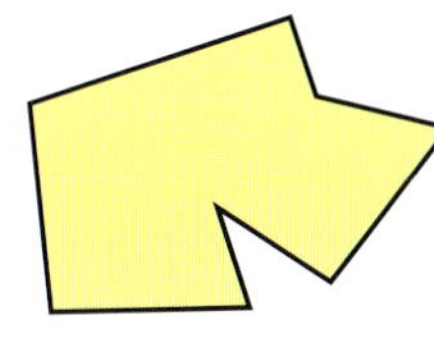

Irregular octagon

See also *polygon*.

parallel lines

Straight lines on the same flat surface that do not meet.

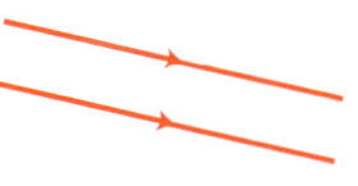

parallelogram

A shape with 4 sides such that the pairs of opposite sides are parallel and equal.

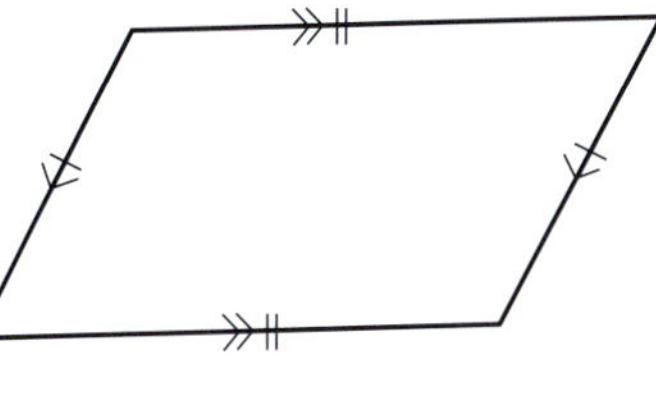

pentagon

A polygon with five sides.

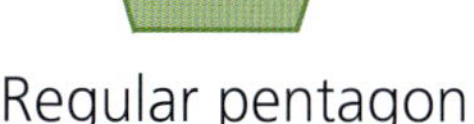

Regular pentagon

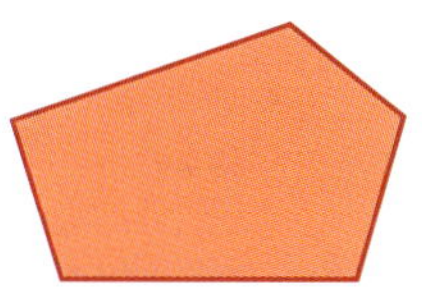

Irregular pentagon

See also *polygon*.

per cent (%)

Out of one hundred.

- $\frac{37}{100} = 0{\cdot}37 = 37\%$ or 37 per cent

perimeter

The distance around the outside of a shape; the boundary.

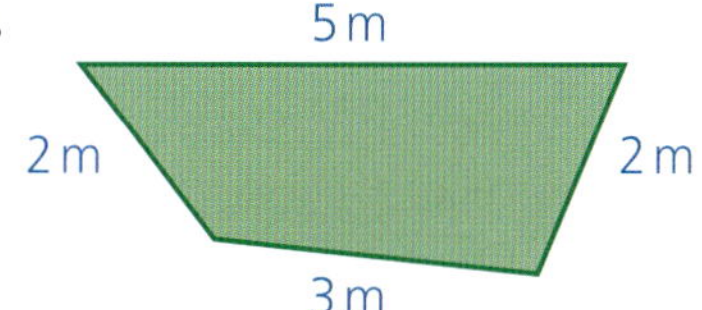

- Perimeter = 2 m + 3 m + 2 m + 5 m
  = 12 m

perpendicular lines

Lines that meet at right angles.

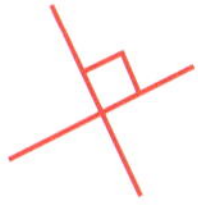

place value

The column value of a digit.

- 396 =

Hundreds	Tens	Ones
3	9	6

pm (post meridiem)

Any time between midday and midnight.

- The time is 20 past 1 in the afternoon. It is 1:20 pm.

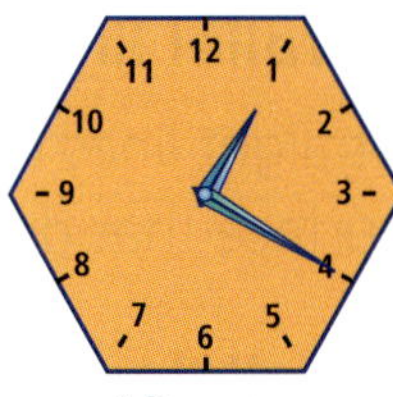

Afternoon

polygon

A two-dimensional shape with three or more straight sides, such as a triangle, quadrilateral, pentagon etc.

prism

A three-dimensional object with a uniform cross-section. The ends are identical shapes and all other faces are rectangles. Prisms are named by the shape of their ends.

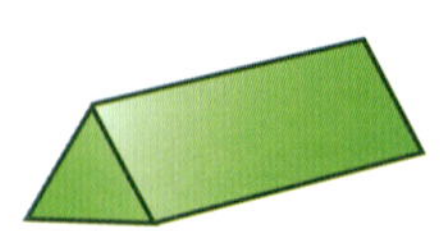

Triangular prism

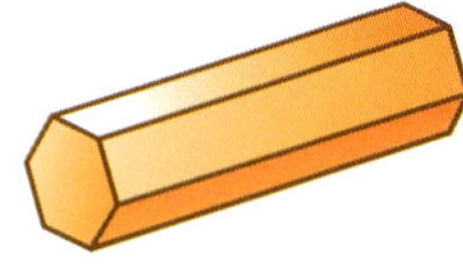

Hexagonal prism

probability

The probability (or chance) of something happening is its likelihood of happening.

- The probability of rolling an even number on a dice is 50%.

product

The answer to a multiplication question.

- The product of 8 and 9 is 72.

protractor

An instrument used for measuring and drawing angles.

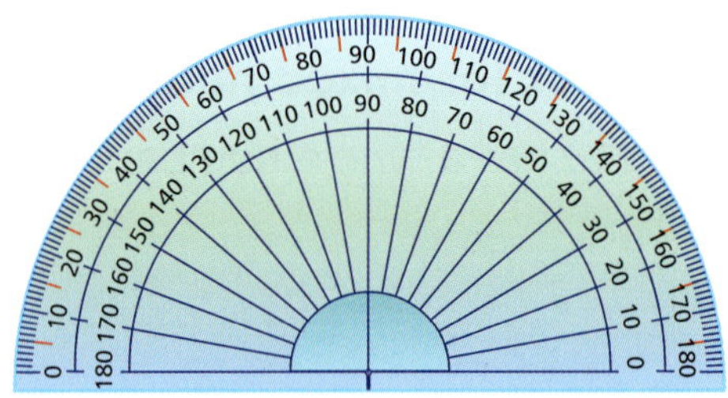

pyramid

A three-dimensional object that has a polygon for a base and triangles for all other faces. Pyramids are named by the shape of their base.

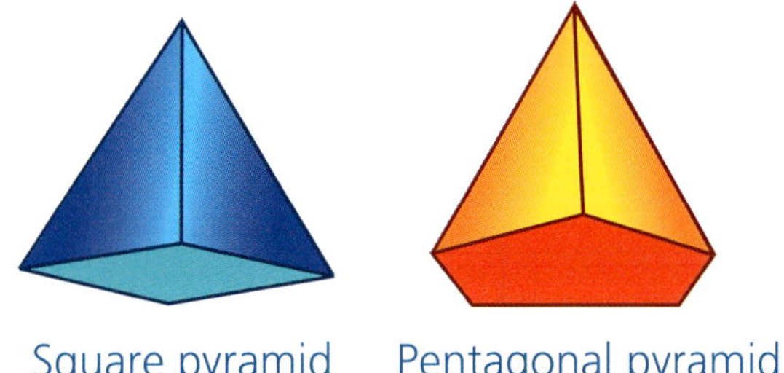

Square pyramid Pentagonal pyramid

quadrilateral

A two-dimensional shape with four straight sides.

quotient

The answer when one number is divided by another.

random selection

Choosing without looking.

Each item has an equal chance of being chosen.

reflection

See *flip*.

regular and irregular shapes

Regular shapes have all sides and all angles equal. Irregular shapes do not.

Regular shape

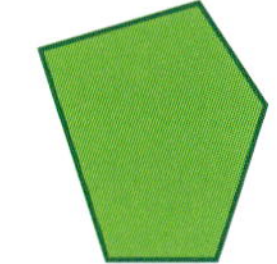

Irregular shape

remainder

The number that is left over after sharing or dividing.

- 22 cups shared among 5 people gives 4 cups each, remainder 2.

rhombus

A shape with 4 sides, opposite sides parallel and all sides equal.

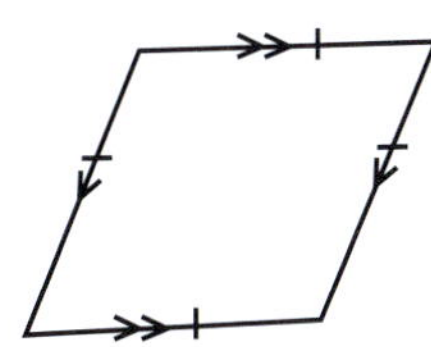

rigid shape

A model that cannot be pushed out of shape because triangles have been used in its construction.

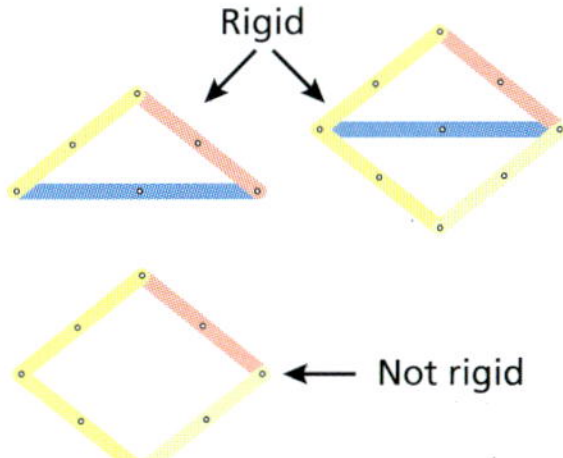

Roman numerals

A number system devised by the ancient Romans.

Roman numerals use letters for numbers:

I	V	X	L	C	D	M
1	5	10	50	100	500	1000

- XXVIII = 28.

rounding

Writing a number to the nearest 5, 10, 100, 1000, …

- 3786 rounded to the nearest 100 is 3800.
- 35 000 rounded to the nearest ten-thousand is 40 000.

skip counting

Counting on, adding the same number each time.

- 5, 10, 15, 20, 25, … is skip counting by 5.

slide (translation)

To move a shape in any direction without changing its orientation.

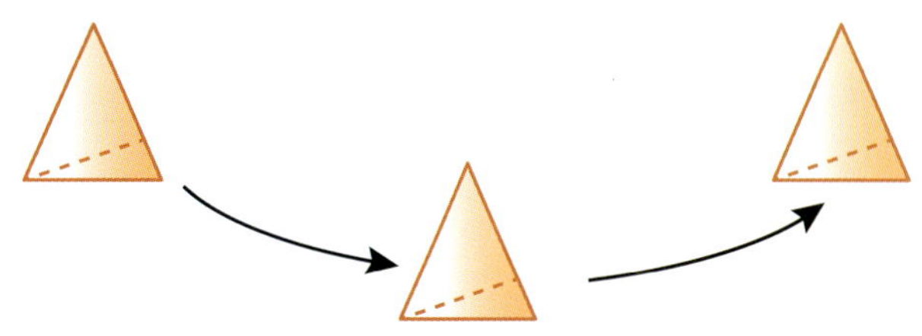

solid

A term used to describe a three-dimensional object.

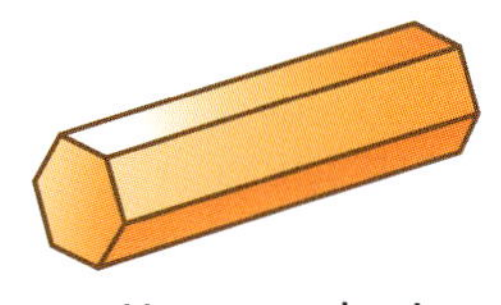

Hexagonal prism

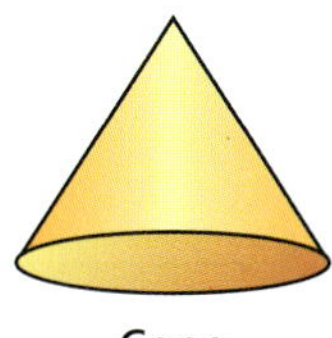

Cone

sphere

A three-dimensional object that is ball-shaped and round. All points on the surface of a sphere are the same distance from its centre.

split strategy

Adding numbers by splitting them into their parts.

- $36 + 52 = 30 + 6 + 50 + 2$
  $= (30 + 50) + (6 + 2)$
  $= 80 + 8$
  $= 88$

spreadsheet

A table produced by a computer program used for organising data allowing rapid calculations and the production of graphs.

square centimetre (cm²)

A unit for measuring area that is equal to a square with sides of 1 cm.

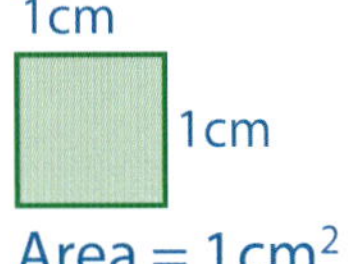

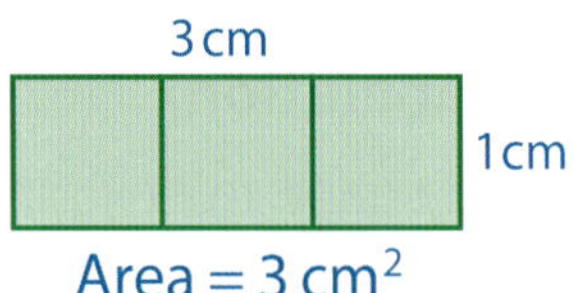

square kilometre (km²)

A unit of area equal to a square with sides of 1 km.

- $1\,km^2 = 1\,000\,000\,m^2$, $1\,km^2 = 100\,ha$

square metre (m²)

A unit of area equal to a square with sides of 1 m.

sum

The answer when you add numbers.

surface

The outside layer of a three-dimensional object.

A surface can be flat or curved.

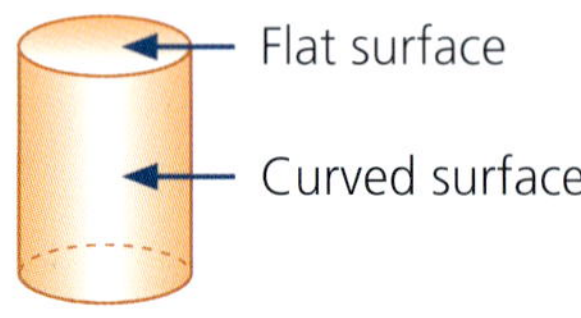

See also *face*.

survey or questionnaire

A list of questions used to discover information.

symmetry

A balanced arrangement.

- Line symmetry

  A property of a figure where one half is the mirror image of the other.

- Line (or Axis) of symmetry

  A line that divides a figure into two parts that are mirror images of each other.

- Rotational symmetry

  A property of a figure where it can be spun about a point so that it repeats its shape more than once in a full turn.

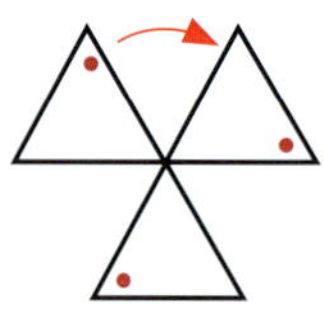

tally

To keep count by making a mark for each item. To make counting easy, the marks are drawn in groups of five, with each fifth mark crossed over the other four marks.

- 𝍸 𝍸 𝍸 ||| = 18

tangram

A traditional Chinese puzzle. A square is cut into seven pieces that can be rearranged to make different pictures.

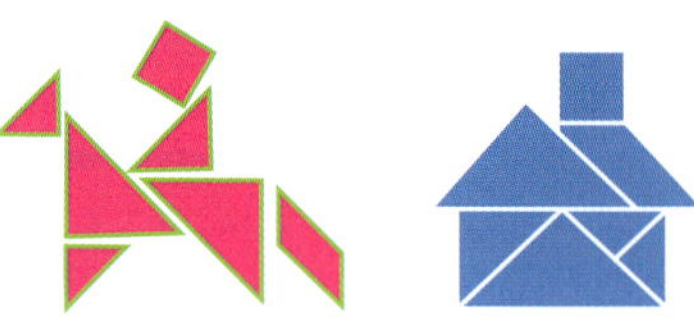

temperature

A measure of how hot or cold something is.

Temperature is usually measured in degrees Celsius (°C).

- Water freezes at 0°C.
- Water boils at 100°C.

tessellation

A pattern of identical shapes that fit together without gaps or overlaps.

thermometer

An instrument used for measuring temperature.

three-dimensional (3D) object

Objects are three-dimensional. They have length, width and height.

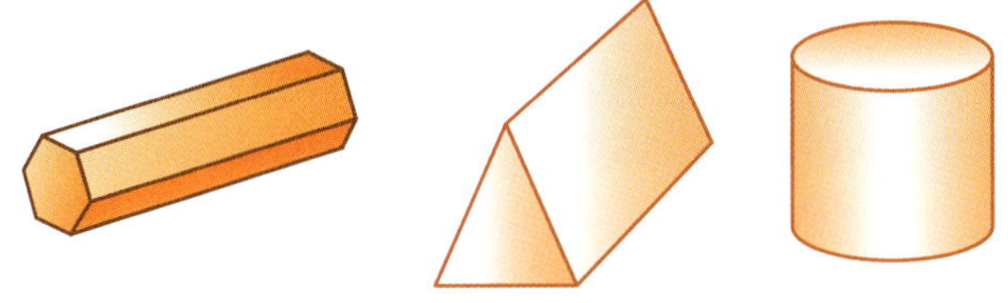

time

- The number of days in each month:

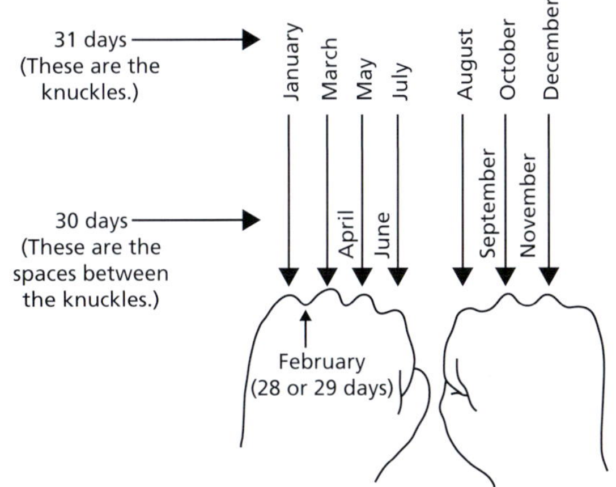

30 days has September, April, June and November. All the rest have 31, except February alone, which has 28 days clear and 29 days each leap year.

- 60 seconds = 1 minute (60 s = 1 min)
  60 minutes = 1 hour (60 min = 1 h)
  24 hours = 1 day
  365 days = 1 year
  366 days = 1 leap year

timeline

Shows a sequence of events in time.

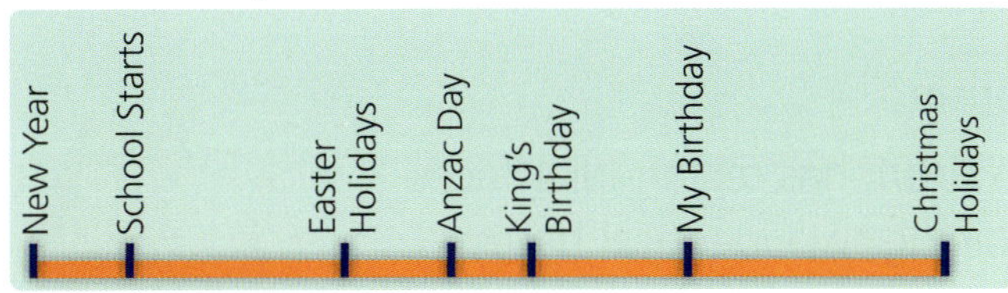

translation

See *slide*.

trapezium

A quadrilateral with one pair of parallel sides.

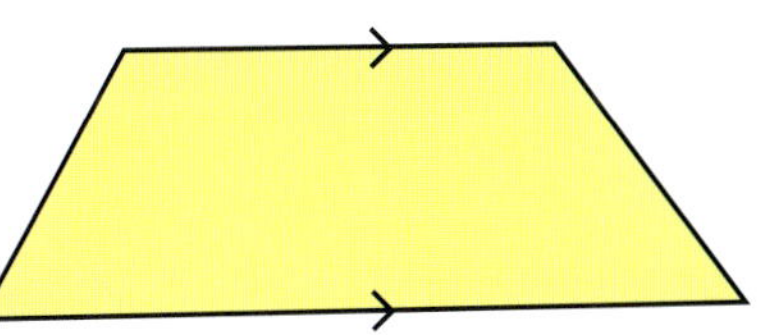

triangle

A two-dimensional shape with three straight sides and three angles.

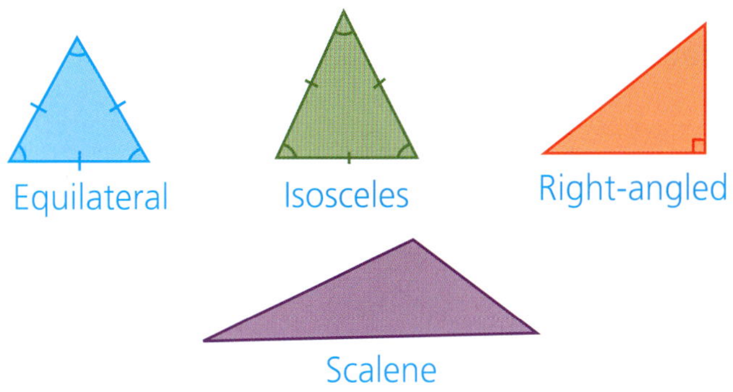

Scalene triangles have no sides equal.
See also *polygon*.

turn (rotation)

To rotate a shape about a given point.

vertex

A point at which two or more lines meet to form a corner on a 2D shape or 3D object.

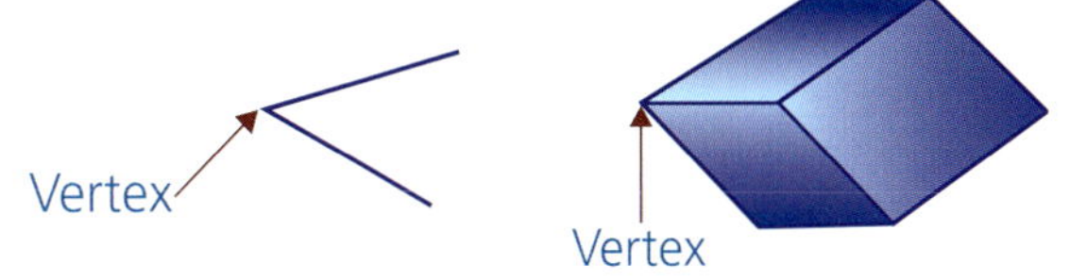

The plural of *vertex* is *vertices*.

vertical

- at right angles to the horizontal.
- straight up and down.
- the direction in which an object falls under gravity.

volume

The amount of space occupied by a 3D object.

Volume = 10 cubic units
1 cubic centimetre = 1 mL

width or breadth (dimensions)

The distance from side to side.

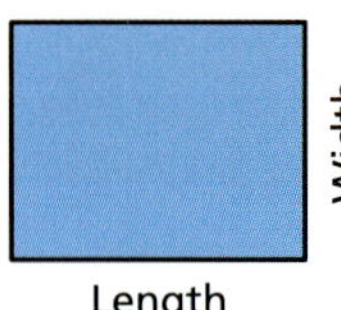

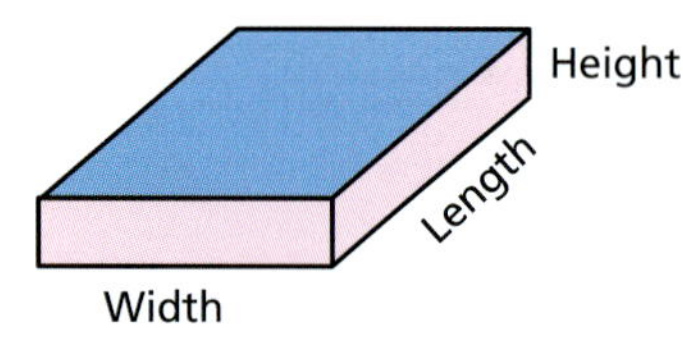

2D shapes (two-dimensional)

Flat shapes are two-dimensional.
They have length and width.

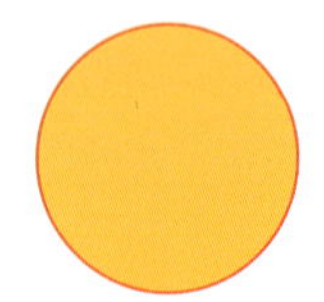

circle
1 curved side

triangle
3 sides
3 corners

square
4 equal sides
4 corners

rectangle
2 equal long sides
and 2 equal short sides,
like a stretched square

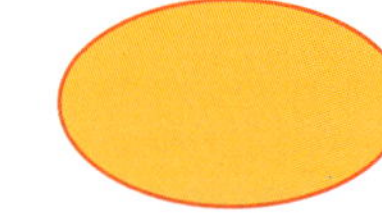

oval
1 curved side, like
a squashed circle

pentagon
5 sides
5 corners

hexagon
6 sides
6 corners

octagon
8 sides
8 corners

quadrilaterals
4 sides
4 corners

parallelogram
two pairs of parallel lines
opposite sides equal

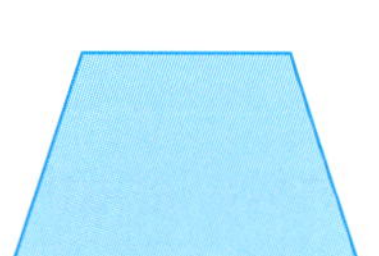

trapezium
one pair of
parallel lines

rhombus
all sides equal
(a diamond)

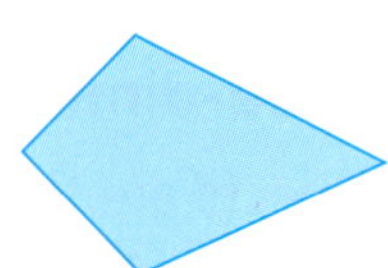

kite
two pairs of
equal sides

All of the blue shapes are quadrilaterals.

3D objects (three-dimensional)

Solid objects are three-dimensional.
They have length, width and height.

sphere

A sphere is curved and round.

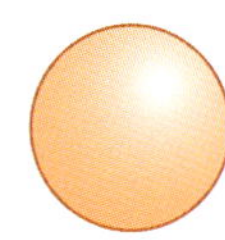

cube

A cube has 6 faces, 8 vertices and 12 straight edges.

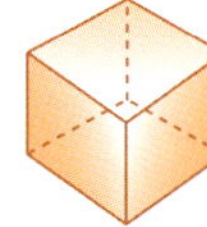

cylinder

A cylinder has 2 flat surfaces and 1 curved surface.

cone

A cone has 1 flat surface and 1 curved surface.

pyramid

A pyramid has triangular faces joined around a base.

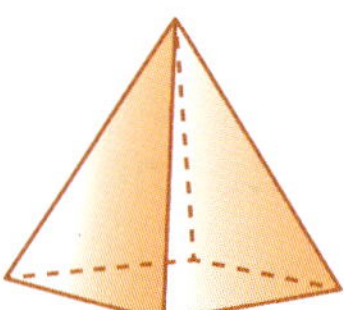

prism

A prism has rectangular faces joining two identical bases.

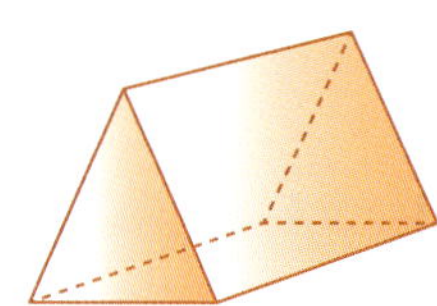

1:01 Numbers to 10 000

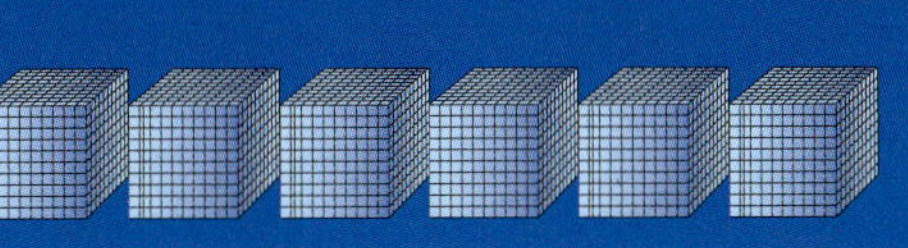

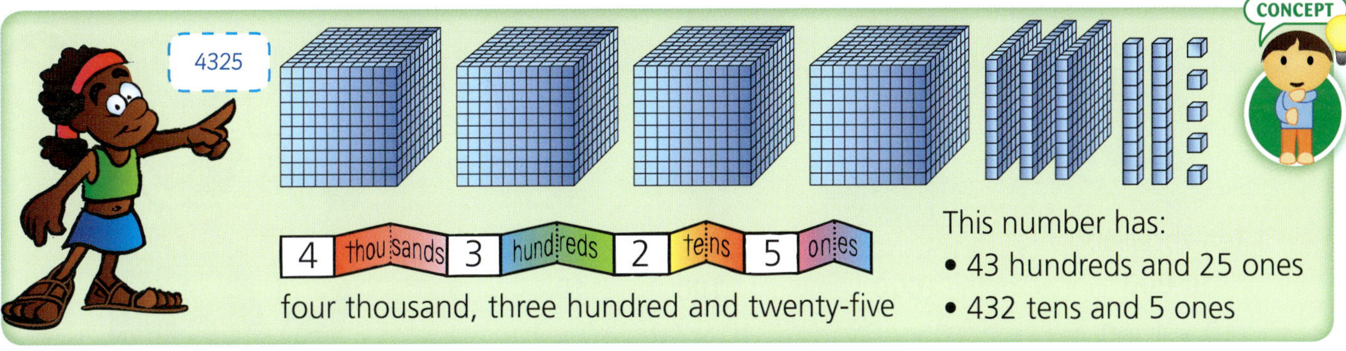

four thousand, three hundred and twenty-five

This number has:
- 43 hundreds and 25 ones
- 432 tens and 5 ones

1 Fill out the numeral expander and write the numeral.

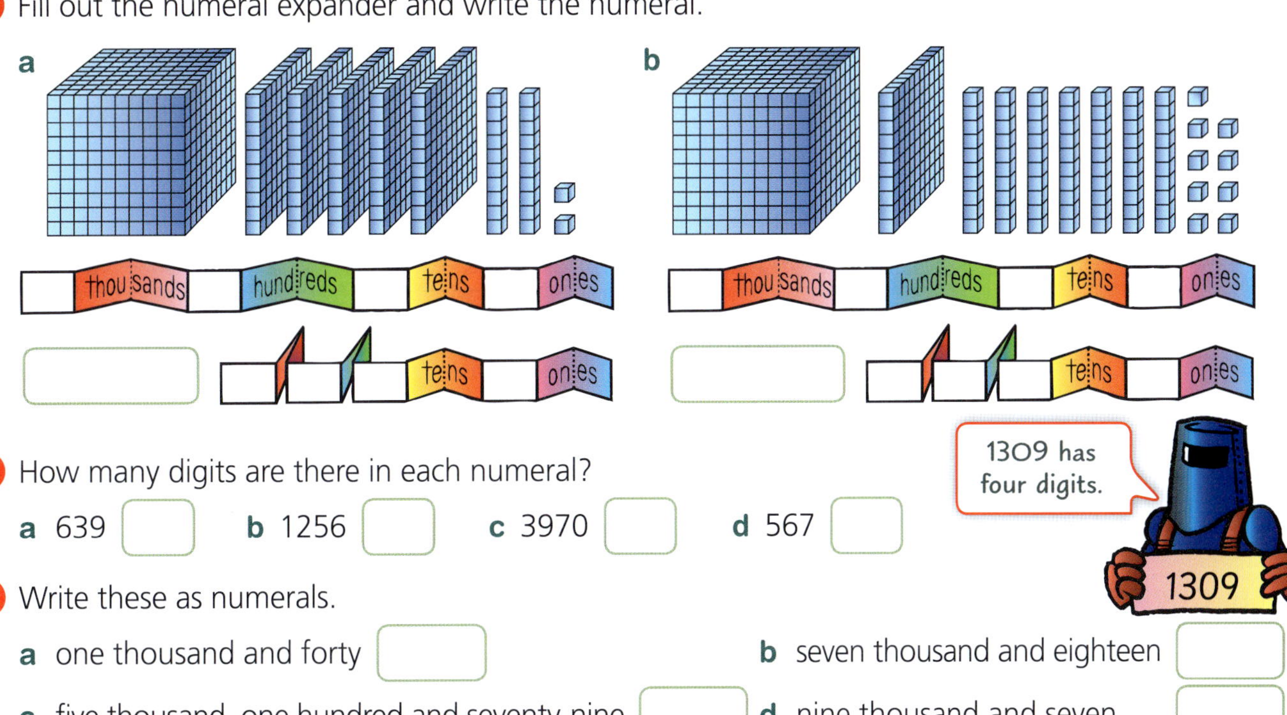

2 How many digits are there in each numeral?

a 639 ☐ b 1256 ☐ c 3970 ☐ d 567 ☐

1309 has four digits.

1309

3 Write these as numerals.

a one thousand and forty ☐
b seven thousand and eighteen ☐
c five thousand, one hundred and seventy-nine ☐
d nine thousand and seven ☐

4 Write in words:

a 4023 ☐
b 9030 ☐

5 Arrange these numbers in ascending order.

a 6426, 6624, 6246 ☐
b 8345, 8453, 8543 ☐

6 Arrange these numbers in descending order.

a 8204, 8042, 8402 ☐
b 2083, 8302, 8203 ☐

7 Does changing the order of the digits in a number change the size of the number? ☐

8 a Write the largest number you can using the digits 5, 2, 8 and 4. ☐

b Write the second largest number you can using the digits 5, 2, 8 and 4. ☐

Ten thousand = 10 000 = 10 × 1000 = 100 × 100 = 1000 × 10. There are 4 zeros in each.

 • *AUSTRALIAN SIGNPOST MATHS NSW 4* • ISBN 9780655709053

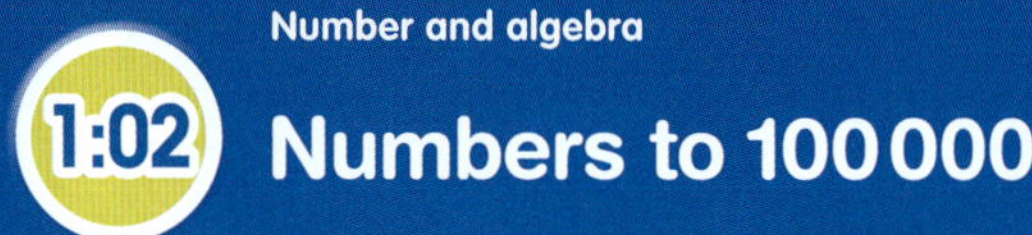

1:02 Numbers to 100 000

We leave a space after the thousands column for numbers with more than 4 digits.

67 208
14 000

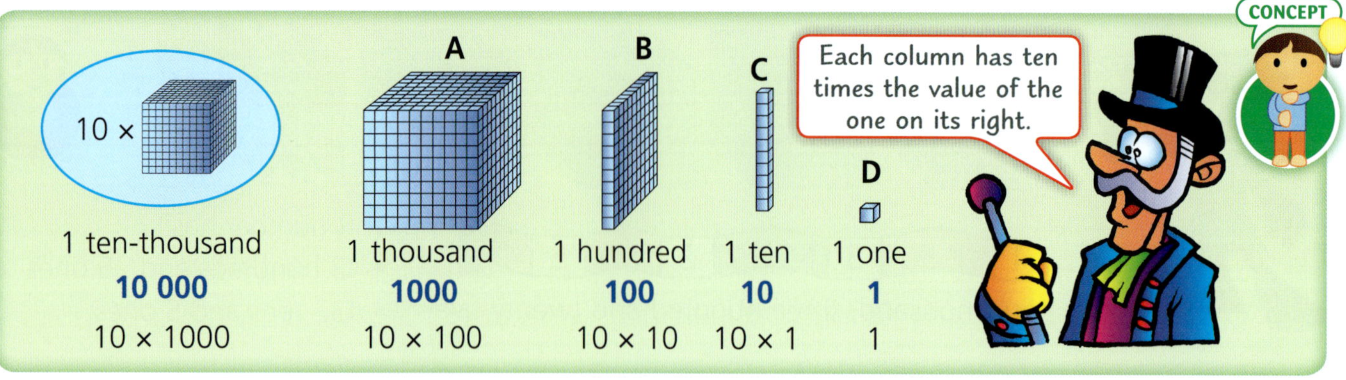

1 How many times as big is the number shown in:

- **a** **A**, compared to the one shown in **B**?
- **b** **B**, compared to the one shown in **C**?
- **c** **C**, compared to the one shown in **D**?
- **d** **A**, compared to the one shown in **C**?
- **e** **B**, compared to the one shown in **D**?
- **f** **A**, compared to the one shown in **D**?

92 thousand			5 hundred and sixty-one		
100 000	10 000	1000	100	10	1
	9	2	5	6	1

This place-value house shows 92 561.

When we multiply by 10 we add a zero. This changes the place value of the digits.

2 Which number is larger:

- **a** **A**: 60 000 + 7000 + 600 + 80 + 1 or **B**: 60 000 + 900 + 90 + 9?
- **b** **C**: 80 000 + 1000 + 200 + 40 + 9 or **D**: 80 000 + 2000 + 100 + 60 + 2?
- **c** **E**: 20 000 + 5000 + 700 + 10 + 8 or **F**: 20 000 + 5000 + 800 + 80 + 1?
- **d** **G**: 50 000 + 3000 + 900 + 90 + 2 or **H**: 50 000 + 9000 + 700 + 90 + 2?

3 **A** 74 186 **B** 79 146 **C** 60 715 **D** 40 207 **E** 97 364 **F** 98 170

- **a** Which number has a 7 that stands for 7000?
- **b** Which numbers contain 6s that have the same value?
- **c** Which numbers contain 9s that have the same value?
- **d** Which numbers contain 7s that have the same value?
- **e** How many times as big is the 7 in **B** compared to the 7 in **E**?

What other questions could you ask?

Wipe out a digit

- A student enters any 5-digit number into a calculator.
- A partner selects any digit to be 'wiped out', i.e. changed to zero.
- Only one operation can be entered into the calculator to wipe out a digit.
- Take turns and score one point for each successful wipe out.

 • *AUSTRALIAN SIGNPOST MATHS NSW 4* • ISBN 9780655709053

Rounding off

We round 15 off to 20 (to the nearest 10).
We round 15000 off to 20000 (to the nearest 10000).

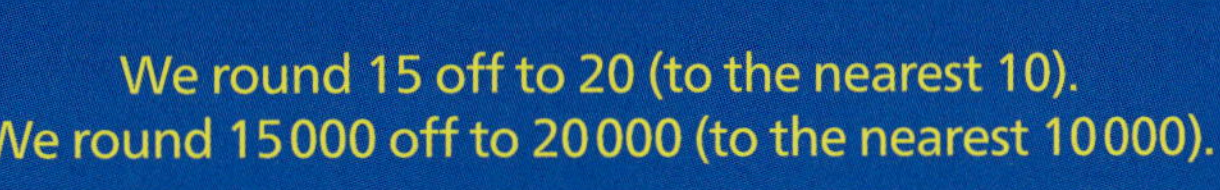

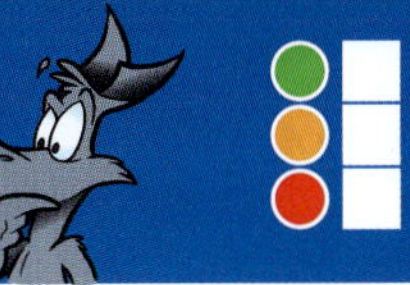

CONCEPT

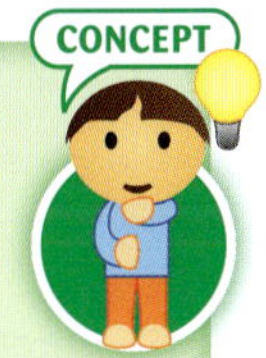

3478 rounds off to 3000 (to the nearest 1000).

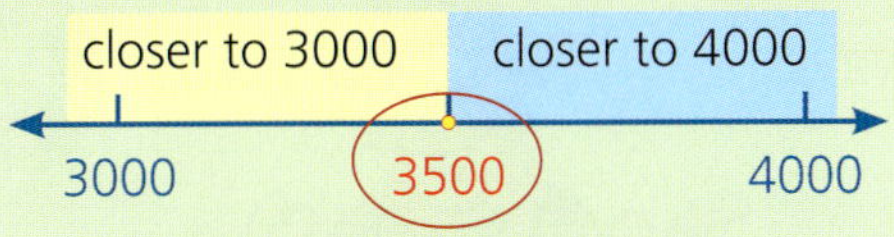

closer to 3000
closer to 4000
3000
3500
4000

3500 rounds up to 4000.

65432 rounds off to 70000 (to the nearest 10000).

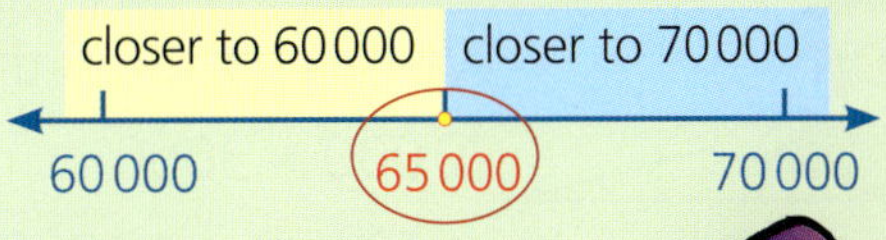

closer to 60000
closer to 70000
60000
65000
70000

65000 rounds up to 70000.

When rounding a number to a particular place, look at the next digit.
If it is 5 or more, round up.
If it is less than 5, round down.

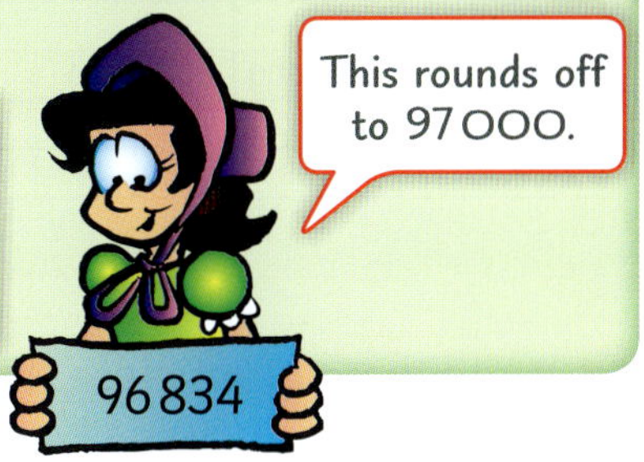

This rounds off to 97000.
96834

1 Round off these numbers to the nearest hundred.

a 3674 ____	b 4237 ____	c 1396 ____	d 9271 ____
e 6549 ____	f 6704 ____	g 8962 ____	h 5854 ____

2 Round off these numbers to the nearest thousand.

a 31569 ____	b 82738 ____	c 10846 ____	d 57249 ____
e 23496 ____	f 52301 ____	g 46972 ____	h 69347 ____

3 Round off these numbers to the nearest ten-thousand.

a 46867 ____	b 82999 ____	c 25000 ____	d 88235 ____
e 92675 ____	f 33951 ____	g 65007 ____	h 74000 ____

4 a Circle numbers that round off to 53000.

53640	52967	52849
52621	52076	53297
53599	53346	52374

b Circle numbers that round off to 80000.

79621	87231	81119
85000	74649	75000
83713	71998	76014

5 Answer **true** or **false** for each statement.

a 4639 rounds off to 4600. ____

b 1854 rounds off to 1800. ____

c 6341 rounds off to 6400. ____

d 9782 rounds off to 9800. ____

e 35000 rounds off to 40000. ____

6

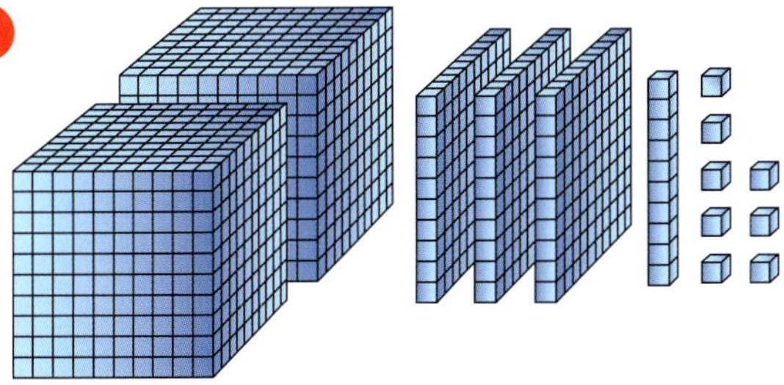

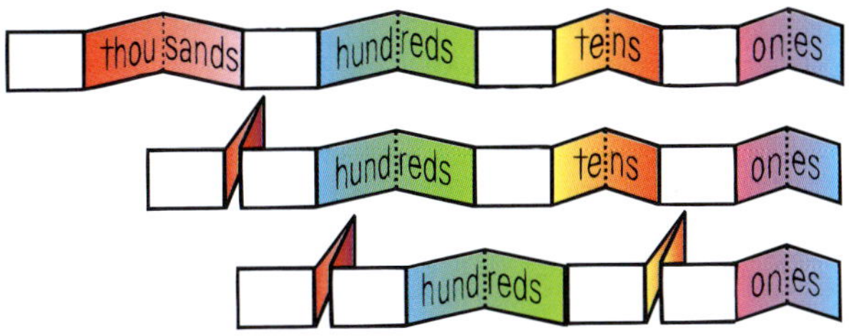

thousands
hundreds
tens
ones
hundreds
tens
ones
hundreds
ones

1:04 Partitioning large numbers

48 000
= 40 000 + 8000 or
30 000 + 18 000

CONCEPT

Thousands					
100 000	10 000	1000	100	10	1
H	T	O	H	T	O
	7	3	0	0	0

This place-value house shows 73 000.
We can partition this in many ways.
70 000 + 3000
or 60 000 + 13 000
or 730 hundreds.

1 Write these numbers in the place-value house then list different ways to partition them.

a 95 000

Thousands					
H	T	O	H	T	O

a 48 000

Thousands					
H	T	O	H	T	O

2 We can write 36 000 as 20 thousands and 16 thousands. Partition these numbers in the same way.

a 42 000

b 58 000

c 37 000

3 **a** 35 000 = 30 000 + ___
= 20 000 + ___

b 83 000 = 80 000 + ___
= 70 000 + ___

c 28 000 = 20 000 + ___
= 10 000 + ___

d 63 000 = 60 000 + ___
= 50 000 + ___

e 72 500 = 70 000 + ___
= 20 000 + ___

f 91 300 = 90 000 + ___
= 50 000 + ___

We can break up numbers in many ways.

4 Rearranging the digits changes the size of a number. Use the digits 6, 2, 7, 9, 2 to:

a Write the smallest number you can.

b Write the second smallest number you can.

c Write the second largest number you can.

Rearranging digits changes the size of the number.

 • *AUSTRALIAN SIGNPOST MATHS NSW 4* • ISBN 9780655709053

Fractions

$\frac{5}{12}$ of this group of stars has been coloured.

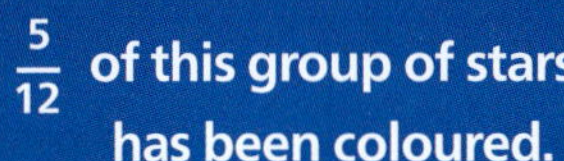

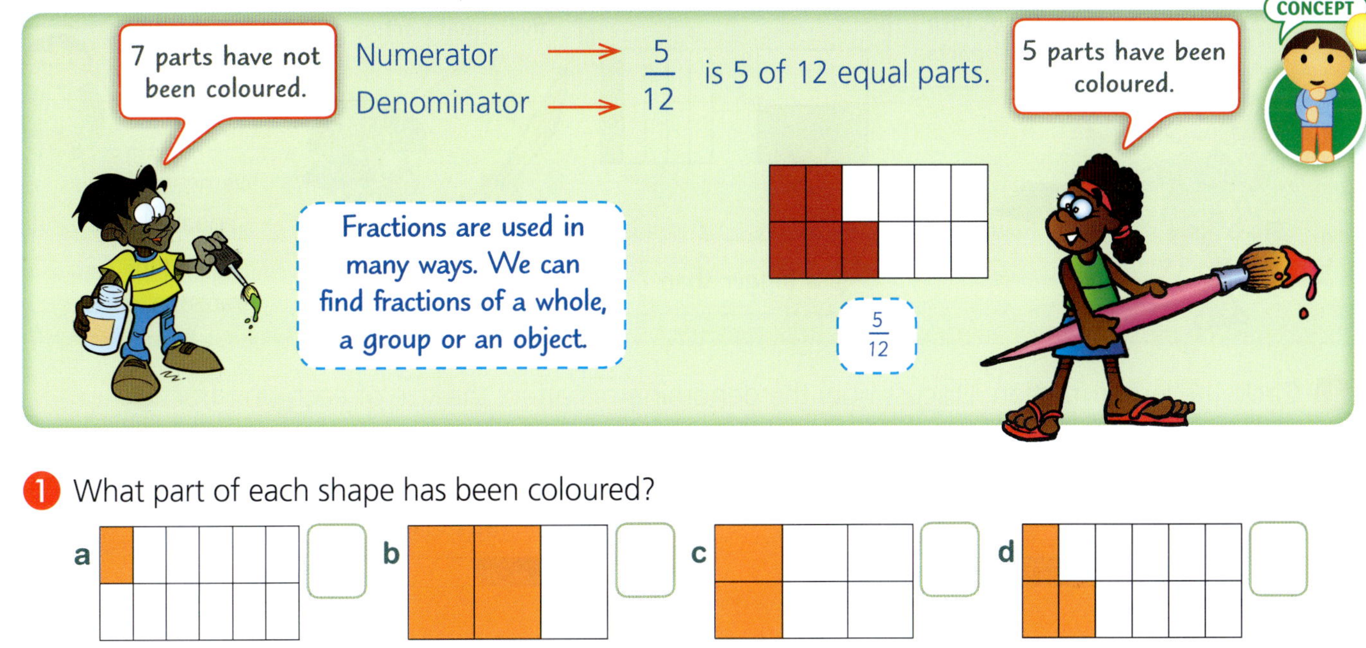

1 What part of each shape has been coloured?

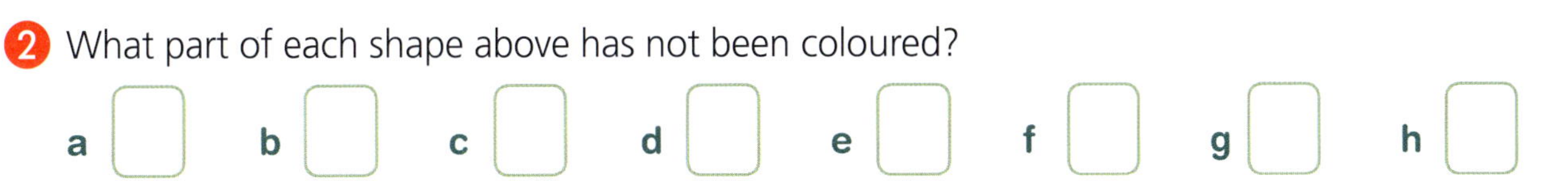

2 What part of each shape above has not been coloured?

a ☐ b ☐ c ☐ d ☐ e ☐ f ☐ g ☐ h ☐

3 Colour part of each shape to match the given fraction.

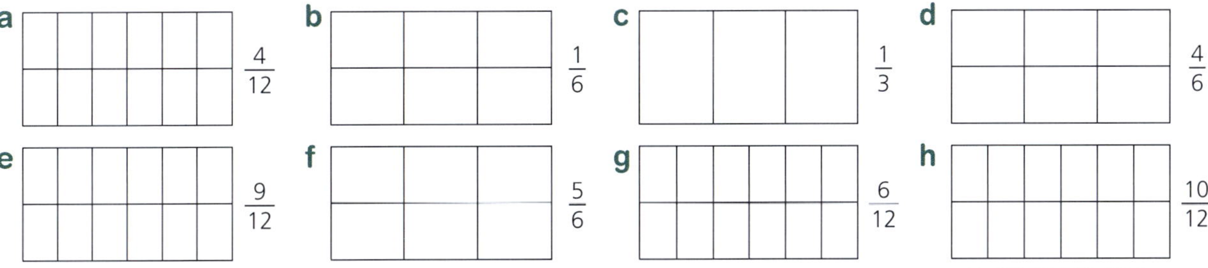

4 What part of each group has been coloured?

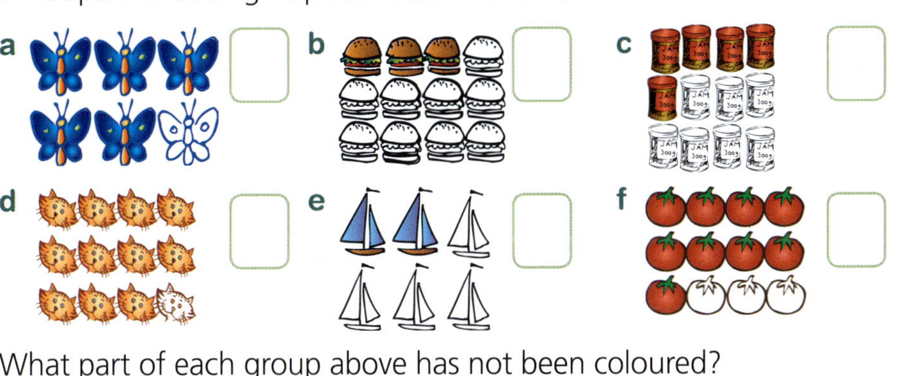

5 What part of each group above has not been coloured?

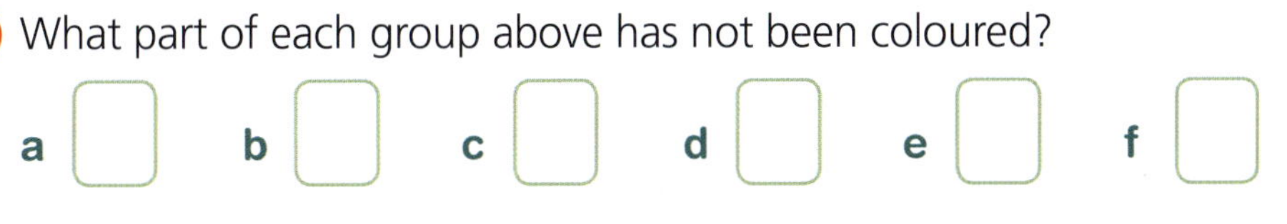

 • • ISBN 9780655709053

1:06 Comparing fractions

one fifth, two fifths, three fifths, ...
$\frac{1}{5}$ $\frac{2}{5}$ $\frac{3}{5}$

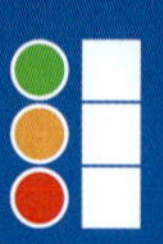

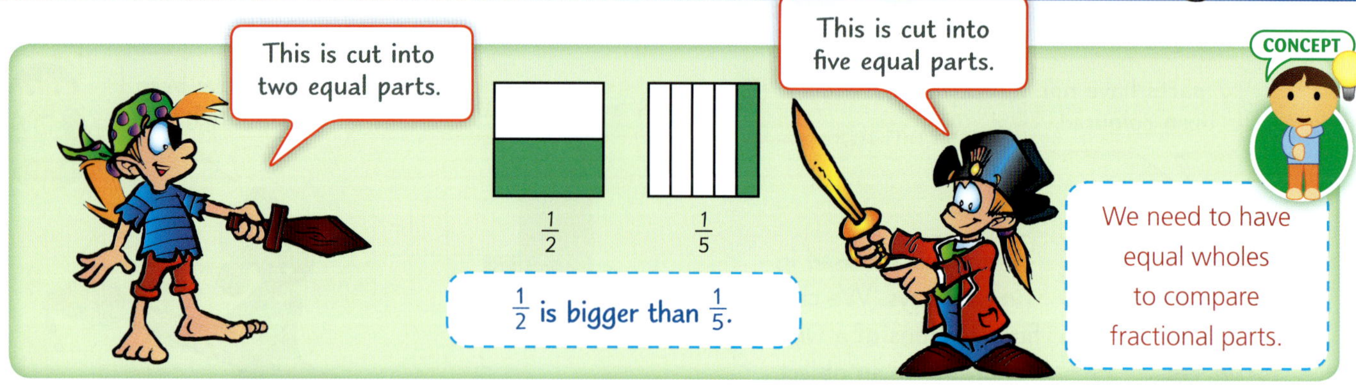

$\frac{1}{2}$ $\frac{1}{5}$

$\frac{1}{2}$ is bigger than $\frac{1}{5}$.

1 Circle the larger fraction. Discuss how the denominators affect the size of each unit fraction.

a $\frac{1}{8}$ $\frac{1}{2}$

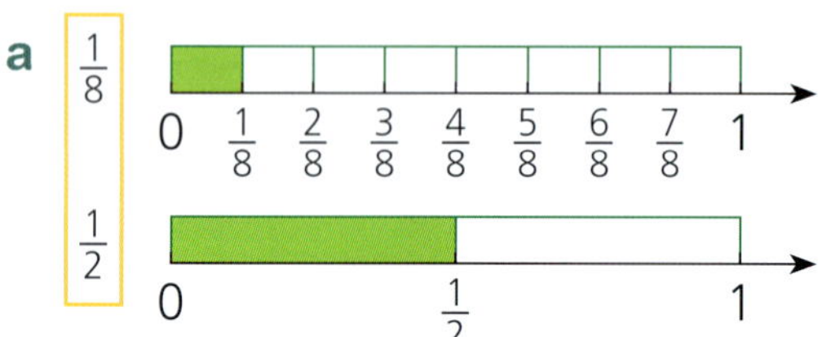

b $\frac{1}{10}$ $\frac{1}{4}$

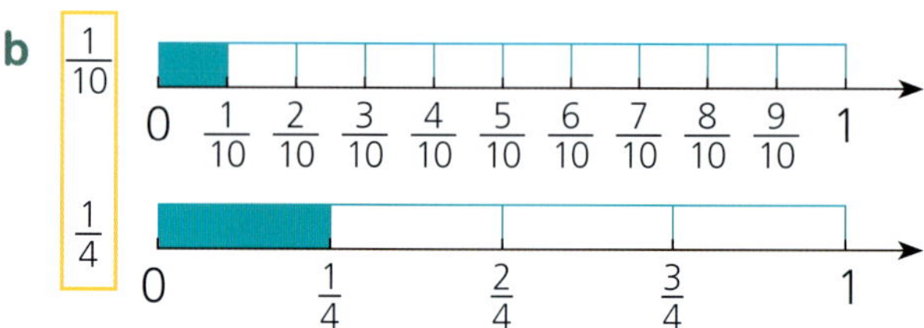

2 Colour part of each shape to match the given fraction.

a $\frac{3}{4}$

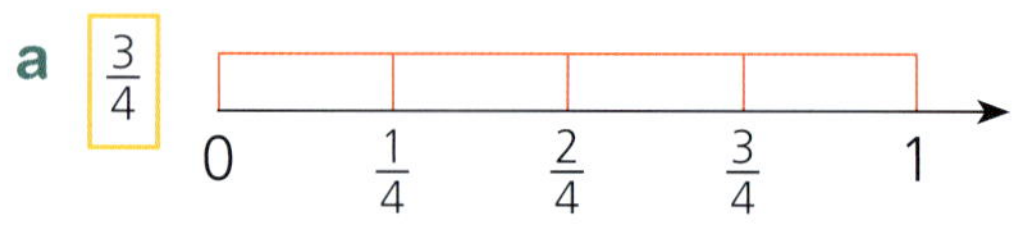

Part coloured: ☐ Part not coloured: ☐

b $\frac{2}{10}$

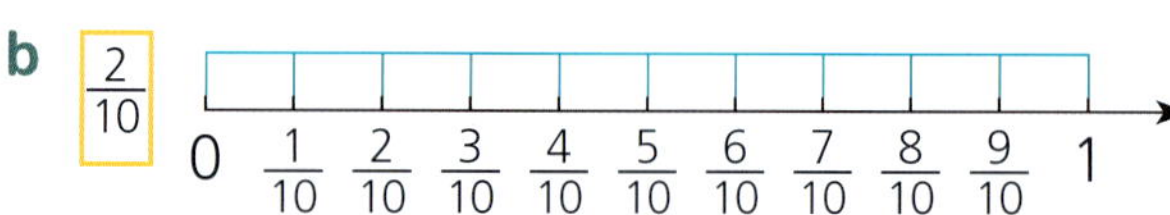

Part coloured: ☐ Part not coloured: ☐

c $\frac{5}{8}$

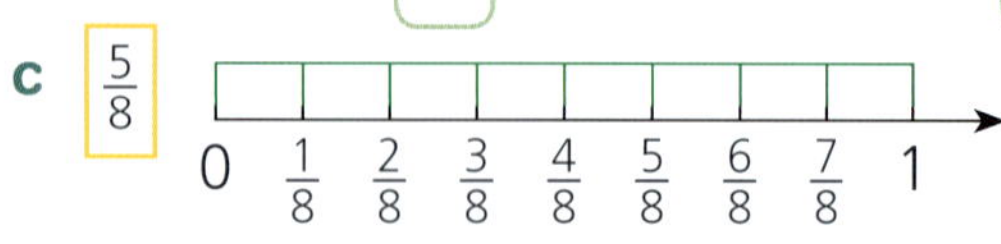

Part coloured: ☐ Part not coloured: ☐

d $\frac{2}{5}$

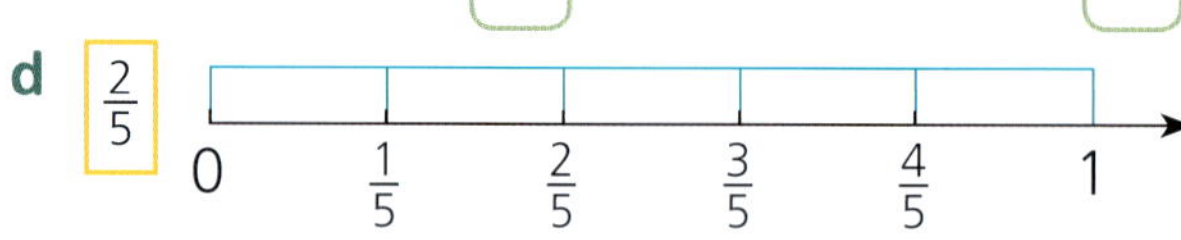

Part coloured: ☐ Part not coloured: ☐

Circle the fractions that are greater than one half.

3 Write true or false for each statement. You could draw these fractions to compare them.

a $\frac{2}{2} = 1$ ☐ **b** $\frac{4}{5} = 1$ ☐ **c** $\frac{8}{8} = 1$ ☐

d $1 = \frac{10}{10}$ ☐ **e** $1 = \frac{3}{8}$ ☐ **f** $1 = \frac{5}{5}$ ☐

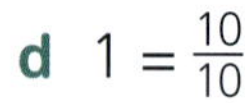

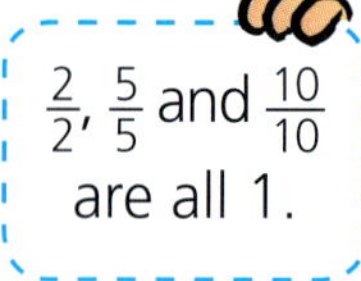

INVESTIGATION

- Ashton, Harry and Riley each coloured half of a strip of paper.
  Explain why each half was a different size.

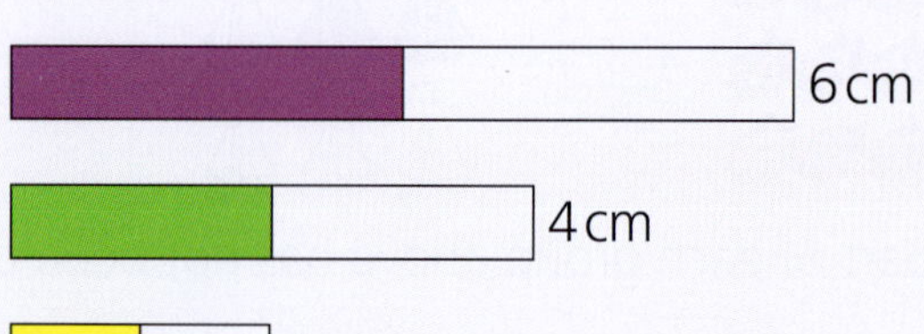

 ISBN 9780655709053

1:07 Fractions beyond 1

$\frac{4}{4} = 1$

$\frac{8}{4} = 2$

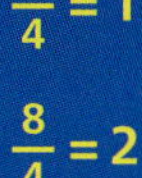

CONCEPT

Scott had 2 halves of a biscuit. Rachel gave him another half. Now he has 3 halves.

$\frac{3}{2} = \frac{2}{2} + \frac{1}{2}$

$= 1 + \frac{1}{2}$

$= 1\frac{1}{2}$

He has $\frac{3}{2}$ or $1\frac{1}{2}$ biscuits.

$\frac{3}{2}$ is called an improper fraction because the numerator is larger than the denominator.
$1\frac{1}{2}$ is called a mixed number.
It has a whole part and a fraction part.

1 Write the mixed number and improper fraction for the parts coloured.

a  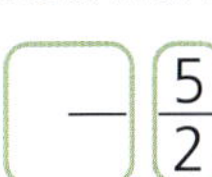 ☐ — $\frac{5}{2}$

5 halves

b    ☐ — ☐

☐ halves

c   ☐ — ☐

☐ halves

d   ☐ — ☐

☐ quarters

e    ☐ — ☐

☐ quarters

f 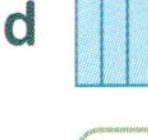  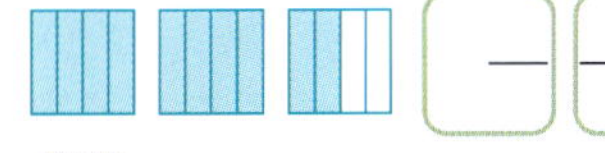 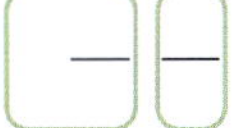 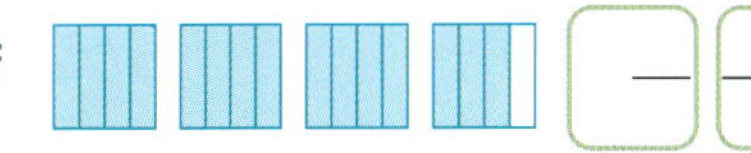 ☐ — ☐

☐ quarters

g   ☐ — ☐

☐ thirds

h 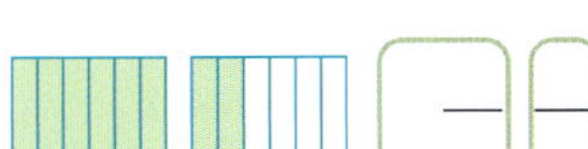  ☐ — ☐

☐ sixths

i  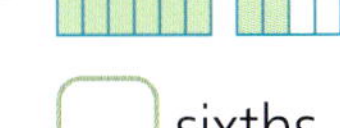  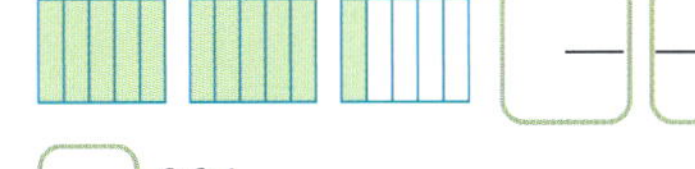 ☐ — ☐

☐ fifths

2 Complete the number line. Practise counting forwards and backwards.

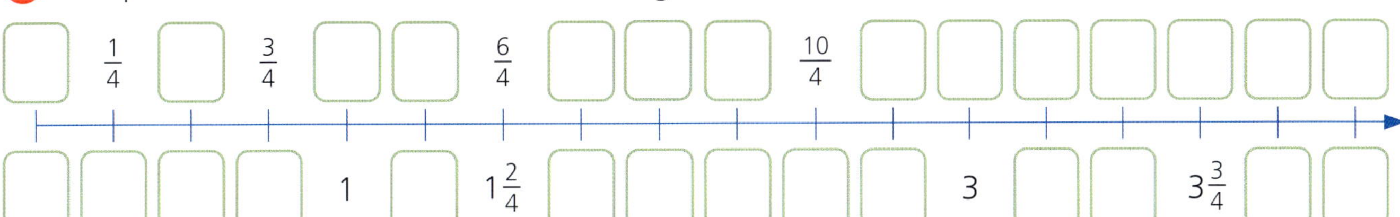

☐	$\frac{1}{4}$	☐	$\frac{3}{4}$	☐	☐	$\frac{6}{4}$	☐	☐	☐	$\frac{10}{4}$	☐	☐	☐	☐	☐	☐	☐
☐	☐	☐	☐	1	☐	$1\frac{2}{4}$	☐	☐	☐	☐	☐	3	☐	☐	$3\frac{3}{4}$	☐	☐

3 Write the improper fraction for:

a $1\frac{1}{2}$ ☐ **b** $2\frac{1}{5}$ ☐ **c** $3\frac{2}{4}$ ☐ **d** $1\frac{4}{5}$ ☐

e $2\frac{3}{4}$ ☐ **f** $2\frac{5}{4}$ ☐ **g** $4\frac{2}{3}$ ☐ **h** $2\frac{5}{8}$ ☐

$2\frac{2}{3}$
$= \frac{3}{3} + \frac{3}{3} + \frac{2}{3}$
$= \frac{8}{3}$

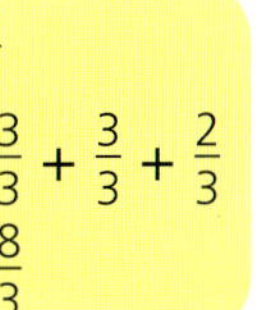

4 Write the mixed number for:

a $\frac{7}{4}$ ☐ **b** $\frac{9}{5}$ ☐ **c** $\frac{11}{4}$ ☐ **d** $\frac{11}{5}$ ☐

e $\frac{8}{5}$ ☐ **f** $\frac{13}{4}$ ☐ **g** $\frac{14}{5}$ ☐ **h** $\frac{17}{4}$ ☐

See *Extra Support 19* (Fraction patterns).

1:08 Fractions beyond 1

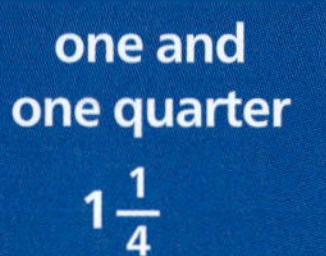

CONCEPT

Caleb's chocolate bar has 3 thirds. Josie gave him one of her thirds. Now he has 4 thirds.

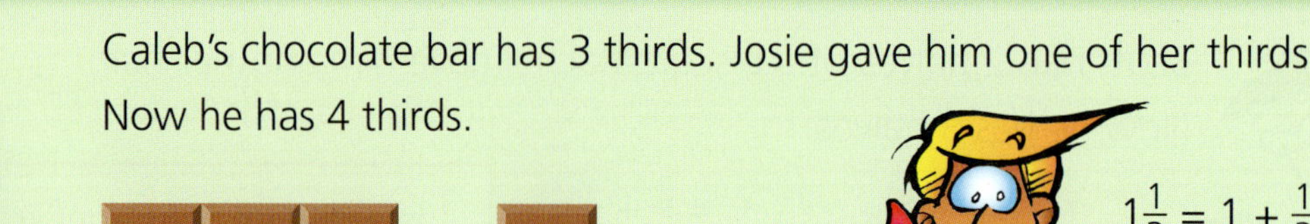

He has $\frac{4}{3}$ or $1\frac{1}{3}$ chocolate bars.

$1\frac{1}{3} = 1 + \frac{1}{3}$

$= \frac{3}{3} + \frac{1}{3}$

$= \frac{4}{3}$

1 a $\frac{1}{3}$, $\frac{2}{3}$, 1, $1\frac{1}{3}$, $1\frac{2}{3}$, 2, $2\frac{1}{3}$, $2\frac{2}{3}$, ☐, ☐, ☐, ☐

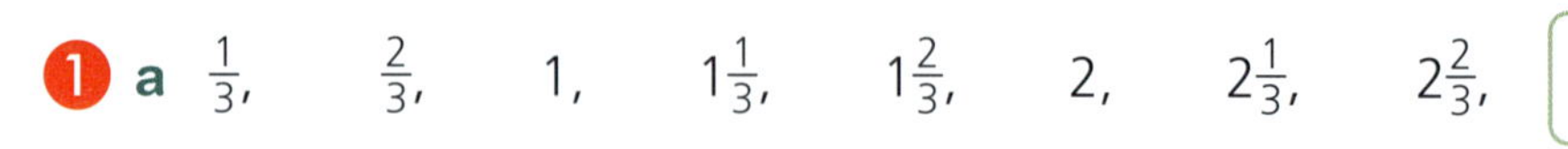

b one-third, two-thirds, three-thirds (or 1), four-thirds, ☐, ☐

2 Write an equivalent whole or mixed number.

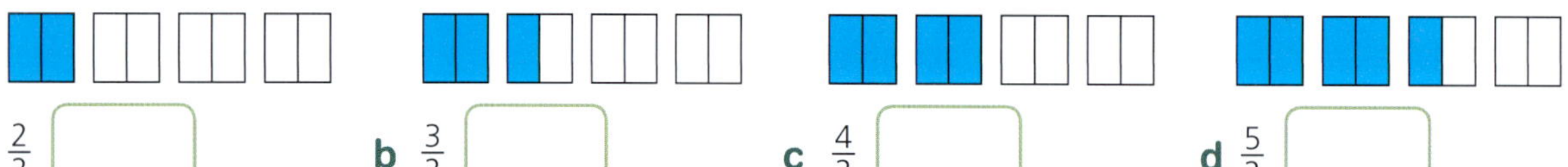

a $\frac{2}{2}$ ☐ b $\frac{3}{2}$ ☐ c $\frac{4}{2}$ ☐ d $\frac{5}{2}$ ☐

3 Write the improper fraction and mixed number for each part.

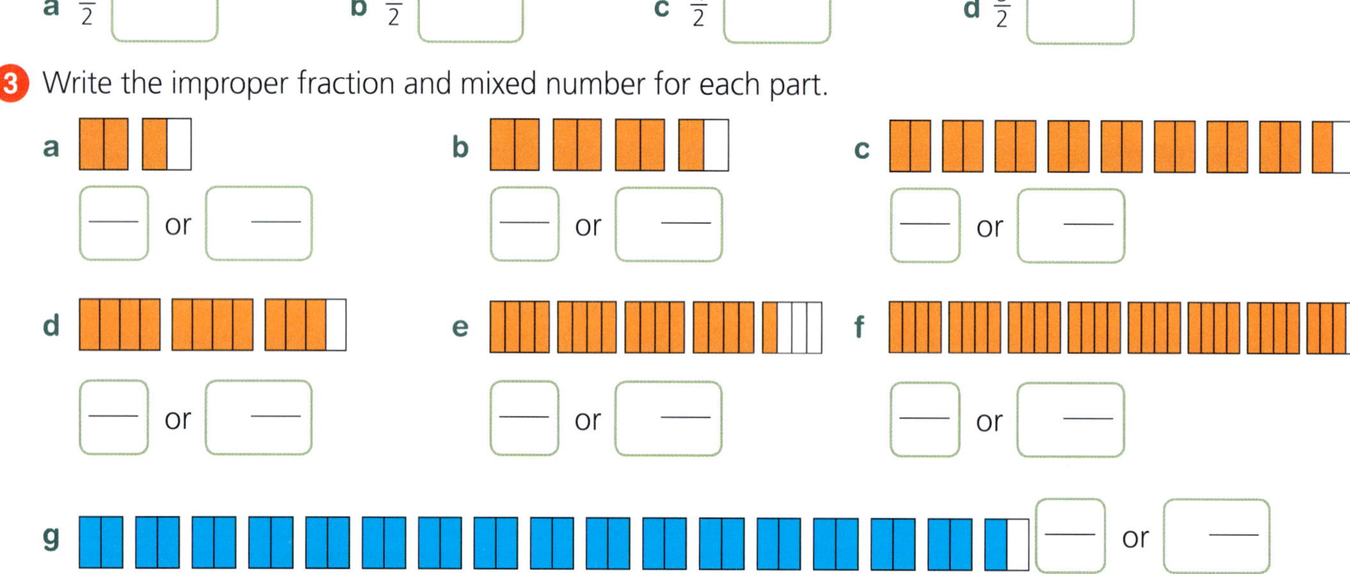

a ☐ or ☐ b ☐ or ☐ c ☐ or ☐

d ☐ or ☐ e ☐ or ☐ f ☐ or ☐

g ☐ or ☐

4 Write the mixed number.

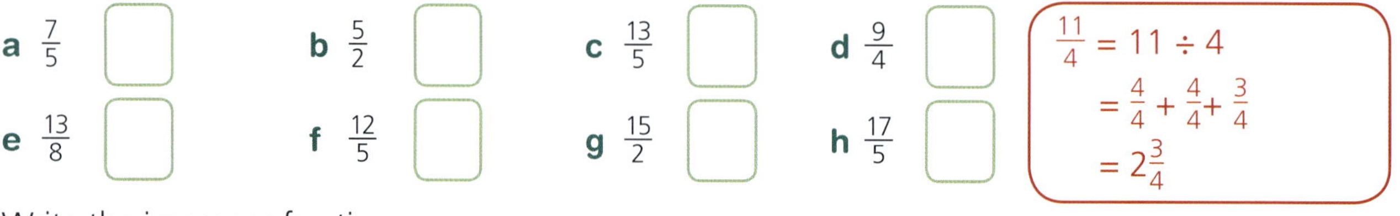

a $\frac{7}{5}$ ☐ b $\frac{5}{2}$ ☐ c $\frac{13}{5}$ ☐ d $\frac{9}{4}$ ☐

e $\frac{13}{8}$ ☐ f $\frac{12}{5}$ ☐ g $\frac{15}{2}$ ☐ h $\frac{17}{5}$ ☐

$\frac{11}{4} = 11 \div 4$

$= \frac{4}{4} + \frac{4}{4} + \frac{3}{4}$

$= 2\frac{3}{4}$

5 Write the improper fraction.

a $1\frac{1}{5}$ ☐ b $5\frac{1}{2}$ ☐ c $3\frac{2}{5}$ ☐ d $6\frac{1}{3}$ ☐

e $1\frac{3}{8}$ ☐ f $2\frac{5}{6}$ ☐ g $4\frac{4}{5}$ ☐ h $1\frac{7}{10}$ ☐

$8\frac{2}{3} = (8 \times 3 + 2)$ thirds

$= \frac{26}{3}$

See *Extra Support 19* (Fraction patterns).

1:09 Numbers to 1000000

75 248 has 5 digits.
137 896 has 6 digits.

CONCEPT

75 248

75 248 can be written as:

- **75** thousands and **248** ones
- **752** hundreds and **48** ones
- **7524** tens and **8** ones

Seventy-five thousand, two hundred and forty-eight

This place-value house separates the thousands from the hundreds, tens and ones.

137 thousand			8 hundred and ninety-six		
100 000	10 000	1000	100	10	1
1	**3**	**7**	**8**	**9**	**6**

Using numeral expanders allows us to see how many hundreds or tens are in a number.

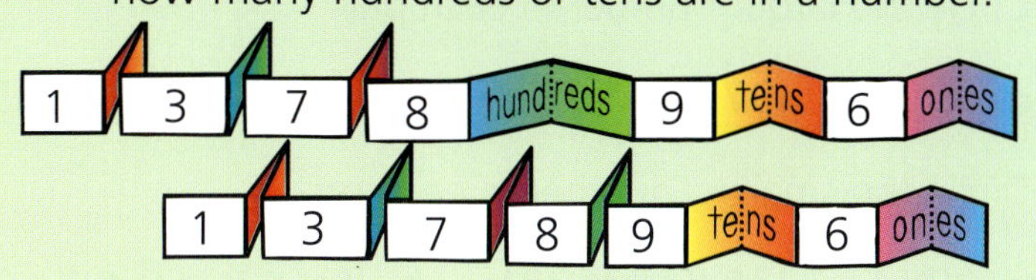

The expanded form of 137 896 is
100 000 + 30 000 + 7000 + 800 + 90 + 6.

1 Read these numbers and then write them in figures on the place-value chart.

a twenty-six thousand, three hundred and twenty-four

b one hundred and sixteen thousand, eight hundred

c five hundred and thirteen thousand and forty-seven

d nine hundred and twenty-six thousand and eleven

Thousands					
H	**T**	**O**	**H**	**T**	**O**

2 Write the numeral for:

a 30 000 + 4 000 + 500 + 20 + 8 ______

b 60 000 + 7 000 + 900 + 30 + 4 ______

c 50 000 + 8 000 + 400 + 60 + 2 ______

d 90 000 + 2 000 + 700 + 40 + 8 ______

e 80 000 + 2 000 + 300 + 50 + 9 ______

f 40 000 + 8 000 + 600 + 70 + 3 ______

g 300 000 + 50 000 + 9 000 + 100 + 80 + 7 ______

h 900 000 + 20 000 + 7 000 + 200 + 30 + 5 ______

i 700 000 + 10 000 + 5 000 + 700 + 20 + 8 ______

Discuss different ways of partitioning these numbers.
857304 = 8573 hundreds and 4 ones

3 When are large numbers like these used?

______

______

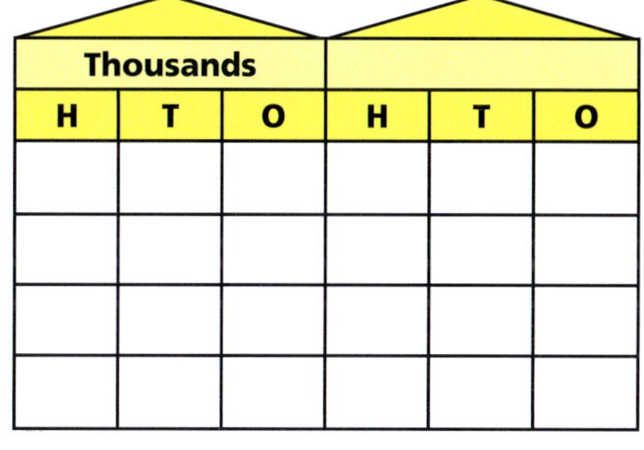

1:10 Numbers to 1000000

To compare numbers, start with the digits on the left of the space.

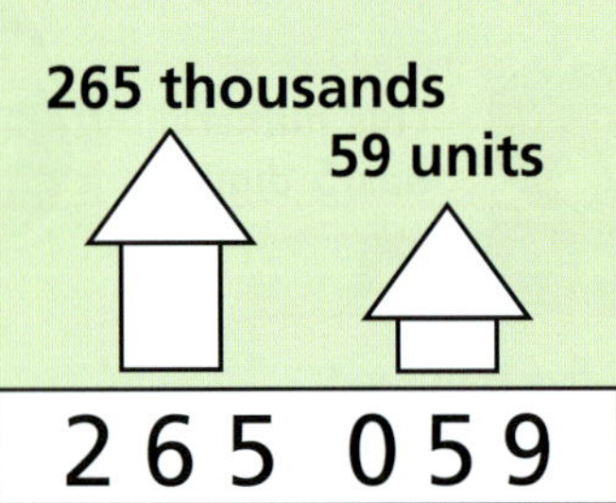

two hundred and sixty-five thousand and fifty-nine

- The value of the 2 is 200000.
- The value of the 6 is 6000.
- The value of the 5 is 5000.
- The value of the 0 is 0.
- The value of the 5 is 50.
- The value of the 9 is 9.

1 Circle the larger number in each pair.

a 49768 49713 **b** 37281 36281 **c** 345022 344997 **d** 897411 978411

2 Circle the smallest number in each group.

a 29642 27849 26301 **b** 72642 69309 70624 **c** 718022 692997 709165

3 Write the numeral for:

a twenty-eight thousand, seven hundred and forty-seven

b fifty thousand, three hundred and seventy-eight

c eight hundred and thirty-nine thousand, six hundred and twenty-five

d four hundred and seventeen thousand, seven hundred and thirteen

Leave a space to the right of the thousands digit.

4 Write the numeral for:

a 500000 + 20000 + 6000 + 400 + 90 + 3

b 800000 + 90000 + 5000 + 600 + 50 + 1

5 Write the value of each coloured digit in these numbers.

a 48603 (8) **b** 91738 (1) **c** 675132 (6)

d 32480 (8) **e** 80965 (9) **f** 401360 (4)

Make the number

- For this game you need a set of playing cards marked with digits 0 to 9.
- The dealer selects a number to be made, e.g. 'Make the number closest to 30000'.
- Five cards are then dealt to each player. The winner is the player able to arrange the five cards closest to the chosen number.
- Each winner scores one point.

Rounding off

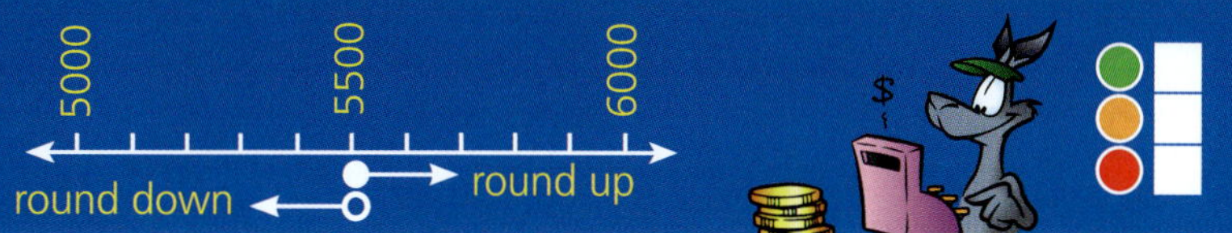

CONCEPT

746 372 rounds off to 700 000 (to the nearest hundred thousand).

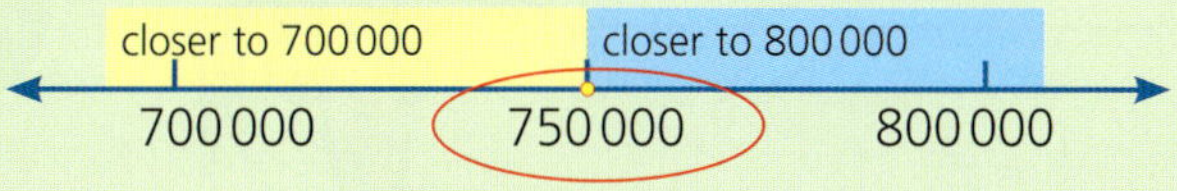

closer to 700 000 | closer to 800 000
700 000 750 000 800 000
746 372 rounds down to 700 000.

When rounding a number to a particular place, look at the next digit.
If it is 5 or more, round up.
If it is less than 5, round down.

Remember, 4 and below round downwards.

1 Round off each number to the nearest hundred thousand.

a 360 000 ______ b 850 000 ______ c 243 600 ______
d 432 000 ______ e 795 800 ______ f 275 382 ______
g 711 493 ______ h 252 978 ______ i 238 003 ______

2 Round off each number to the nearest ten-thousand.

a 72 500 ______ b 36 900 ______ c 83 928 ______
d 45 297 ______ e 57 803 ______ f 19 287 ______
g 94 603 ______ h 62 058 ______ i 27 847 ______

3 Arrange these numbers in ascending order.

a 369 204, 347 291, 383 978 ______
b 836 736, 863 846, 834 820 ______
c 389 245, 387 462, 380 672 ______

Ascending means smallest to largest. *Descending* means largest to smallest.

4 Write the value of each coloured digit.

a 8**5**3 638 ______ b 4**8**6 274 ______
c 526 **9**43 ______ d 9**0**4 200 ______
e 9**1**7 400 ______ f **6**37 268 ______

ACTIVITY

- List three things that would cost more than $1 000 000.

______
______

1:12 Equivalent fractions

Fold the paper, fold again and fold again.

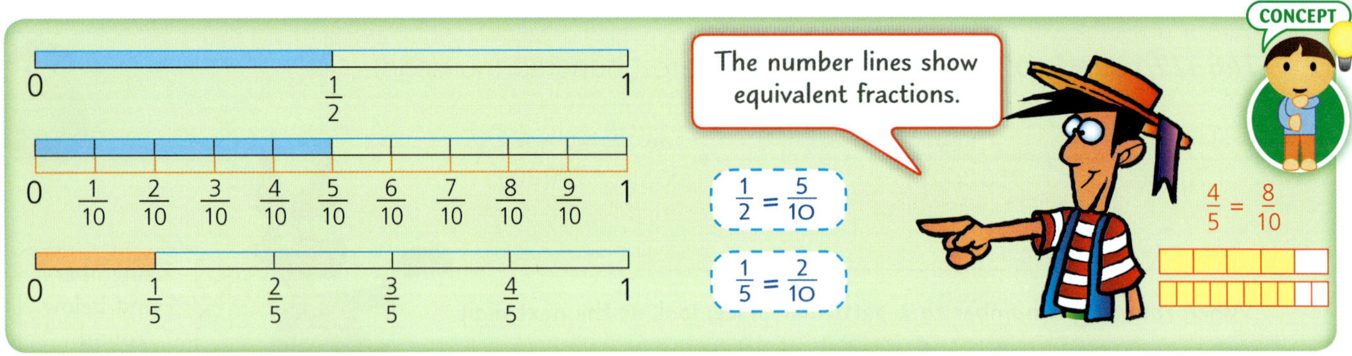

1. Use the number lines to show an equivalent fraction for:

   a $\frac{1}{5}$ = ☐ b $\frac{4}{10}$ = ☐ c $\frac{4}{5}$ = ☐ d $\frac{6}{10}$ = ☐

   e $\frac{5}{10}$ = ☐ f $\frac{2}{5}$ = ☐ g $\frac{1}{2}$ = ☐ h $\frac{10}{10}$ = ☐

2. Use the number lines above to compare the two fractions. Circle the smaller fraction.

   a $\frac{1}{5}$ $\frac{1}{10}$ b $\frac{6}{10}$ $\frac{1}{2}$ c $\frac{8}{10}$ $\frac{3}{5}$ d $\frac{4}{5}$ $\frac{9}{10}$

3. Complete the number lines. Count forwards and backwards.

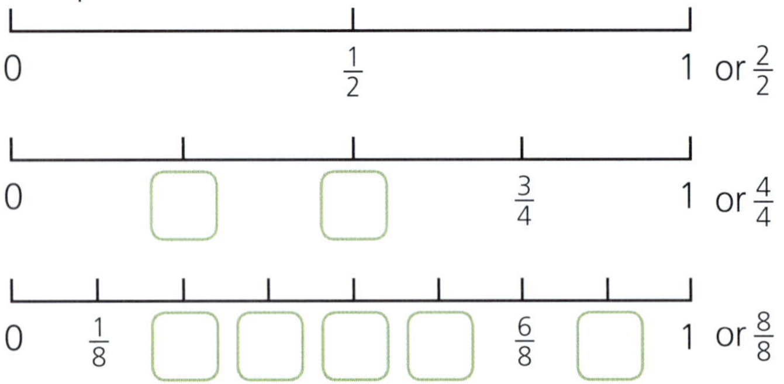

4. Use the number lines above to show an equivalent fraction for:

   a $\frac{1}{4}$ = ☐ b $\frac{4}{8}$ = ☐ c $\frac{2}{4}$ = ☐ d $\frac{1}{2}$ = ☐

   e $\frac{6}{8}$ = ☐ f $\frac{3}{4}$ = ☐ g $\frac{2}{8}$ = ☐ h $\frac{8}{8}$ = ☐

Equivalent fractions are equal fractions.

5. True or false?

   a $\frac{6}{6} = \frac{3}{3}$ ☐

   b $\frac{2}{6} = \frac{1}{3}$ ☐

   c $\frac{1}{3} = \frac{1}{6}$ ☐

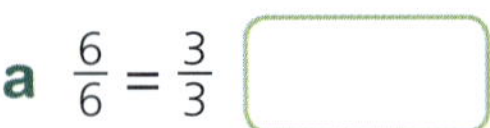
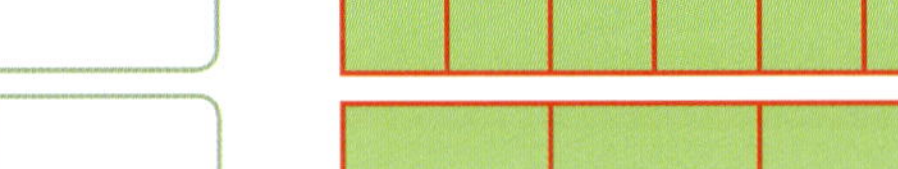

   d Is $\frac{1}{6}$ half of $\frac{1}{3}$? ☐

6. How many oranges do I have?

   a I have 2 halves of an orange. ☐

   b I have 3 thirds of an orange. ☐

   c I have 4 quarters of an orange. ☐

   d I have 8 quarters of an orange. ☐

1:13 Equivalent fractions

$\frac{3}{4}$ is 3 in each 4, so this would also be 6 in each 8.

CONCEPT

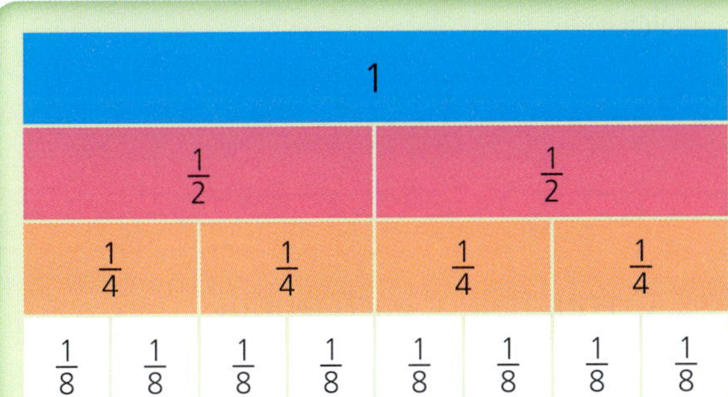

1					
$\frac{1}{2}$			$\frac{1}{2}$		
$\frac{1}{3}$		$\frac{1}{3}$		$\frac{1}{3}$	
$\frac{1}{6}$	$\frac{1}{6}$	$\frac{1}{6}$	$\frac{1}{6}$	$\frac{1}{6}$	$\frac{1}{6}$

1 What fraction is equal to:

a $\frac{2}{4}$? ☐ **b** $\frac{4}{8}$? ☐

c $\frac{6}{8}$? ☐ **d** $\frac{4}{4}$? ☐

e 1 ? ☐ **f** $\frac{1}{2}$? ☐

2 What fraction is equal to:

a $\frac{2}{6}$? ☐ **b** $\frac{4}{6}$? ☐

c $\frac{6}{6}$? ☐ **d** $\frac{3}{3}$? ☐

e $\frac{1}{3}$? ☐ **f** $\frac{2}{3}$? ☐

3 True (**T**) or false (**F**)?

a $\frac{1}{2} = \frac{2}{4}$ ☐ **b** $\frac{3}{4} = \frac{6}{8}$ ☐

c $\frac{4}{8} = \frac{2}{4}$ ☐ **d** $\frac{5}{8} = \frac{3}{4}$ ☐

e $\frac{8}{8} = \frac{4}{4}$ ☐ **f** $\frac{2}{2} = 1$ ☐

4 True (**T**) or false (**F**)?

a $\frac{2}{3} = \frac{4}{6}$ ☐ **b** $\frac{1}{3} = \frac{2}{6}$ ☐

c $\frac{3}{3} = \frac{6}{6}$ ☐ **d** $\frac{1}{6} = \frac{1}{3}$ ☐

e $\frac{3}{6} = \frac{2}{3}$ ☐ **f** $\frac{6}{6} = 1$ ☐

5 Complete each pattern.

a $\frac{1}{3}, \frac{2}{3}, \frac{3}{3}$, ☐, ☐, ☐, ☐

b $\frac{1}{4}, \frac{2}{4}, \frac{3}{4}$, ☐, ☐, ☐, ☐, ☐

c $\frac{1}{6}, \frac{2}{6}, \frac{3}{6}$, ☐, ☐, ☐, ☐, ☐, ☐

d $\frac{1}{8}, \frac{2}{8}, \frac{3}{8}$, ☐, ☐, ☐, ☐, ☐, ☐, ☐

1 whole is the same as $\frac{2}{2}, \frac{3}{3}, \frac{4}{4}, \frac{6}{6}$ or $\frac{8}{8}$.

6

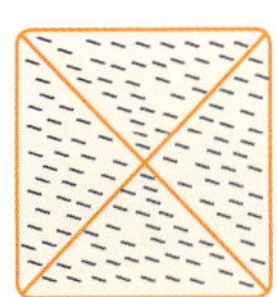

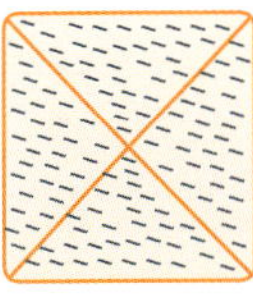

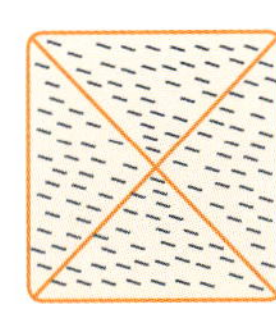

Count by quarters. One quarter, two quarters,

☐, ☐,
☐, ☐

FUN SPOT

- Cut 5 strips of paper the same length to construct your own fraction wall.
- Use one strip at a time to make separate strips folded into:
  - halves
  - quarters
  - eighths
  - thirds
  - sixths
- Paste these onto a large sheet of paper.

See *Extra Support 19* (Fraction patterns).

1:14 Comparing fractions

one third, two thirds, three thirds,…
$\frac{1}{3}$ $\frac{2}{3}$ $\frac{3}{3}$

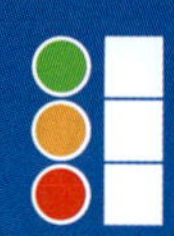

1 Draw lines to cut each shape into the correct parts, then colour:

a 2 halves b 3 thirds c 4 quarters d 8 eighths

2 Use 1 as a benchmark. Label the halves and quarters on these number lines.

a 0 ☐ ☐ ☐ 1

b 0 ☐ ☐ ☐ 1 ☐ ☐ ☐ 2

c 0 ☐ ☐ ☐ 1 ☐ ☐ ☐ 2 ☐ ☐ ☐

Where can fractions be found?

3 Colour half of each length.

a

b

c

Is each half the same size? ☐

Colour a quarter of each length.

d

e

f

Is each quarter the same size? ☐

4 a Andrew cut a 10 m length of wood into halves. How long was each half? ☐ m

b David cut a 14 m length of wood into halves. How long was each half? ☐ m

What is half of: c 8 m? ☐ d 4 m? ☐ e 2 m? ☐

INVESTIGATION

- Lydia and Isaac each had a length of paper. They each cut their length into halves. They found that their halves were not the same length. Discuss how this is possible.
- Jasmine ate a quarter of a cake. Matilda ate a quarter of another cake. Jasmine ate more cake than Matilda. Explain how this is possible.
- Cut strips of paper or pieces of food of different sizes in half. Compare the size of each half.

Conclusion: We can only compare fractions when the wholes are equal.

Tenths and fifths

$\frac{\square}{10}$ are yellow. $\frac{\square}{5}$ are blue.

1. Use the number line to write these decimals as tenths.

   a $0·3 = \frac{\square}{10}$ b $0·5 = \frac{\square}{10}$ c $0·9 = \frac{\square}{10}$ d $0·7 = \frac{\square}{10}$ e $0·6 = \frac{\square}{10}$

2. Write the decimal for:

   a $\frac{2}{10}$ ☐ b $\frac{5}{10}$ ☐ c $\frac{1}{10}$ ☐ d $\frac{9}{10}$ ☐
   e $\frac{8}{10}$ ☐ f $\frac{3}{10}$ ☐ g $\frac{7}{10}$ ☐ h $\frac{10}{10}$ ☐
   i $\frac{0}{10}$ ☐ j $\frac{4}{10}$ ☐ k $\frac{6}{10}$ ☐

3. Cut a straw into 5 equal parts. Label each part.

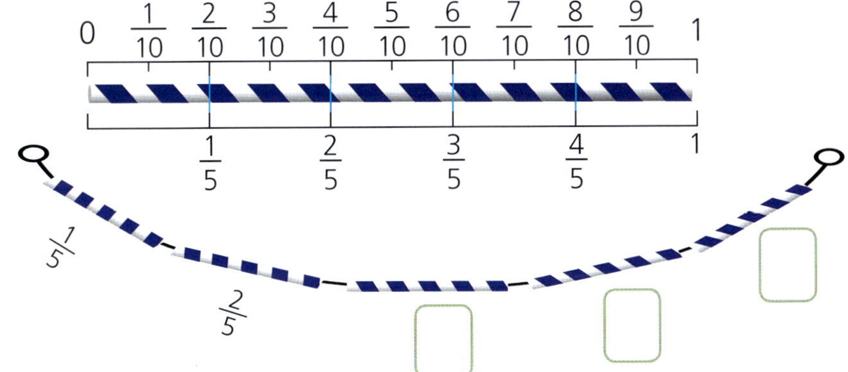

CONCEPT

$\frac{1}{5} = \frac{2}{10}$

$\frac{1}{5} = \frac{2}{10}$
$\frac{2}{5} = \frac{4}{10}$
$\frac{3}{5} = \frac{6}{10}$
$\frac{4}{5} = \frac{8}{10}$
$\frac{5}{5} = \frac{10}{10}$ or 1 whole

4. Write these as fifths.

   a one whole $\frac{\square}{5}$ b 2 tenths $\frac{\square}{5}$ c 4 tenths $\frac{\square}{5}$
   d 8 tenths $\frac{\square}{5}$ e 6 tenths $\frac{\square}{5}$ f 10 tenths $\frac{\square}{5}$

1 fifth is 1 of 5 equal parts.

5. Write these as tenths.

   a $\frac{2}{5}$ ☐ b $\frac{4}{5}$ ☐ c $\frac{3}{5}$ ☐ d $\frac{1}{5}$ ☐

1:16 Place value using tenths

$\frac{\square}{10}$ is yellow. $\frac{\square}{10}$ are red.

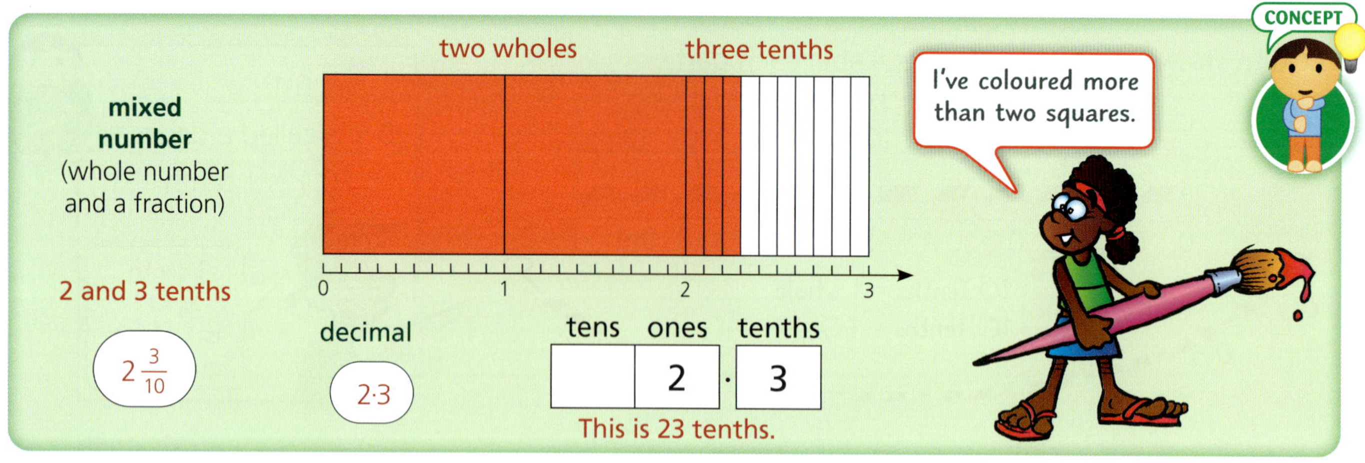

1 Write the decimal for:

a

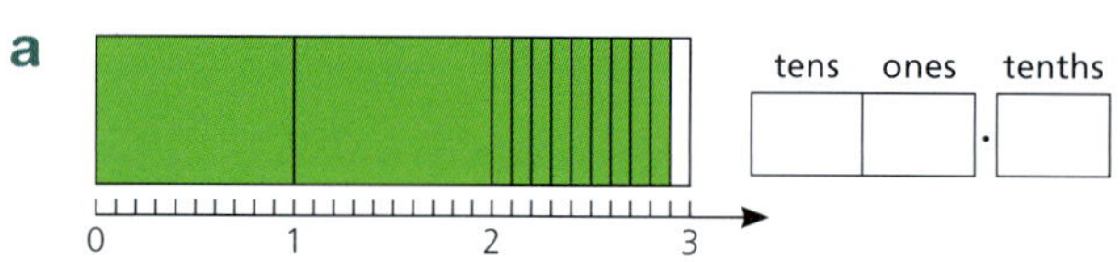

b

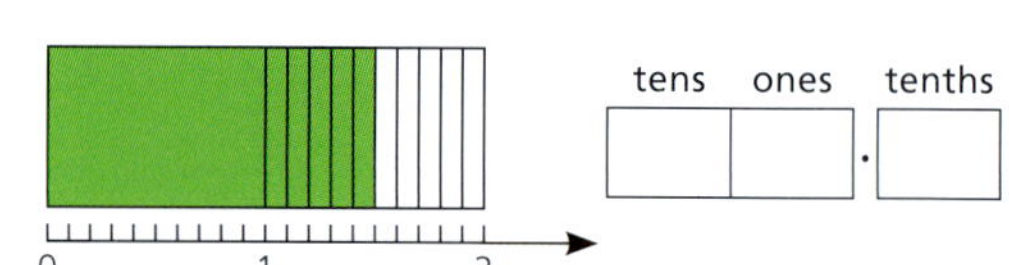

2 Write the decimal for:

a $\frac{1}{10}$ ☐ **b** $\frac{3}{10}$ ☐ **c** $\frac{5}{10}$ ☐

d $\frac{4}{10}$ ☐ **e** $\frac{2}{10}$ ☐ **f** $\frac{8}{10}$ ☐

g $\frac{9}{10}$ ☐ **h** $\frac{7}{10}$ ☐ **i** $\frac{10}{10}$ ☐

three tenths
0·3
decimal point

3 Write the decimal for:

a $1\frac{1}{10}$ ☐ **b** $1\frac{6}{10}$ ☐ **c** $1\frac{2}{10}$ ☐

d $2\frac{3}{10}$ ☐ **e** $2\frac{4}{10}$ ☐ **f** $2\frac{9}{10}$ ☐

g $3\frac{5}{10}$ ☐ **h** $3\frac{8}{10}$ ☐ **i** $3\frac{7}{10}$ ☐

$1\frac{3}{10} = 1·3$

$2\frac{6}{10} = 2·6$

$3\frac{9}{10} = 3·9$

4 Write the fraction (or mixed number) for:

a 0·5 ☐ **b** 0·7 ☐ **c** 0·2 ☐

d 1·4 ☐ **e** 3·1 ☐ **f** 2·8 ☐

g 6·9 ☐ **h** 5·3 ☐ **i** 7·6 ☐

j 2·5 ☐ **k** 5·4 ☐ **l** 6·7 ☐

m 0·9 ☐ **n** 1·9 ☐ **o** 2·9 ☐

5 Write as a decimal.

a 4 ones and 1 tenth

= ☐

b 8 ones and 3 tenths

= ☐

c 5 ones and 2 tenths

= ☐

1:17 Decimals

0·1 is the same as 0·10.

$0.1 is the same as $0.10.

CONCEPT

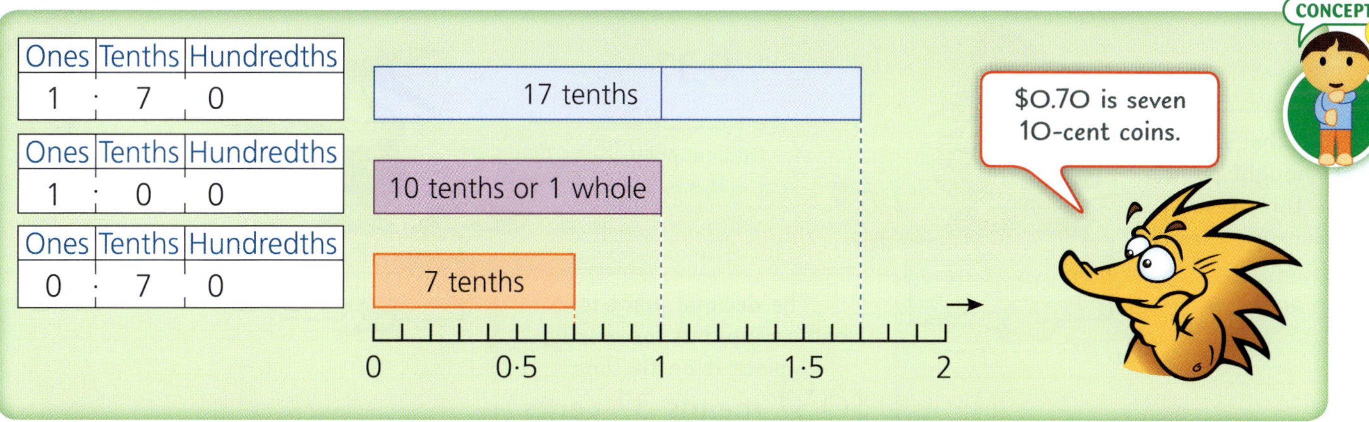

1 Write the decimal for:

a $\frac{7}{10}$ ☐ **b** $\frac{5}{10}$ ☐ **c** $\frac{6}{10}$ ☐ **d** $\frac{1}{10}$ ☐

e $\frac{8}{10}$ ☐ **f** $\frac{9}{10}$ ☐ **g** $\frac{2}{10}$ ☐ **h** $\frac{4}{10}$ ☐

i $1\frac{1}{10}$ ☐ **j** $1\frac{3}{10}$ ☐ **k** $1\frac{9}{10}$ ☐ **l** $1\frac{8}{10}$ ☐

2 Match each fraction with the correct decimal.

a

$\frac{5}{10}$	0·6
$\frac{1}{10}$	0·5
$\frac{6}{10}$	0·1

b

$\frac{8}{10}$	0·9
$\frac{4}{10}$	0·4
$\frac{9}{10}$	0·8

c

$1\frac{2}{10}$	2·3
$2\frac{7}{10}$	2·7
$2\frac{3}{10}$	1·2

3 Use decimals to write:

a 9 tenths ☐ **b** 7 tenths ☐ **c** 6 tenths ☐ **d** 2 tenths ☐

e 8 tenths ☐ **f** 3 tenths ☐ **g** 5 tenths ☐ **h** 10 tenths ☐

i zero point one ☐ **j** zero point eight ☐ **k** zero point five ☐

l one point nine ☐ **m** one point three ☐ **n** one point zero ☐

4 Complete the number lines.

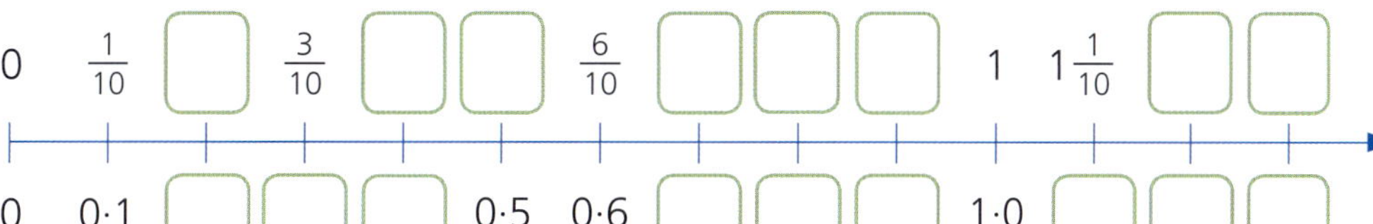

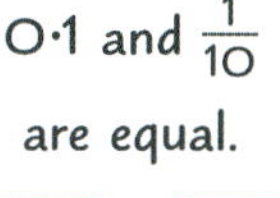

0·1 = 0·10
0·2 = 0·20
0·3 = 0·30
0·4 = 0·40

5 Tick the larger decimal.

a

0·2	
0·7	

b

0·40	
0·6	

c

0·5	
0·4	

d

0·9	
0·80	

Decimals

$0.05 is $$\frac{5}{100}$. $0.10 is $$\frac{10}{100}$.

$0.20 is $$\frac{20}{100}$. $0.50 is $$\frac{50}{100}$.

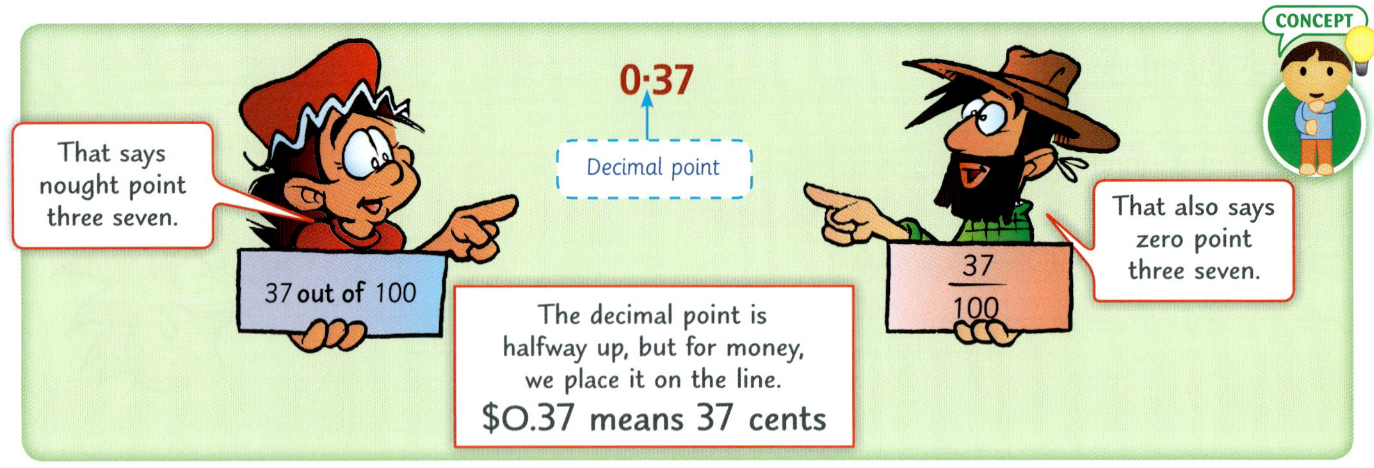

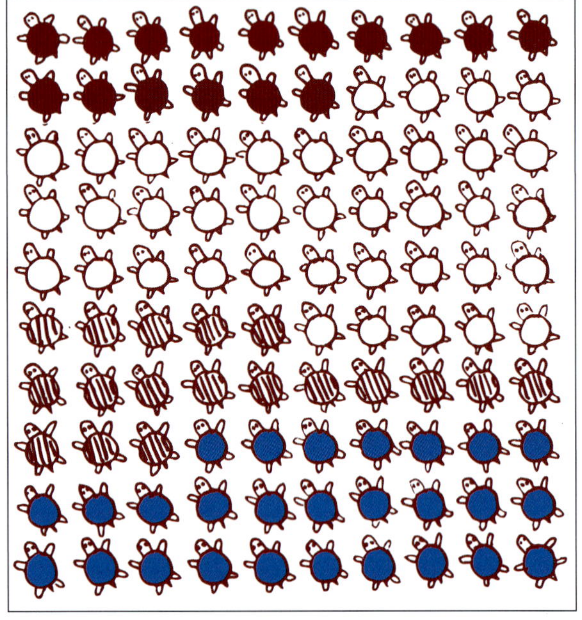

1 How many turtles are inside the box? ☐

2 What part of the group of turtles:

a is [turtle]?
☐ out of 100 ☐/100 0·☐

b is [turtle]?
☐ out of 100 ☐/100 0·☐

c is [turtle]?
☐ out of 100 ☐/100 0·☐

d is [turtle] and [turtle] together?
☐ out of 100 ☐/100 0·☐

3 What part of the group is [turtle]? 0·☐

4 Write the decimal and fraction shown on each hundred square.

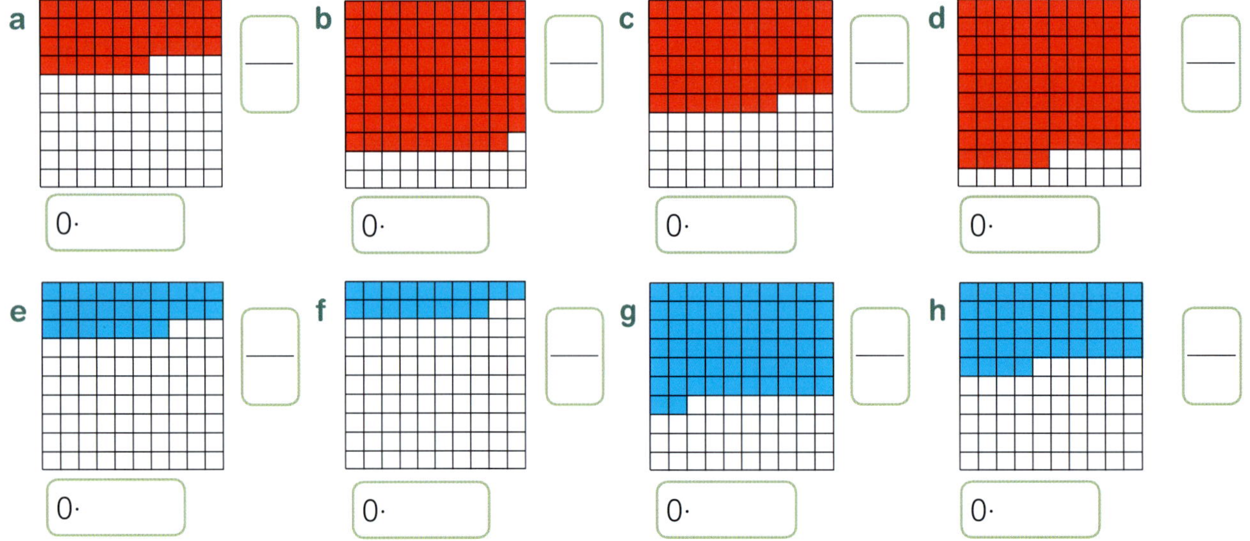

1:19 Decimals and place value

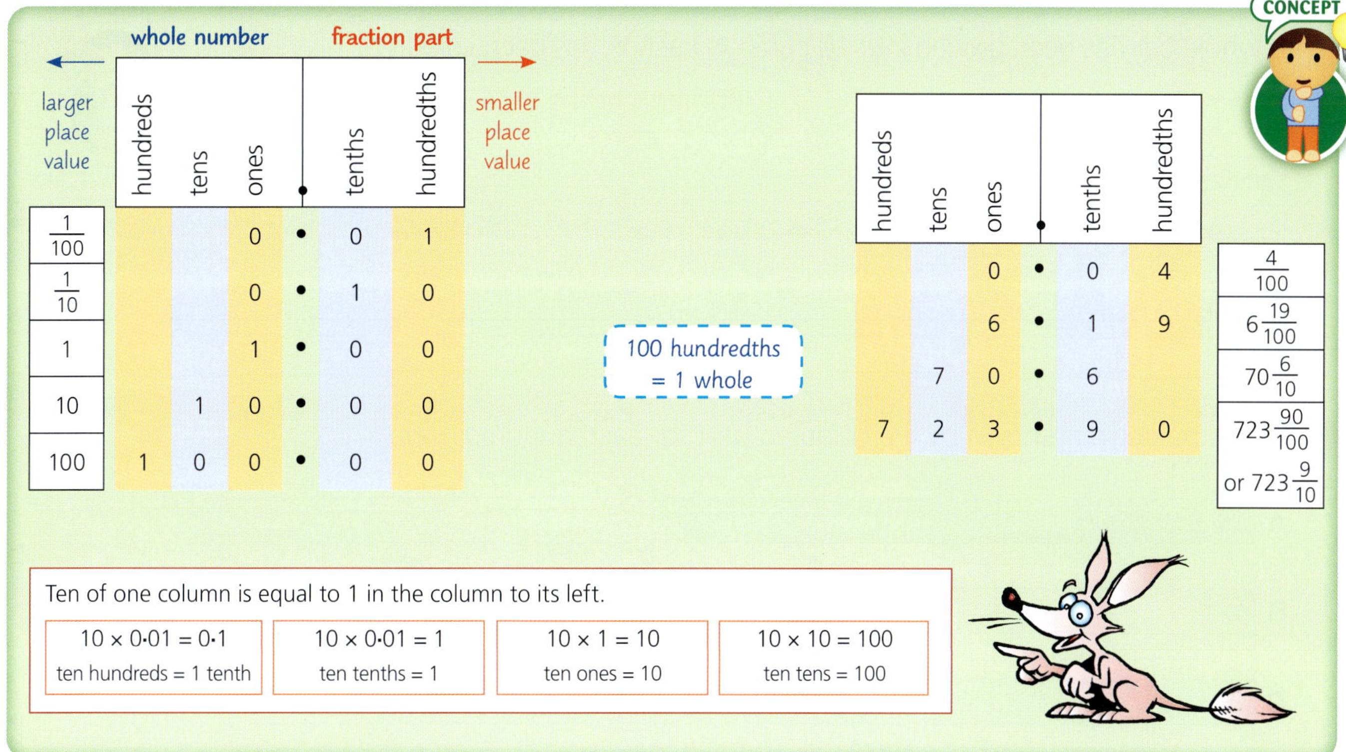

larger place value ← whole number | fraction part → smaller place value

	hundreds	tens	ones	•	tenths	hundredths
$\frac{1}{100}$			0	•	0	1
$\frac{1}{10}$			0	•	1	0
1			1	•	0	0
10		1	0	•	0	0
100	1	0	0	•	0	0

100 hundredths = 1 whole

hundreds	tens	ones	•	tenths	hundredths	
		0	•	0	4	$\frac{4}{100}$
		6	•	1	9	$6\frac{19}{100}$
	7	0	•	6		$70\frac{6}{10}$
7	2	3	•	9	0	$723\frac{90}{100}$ or $723\frac{9}{10}$

Ten of one column is equal to 1 in the column to its left.

10 × 0·01 = 0·1	10 × 0·01 = 1	10 × 1 = 10	10 × 10 = 100
ten hundreds = 1 tenth	ten tenths = 1	ten ones = 10	ten tens = 100

1 Write the decimal for each fraction.

		hundreds	tens	ones	•	tenths	hundredths
a	$\frac{4}{10}$				•		
b	$\frac{90}{100}$				•		
c	$\frac{20}{100}$				•		
d	$\frac{8}{10}$				•		
e	$\frac{52}{100}$				•		
f	$\frac{37}{100}$				•		

2 Write the decimal for each mixed number.

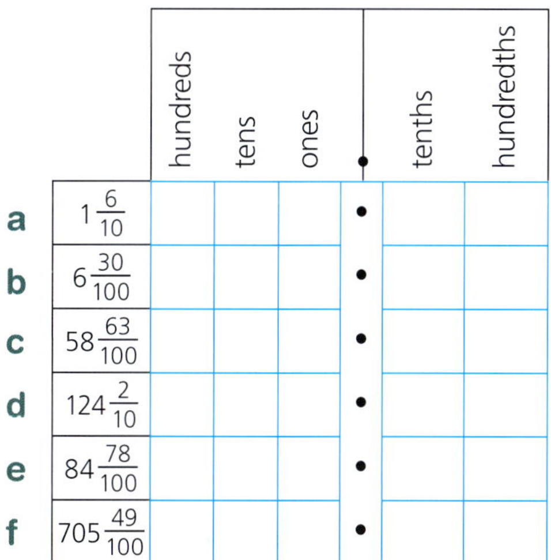

		hundreds	tens	ones	•	tenths	hundredths
a	$1\frac{6}{10}$				•		
b	$6\frac{30}{100}$				•		
c	$58\frac{63}{100}$				•		
d	$124\frac{2}{10}$				•		
e	$84\frac{78}{100}$				•		
f	$705\frac{49}{100}$				•		

3 13 tenths = 1 and 3 tenths = 1·3 Write these tenths as decimals.

a 15 tenths ☐ **b** 24 tenths ☐ **c** 62 tenths ☐ **d** 84 tenths ☐

4 0·25 is 2 tenths and 5 hundredths or 25 hundredths. Partition these decimals in the same way.

a 0·46 = ☐ tenths and ☐ hundredths 0·46 = ☐ hundredths

b 0·73 = ☐ tenths and ☐ hundredths 0·73 = ☐ hundredths

 • *AUSTRALIAN SIGNPOST MATHS NSW 4* • ISBN 9780655709053

1:20 Comparing decimals

$\frac{20}{100}$ is 0·20 or 0·2. $\frac{35}{100}$ is 0·35.
$\frac{2}{100}$ is 0·02. $\frac{5}{100}$ is 0·05.

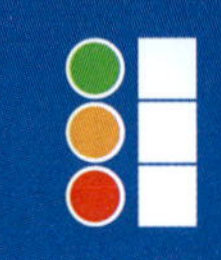

CONCEPT

This whole bar has been divided into 10 parts. A fraction has been coloured.

30 hundredths or 0·30 (0·3 or 3 tenths)

8 hundredths or 0·08

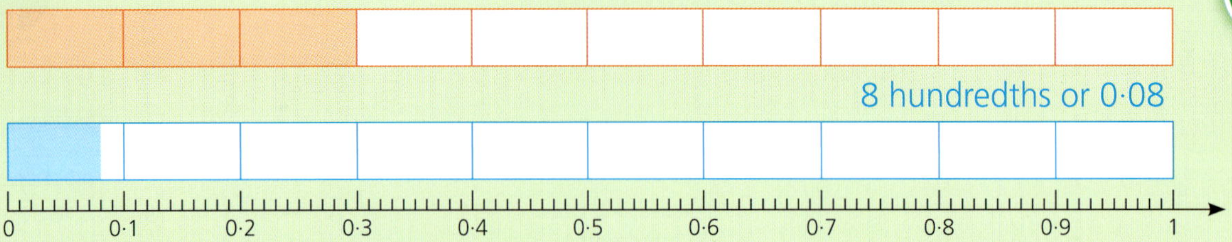

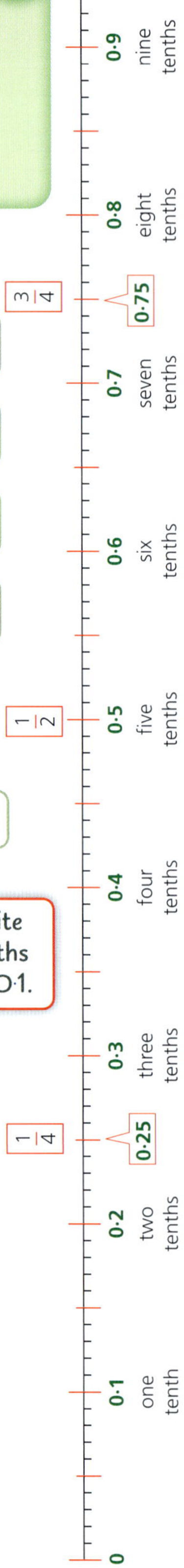

0 0·1 0·2 0·3 0·4 0·5 0·6 0·7 0·8 0·9 1

1 Write the decimal shown by the coloured part for each hundreds strip.

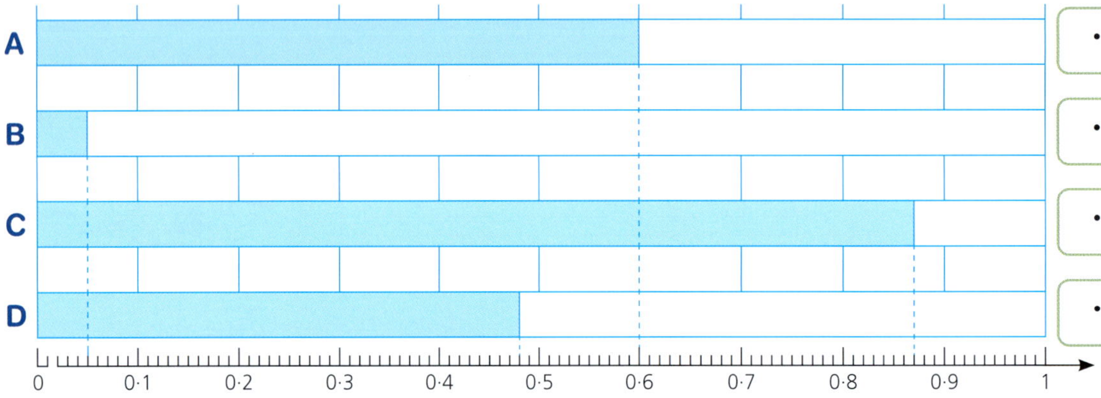

A ☐·☐

B ☐·☐

C ☐·☐

D ☐·☐

0 0·1 0·2 0·3 0·4 0·5 0·6 0·7 0·8 0·9 1

2 Which blue bar shows the largest fraction coloured?

a A, B or C? ☐ b A, B or D? ☐ c A, C or D? ☐ d A or D? ☐

3 Place a dot on these decimals on the number line to the right:

A 0·4 B 0·78 C 0·21 D 0·03 E 0·89 F 0·46

4 Tick the larger number. Use the number line to help you.

a	0·25	☐	b	0·9	☐	c	0·3	☐	d	1·2	☐
	0·5	☐		0·88	☐		0·14	☐		1·21	☐
e	2·23	☐	f	1·5	☐	g	0·3	☐	h	0·07	☐
	2·3	☐		2·4	☐		0·03	☐		0·7	☐
i	1·05	☐	j	0·2	☐	k	1·8	☐	l	0·45	☐
	1·5	☐		$\frac{1}{4}$	☐		$\frac{1}{4}$	☐		$\frac{1}{2}$	☐
m	0·55	☐									
	$\frac{1}{2}$	☐									

You can write 10 hundredths as 0·10 or 0·1.

10 hundredths
0·10
0·1

Number line (0 to 1): 0; 0·1 one tenth; 0·2 two tenths; 0·25 $\frac{1}{4}$; 0·3 three tenths; 0·4 four tenths; 0·5 five tenths $\frac{1}{2}$; 0·6 six tenths; 0·7 seven tenths; 0·75 $\frac{3}{4}$; 0·8 eight tenths; 0·9 nine tenths; 1

5 Write the decimal that follows:

a 0·26, 0·27, ☐ b 0·83, 0·84, ☐ c 0·47, 0·48, ☐

 AUSTRALIAN SIGNPOST MATHS NSW 4 • ISBN 9780655709053

1:21 Place value to hundredths

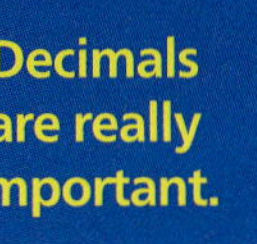

CONCEPT

	whole number				fraction part	
hundreds	tens	ones		tenths	hundredths	meaning
		0	•	4		4 tenths
		0	•	4	0	40 hundredths or 4 tenths
		2	•	5		2 ones and 5 tenths
		2	•	5	0	2 ones and 50 hundredths
		1	•	6	8	1 one and 68 hundredths
	1	6	•	8	0	16 ones and 80 hundredths
		9	•	2	5	9 ones and 25 hundredths
$2	4	0	•	7	5	240 dollars and 75 cents

← larger place value

smaller place value →

decimal point

The value of the 4 in the tenths column is 4 tenths.

My value is 10 x higher in the ones column than in the tenths column.

I don't need to be written in the hundredths column for 16·80.

- 1·68 is read as one point six eight.
- The decimal point separates the whole number part from the fraction part.

1 Write the decimal for:

a 7 tenths ☐ **b** 3 tenths ☐ **c** 2 tenths ☐

d 9 and 2 tenths ☐ **e** 8 and 4 tenths ☐ **f** 10 and 9 tenths ☐

g 49 hundredths ☐ **h** 28 hundredths ☐ **i** 37 hundredths ☐

j 384 and 4 tenths ☐ **k** 458 and 25 hundredths ☐

l 30 and 5 tenths ☐ **m** 703 and 7 hundredths ☐

n 95 cents ☐ **o** 52 dollars and 9 cents ☐

2 **a** Circle these positions on the number line: 0, 0·25, 0·5, 0·75 and 1.

b Put blue dots to show the position of 0·5, 0·05 and 0·55 on the number line.

c Put red dots on the number line to show the positions of 0·37, 0·62, 0·87, 0·07, 0·53.

d Place a cross on the number line to show the positions of 1·0, 0·1, 0·01.

3 **a** Is one tenth equal to 10 hundredths? ☐ **b** Is 0·5 larger than 0·45? ☐

c Is five tenths larger than 9 hundredths? ☐ **d** Is 0·8 larger than 0·65? ☐

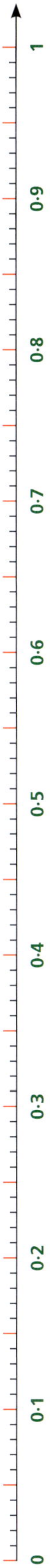

Number line: 0, 0·1, 0·2, 0·3, 0·4, 0·5, 0·6, 0·7, 0·8, 0·9, 1

 • *AUSTRALIAN SIGNPOST MATHS NSW 4* • ISBN 9780655709053

1:22 Place value to hundedths

CONCEPT

This number is 578·96.

This diagram shows the symmetry on both sides of the ones.

hundreds	tens	ones	·	tenths	hundredths
5	7	8	·	9	6

1 Write each number on the place-value chart.

	Ones		Tenths	Hundredths
a two point five nine		·		
b six point seven three		·		
c nine point four one		·		
d five point two six		·		
e eight point four eight		·		
f seven point one three		·		
g six point seven nine		·		

2·59 metres is 2 metres and 59 hundredths of the next metre

2 3·46 has 3 ones, 4 tenths and 6 hundredths. Write the number that has:

a 12 ones and 56 hundredths ☐

b 35 ones, 7 tenths and 2 hundredths ☐

c 38 ones and 37 hundredths ☐

d 17 ones, 2 tenths and 9 hundredths ☐

e 52 ones and 19 hundredths ☐

f 46 ones, 3 tenths and 0 hundredths ☐

g 92 ones and 7 hundredths ☐

h 8 ones, 0 tenths and 6 hundredths ☐

3 Write the value for each coloured digit.

a 4·3**2** ☐ **b** 8·**4**7 ☐ **c** **3**·95 ☐ **d** 5·3**8** ☐ **e** **1**·76 ☐

f 7·**5**1 ☐ **g** **2**·84 ☐ **h** 9·6**2** ☐ **i** 1·**6**9 ☐ **j** 6·5**1** ☐

FUN SPOT

Digit game

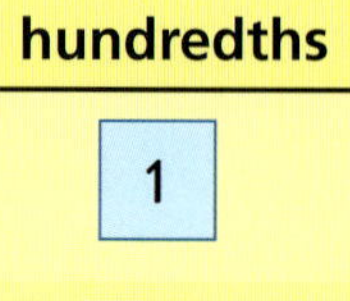

- In turn, each player receives one numeral card from a dealer and places it in one column of a place-value chart.
- Two more cards are received and placed in the same way.
- The player with the largest number wins a point.

1:23 Reading and writing decimals

Is 1·25 larger than 1·5?

CONCEPT

We say: two hundred and seventy-five point six four.

hundreds	tens	ones		tenths	hundredths
2	7	5	•	6	4
1	3	6	•	0	8
		9	•	4	0
	8	1	•	7	
		0	•	6	2

We can partition these decimals in different ways.

- 275·64 has 27 tens, 5 ones and 64 hundredths
- 136·08 has 136 ones and 8 hundredths
- 9·40 = 9·4 The zero is not necessary, because 40 hundredths is the same as 4 tenths.
- 0·62 has 6 tenths and 2 hundredths.

1 Use numerals to write:

a nineteen point seven five
b forty point nine one
c sixty-seven point eight two
d thirty point zero six
e fifty-two point one four
f twenty-seven point four three

2 Complete the following.

a 0·86 ☐ tenths and ☐ hundredths
b 0·09 ☐ tenths and ☐ hundredths
c 0·60 ☐ tenths and ☐ hundredths

3 Write the number represented by:

a 6 hundreds, 2 tens, 9 ones, 3 tenths and 7 hundredths
b 4 hundreds, 6 tens, 3 ones, 0 tenths and 9 hundredths
c 7 hundreds, 3 tens, 1 one and 6 tenths
d 9 hundreds, 5 tens, 7 ones, 4 tenths and 2 hundredths
e five and six tenths
f ten and three tenths
g two and eight tenths
h seven and nine tenths

$2.75 is read 'two dollars seventy-five'.
2·75 metres is read 'two point seven five metres.

4 Write the value for each coloured digit.

a 164·21 **b** 359·73 **c** 847·35 **d** 652·47
e 278·52 **f** 247·38 **g** 516·69 **h** 759·57
i 316·84 **j** 472·19 **k** 792·62 **l** 134·85

 ISBN 9780655709053

2:01 Number patterns

Skip counting helps you remember the multiplication tables.

Use skip counting to continue the patterns on this page. Add on the same number each time.

1
- **a** 1, 2, 3, 4, ___, ___, ___, ___, ___, ___, ___
- **b** 2, 4, 6, 8, ___, ___, ___, ___, ___, ___, ___
- **c** 3, 6, 9, 12, ___, ___, ___, ___, ___, ___, ___
- **d** 4, 8, 12, 16, ___, ___, ___, ___, ___, ___, ___
- **e** 5, 10, 15, 20, ___, ___, ___, ___, ___, ___, ___
- **f** 6, 12, 18, 24, ___, ___, ___, ___, ___, ___, ___
- **g** 7, 14, 21, 28, ___, ___, ___, ___, ___, ___, ___
- **h** 8, 16, 24, 32, ___, ___, ___, ___, ___, ___, ___
- **i** 9, 18, 27, 36, ___, ___, ___, ___, ___, ___, ___
- **j** 10, 20, 30, 40, ___, ___, ___, ___, ___, ___, ___

2
- **a** 9, 10, 11, ___, ___
- **b** 18, 20, 22, ___, ___
- **c** 27, 30, 33, ___, ___
- **d** 36, 40, 44, ___, ___
- **e** 45, 50, 55, ___, ___
- **f** 54, 60, 66, ___, ___
- **g** 63, 70, 77, ___, ___
- **h** 72, 80, 88, ___, ___
- **i** 81, 90, 99, ___, ___
- **j** 90, 100, 110, ___, ___

You could use me.

3 Consider your answers to Question 1. Explain the pattern made by the last digits of each number in part:

- **a** **b** ___
- **b** **d** ___
- **c** **e** ___
- **d** **f** ___
- **e** **h** ___
- **f** **i** ___
- **g** **j** ___

4 Make two number patterns of your own.

- **a** ___, ___, ___, ___
- **b** ___, ___, ___, ___

Multiplication tables revision

Step 1: Have someone test you.

Step 2: For each table you don't know, make a card with the question on one side and the answer on the other.

Step 3: Carry these cards with you, testing yourself until you know them.

Use these steps to learn your 1, 2, 3, 5 and 10 times tables.

1 Use skip counting to complete.

×	0	1	2	3	4	5	6	7	8	9	10
1											
2											
3											
5											
10											

2 Complete these number wheels.

a

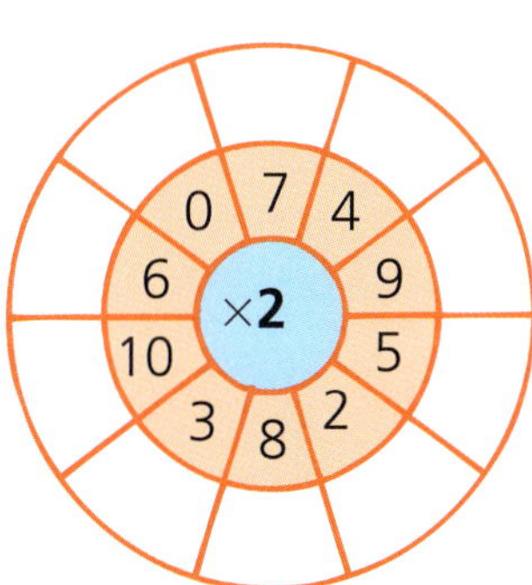

b

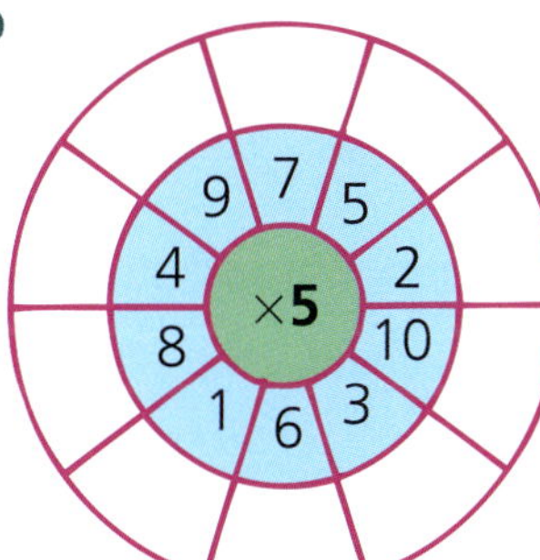

c

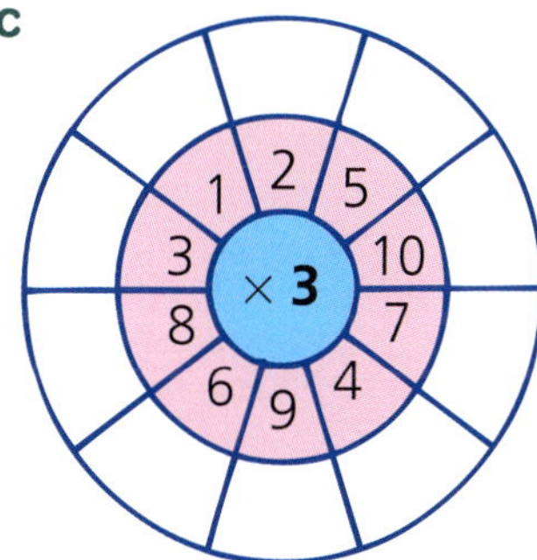

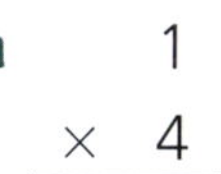

3

a 1×4 = ___

b 5×6 = ___

c 10×7 = ___

d 2×5 = ___

e 2×6 = ___

f 1×8 = ___

g 10×6 = ___

h 2×7 = ___

Multiplication cards

- Cards marked 1 to 10 are placed face down in a pile.
- One card is turned at a time. The first to correctly multiply the card by 5, keeps the card. The player with the most cards wins.

 • *AUSTRALIAN SIGNPOST MATHS NSW 4* • ISBN 9780655709053

× 4 tables

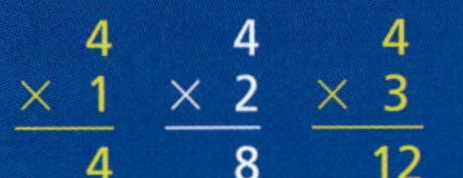
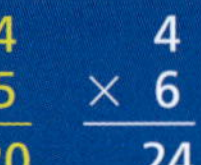
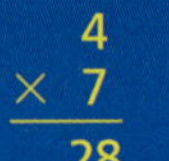
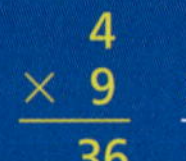
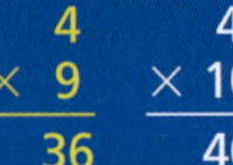

4	4	4	4	4	4	4	4	4	4
× 1	× 2	× 3	× 4	× 5	× 6	× 7	× 8	× 9	× 10
4	8	12	16	20	24	28	32	36	40

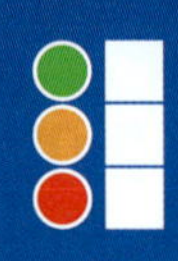

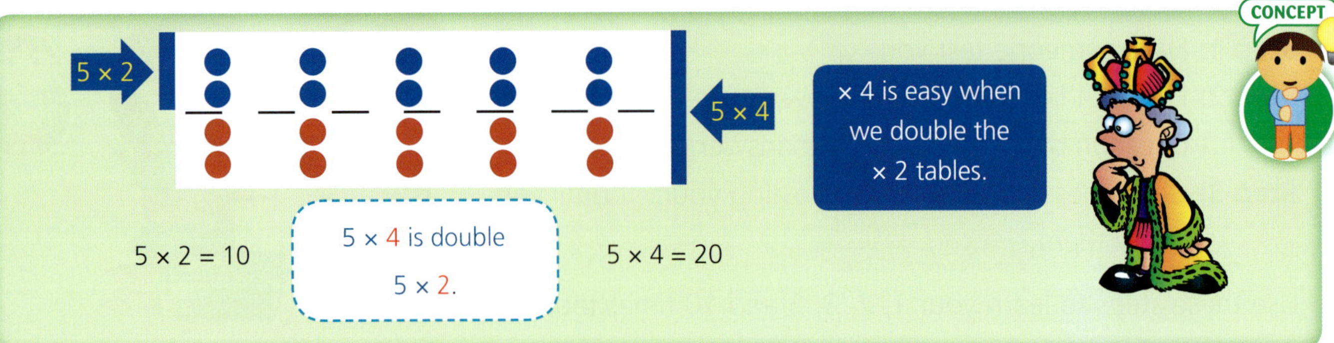

1. **a** 1 × 2 = ☐ 1 × 4 = ☐ **b** 7 × 2 = ☐ 7 × 4 = ☐ **c** 10 × 2 = ☐ 10 × 4 = ☐ **d** 8 × 2 = ☐ 8 × 4 = ☐

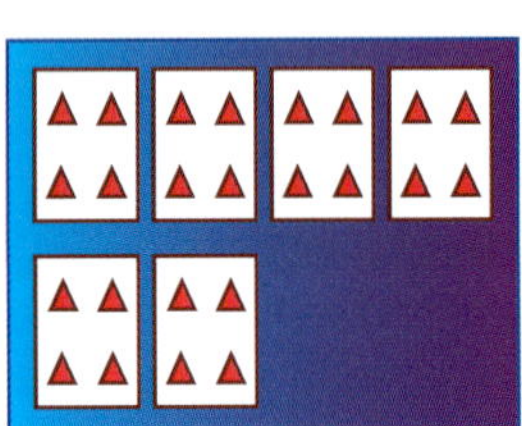

2. **a** 6 groups of 4 = ☐

b 9 groups of 4 = ☐

Use skip counting to complete.

c 4 groups of 4 = ☐

d 7 groups of 4 = ☐

e 8 groups of 4 = ☐

3. Complete the table.

×	0	1	2	3	4	5	6	7	8	9	10
2											
4											

4. **a** 3 groups of 4 cars

☐ × ☐ = ☐

b 5 groups of 4 cars

☐ × ☐ = ☐

c 10 groups of 4 cars

☐ × ☐ = ☐

d 11 groups of 4 cars

☐ × ☐ = ☐

5. Complete these number wheels.

All answers to × 4 tables end in 2, 4, 6, 8 or 0.

a

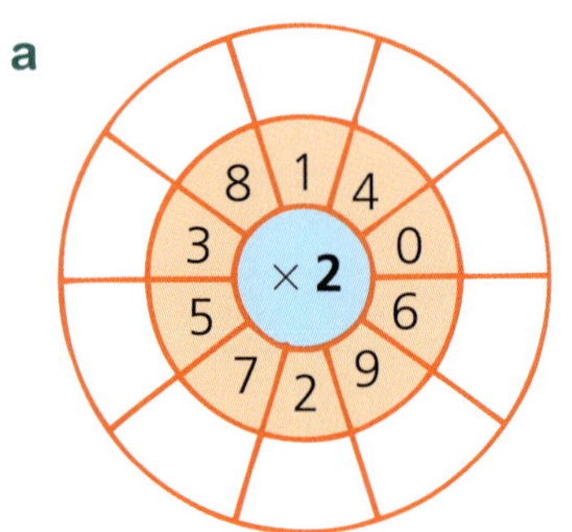

b

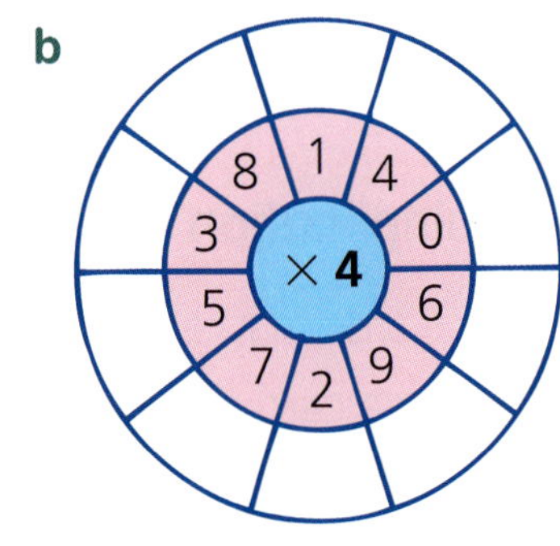

 • *AUSTRALIAN SIGNPOST MATHS NSW 4* • ISBN 9780655709053

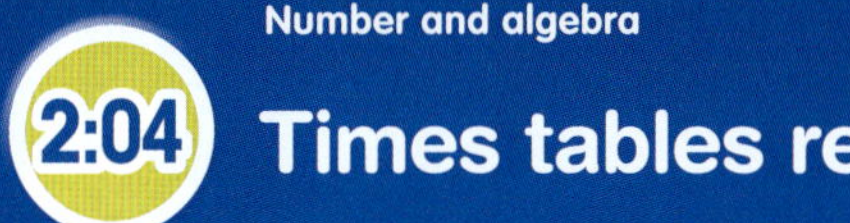

Times tables review

If you know that 6 × 5 = 30
then 7 × 5 = (6 × 5) + 5 = 35.

Start 4 8 10 12 16 20 24 28 30 32 36 40 44 48 50 60 70 80 90 100

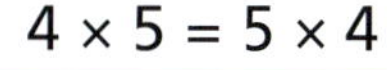

- Any number times 1 stays the same. 9 × 1 = 9
- Any number times 0 is equal to 0. 9 × 0 = 0
- To multiply by 4, we can double and double again.
  6 × 4 = (6 × 2) × 2 = 12 × 2 = 24
- To multiply by 10, place a zero and the end. 7 × 10 = 70
- To multiply by 5, you can multiply by 10 and halve the answer.
  7 × 5 = half of 7 × 10 = 35

4 × 5 = 5 × 4

1 Join each question to its answer using a pencil and ruler.

a

× 4	
0 × 4	4
1 × 4	12
2 × 4	0
3 × 4	20
4 × 4	8
5 × 4	16
6 × 4	36
7 × 4	24
8 × 4	40
9 × 4	28
10 × 4	32

b

× 4	
3 × 4	0
0 × 4	12
5 × 4	4
1 × 4	28
7 × 4	20
2 × 4	32
8 × 4	40
4 × 4	8
6 × 4	36
10 × 4	24
9 × 4	16

c

×	
6 × 10	0
3 × 1	10
4 × 0	2
5 × 2	3
2 × 1	60
7 × 2	12
4 × 10	10
6 × 2	80
10 × 1	14
9 × 2	40
8 × 10	18

× 2 answers end in: 0, 2, 4, 6, or 8.

× 10 answers end in: 0.

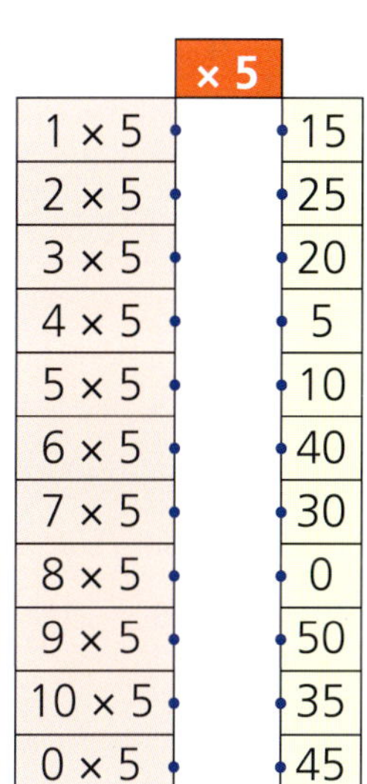

d

× 5	
1 × 5	15
2 × 5	25
3 × 5	20
4 × 5	5
5 × 5	10
6 × 5	40
7 × 5	30
8 × 5	0
9 × 5	50
10 × 5	35
0 × 5	45

e

× 5	
1 × 5	50
6 × 5	10
10 × 5	5
5 × 5	40
8 × 5	30
0 × 5	45
2 × 5	25
9 × 5	35
3 × 5	20
7 × 5	0
4 × 5	15

f

×	
7 × 10	15
6 × 5	32
3 × 5	8
8 × 4	70
4 × 2	30
7 × 4	25
5 × 5	24
6 × 4	28
1 × 5	5
7 × 2	36
9 × 4	14

× 5 answers end in: 5 or 0.

40 is
☐ × 10
☐ × 4
☐ × 5

 • *AUSTRALIAN SIGNPOST MATHS NSW 4* • ISBN 9780655709053

2:05 Addition, no trading

7 tens and 2 ones
+ 2 tens and 3 ones

CONCEPT

- 34 planes took off during the day and 12 during the night. How many planes took off?

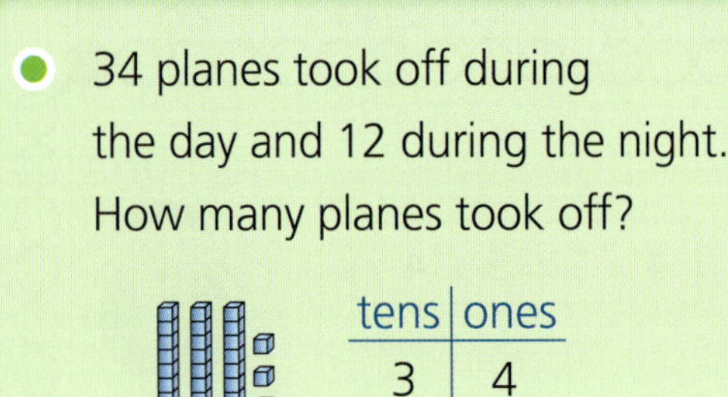

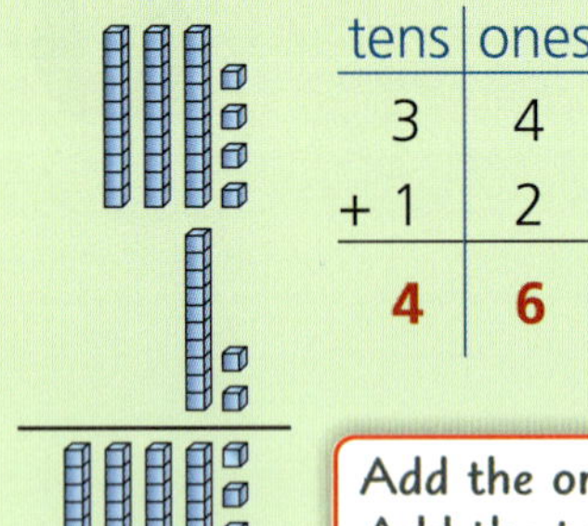

tens	ones
3	4
+ 1	2
4	**6**

Add the ones.
Add the tens.

tens	ones
1	4
3	2
+ 2	3
6	**9**

1 Use the split strategy or place-value blocks to answer these.

a

tens	ones
9	2
+	6

b

tens	ones
4	2
+ 5	1

c

tens	ones
3	5
+ 6	2

d

tens	ones
1	5
+ 2	3

e

tens	ones
$5	0
+ $1	9

f

tens	ones
$2	3
+ $1	5

g

tens	ones
$4	4
+ $4	4

h

tens	ones
$2	7
+ $5	1

2 Use the split strategy or place-value blocks to answer these.

a

tens	ones
3	1
1	6
+ 2	2

b

tens	ones
2	3
4	2
+ 1	0

c

tens	ones
4	1
2	2
+ 1	3

d

tens	ones
2	4
1	4
+ 3	1

e

tens	ones
3	0
1	4
+ 3	2

f

tens	ones
4	2
1	5
+ 2	1

g

tens	ones
2	5
3	1
+ 1	3

h

tens	ones
3	2
4	1
+ 1	5

i

tens	ones
$5	1
$1	4
+ $2	2

j

tens	ones
$3	3
$4	0
+ $1	5

k

tens	ones
$2	0
$3	6
+ $2	1

l

tens	ones
$4	3
$3	1
+ $2	5

See *Extra Support 1* (Addition and subtraction facts).

2:06 Addition and subtraction, no trading

- I bought 37 apples and sold 24.
  How many were left?

  3 tens and 7 ones
  − 2 tens and 4 ones

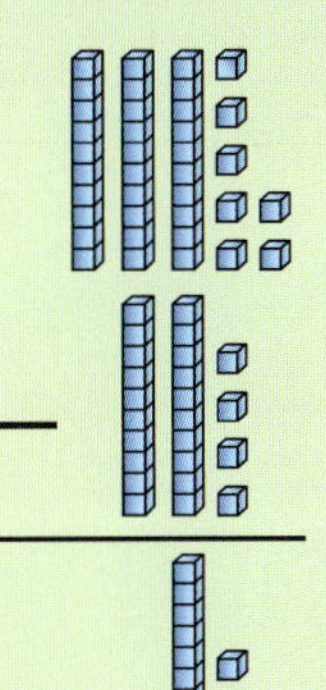

tens	ones
3	7
− 2	4
1	3

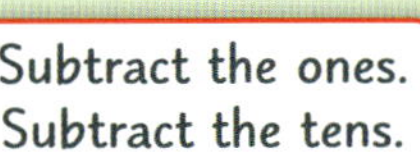

1 **a**

tens	ones
5	7
− 3	4

b

tens	ones
5	6
− 2	1

c

tens	ones
4	7
− 1	5

d

tens	ones
7	8
− 4	1

e

tens	ones
7	5
− 7	4

f

tens	ones
6	9
− 4	3

g

tens	ones
4	4
− 1	1

h

tens	ones
6	3
− 5	3

i

tens	ones
$8	4
− $8	0

j

tens	ones
$7	3
− $4	3

k

tens	ones
$9	9
− $3	2

l

tens	ones
$6	8
− $2	4

2 Model the question, write it as an algorithm, then find the answer.

a 23 candles
11 candles
54 candles
How many altogether?

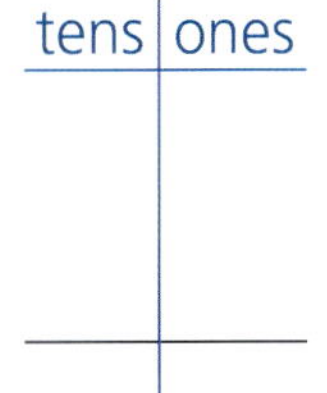

tens	ones

b 30 lollies
25 lollies
14 lollies
How many altogether?

tens	ones

3 **a** I paid $23 for a shirt and $56 for pants.
How much did I spend?

b There are 14 boys and 13 girls in our class.
How many in our class?

4 Complete each number sentence.

a 47 birds, 35 fly away.
How many remain? =

b 56 books, 34 covered.
How many more to cover? =

c 74 needed, 61 collected.
How many more to collect? =

See *Extra Support 1* (Addition and subtraction facts).

2:07 Addition to 99 with trading

5 tens 14 ones
50 + 10 + 4
6 tens 4 ones

CONCEPT

- Thirty-eight ducks and twenty-six chickens were in the yard. How many birds were there altogether?

Find:
How many birds?

Number sentence:
38 + 26 = ☐

Answer:
64 birds were in the yard.

3	8
+ 2	6
1	4 (sum of ones)
+ 5	0 (sum of tens)
6	4

We trade 10 ones for 1 ten.

tens	ones
1	
3	8
+ 2	6
6	4

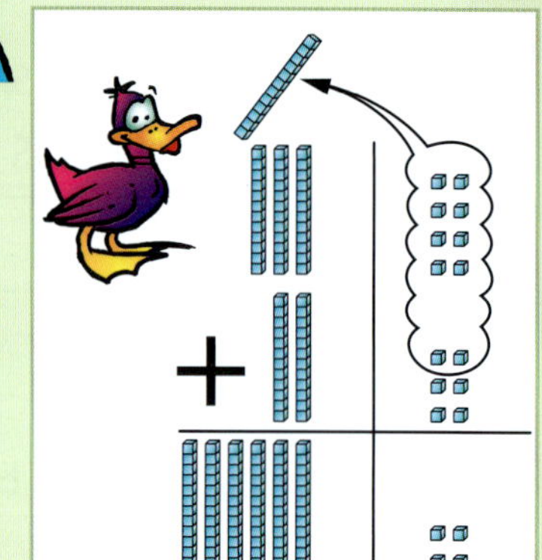

Show the trading on these algorithms.

1

	a	b	c	d
tens ones	2 2	3 3	1 5	2 6
	+ 1 9	+ 5 7	+ 5 8	+ 5 8

	e	f	g	h
tens ones	1 6	4 4	6 2	7 6
	+ 2 7	+ 3 8	+ 2 8	+ 1 9

	i	j	k	l
tens ones	3	8 1	2 5	5 7
	+ 8 9	+ 9	+ 2 6	+ 2 7

2

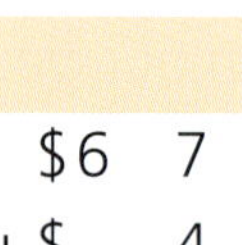

	a	b	c	d
tens ones	$6 7	$ 8	$2 8	$4 5
	+ $ 4	+ $5 4	+ $3 8	+ $1 7

3
a I have 42 English coins and 19 Turkish coins. How many coins do I have? ☐ coins
b We have 26 budgerigars and 58 finches. How many birds do we have? ☐ birds
c Hudson has 37 lizards and 18 snakes. How many reptiles does he have? ☐ reptiles

See *Extra Support 1* (Addition and subtraction facts).

 • *AUSTRALIAN SIGNPOST MATHS NSW 4* • ISBN 9780655709053

2:08 Addition to 99 with trading

3 tens 12 ones
30 + 10 + 2
4 tens 2 ones

1

a tens ones

tens	ones
4	8
+ 4	6

b tens ones

tens	ones
7	4
+ 1	6

c tens ones

tens	ones
2	2
+ 7	5

d tens ones

tens	ones
1	5
+ 5	9

e tens ones

tens	ones
8	6
+ 1	3

f tens ones

tens	ones
4	9
+ 3	7

g tens ones

tens	ones
5	7
+ 2	8

h tens ones

tens	ones
2	6
+ 6	6

i tens ones

tens	ones
$6	4
+ $2	9

j tens ones

tens	ones
$1	8
+ $5	3

k tens ones

tens	ones
$3	8
+ $3	8

l tens ones

tens	ones
$4	9
+ $2	2

Example

How many rulers were in the classroom if 27 were on the desks and 35 were still in the cupboard?

Find:

How many rulers?

Number sentence:

27 + 35 = ☐

Answer:

There were 62 rulers in the classroom.

Working:

tens	ones
1	
2	7
+ 3	5
6	2

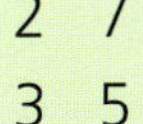

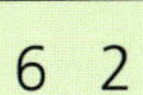

Algorithms are also useful.

```
   2 7
 + 3 5
   1 2   sum of ones
 + 5 0   sum of tens
   6 2
```

2 Answer these questions, setting them out as shown above.

a A group of emus has 13 females and 17 males. How many emus are there altogether?

Answer: ☐ emus

tens ones

b There were 37 kiwis in the zoo. 46 more were hatched. How many kiwis are in the zoo now?

Answer: ☐ kiwis

tens ones

c A woman needed 20 metres of pink ribbon and 34 metres of blue ribbon. How much ribbon did she need?

Answer: ☐ metres

tens ones

d 28 finches and 12 doves were kept in a large aviary. How many birds were there altogether?

Answer: ☐ birds

tens ones

See *Extra Support 1* (Addition and subtraction facts).

 • *AUSTRALIAN SIGNPOST MATHS NSW 4* • ISBN 9780655709053

2:09 Jump strategy, +

28 + 40 = ☐ 28 + 50 = ☐
28 + 10 = ☐ 28 + 20 = ☐
49 + 20 = ☐ 49 + 30 = ☐

CONCEPT

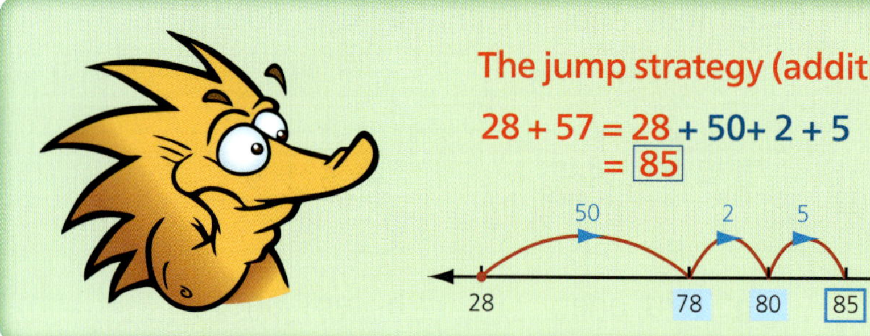

The jump strategy (addition)

28 + 57 = 28 + 50 + 2 + 5
= 85

Steps

1. Add the tens.
2. Jump to the next 10 if you can.
3. Add on anything left over.

To add 7, we add 2 then 5.

1 Use the jump strategy to answer these questions.

a 28 + 27 ☐ To add 7, we add 2 then 5.

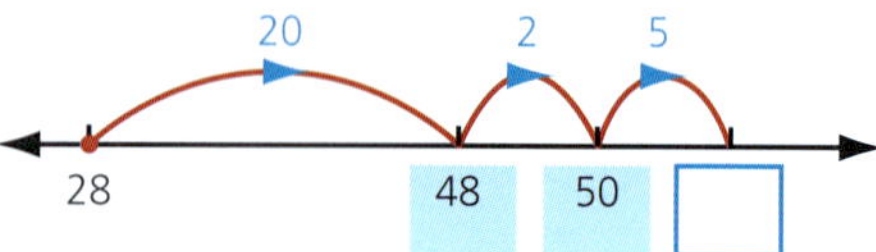

b 49 + 34 ☐ To add 4, we add 1 then 3.

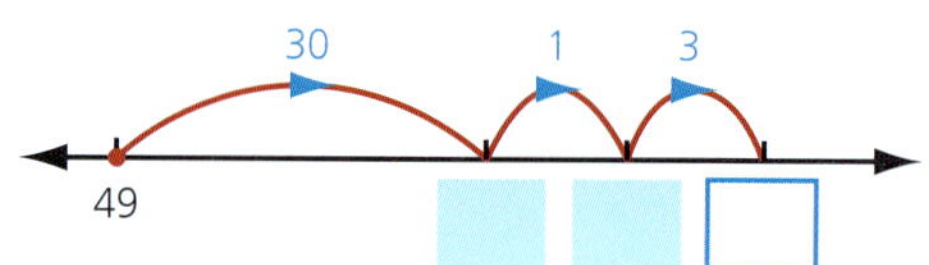

c 15 + 69 ☐

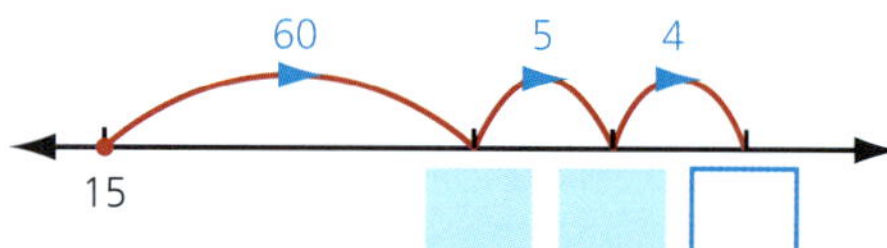

d 57 + 27 ☐

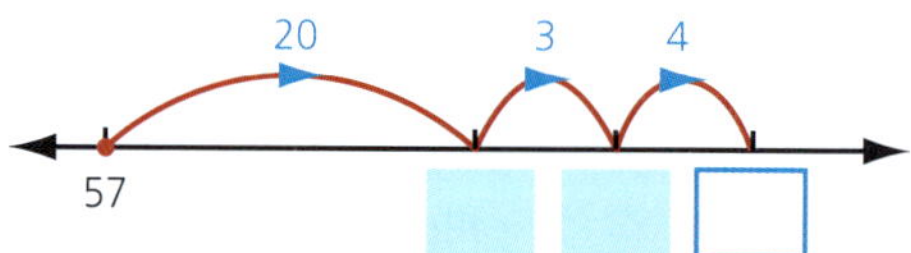

e 46 + 38 ☐

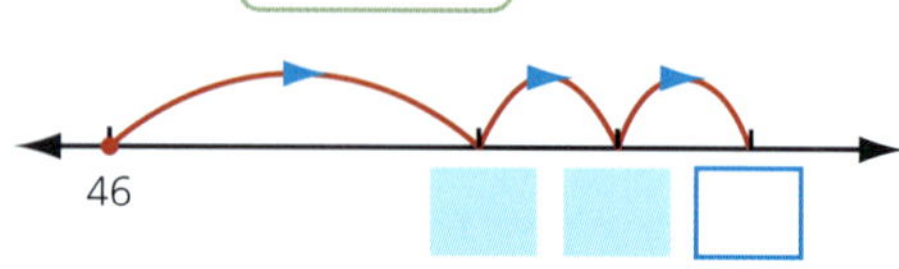

f 49 + 34 ☐

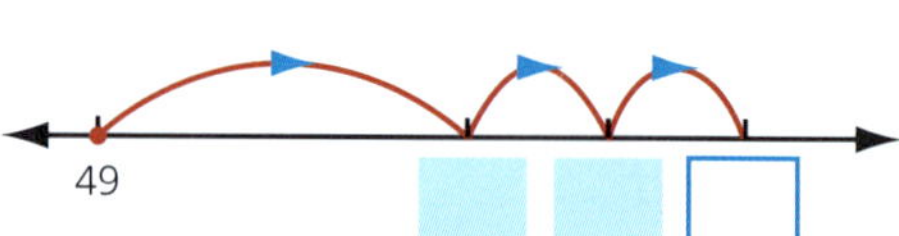

2 Use the jump strategy to answer these questions.

a 29 + 29 ☐

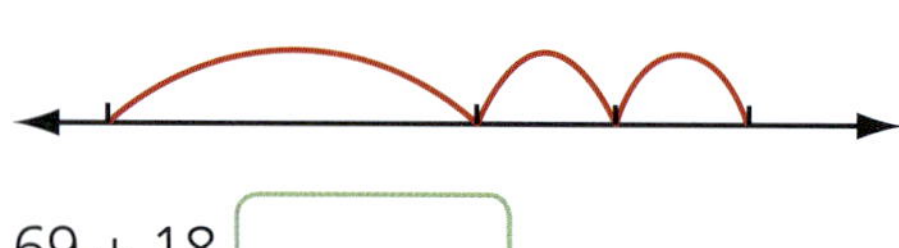

b 48 + 23 ☐

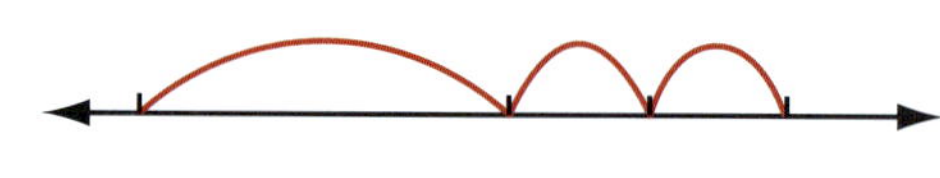

c 69 + 18 ☐

d 36 + 45 ☐

Do these on your own paper or in your head.

e 37 + 45 ☐

f 18 + 58 ☐

g 53 + 39 ☐

h 28 + 47 ☐

See *Extra Support 2* (Building to the next 10).

Jump strategy, –

52 – 20 = ☐ 52 – 30 = ☐
72 – 10 = ☐ 72 – 20 = ☐
41 – 20 = ☐ 41 – 30 = ☐

CONCEPT

The jump strategy (subtraction)

52 – 27 = 52 – 20 – 2 – 5
= 85

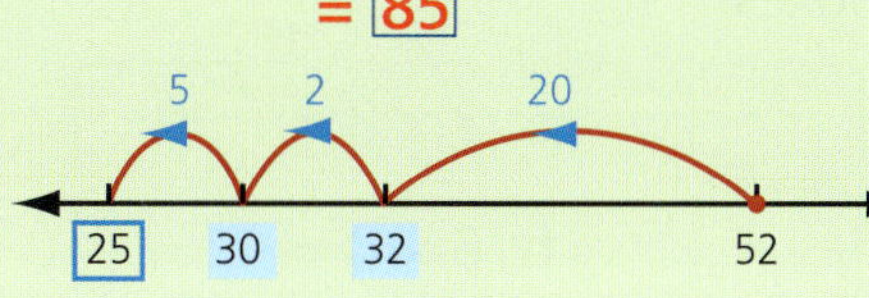

Steps

1. Subtract the tens.
2. Jump back to the next 10.
3. Take away anything left over.

To take away 7, we take away 2 then 5.

1 Use the jump strategy to answer these questions.

a 72 – 15 ☐

To take away 5, we take away 2 then 3.

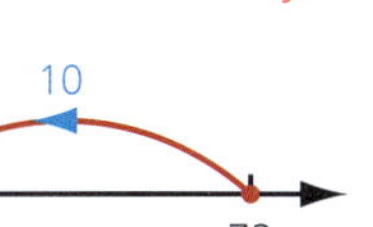

b 41 – 28 ☐

To take away 8, we take away 1 then 7.

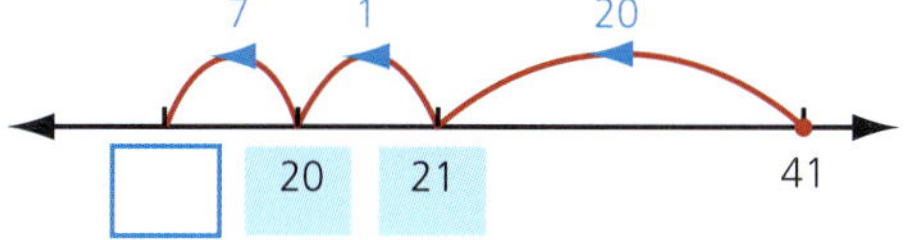

c 53 – 26 ☐

To take away 6, we take away 2 then 4.

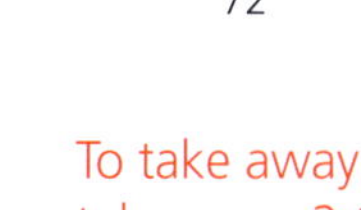

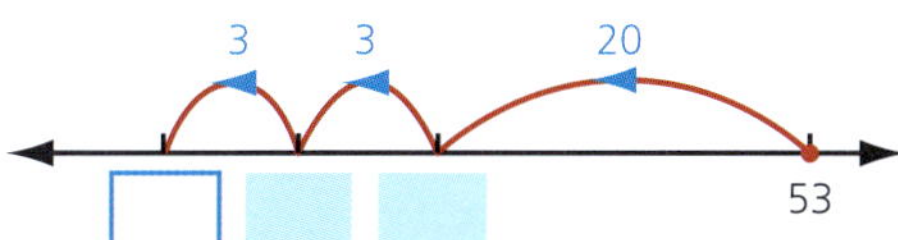

d 83 – 39 ☐

To take away 9, we take away 3 then 6.

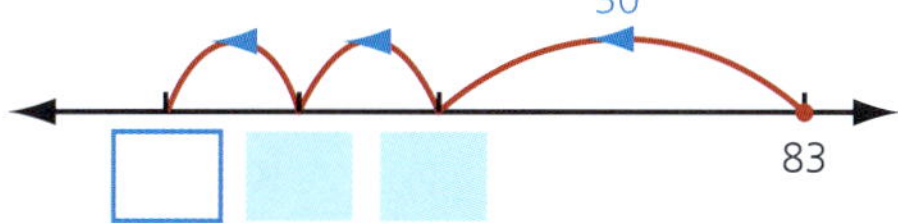

e 65 – 48 ☐

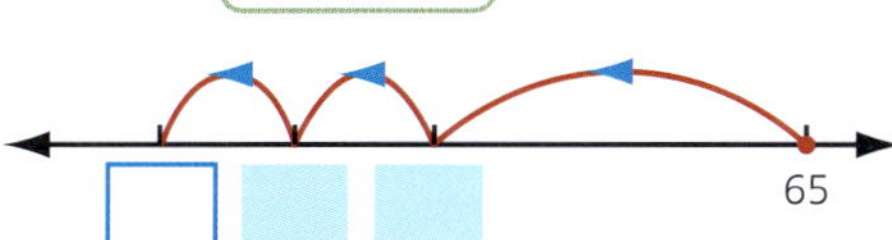

f 94 – 37 ☐

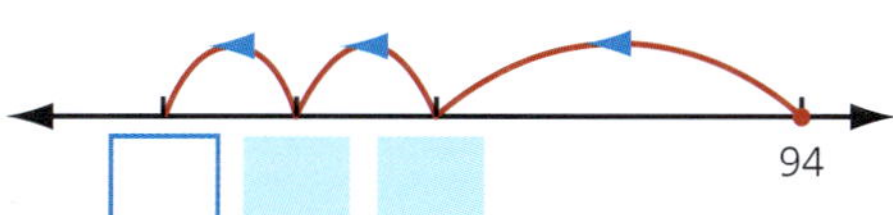

2 Use the jump strategy to answer these questions.

a 64 – 29 ☐

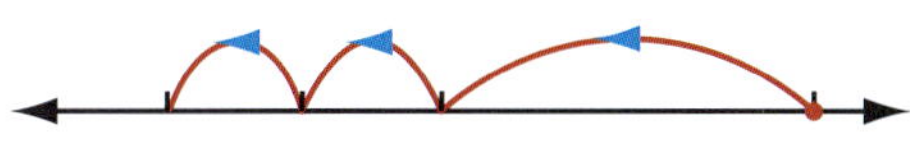

b 71 – 44 ☐

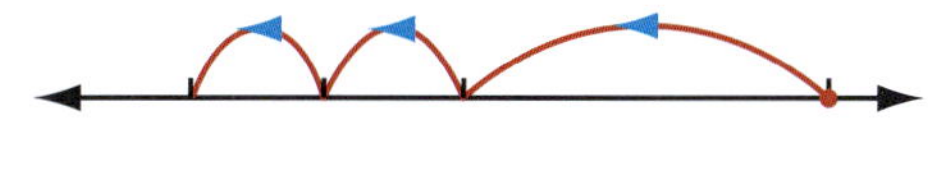

c 82 – 56 ☐

d 77 – 38 ☐

Do these on your own paper or in your head.

e 63 – 27 ☐

f 55 – 39 ☐

g 42 – 24 ☐

h 81 – 43 ☐

i 93 – 27 ☐

j 76 – 27 ☐

2:11 × 8 tables

Sing multiplication songs to learn your tables.

★★★★ ★★★★	★★★★ ★★★★	★★★★ ★★★★	★★★★ ★★★★	★★★★ ★★★★	★★★★ ★★★★	★★★★ ★★★★	★★★★ ★★★★	★★★★ ★★★★	★★★★ ★★★★

1 Count the groups of 8 to fill in the boxes.

a 1 × 8 = ☐ **b** 2 × 8 = ☐ **c** 3 × 8 = ☐

d 4 × 8 = ☐ **e** 5 × 8 = ☐ **f** 6 × 8 = ☐

g 7 × 8 = ☐ **h** 8 × 8 = ☐ **i** 9 × 8 = ☐

Doubling the answers to '×4' gives the answers to '×8'.

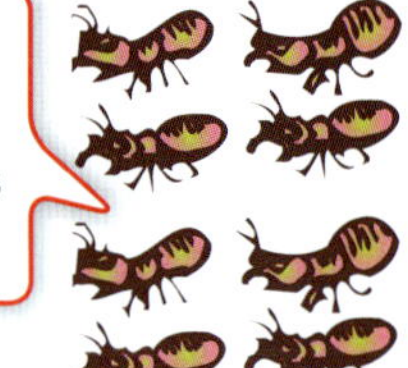

j 10 × 4 = ☐ so 10 × 8 = ☐ **k** 1 × 4 = ☐ so 1 × 8 = ☐

l 2 × 4 = ☐ so 2 × 8 = ☐ **m** 3 × 4 = ☐ so 3 × 8 = ☐

n 6 × 4 = ☐ so 6 × 8 = ☐ **o** 5 × 4 = ☐ so 5 × 8 = ☐

2 Complete:

a 3 groups of 8 = ☐ **b** 6 rows of 8 = ☐ **c** 5 eights = ☐

d 4 groups of 8 = ☐ **e** 7 lots of 8 = ☐ **f** 8 eights = ☐

g 1 group of 8 = ☐ **h** 9 rows of 8 = ☐ **i** 2 × 8 = ☐

j 0 groups of 8 = ☐ **k** 10 rows of 8 = ☐ **l** 11 × 8 = ☐

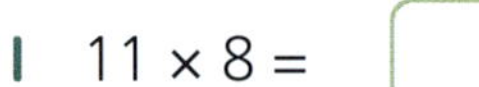

CONCEPT

Skip counting by 3

3, 6, 9, 12, 15, 18, 21, 24, 27, 30, ...

Skip counting by 4

4, 8, 12, 16, 20, 24, 28, 32, 36, 40, ...

Skip counting by 8

8, 16, 24, 32, 40, 48, 56, 64, 72, 80, ...

Practise skip counting, just as you would learn a song.

7 × 8
= (5 × 8) + (2 × 8)
= 40 + 16
= 56

3 Do as many as you can without skip counting.

×	0	1	2	3	4	5	6	7	8	9	10
8											

×	5	3	7	4	2	9	10	1	8	6	0
2											
4											
8											
3											

 • *AUSTRALIAN SIGNPOST MATHS NSW 4* • ISBN 9780655709053

× 8 tables

If you know that 6 × 5 = 30, then 7 × 5 = (6 × 5) + 5 = 35.

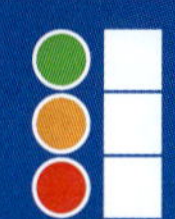

CONCEPT

- The pattern of the last digit of the × 8 tables is 8, 6, 4, 2, 0. 8, 16, 24, 32, 40, 48, 56, ...
- To multiply by 4, we can double and double again. 6 × 4 = (6 × 2) × 2 = 12 × 2 = 24
- To multiply by 8, we can multiply by 4, then double. 6 × 8 = (6 × 4) × 2 = 24 × 2 = 48
- To multiply by 5, you can multiply by 10 and halve the answer. 7 × 5 = half of 7 × 1 0 = 35

1 Join each question to its answer, using a pencil and ruler.

a

× 8	
0 × 8	16
1 × 8	24
2 × 8	0
3 × 8	48
4 × 8	8
5 × 8	32
6 × 8	56
7 × 8	80
8 × 8	40
9 × 8	64
10 × 8	72

b

× 8	
3 × 8	0
0 × 8	24
5 × 8	56
1 × 8	64
7 × 8	32
2 × 8	8
8 × 8	40
4 × 8	80
6 × 8	16
10 × 8	72
9 × 8	48

c

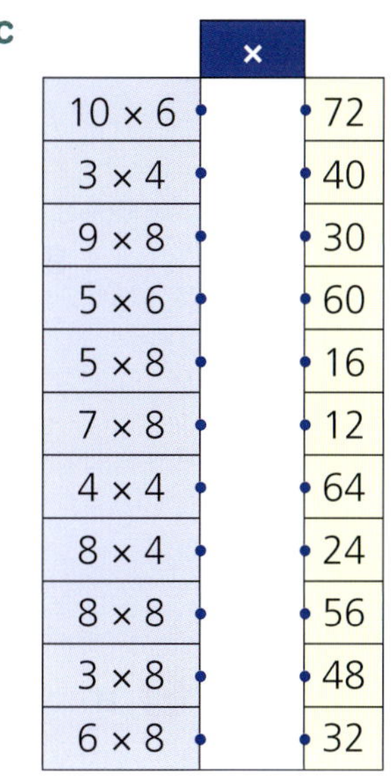

×	
10 × 6	72
3 × 4	40
9 × 8	30
5 × 6	60
5 × 8	16
7 × 8	12
4 × 4	64
8 × 4	24
8 × 8	56
3 × 8	48
6 × 8	32

× 8 answers end in: 8, 6, 4, 2, or 0.

× 10 answers end in: 0.

d

× 5	
1 × 5	10
2 × 5	20
3 × 5	5
4 × 5	35
5 × 5	0
6 × 5	15
7 × 5	30
8 × 5	25
9 × 5	50
10 × 5	40
0 × 5	45

e

× 3	
1 × 3	24
6 × 3	30
10 × 3	0
5 × 3	3
8 × 3	18
0 × 3	15
2 × 3	27
9 × 3	21
3 × 3	12
7 × 3	6
4 × 3	9

f

× 4	
7 × 4	24
6 × 4	28
3 × 4	32
8 × 4	16
4 × 4	32
8 × 4	20
5 × 4	12
6 × 4	36
1 × 4	28
7 × 4	4
9 × 4	24

× 5 answers end in: 5 or 0.

24 is
12 × 2
6 × 4
3 × 8

40
48
50
56
60
64
70
72

 • *AUSTRALIAN SIGNPOST MATHS NSW 4* • ISBN 9780655709053

2:13 Addition, trading 2 tens

4 tens 24 ones
40 + 20 + 4
6 tens 4 ones

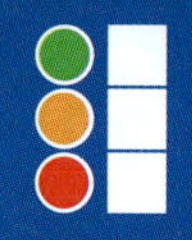

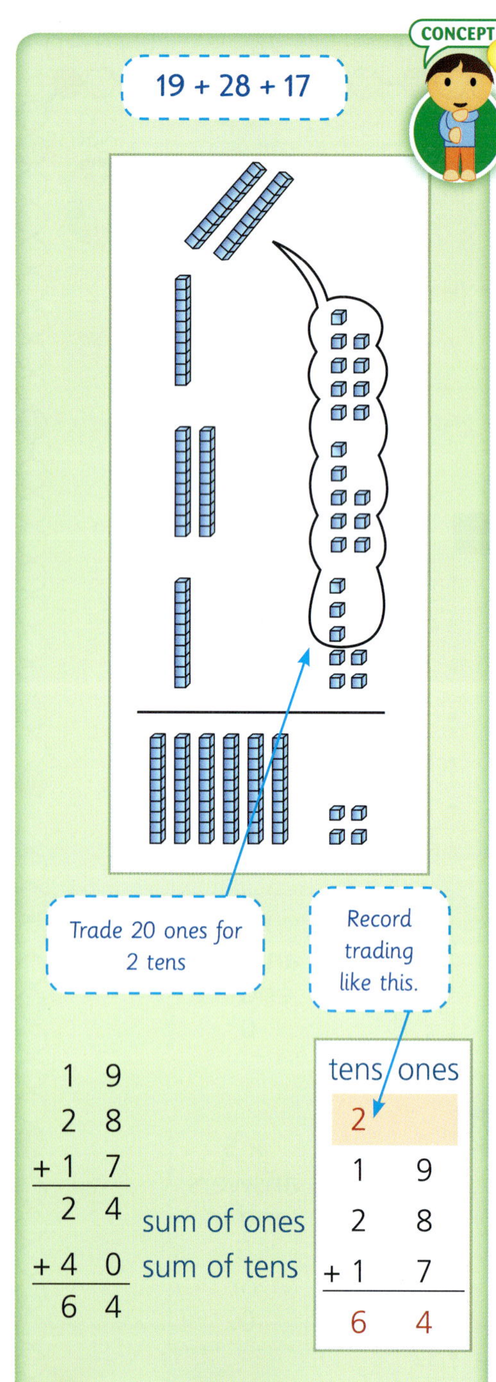

	1	9	
	2	8	
+	1	7	
	2	4	sum of ones
+	4	0	sum of tens
	6	4	

tens	ones
2	
1	9
2	8
+ 1	7
6	4

Check your answers with a calculator.

1

a

tens	ones
1	3
2	4
+ 2	5

b

tens	ones
2	6
3	3
+ 1	5

c

tens	ones
1	5
3	7
+ 2	9

d

tens	ones
3	8
2	7
+ 3	8

e

tens	ones
2	3
1	4
+ 3	6

f

tens	ones
	9
3	8
+ 2	9

g

tens	ones
4	4
3	4
+ 1	8

h

tens	ones
3	9
2	8
+ 1	5

i

tens	ones
2	8
2	8
+ 2	8

2

a

tens	ones
3	9
2	4
+ 1	3

b

tens	ones
2	8
3	6
+ 1	5

c

tens	ones
2	7
3	7
+ 2	8

d

tens	ones
3	7
2	9
+ 1	6

e

tens	ones
$1	4
$1	8
$2	6
+ $3	3

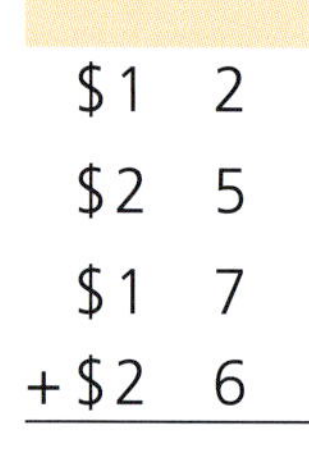

f

tens	ones
$1	2
$2	5
$1	7
+ $2	6

- Adding 3 odd numbers gives an ______ number.

 • *AUSTRALIAN SIGNPOST MATHS NSW 4* • ISBN 9780655709053

2:14 Addition involving hundreds

12 tens
100 + 20
1 hundred 2 tens

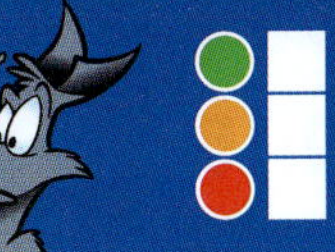

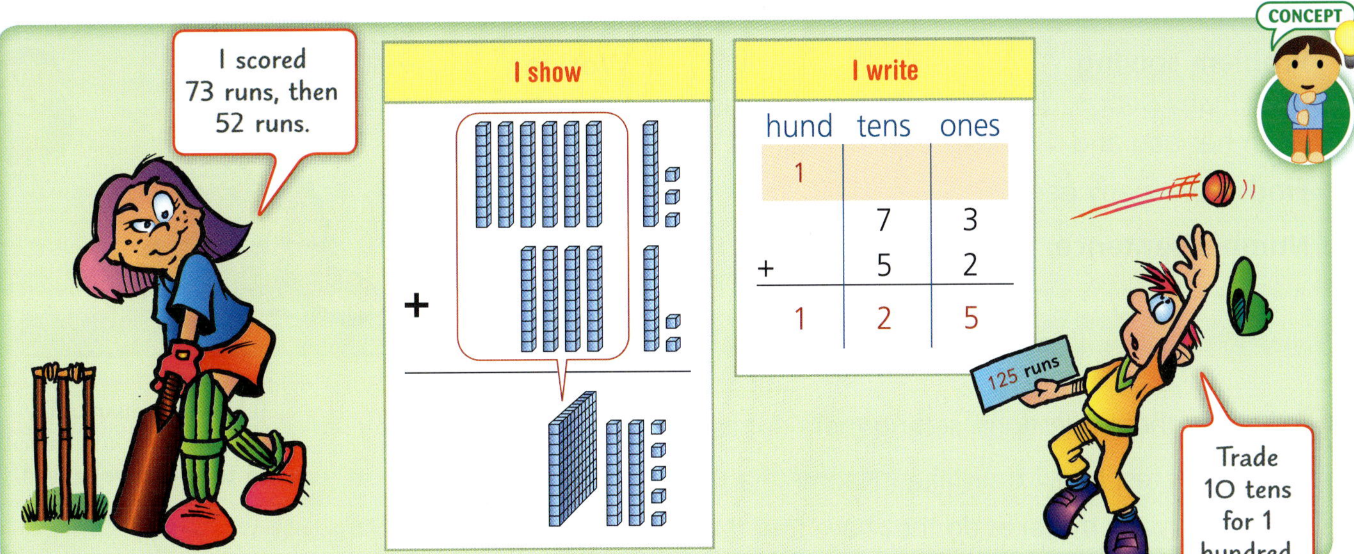

1 Model these with place-value blocks, then fill in the boxes.

a 61 books ☐ + ☐ = ☐
88 books
How many books altogether? ☐

b 94 stickers ☐ + ☐ = ☐
53 stickers
How many stickers altogether? ☐

2

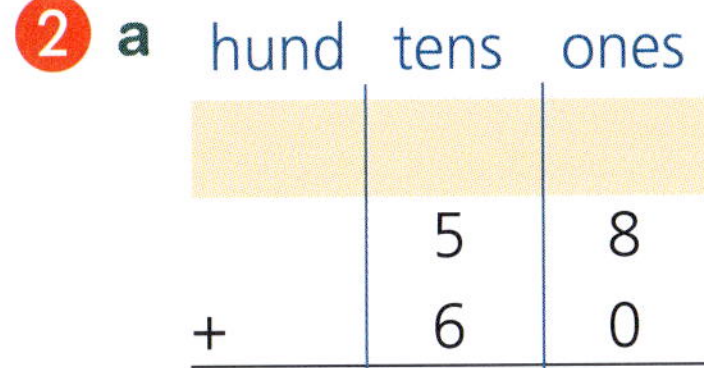

a

	hund	tens	ones
		5	8
+		6	0

b

	hund	tens	ones
		9	2
+		4	6

c

	hund	tens	ones
		8	5
+		7	2

d

	hund	tens	ones
		6	3
+		4	3

e

	hund	tens	ones
		7	4
+		8	5

f

	hund	tens	ones
		3	7
+		9	1

g

	hund	tens	ones
		9	4
+		6	1

h

	hund	tens	ones
		6	3
+		6	4

i

	hund	tens	ones
		7	2
+		5	7

3 In each part of Questions 1 and 2, estimate the answer by rounding off each number to the nearest ten and then adding.
In each case, ask: 'Is my answer reasonable?' If it is not, do the question again.

2:15 Addition problems to 99

Underline important words in the problem.

Problem solving

How many pencils does Molly have if she has 24 in her bag and 47 in her desk?

Find: How many pencils?

Number sentence: 24 + 47 = ☐

Answer: Molly has 71 pencils.

Working

tens	ones
1	
2	4
+ 4	7
7	1

Use these blanks for working. Work in pencil so they can be reused.

1 Answer these questions, setting them out as shown above.

a Luke's test had 27 mistakes. Naomi's had 22 mistakes. How many mistakes do they have together? ☐ mistakes

b Brianna had 56 pet ants. Jordan caught 8 more and gave them to her. How many did Brianna have then? ☐ ants

c Wen, an ancient Chinese king, began the first zoo 3000 years ago. He received 56 animals from the north and 27 from the south. How many animals did he receive altogether? ☐ animals

d At night, an owl can see about 100 times better than a human. In one week an owl caught 53 mice. In the next week it caught 38. How many mice did it catch altogether? ☐ mice

e At a waterhole, Michelle photographed 31 magpie geese, 12 Burdekin ducks and 8 pied herons. How many birds did she photograph altogether? ☐ birds

f A family of 18 bandicoots lived near 13 possums and 6 native cats. How many animals were there altogether? ☐ animals

2 a Alan saw three varieties of finch in one paddock. There were 35 zebra finches, 15 double-bar finches and 27 spice finches. How many were there altogether? ☐ finches

b On Phillip Island, 37 penguins came ashore before 6 pm. In the next hour 8 more arrived. How many had arrived by 7 pm? ☐ penguins

c Consecutive numbers follow one after the other. Find the sum of the consecutive numbers 28, 29 and 30. ☐ is the sum

d In a Test cricket series, Eric batted three times. His scores were 44, 28 and 19. What was his total score? ☐ runs

tens	ones

tens	ones

tens	ones

 • *AUSTRALIAN SIGNPOST MATHS NSW 4* • ISBN 9780655709053

2:16 × 3, × 6 tables

Carry cards with you, so you can learn your tables.

★★★ ★★★	★★★ ★★★	★★★ ★★★	★★★ ★★★	★★★ ★★★	★★★ ★★★	★★★ ★★★	★★★ ★★★	★★★ ★★★	★★★ ★★★

1 Count the groups of 6 to fill in the boxes.

Doubling the answers to '×3' gives the answers to '×6'?

a $1 \times 6 =$ ☐ b $2 \times 6 =$ ☐ c $3 \times 6 =$ ☐

d $4 \times 6 =$ ☐ e $5 \times 6 =$ ☐ f $6 \times 6 =$ ☐

g $7 \times 6 =$ ☐ h $8 \times 6 =$ ☐ i $9 \times 6 =$ ☐

j $10 \times 3 =$ ☐ so $10 \times 6 =$ ☐ k $1 \times 3 =$ ☐ so $1 \times 6 =$ ☐

l $2 \times 3 =$ ☐ so $2 \times 6 =$ ☐ m $3 \times 3 =$ ☐ so $3 \times 6 =$ ☐

n $6 \times 3 =$ ☐ so $6 \times 6 =$ ☐ o $5 \times 3 =$ ☐ so $5 \times 6 =$ ☐

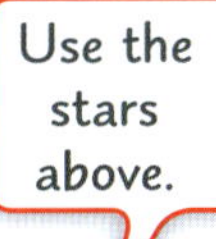

2 Complete:

a 3 groups of 6 = ☐ b 6 rows of 6 = ☐ c 5 sixes = ☐

d 4 groups of 6 = ☐ e 7 lots of 6 = ☐ f 8 sixes = ☐

g 1 group of 6 = ☐ h 9 rows of 6 = ☐ i $2 \times 6 =$ ☐

j 0 groups of 6 = ☐ k 10 rows of 6 = ☐ l $11 \times 6 =$ ☐

CONCEPT

- The numbers in Skip counting by 6 are double the numbers in Skip counting by 3.

Skip counting by 3

3, 6, 9, 12, 15, 18, 21, 24, 27, 30, ...

Skip counting by 6

6, 12, 18, 24, 30, 36, 42, 48, 54, 60, ...

Practise skip counting, just as you would learn a song.

7×6
$= (5 \times 6) + (2 \times 6)$
$= 30 + 12$
$= 42$

3 Do as many as you can without skip counting.

×	0	1	2	3	4	5	6	7	8	9	10
3											
6											

×	5	3	7	4	2	9	10	1	8	6	0
3											
6											

2:17 × 3 and × 6 tables

Rub out the pencil lines and do the questions again.

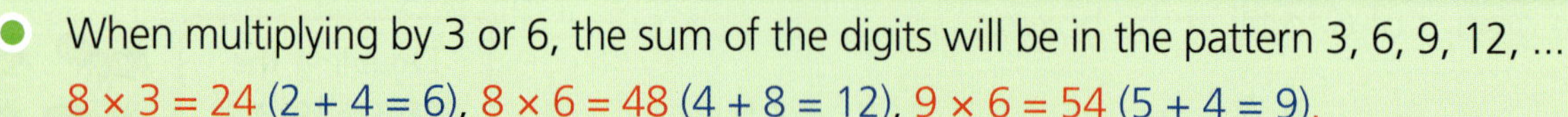

- When multiplying by 3 or 6, the sum of the digits will be in the pattern 3, 6, 9, 12, … .
  8 × 3 = 24 (2 + 4 = 6), 8 × 6 = 48 (4 + 8 = 12), 9 × 6 = 54 (5 + 4 = 9).
- To multiply by 6, you could multiply by 3, then double. 6 × 3 = 18 so 6 × 6 = 2 × 18 = 36.
- If you know that 3 × 6 = 18, then you know that 6 × 3 = 18. 6 × 8 = 8 × 6 = 48.

1 Join each question to its answer using a pencil and ruler.

a

	× 3	
0 × 3		6
1 × 3		9
2 × 3		0
3 × 3		18
4 × 3		3
5 × 3		12
6 × 3		21
7 × 3		30
8 × 3		15
9 × 3		24
10 × 3		27

b

	× 3	
3 × 3		0
0 × 3		9
5 × 3		21
1 × 3		24
7 × 3		12
2 × 3		3
8 × 3		15
4 × 3		30
6 × 3		6
10 × 3		27
9 × 3		18

c

	×	
8 × 5		27
7 × 2		80
9 × 3		56
7 × 8		40
8 × 10		0
6 × 1		14
4 × 0		24
9 × 5		35
8 × 3		6
7 × 5		72
9 × 8		45

× 2
× 4
× 8
answers end in: 8, 6, 4, 2, or 0.

× 10
answers end in: 0.

d

	× 6	
1 × 6		12
2 × 6		24
3 × 6		6
4 × 6		42
5 × 6		0
6 × 6		18
7 × 6		36
8 × 6		30
9 × 6		60
10 × 6		48
0 × 6		54

e

	× 6	
1 × 6		48
6 × 6		60
10 × 6		0
5 × 6		6
8 × 6		36
0 × 6		30
2 × 6		54
9 × 6		42
3 × 6		24
7 × 6		12
4 × 6		18

f

	×	
7 × 3		42
7 × 6		21
6 × 3		36
6 × 6		24
8 × 3		48
8 × 6		15
5 × 3		18
5 × 6		12
9 × 3		54
9 × 6		27
4 × 3		30

× 5
answers end in: 5 or 0.

24 is
8 × 3
4 × 6
3 × 8

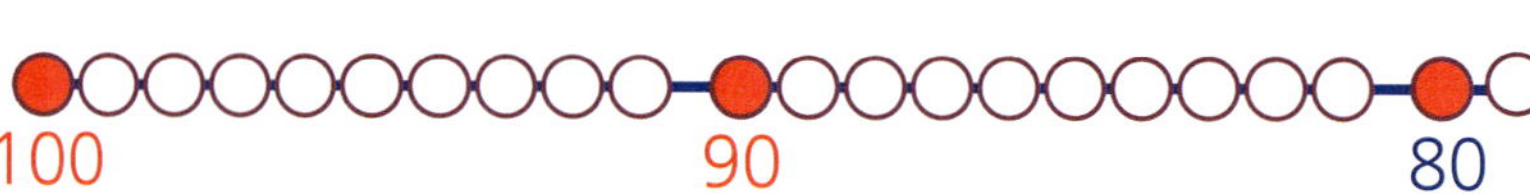

 • *AUSTRALIAN SIGNPOST MATHS NSW 4* • ISBN 9780655709053

2:18 Subtraction with trading

7 tens and 2 ones is the same as 6 tens and 12 ones.

CONCEPT

When adding, we trade 10 ones for 1 ten.

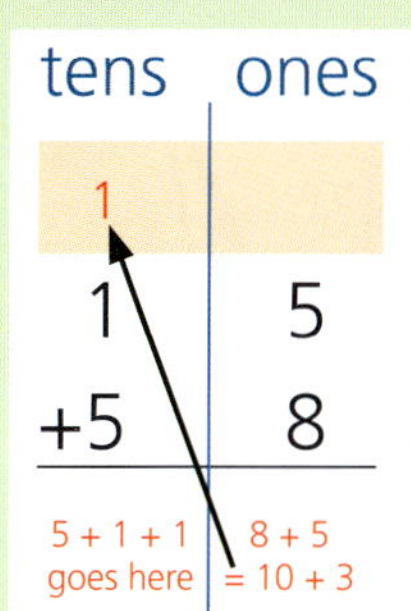

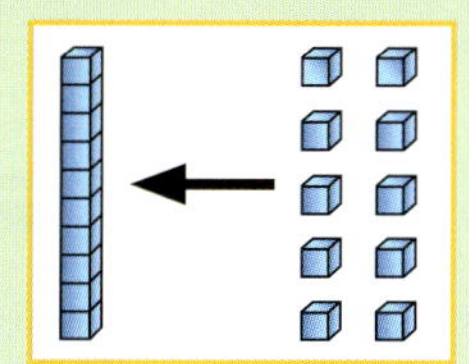

We change ten of the 13 ones into 1 ten. That leaves 3 in the ones place.

When subtracting, we trade 1 ten for 10 ones.

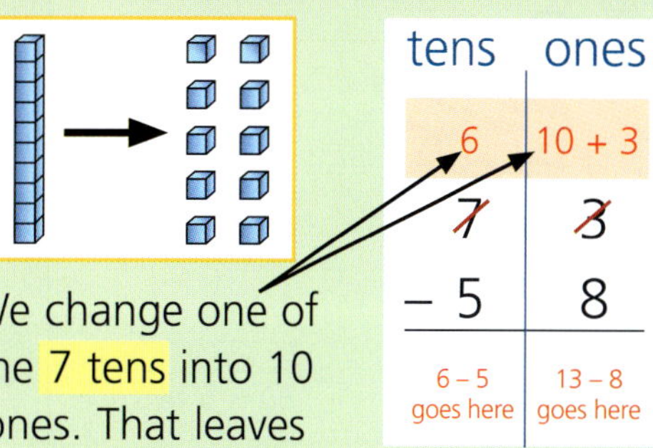

We change one of the 7 tens into 10 ones. That leaves 6 in the tens place.

Trading down

1 34 cakes, 18 eaten. How many left?

2 I can't take 8 ones from 4 ones. Trade 1 ten for 10 ones.

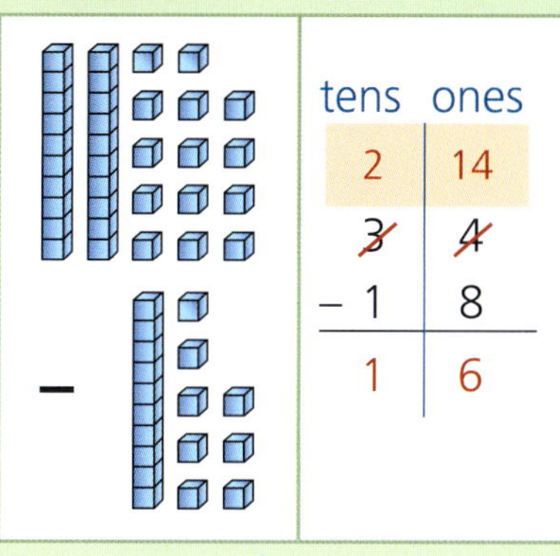

tens	ones
2	14
~~3~~	~~4~~
− 1	8
1	6

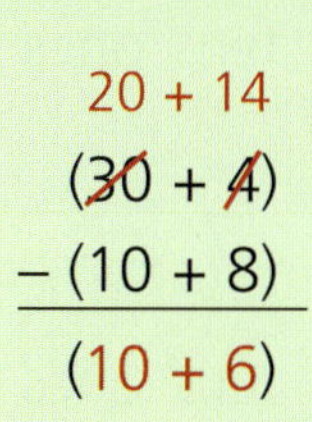

20 + 14
(~~30~~ + ~~4~~)
− (10 + 8)
(10 + 6)

1 You may use place-value blocks to do these. Estimate your answer first.

	tens	ones
a	4	3
	− 1	7
b	6	5
	− 2	9
c	9	1
	− 5	4
d	7	2
	− 2	8
e	4	6
	− 2	7
f	5	6
	− 3	8
g	9	1
	− 1	8
h	8	6
	− 3	9
i	7	2
	− 3	4
j	6	1
	− 4	3

2 **a** Paul has 43 animal cards. I have 17 cards. How many more cards has Paul?

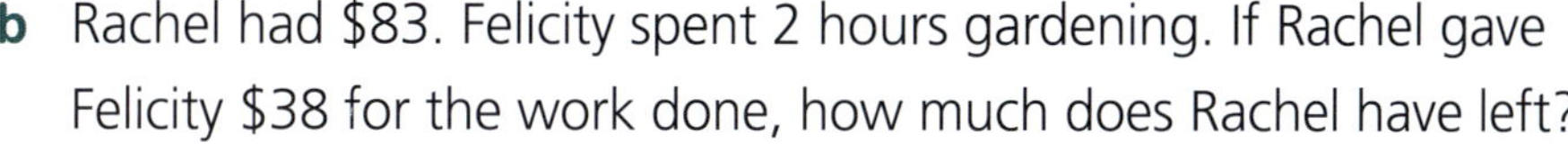

b Rachel had $83. Felicity spent 2 hours gardening. If Rachel gave Felicity $38 for the work done, how much does Rachel have left?

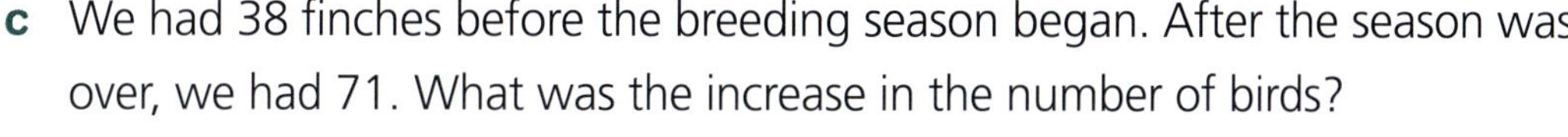

c We had 38 finches before the breeding season began. After the season was over, we had 71. What was the increase in the number of birds?

d 28 cm was cut from a wooden stick 85 cm long. How much was left?

2:19 Subtracting from tens

6 tens is the same as 5 tens and 10 ones.

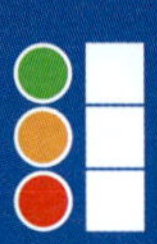

1 Show trading down to 1 ten.

a tens ones
5 0

b tens ones
7 0

c tens ones
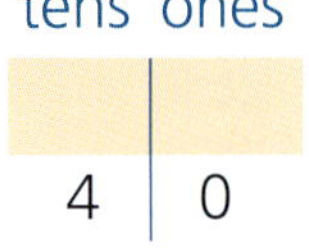
4 0

d tens ones
9 0

2

a tens ones
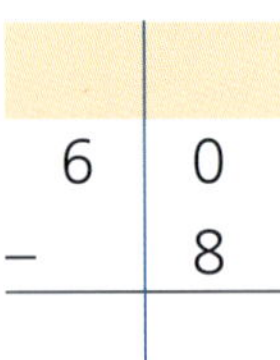
6 0
– 8

b tens ones
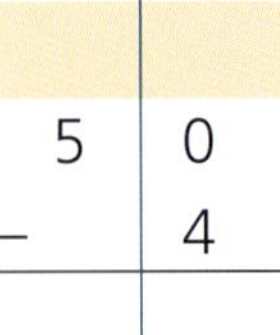
5 0
– 4

c tens ones
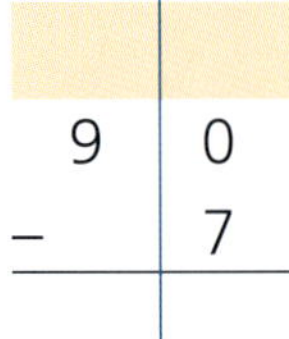
9 0
– 7

We don't need to write 'tens' and 'ones'.

d tens ones
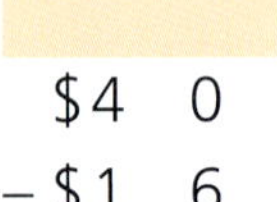
\$4 0
– \$1 6

e tens ones
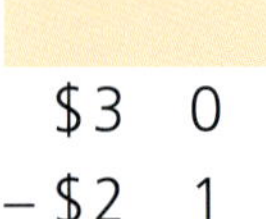
\$3 0
– \$2 1

f tens ones
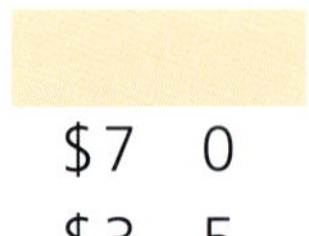
\$7 0
– \$3 5

g tens ones
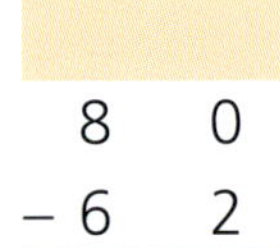
8 0
– 6 2

h tens ones

2 0
– 1 3

i tens ones
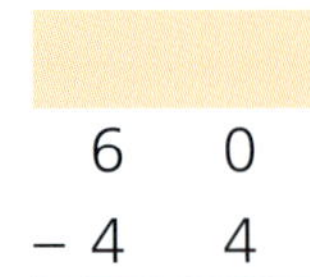
6 0
– 4 4

j tens ones
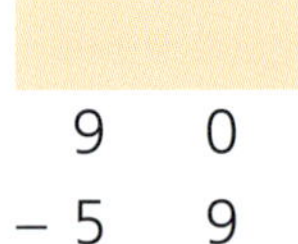
9 0
– 5 9

k tens ones
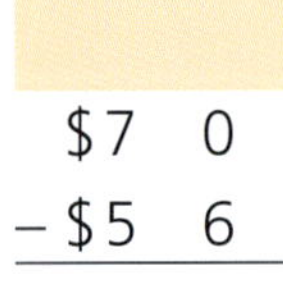
\$7 0
– \$5 6

l tens ones
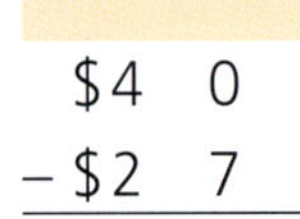
\$4 0
– \$2 7

m tens ones
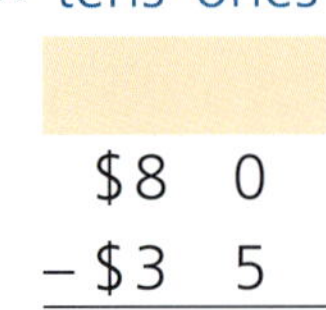
\$8 0
– \$3 5

n tens ones
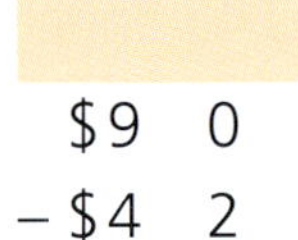
\$9 0
– \$4 2

3 Scott had \$90. Lachlan spent 2 hours cleaning the home. Scott gave Lachlan \$28 for the work he did. How much does Scott have left?

 ISBN 9780655709053

2:20 Subtracting with trading

3 tens 3 ones
is the same as
2 tens and 13 ones.

1

a

tens	ones
3	1
− 2	5

b

tens	ones
2	3
− 1	6

c

tens	ones
4	6
− 3	8

d

tens	ones
3	4
− 2	7

e

tens	ones
5	2
− 3	4

f

tens	ones
7	5
− 5	9

g

tens	ones
6	7
− 4	8

h

tens	ones
5	2
− 3	7

i

tens	ones
8	4
− 6	8

j

tens	ones
6	8
− 4	9

k

tens	ones
9	1
− 5	3

l

tens	ones
7	3
− 2	9

m

tens	ones
3	7
−	9

n

tens	ones
4	4
− 1	5

o

tens	ones
3	8
− 1	9

p

tens	ones
6	2
−	7

q

tens	ones
$5	5
− $2	9

r

tens	ones
$7	2
− $5	4

s

tens	ones
$8	0
− $4	3

Use a calculator to check your answers.

 • *AUSTRALIAN SIGNPOST MATHS NSW 4* • ISBN 9780655709053

To add 9, add 10 then take away 1.

27 + 9
27 + 10 – 1

Skip counting by 9 (The 2 digits add to make 9 each time.)

9, 19, 27, 36, 45, 54, 63, 72, 81, 90, . . .

As the tens digit goes up by 1, the ones digit comes down by 1.

  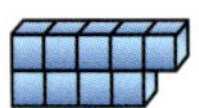 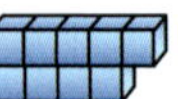 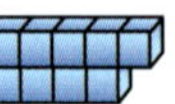 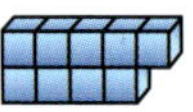 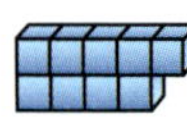 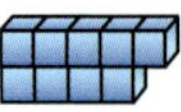 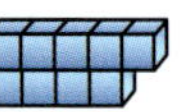 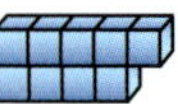

1 Use the blocks above to complete these × 9 tables.

- **a** 1 × 9 = ☐
- **b** 2 × 9 = ☐
- **c** 3 × 9 = ☐
- **d** 4 × 9 = ☐
- **e** 5 × 9 = ☐
- **f** 6 × 9 = ☐
- **g** 7 × 9 = ☐
- **h** 8 × 9 = ☐
- **i** 9 × 9 = ☐
- **j** 10 × 9 = ☐

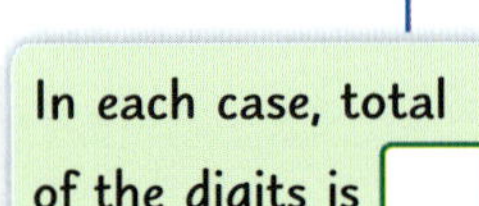

2 Use the method in the concept box to do these.

- **a** 10 × 9 = ☐
- **b** 9 × 9 = ☐
- **c** 8 × 9 = ☐
- **d** 7 × 9 = ☐
- **e** 6 × 9 = ☐
- **f** 5 × 9 = ☐
- **g** 4 × 9 = ☐
- **h** 3 × 9 = ☐
- **i** 2 × 9 = ☐
- **j** 1 × 9 = ☐

CONCEPT

4 × 9 is
4 × 10 take away 4.
4 × 9 = 40 – 4

3

a 5 × 9 = ☐	**b** 9 × 9 = ☐	**c** 7 × 9 = ☐
d 8 × 9 = ☐	**e** 4 × 9 = ☐	**f** 1 × 9 = ☐
g 3 × 9 = ☐	**h** 6 × 9 = ☐	**i** 2 × 9 = ☐

4 Do as many as you can without skip counting.

×	0	1	2	3	4	5	6	7	8	9	10
3											
9											

×	5	3	7	4	2	9	10	1	8	6	0
3											
9											

 • *AUSTRALIAN SIGNPOST MATHS NSW 4* • ISBN 9780655709053

× 9 tables

3 × 9 = 9 × 3 4 × 9 = 9 × 4 5 × 9 = 9 × 5
6 × 9 = 9 × 6 8 × 9 = 9 × 8

Start

CONCEPT

- When multiplying by 9, you could multiply by 10, then subtract the original number.
  6 × 9 = (6 × 10) − 6 = 60 − 6 = 54, 7 × 9 = (7 × 10) − 7 = 70 − 7 = 63
- When multiplying by 9, the sum of the digits in the answer will be 9, 18 (or 27 …).
  6 × 9 = 54, … (5 + 4 = 9), 8 × 9 = 72, … (7 + 2 = 9), 11 × 9 = 99, … (9 + 9 = 18)

1 Join each question to its answer using a pencil and ruler.

a

× 9	
0 × 9	18
1 × 9	27
2 × 9	0
3 × 9	54
4 × 9	9
5 × 9	36
6 × 9	63
7 × 9	90
8 × 9	45
9 × 9	72
10 × 9	81

b

× 9	
3 × 9	0
0 × 9	27
5 × 9	63
1 × 9	72
7 × 9	36
2 × 9	9
8 × 9	45
4 × 9	90
6 × 9	18
10 × 9	81
9 × 9	54

c

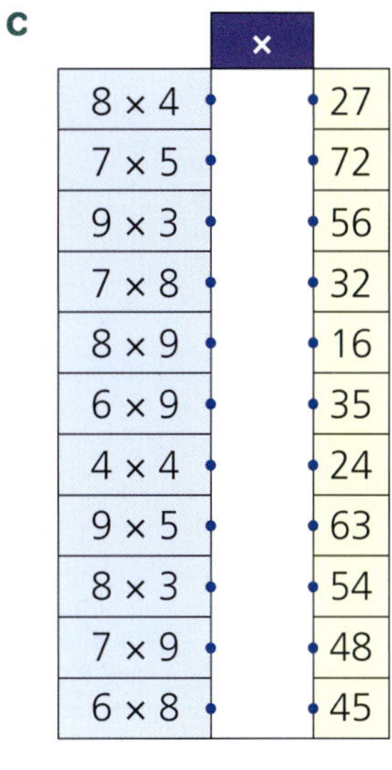

×	
8 × 4	27
7 × 5	72
9 × 3	56
7 × 8	32
8 × 9	16
6 × 9	35
4 × 4	24
9 × 5	63
8 × 3	54
7 × 9	48
6 × 8	45

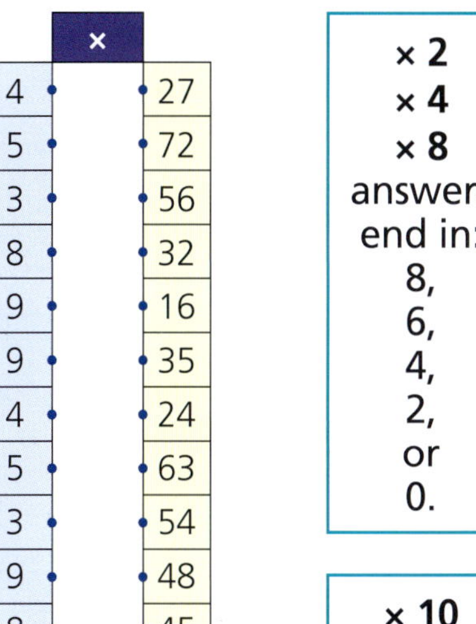

× 2
× 4
× 8
answers end in: 8, 6, 4, 2, or 0.

× 10
answers end in: 0.

× 5
answers end in: 5 or 0.

d

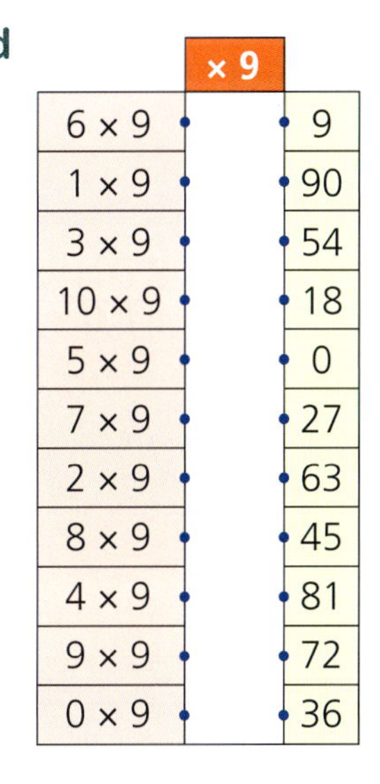

× 9	
6 × 9	9
1 × 9	90
3 × 9	54
10 × 9	18
5 × 9	0
7 × 9	27
2 × 9	63
8 × 9	45
4 × 9	81
9 × 9	72
0 × 9	36

e

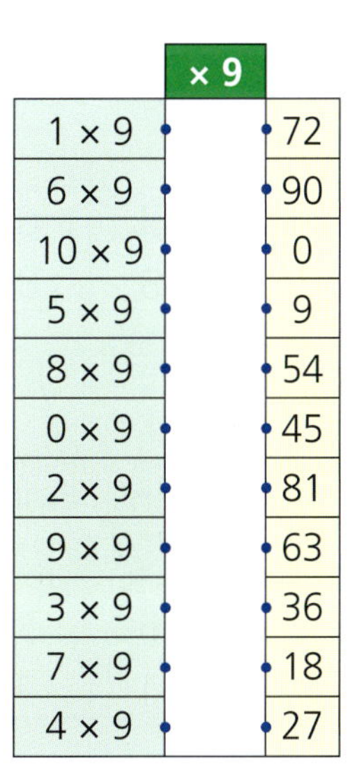

× 9	
1 × 9	72
6 × 9	90
10 × 9	0
5 × 9	9
8 × 9	54
0 × 9	45
2 × 9	81
9 × 9	63
3 × 9	36
7 × 9	18
4 × 9	27

f

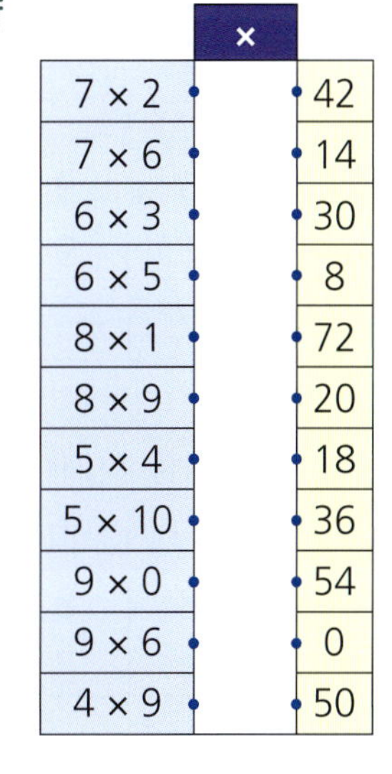

×	
7 × 2	42
7 × 6	14
6 × 3	30
6 × 5	8
8 × 1	72
8 × 9	20
5 × 4	18
5 × 10	36
9 × 0	54
9 × 6	0
4 × 9	50

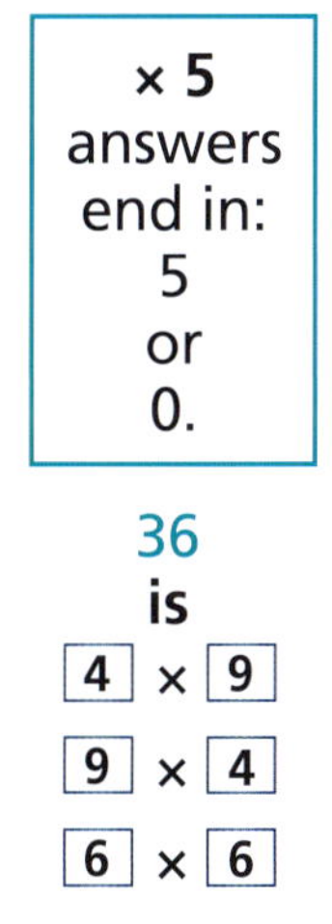

36 is
4 × 9
9 × 4
6 × 6

2:23 Addition to 999

Trade 10 ones for 1 ten.
Trade 10 tens for 1 hundred.

CONCEPT

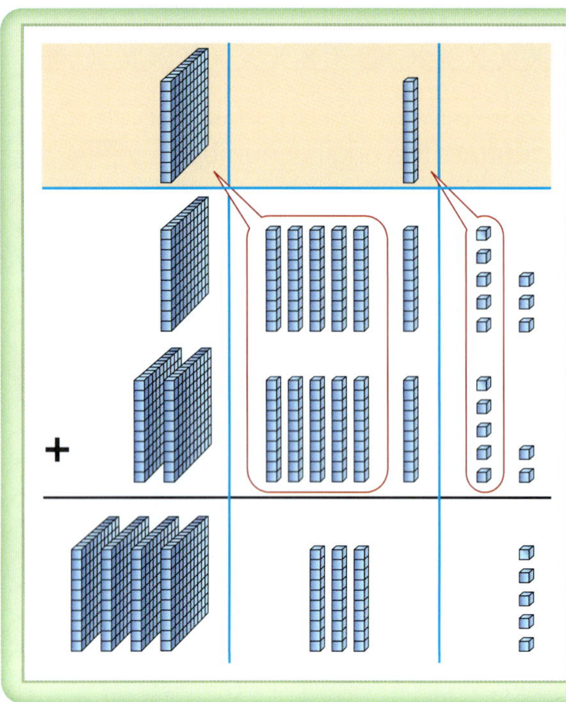

168 sheep and 267 cattle are on sale.
How many animals are there altogether?

hund	tens	ones
1	1	
1	6	8
+ 2	6	7
4	3	5

```
  1 6 8
+ 2 6 7
    1 5   sum of ones
  1 2 0   sum of tens
  3 0 0   sum of hundreds
  4 3 5
```

There are 435 animals altogether.
We can check the answer by rounding to the nearest 100 (or 10).
200 + 300 = 500
435 is reasonably close to 500.

1

a

hund	tens	ones
	6	1
+	9	3

b

hund	tens	ones
	7	2
+	4	5

c

hund	tens	ones
	3	0
+	7	8

d

hund	tens	ones
2	5	8
+	2	5

e

hund	tens	ones
	7	6
+ 7	1	4

f

hund	tens	ones
3	6	9
+	1	9

g

hund	tens	ones
4	3	6
+	8	0

h

hund	tens	ones
4	2	5
+	8	5

i

hund	tens	ones
	8	7
+ 3	4	1

j

hund	tens	ones
1	8	8
+ 1	4	3

k

hund	tens	ones
3	6	5
+ 1	4	9

l

hund	tens	ones
4	5	9
+ 2	7	4

2 362 women and 298 men. How many men and women were there altogether? ☐

- Check your answer by rounding each number to the nearest 100 (or 10) then adding. If your answer is not reasonable, do the question again.
- Keep a lookout for questions that will be easier to solve using mental strategies.

See *Extra Support 5* (Addition of money), *Extra Support 6 and 7* (Addition to 9999), *Extra Support 8* (Addition to 999 999).

2:24 Addition to 999

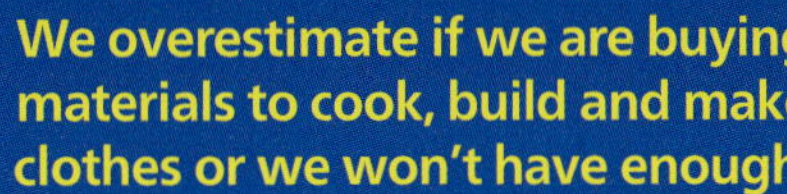

CONCEPT

- We can round off to check our answers.
  We round down if the digit is 4 or less. We round up if the digit is 5 or more.
- When both numbers are rounded up, the answer is an **overestimate**.
  482 + 257 = 739
  500 + 300 = 800
  Here the estimate is more than the answer.
- When both numbers are rounded down, the answer is an **underestimate**.
  319 + 443 = 762
  300 + 400 = 700
  Here the estimate is less than the answer.

1

a

	H	T	U
	2	8	3
+		4	5

b

	H	T	U
	5	3	1
+		7	0

c

	H	T	U
		8	2
+	7	3	3

d

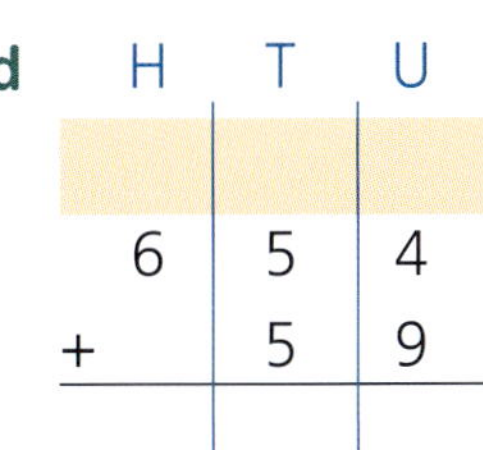

	H	T	U
	6	5	4
+		5	9

e

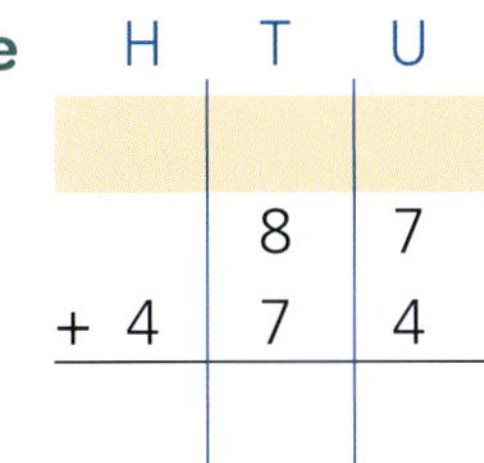

	H	T	U
		8	7
+	4	7	4

f

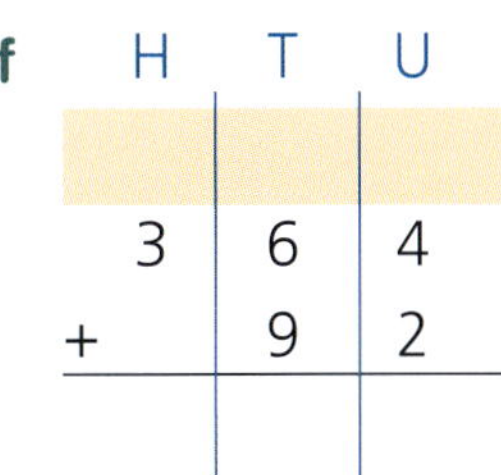

	H	T	U
	3	6	4
+		9	2

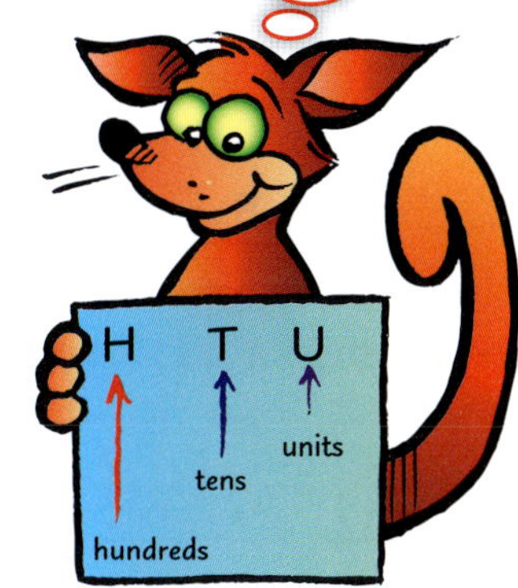

g

	H	T	U
	1	3	8
+	2	0	4

h

	H	T	U
	3	1	6
+	1	4	7

i

	H	T	U
	3	4	6
+	2	2	4

j

	H	T	U
	1	8	4
+	1	0	9

2

a

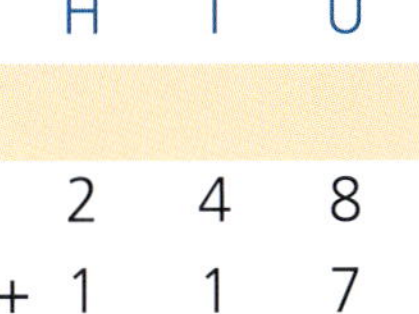

	H	T	U
	2	4	8
+	1	1	7

b

	H	T	U
		7	4
+	5	3	1

c

	H	T	U
	4	1	9
+	2	0	9

d

	H	T	U
	1	6	8
+	6	1	1

e

	H	T	U
	2	4	8
+	1	6	6

f

	H	T	U
	2	2	7
+	5	9	2

See *Extra Support 5* (Addition of money), *Extra Support 6 and 7* (Addition to 9999), *Extra Support 8* (Addition to 999 999).

Writing algorithms

To estimate, round each number to the nearest hundred, then add.

$$\begin{array}{r} 600 \\ +200 \\ \hline \end{array}$$

CONCEPT

583 apples and 179 oranges were sold. How many pieces of fruit were sold altogether?

All of these are ways of setting out the same sum.

H	T	U
1	1	
5	8	3
+ 1	7	9
7	6	2

$$\begin{array}{r} {}^{1}5\;{}^{1}8\;3 \\ +\;1\;7\;9 \\ \hline 7\;6\;2 \end{array}$$

Trade 10 ones for 1 ten.

Trade 10 tens for 1 hundred.

$$\begin{array}{rl} 583 & \\ +179 & \\ \hline 12 & \text{sum of ones} \\ 150 & \text{sum of tens} \\ 600 & \text{sum of hundreds} \\ \hline 762 & \end{array}$$

762 pieces of fruit were sold altogether.

1

a $\begin{array}{r} 250 \\ +\;\;84 \\ \hline \end{array}$ **b** $\begin{array}{r} 534 \\ +128 \\ \hline \end{array}$ **c** $\begin{array}{r} 154 \\ +207 \\ \hline \end{array}$ **d** $\begin{array}{r} 92 \\ +340 \\ \hline \end{array}$ **e** $\begin{array}{r} 245 \\ +370 \\ \hline \end{array}$

f $\begin{array}{r} 365 \\ +166 \\ \hline \end{array}$ **g** $\begin{array}{r} 209 \\ +583 \\ \hline \end{array}$ **h** $\begin{array}{r} 345 \\ +312 \\ \hline \end{array}$ **i** $\begin{array}{r} 507 \\ +220 \\ \hline \end{array}$ **j** $\begin{array}{r} 365 \\ +397 \\ \hline \end{array}$

k $\begin{array}{r} 188 \\ +133 \\ \hline \end{array}$ **l** $\begin{array}{r} 365 \\ +366 \\ \hline \end{array}$ **m** $\begin{array}{r} 509 \\ +296 \\ \hline \end{array}$ **n** $\begin{array}{r} 381 \\ +259 \\ \hline \end{array}$ **o** $\begin{array}{r} 777 \\ +185 \\ \hline \end{array}$

2 Estimate each answer and use the estimate to check your answers.

a Luke watched 287 minutes of television on Saturday and 145 minutes on Sunday. How much did he watch altogether? Give your answer in minutes.

b The attendances at two concerts on Sunday were 156 and 218. How many people attended altogether?

c This year farmer McDonald sold 180 bags of corn. Last year she sold 17 bags more than this. How many bags were sold in the two years?

d Rex and Lyn bought the house next door and added 346 square metres to their original block of 575 square metres. How large is the block now?

3 Use mental strategies and estimation to check your answers to Question 1.

See *Extra Support 5* (Addition of money), *Extra Support 6 and 7* (Addition to 9999), *Extra Support 8* (Addition to 999 999).

AUSTRALIAN SIGNPOST MATHS NSW 4 • ISBN 9780655709053

2:26 What's the rule?

The rule is applied to each number to get the next one in the pattern.

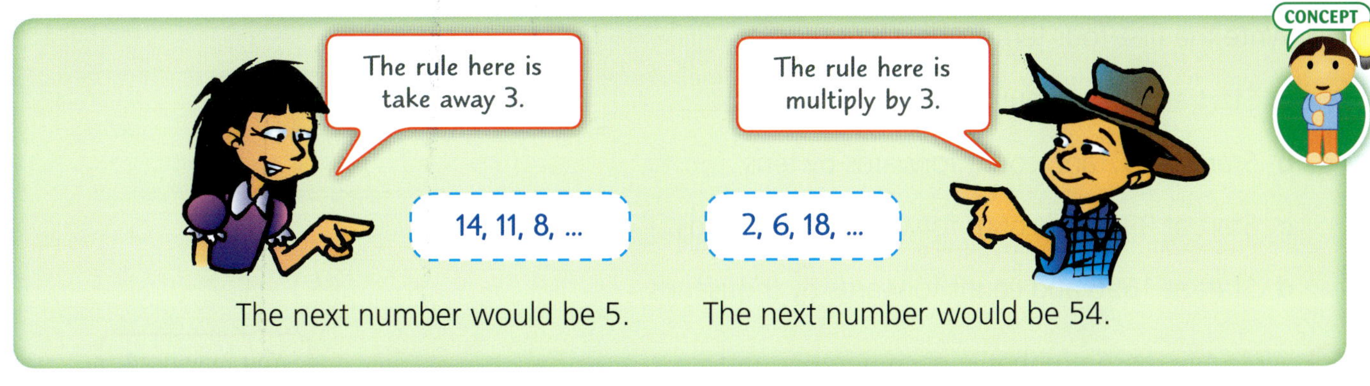

The next number would be 5. The next number would be 54.

1 Write the next number in each pattern.

a 2, 4, 6, ☐ **b** 1, 5, 9, ☐ **c** 20, 18, 16, ☐

d 3, 6, 12, ☐ **e** 27, 9, 3, ☐ **f** 1, 5, 25, ☐

g 99, 98, 97, ☐ **h** 9, 16, 23, ☐ **i** 80, 40, 20, ☐

2 Write the rule for each part of Question 1.

a ☐ **b** ☐ **c** ☐

d ☐ **e** ☐ **f** ☐

g ☐ **h** ☐ **i** ☐

3 Continue each pattern by following the rule.

a Add 7. 0, ☐, ☐, ☐ **b** Subtract 5. 26, ☐, ☐, ☐

c Multiply by 4. 1, ☐, ☐, ☐ **d** Divide by 2. 88, ☐, ☐, ☐

e Add 11. 23, ☐, ☐, ☐ **f** Subtract 9. 47, ☐, ☐, ☐

g Multiply by 2. 6, ☐, ☐, ☐ **h** Divide by 3. 27, ☐, ☐, ☐

4 Write the pattern for the number of lines used in the pictures and write the rule used (like 'add 3').

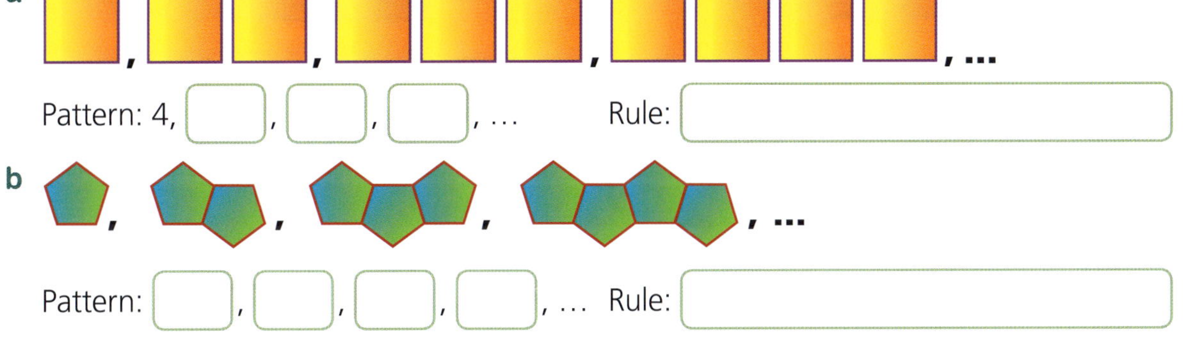

a Pattern: 4, ☐, ☐, ☐, … Rule: ☐

b Pattern: ☐, ☐, ☐, ☐, … Rule: ☐

 • *AUSTRALIAN SIGNPOST MATHS NSW 4* • ISBN 9780655709053

2:27 Number patterns

1 Write the first four terms of each pattern.

a Start at 40 and count backwards by fives.

b Start at 137 and count forwards by tens.

c Start at 995 and count forwards by hundreds.

d Start at 1696 and count forwards by thousands.

2 Write the tenth number in each number pattern.

a 14, 21, 28, 35, …

b 189, 179, 169, 159, …

c 40, 80, 120, 160, …

d 16, 24, 32, 40, …

e 643, 743, 843, 943, …

f 950, 900, 850, 800, …

g $1\frac{1}{4}$, $1\frac{1}{2}$, $1\frac{3}{4}$, 2, …

h $6\frac{1}{2}$, 6, $5\frac{1}{2}$, 5, …

3 Complete each number pattern.

a 20, ___, 60, 80, ___, ___

b 479, 489, ___, ___, 519, ___

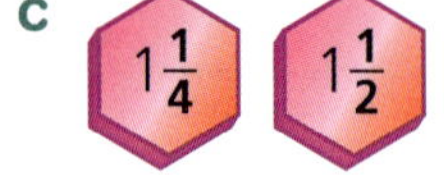

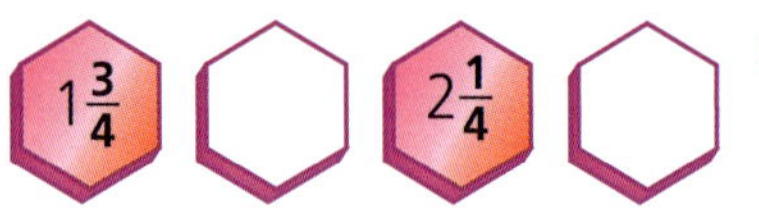

c $1\frac{1}{4}$, $1\frac{1}{2}$, $1\frac{3}{4}$, ___, $2\frac{1}{4}$, ___

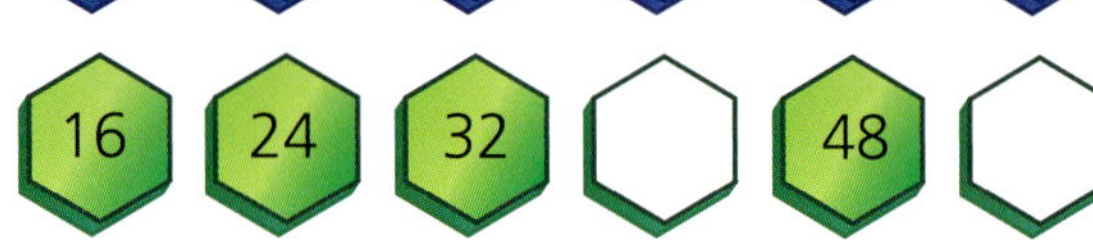

d 16, 24, 32, ___, 48, ___

4 Fill in the missing measurements for each bottle.

a

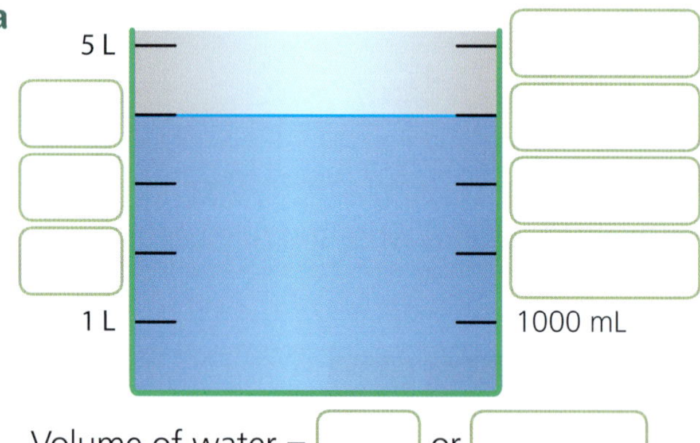

Volume of water = ___ or ___.

b

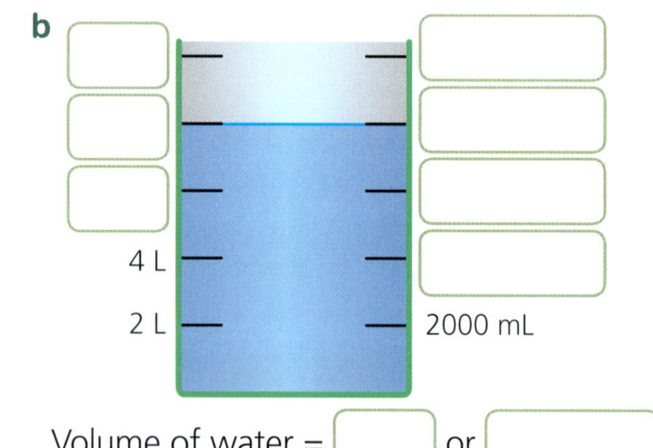

Volume of water = ___ or ___.

5 Continue each pattern.

a 1 kg, 2 kg, 3 kg, ___, ___

b 1000 g, 2000 g, 3000 g, ___, ___

c 5 km, 6 km, 7 km, ___, ___

d 5000 m, 6000 m, 7000 m, ___, ___

e 2 kg, 4 kg, 6 kg, ___, ___

f 2000 g, 4000 g, 6000 g, ___, ___

 • *AUSTRALIAN SIGNPOST MATHS NSW 4* • ISBN 9780655709053

× 7 tables

$7 \times 7 = (5 \times 7) + (2 \times 7)$
$= 35 + 14$
$= 49$

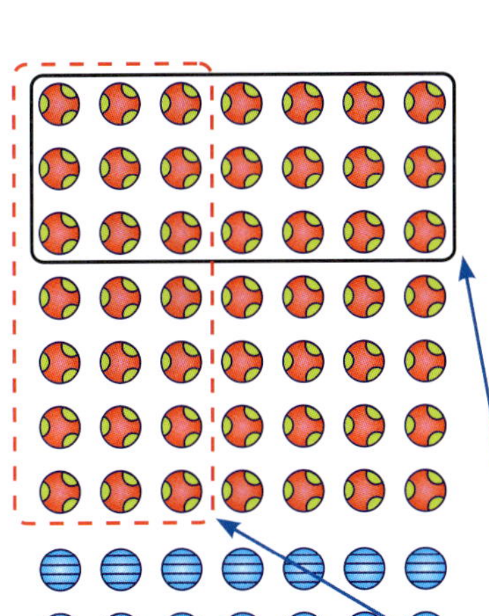

1 Count the rows and fill in the boxes.

a 7 rows of 3 = ☐ **b** 3 rows of 7 = ☐

c $7 \times 4 =$ ☐ **d** $4 \times 7 =$ ☐

e $7 \times 5 =$ ☐ **f** $5 \times 7 =$ ☐

g $7 \times 6 =$ ☐ **h** $6 \times 7 =$ ☐

i $7 \times 8 =$ ☐ **j** $8 \times 7 =$ ☐

k $9 \times 7 =$ ☐

l $10 \times 7 =$ ☐

Changing the order does not change the answer.

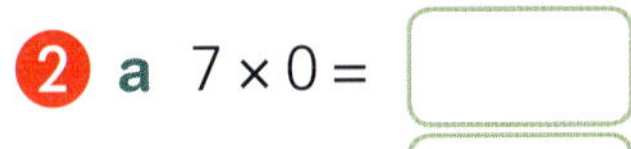

2 **a** $7 \times 0 =$ ☐ **b** $0 \times 7 =$ ☐ **c** $7 \times 1 =$ ☐ **d** $1 \times 7 =$ ☐

e $7 \times 2 =$ ☐ **f** $2 \times 7 =$ ☐ **g** $7 \times 3 =$ ☐ **h** $3 \times 7 =$ ☐

i $5 \times 8 =$ ☐ **j** $9 \times 8 =$ ☐ **k** $6 \times 8 =$ ☐ **l** $8 \times 8 =$ ☐

3 **a** 7×4 **b** 7×6

c 7×8 **d** 7×7

e 7×10 **f** 7×9

g 6×7 **h** 9×7

×	0	1	2	3	4	5	6	7	8	9	10
4											
2											
5											
8											
1											
6											
3											
0											
9											
10											
7											

4 Try to memorise the answers.

×	0	1	2	3	4	5	6	7	8	9	10
7											

×	5	3	7	4	2	9	10	1	8	6	0
7											

  • ISBN 9780655709053

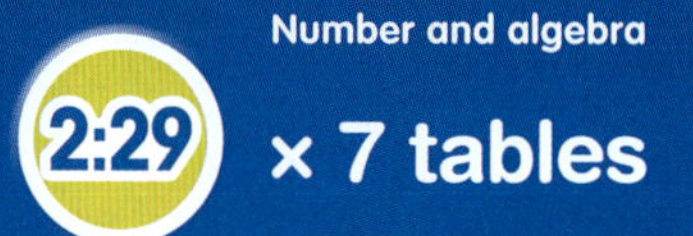

× 7 tables

This is the last of the multiplication tables you need to learn.
Make sure you know × 2 up to × 10 tables.

Start 7 10 14 20 21 28 30 35 40 42 49 50 56 60 63 70 77

CONCEPT

- If we know the other times tables we have met so far, the only new one would be $7 \times 7 = 49$

$7 \times 2 = 2 \times 7 = 14$, $7 \times 3 = 3 \times 7 = 21$, $7 \times 4 = 4 \times 7 = 28$, $7 \times 5 = 5 \times 7 = 35$,
$7 \times 6 = 6 \times 7 = 42$, $7 \times 8 = 8 \times 7 = 56$, $7 \times 9 = 9 \times 7 = 63$, $7 \times 10 = 10 \times 7 = 70$

1 Join each question to its answer using a pencil and ruler.

a

	× 7	
0 × 7		14
1 × 7		21
2 × 7		0
3 × 7		42
4 × 7		7
5 × 7		28
6 × 7		49
7 × 7		70
8 × 7		35
9 × 7		56
10 × 7		63

b

	× 7	
3 × 7		0
0 × 7		21
5 × 7		63
1 × 7		56
7 × 7		28
2 × 7		7
8 × 7		35
4 × 7		70
6 × 7		14
10 × 7		63
9 × 7		42

c

	×	
9 × 4		21
6 × 7		72
7 × 3		32
4 × 8		36
8 × 9		28
7 × 7		42
4 × 7		56
9 × 5		63
8 × 7		49
7 × 9		24
6 × 4		45

× 2
× 4
× 8
answers end in: 8, 6, 4, 2, or 0.

× 10
answers end in: 0.

d

	× 7	
6 × 7		7
1 × 7		70
3 × 7		42
10 × 7		14
5 × 7		0
7 × 7		21
2 × 7		49
8 × 7		35
4 × 7		63
9 × 7		56
0 × 7		28

e

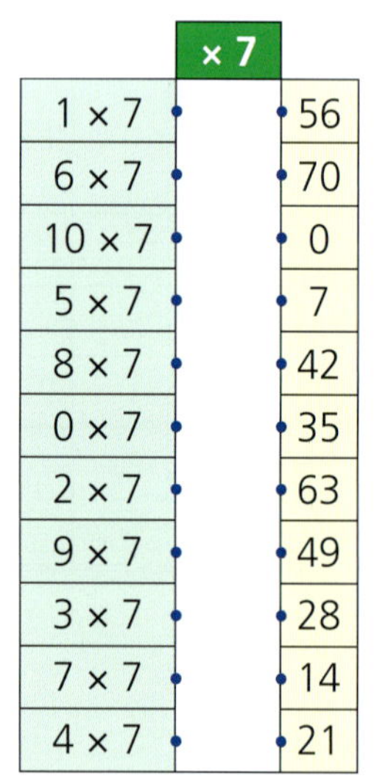

	× 7	
1 × 7		56
6 × 7		70
10 × 7		0
5 × 7		7
8 × 7		42
0 × 7		35
2 × 7		63
9 × 7		49
3 × 7		28
7 × 7		14
4 × 7		21

f

	×	
7 × 8		42
7 × 6		56
3 × 7		30
6 × 5		70
10 × 7		72
8 × 9		20
5 × 4		21
5 × 7		36
9 × 7		54
9 × 6		63
4 × 9		35

× 5
answers end in: 5 or 0.

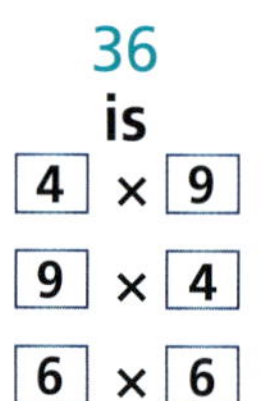

 • *AUSTRALIAN SIGNPOST MATHS NSW 4* • ISBN 9780655709053

Multiplication tables review

Let's learn them all.

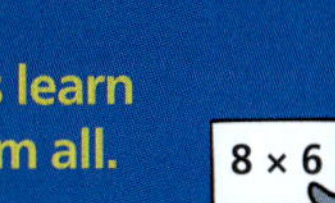

1 Complete these multiplication webs.

a

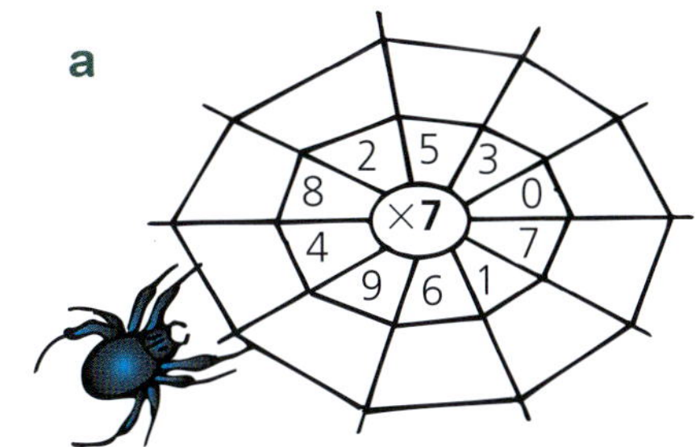

b

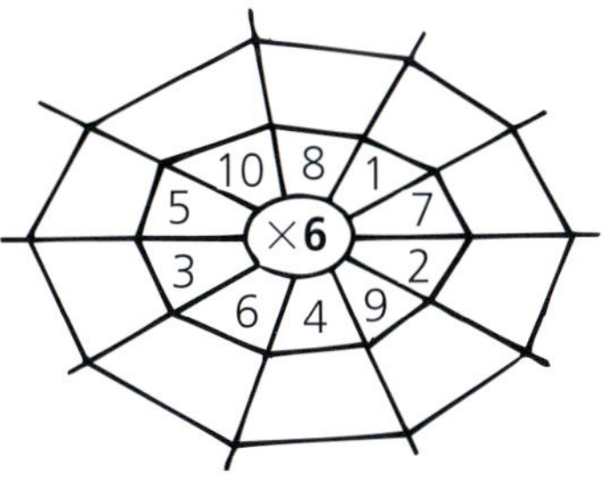

c

2

a 4 × 7 = ☐	**b** 7 × 4 = ☐	**c** 5 × 9 = ☐
d 10 × 9 = ☐	**e** 9 × 10 = ☐	**f** 3 × 9 = ☐
g 6 × 9 = ☐	**h** 9 × 6 = ☐	**i** 4 × 9 = ☐
j 8 × 9 = ☐	**k** 7 × 9 = ☐	**l** 9 × 9 = ☐
m 9 × 3 = ☐	**n** 7 × 7 = ☐	**o** 9 × 8 = ☐
p 9 × 7 = ☐	**q** 9 × 5 = ☐	**r** 9 × 4 = ☐

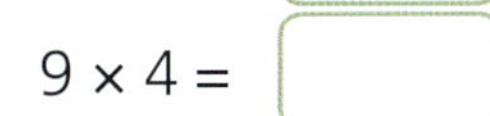

3

a 6×2

b 6×5

c 6×3

d 3×4

e 3×10

f 3×6

g 3×2

h 3×8

3 × 9 = 27 → 2 + 7 = 9

4 × 9 = 36 → 3 + 6 = 9

The answer to a multiplication question is called the **product**.

4

a The product of 7 and 6 = ☐

b The product of 0 and 6 = ☐

c The product of 7 and 3 = ☐

d The product of 5 and 9 = ☐

e The product of 6 and 6 = ☐

f The product of 8 and 6 = ☐

5

×	5	3	7	4	2	9	10	1	8	6	0
3											
9											

 ISBN 9780655709053

Subtraction without trading to 999

I write

	hund	tens	ones
	4	3	8
–	2	1	6
	2	2	2

1 **a**

	4 hundreds	7 tens	6 ones
–	2 hundreds	3 tens	1 one

b

	8 hundreds	9 tens	7 ones
–	2 hundreds	5 tens	2 ones

c

	hund	tens	ones
	8	5	2
–	7	2	1

d

	hund	tens	ones
	9	6	7
–	2	3	4

e

	hund	tens	ones
	9	9	8
–	4	6	5

f

	hund	tens	ones
	3	4	2
–		1	1

g

	hund	tens	ones
	6	9	8
–		2	4

h

	hund	tens	ones
	9	4	5
–		1	1

i

	hund	tens	ones
	6	8	6
–			4

j

	hund	tens	ones
	7	4	7
–			4

k

	hund	tens	ones
	3	6	9
–			7

l

	hund	tens	ones
	5	5	9
–	4	3	0

m

	hund	tens	ones
	1	7	3
–		5	0

n

	hund	tens	ones
	6	4	6
–	2	0	3

o

	H	T	O
	7	7	8
–	6	0	0

p

	H	T	O
	5	2	9
–	1	0	0

q

	H	T	O
	1	8	3
–	1	1	3

r

	H	T	O
	5	8	7
–	3	8	2

2 Use mental strategies and estimation to check each answer in Question 1.

- Make up a problem to match each of the sums in parts **c**, **d**, **e** and **f**.

 • *AUSTRALIAN SIGNPOST MATHS NSW 4* • ISBN 9780655709053

2:32 Subtraction with trading to 999

U stands for *units* or *ones*.

CONCEPT

28 of my 384 stamps are Chinese. How many are not Chinese?

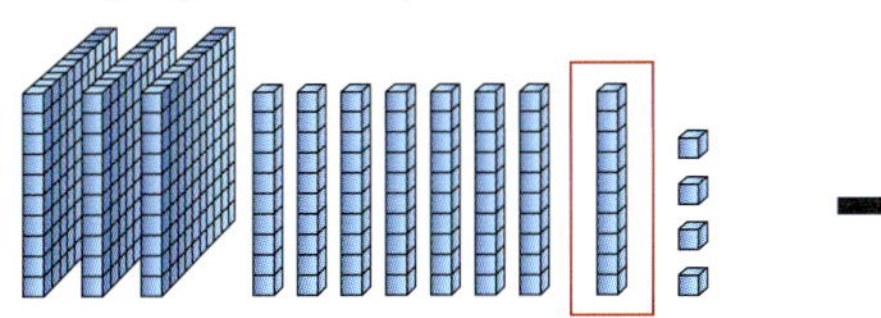

We can't take 8 ones from 4 ones, so trade 1 ten for 10 ones.

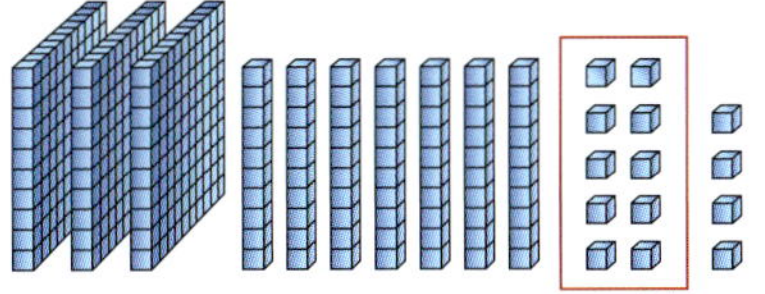

From this we take 2 tens and 8 ones.

	70	14
300 +	~~80~~ +	~~4~~

hund	tens	ones
	7	14
3	~~8~~	~~4~~
−	2	8
3	5	6

1

	H	T	U
a	5	8	1
−		5	3
b	3	4	3
−		2	8
c	2	9	6
−		6	7
d	4	6	0
−		3	9
e	2	7	3
−			9
f	1	6	6
−		5	8
g	8	4	4
−			8
h	9	7	3
−		6	5
i	7	5	0
−		3	9
j	3	4	1
−		2	6
k	2	8	0
−		3	2
l	6	4	7
−		1	9

m	8	3	5
−	1	0	8
n	8	9	1
−	8	3	6
o	5	2	0
−	4	1	5
p	6	8	4
−		7	6
q	2	1	4
−	2	0	8
r	7	8	4
−		5	0
s	3	9	1
−	3	7	5

Use estimation or mental strategies to check your answers.

See *Extra Support 9* (Subtraction of money), *Extra Support 10* (Subtraction with trading to 9999), *Extra Support 11* (Four-digit subtraction from 1000s), *Extra Support 12* (Subtraction to 999 999).

 • *AUSTRALIAN SIGNPOST MATHS NSW 4* • ISBN 9780655709053

2:33 Subtraction with trading to 999

Trade 1 hundred for 10 tens.

CONCEPT

354 of the 718 birds in the zoo are parrots. How many are not parrots?

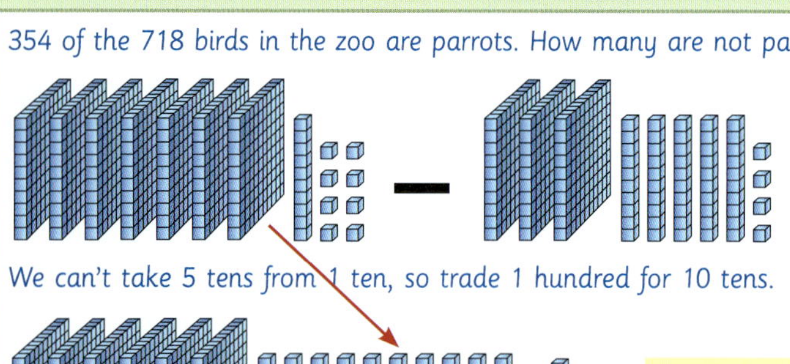

We can't take 5 tens from 1 ten, so trade 1 hundred for 10 tens.

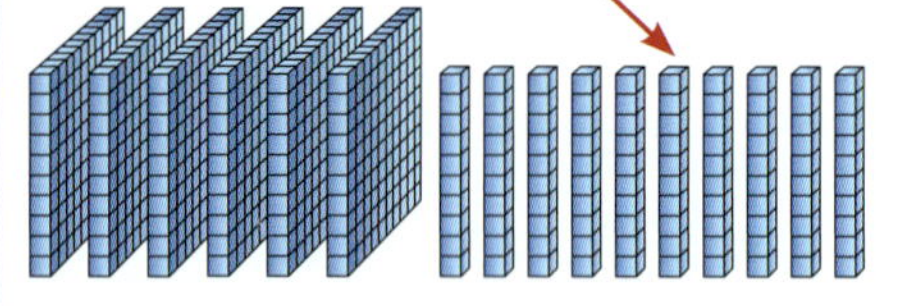

600 110
~~700~~ + ~~10~~ + 8

From this we take 3 hundreds, 5 tens and 4 ones.

Hund	Tens	Ones
6	11	
~~7~~	~~1~~	8
− 3	5	4
3	6	4

1

a

H	T	U
6	1	7
− 1	5	3

b

H	T	U
8	2	6
− 5	7	1

c

H	T	U
4	3	4
− 2	4	0

d

H	T	U
7	2	9
−	3	8

e

H	T	U
5	2	8
− 1	5	2

f

H	T	U
6	0	7
− 3	5	2

g

H	T	U
6	8	5
−	9	1

h

H	T	U
2	1	5
− 1	7	5

i

H	T	U
4	5	0
− 1	3	9

j

H	T	U
6	1	7
− 3	2	6

k

H	T	U
5	0	4
− 1	9	2

l

H	T	U
9	4	7
− 3	0	9

m

  7 3 3
− 1 0 8

n

  9 1 6
− 8 3 6

o

  6 0 8
− 4 1 5

p

  4 1 4
− 2 0 8

q

  9 8 4
− 5 5 0

r

  8 6 6
− 3 7 5

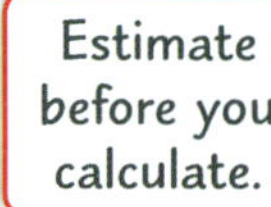

See *Extra Support 9* (Subtraction of money), *Extra Support 10* (Subtraction with trading to 9999), *Extra Support 11* (Four-digit subtraction from 1000s), *Extra Support 12* (Subtraction to 999 999).

2:34 Subtraction with 2 trades to 999

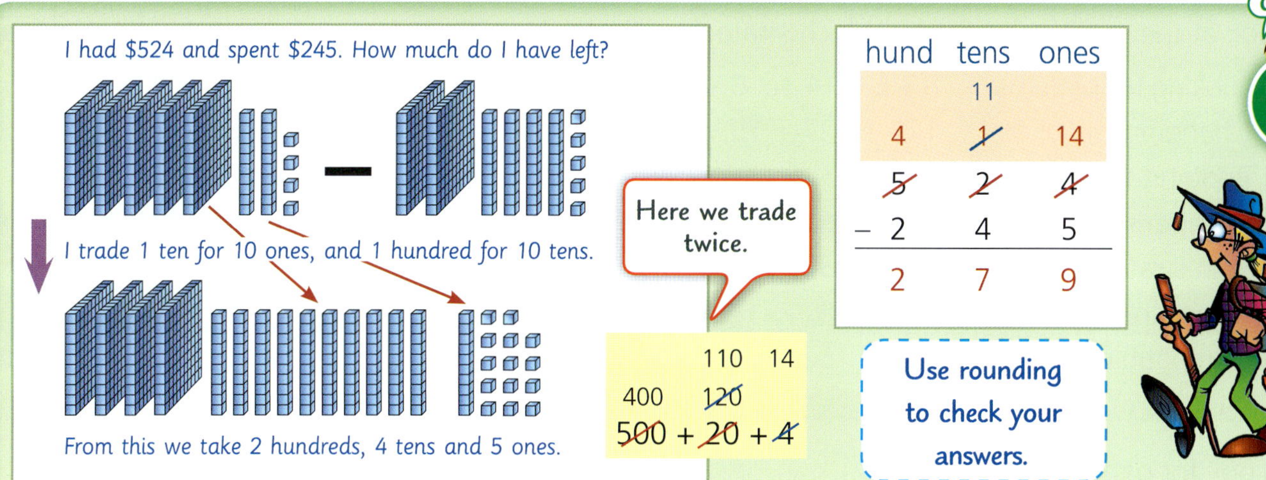

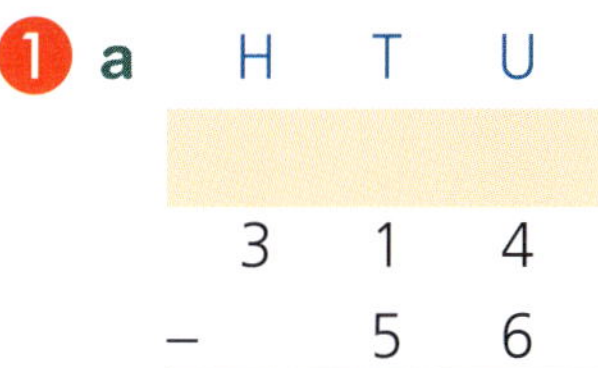

1

a
H	T	U
3	1	4
−	5	6

b
H	T	U
2	4	6
−	6	7

c
H	T	U
1	3	2
−	9	8

d
H	T	U
7	3	5
−	8	9

e
H	T	U
4	3	0
− 1	5	6

f
H	T	U
3	4	1
− 2	7	8

g
H	T	U
6	2	4
− 1	3	5

h
H	T	U
9	2	2
− 3	3	3

i
H	T	U
7	1	5
− 5	7	7

j
H	T	U
4	7	0
− 2	9	3

k
H	T	U
8	4	2
− 1	8	3

l
H	T	U
9	1	1
− 3	4	4

m
$$\begin{array}{r} 614 \\ -\ 585 \\ \hline \end{array}$$

n
$$\begin{array}{r} 528 \\ -\ 429 \\ \hline \end{array}$$

o
$$\begin{array}{r} 755 \\ -\ 668 \\ \hline \end{array}$$

p
$$\begin{array}{r} 415 \\ -\ 387 \\ \hline \end{array}$$

q
$$\begin{array}{r} 706 \\ -\ 249 \\ \hline \end{array}$$

r
$$\begin{array}{r} 601 \\ -\ 184 \\ \hline \end{array}$$

s
$$\begin{array}{r} 506 \\ -\ 278 \\ \hline \end{array}$$

In Questions 1q–1s, start by trading 1 hundred for 10 tens.

See *Extra Support 9* (Subtraction of money), *Extra Support 10* (Subtraction with trading to 9999), *Extra Support 11* (Four-digit subtraction from 1000s), *Extra Support 12* (Subtraction to 999 999).

Mental strategies, +

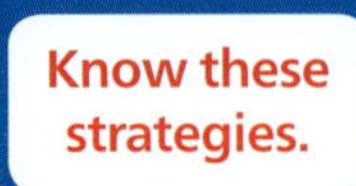

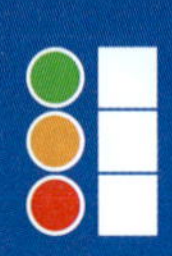

Look at the question and ask, 'Which strategy will work best?'

A Looking for patterns	8 + 6 = 14 so 8 + 26 = 34,	3 + 8 = 11 so 300 + 800 = 1100		
B Changing the order	115 + 137 + 15	= 115 + 15 + 137		= 130 + 137
C Bridging to 10s	148 + 7	= 148 + 2 + 5		= 150 + 5
D Compensation	318 + 98	= 318 +100 – 2		= 418 – 2
E Split strategy	316 + 432	= (300 + 400) + (10 + 30) + (6 + 2)		= 700 + 40 + 8
F Jump strategy	257 + 48	= 257 + 40 + 8		= 297 + 8
G Compatible numbers	560 + 162	= (550 + 10) + (150 + 12)		= 700 + 22

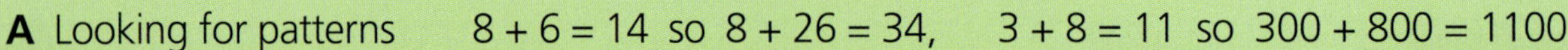

1 Look for patterns. (**A**)

a 5 + 76 ☐ **b** 5 + 83 ☐ **c** 400 + 800 ☐

2 Change the order. (**B**)

a 199 + 59 + 11 ☐ **b** 630 + 9 + 70 ☐ **c** 176 + 59 + 4 ☐

3 Bridge to 10. (**C**)

a 538 + 6 ☐ **b** 788 + 7 ☐ **c** 844 + 8 ☐

Make sure you know addition facts.

See Extra Support page 164.

4 Round off then compensate. (**D**)

a 362 + 39 ☐ **b** 288 + 98 ☐ **c** 603 + 49 ☐

5 Use the split strategy. (**E**)

a 426 + 113 ☐ **b** 235 + 662 ☐ **c** 714 + 263 ☐

d 934 + 51 ☐ **e** 63 + 725 ☐ **f** 72 + 806 ☐

6 Use the jump strategy. (**F**)

a 238 + 56 ☐ **b** 418 + 38 ☐ **c** 369 + 47 ☐

7 Look for compatible numbers. (**G**)

a 452 + 259 ☐ **b** 185 + 723 ☐ **c** 564 + 259 ☐

8 Complete the additions. Write the strategy you used (from **A** to **G** above).

a 342 + 57 ☐ ☐ **b** 72 + 9 + 18 ☐ ☐ **c** 424 + 7 ☐ ☐

d 65 + 19 ☐ ☐ **e** 800 + 900 ☐ ☐ **f** 537 + 46 ☐ ☐

Discuss how and why you chose each strategy.

See *Extra Support 2* (Building to the next 10).

2:36 Mental strategies, + and –

Practise looking for the best strategy?

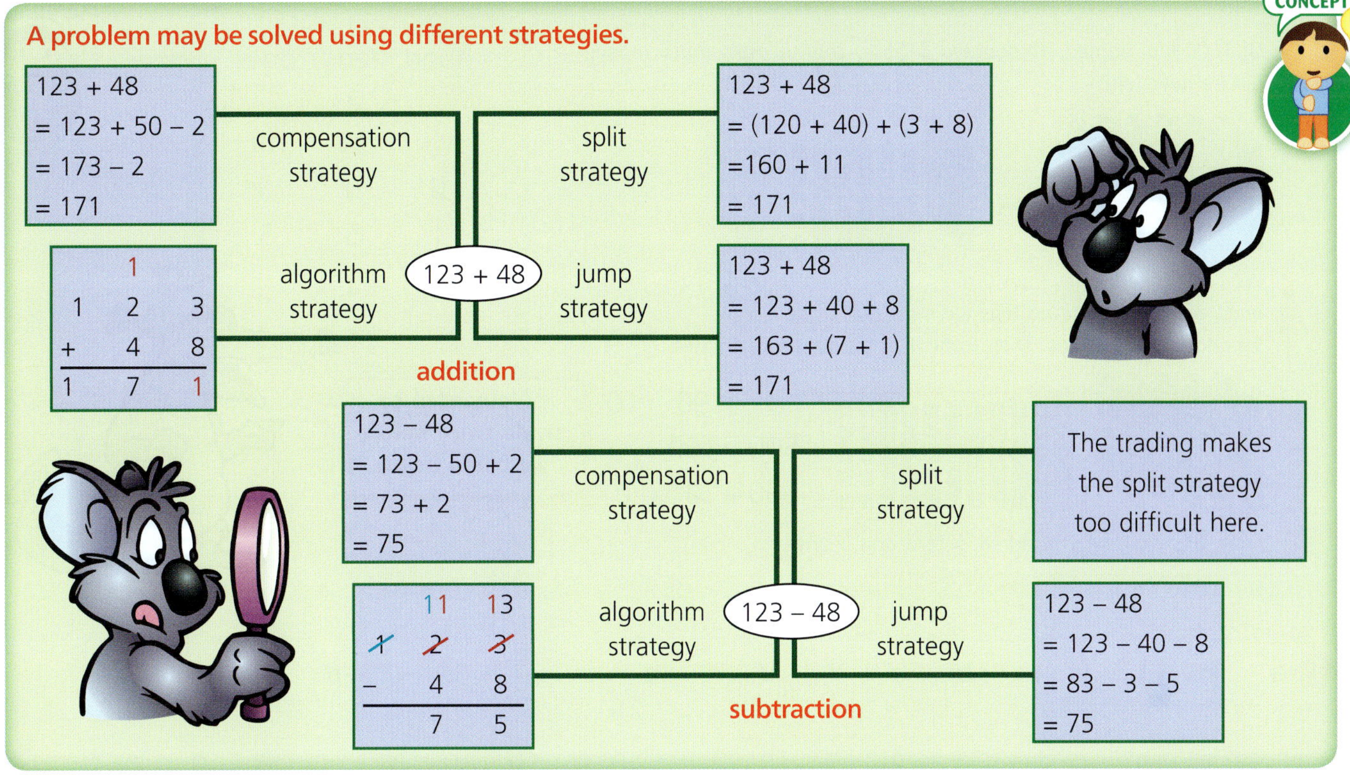

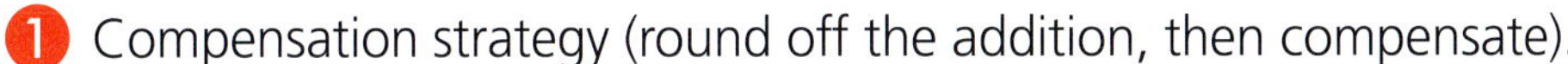

1 Compensation strategy (round off the addition, then compensate).

- **a** 241 + 48
- **b** 513 + 9
- **c** 537 + 98
- **d** 374 + 49
- **e** 732 + 48
- **f** 277 + 95
- **g** 543 + 98
- **h** 587 + 95
- **i** 429 + 97

To add 95, add 100 and subtract 5.

2 Building to 100 (combine tens to make 100).

- **a** 745 + 63
- **b** 154 + 54
- **c** 842 + 69
- **d** 473 + 42
- **e** 735 + 80
- **f** 436 + 75
- **g** 823 + 94
- **h** 712 + 95
- **i** 663 + 65

3 Compensation strategy (round off the subtraction, then compensate).

- **a** 783 – 49
- **b** 260 – 48
- **c** 667 – 98
- **d** 374 – 48
- **e** 732 – 47
- **f** 277 – 99
- **g** 543 – 98
- **h** 587 – 49
- **i** 429 – 96

To subtract 96, take away 100 and add 4.

4 Choose your own strategy.

- **a** 783 – 59
- **b** 163 – 42
- **c** 627 – 19
- **d** 555 – 19
- **e** 664 – 490
- **f** 852 – 39
- **g** 548 – 36
- **h** 283 – 47
- **i** 892 – 48

  ISBN 9780655709053

2:37 Subtraction from hundreds

1 hundred is the same as 9 tens and 10 ones.

CONCEPT

Of $600 Kim earned, he donated $155 to charity. How much money did he have left?

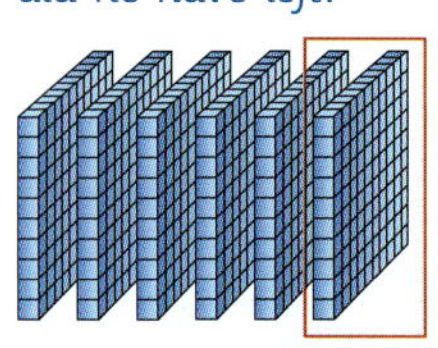

We can't take 5 ones from 0 ones, so we need to trade 1 ten for 10 ones. Since there are no tens we must first trade 1 hundred for 10 tens. Then trade 1 of the tens for 10 ones.

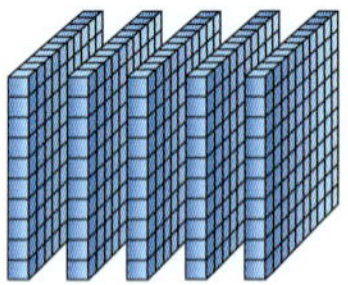
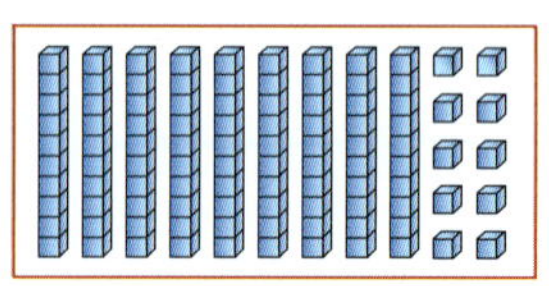

	90	10
500	~~100~~	
~~600~~ +	~~0~~ +	~~0~~

From this we take 1 hundred, 5 tens and 5 ones.

	hund	tens	ones
		9	
	5	~~10~~	10
	~~6~~	~~0~~	~~0~~
−	1	5	5
	4	4	5

1

a

	H	T	U
	1	0	0
−		2	7

b

	H	T	U
	2	0	0
−		3	8

c

	H	T	U
	9	0	0
−		6	1

d

	H	T	U
	6	0	0
−		5	5

e $700 - 302$

f $900 - 793$

g $400 - 106$

h $300 - 253$

2

a $600 - 534$

b $500 - 399$

c $800 - 674$

d $700 - 668$

3 Estimate each answer and use the estimates to check your answers.

a Chloe needed 600 points to qualify for a state team. She earned only 487. How far short of her target was she? ☐ points

b Blackburn Post Office was sent 900 stamp albums to sell. If 481 were sold in the first month, how many were left? ☐ albums

c In our class library we have 400 books. I have read 147. How many have I not read? ☐ books

We could write 600 as 599 + 1.

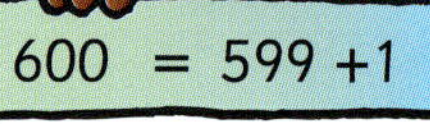

Subtraction from hundreds strategy

$1000 = $999 + $1

CONCEPT

700 − 137
= 699 + 1 − 137
= 699 − 137 + 1
= 562 + 1
= 563

OR

700	→	699 + 1
− 137		− 137
		562 + 1
		= 563

1

	H	T	U	
a		9	9	+ 1
	~~1~~	~~0~~	~~0~~	
−		3	7	
				+ 1
=				

	H	T	U	
b	2	9	9	+ 1
	~~3~~	~~0~~	~~0~~	
−		4	8	
				+ 1
=				

	H	T	U	
c	8	9	9	+ 1
	~~9~~	~~0~~	~~0~~	
−		7	1	
				+ 1
=				

d
~~7 0 0~~ + 1
− 4 6 9
+ 1
= ______

e
~~5 0 0~~ + 1
− 2 8 5
+ 1
= ______

f
~~2 0 0~~ + 1
− 1 3 7
+ 1
= ______

g
+ 1
4 0 0
− 3 2 1
+ 1
= ______

h
+ 1
6 0 0
− 2 9 3
+ 1
= ______

i
+ 1
8 0 0
− 5 4 6
+ 1
= ______

j
6 0 0
− 2 7 1
+
= ______

k
9 0 0
− 3 4 9
+
= ______

l
5 0 0
− 1 5 6
+
= ______

2 I took $1000 to the show. How much would I have left if I spent:

a $297? ______ **b** $174? ______ **c** $856? ______ **d** $324? ______

 • *AUSTRALIAN SIGNPOST MATHS NSW 4* • ISBN 9780655709053

2:39 Division as repeated subtraction

How many groups?

CONCEPT

How can I find how many groups of 3 mushrooms?

15		
3	3	...

Put a small mark after each 3 mushrooms. Count the groups of 3.

15	
36	
24	
30	
48	

1 How many groups of 3 could be made from each of these?

a ☐ groups

b ☐ groups

c ☐ groups

2
a How many groups of 5 mushrooms are in 15? ☐ groups. So 15 ÷ 5 = ☐

b How many groups of 5 candles are in 30? ☐ groups. So 30 ÷ 5 = ☐

c How many groups of 3 mushrooms are in 15? ☐ groups. So 15 ÷ 3 = ☐

d How many groups of 6 tacks are in 36? ☐ groups. So 36 ÷ 6 = ☐

e How many groups of 3 candles are in 30? ☐ groups. So 30 ÷ 3 = ☐

f How many groups of 4 tacks are in 36? ☐ groups. So 36 ÷ 4 = ☐

g How many groups of 4 footballs are in 24? ☐ groups. So 24 ÷ 4 = ☐

h How many groups of 6 notes are in 48? ☐ groups. So 48 ÷ 6 = ☐

i How many groups of 9 tacks are in 36? ☐ groups. So 36 ÷ 9 = ☐

j How many groups of 8 footballs are in 24? ☐ groups. So 24 ÷ 8 = ☐

k How many groups of 8 notes are in 48? ☐ groups. So 48 ÷ 8 = ☐

3 Use counters or place-value blocks to answer these.

a 42 apples are put in groups of 6. How many groups are there? ☐, 42 ÷ 6 = ☐

b 5 cakes fill one box. How many boxes can be filled with 35 cakes? ☐, 35 ÷ 5 = ☐

c A table seats 4 people. How many tables are needed to seat 32? ☐, 32 ÷ 4 = ☐

Understanding division

How many groups?
or
How many in each share?

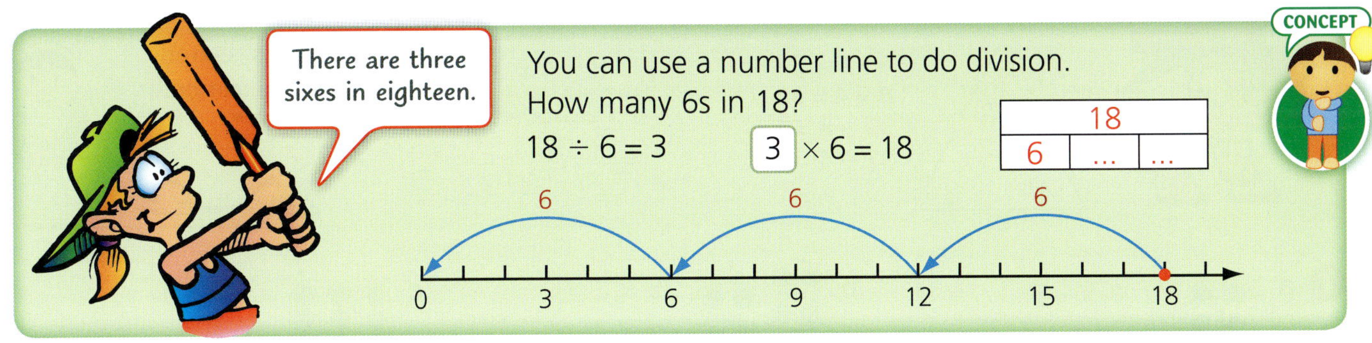

1 Use the number line above to find the answers.

a How many 3s are in 18?

$18 \div 3 =$ ☐

b How many 9s are in 18?

$18 \div 9 =$ ☐

c How many 2s are in 18?

$18 \div 2 =$ ☐

d How many 18s are in 18?

$18 \div 18 =$ ☐

2 Use this number line to find the answers.

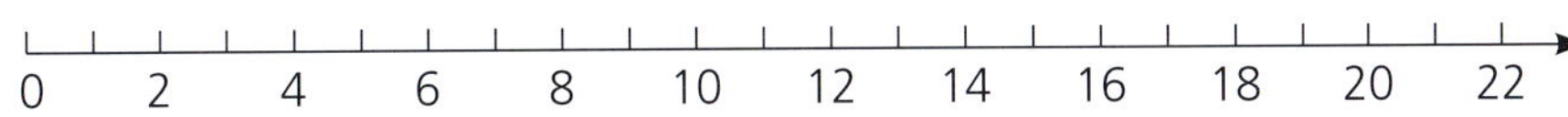

a How many 4s in 24?

$24 \div 4 =$ ☐

b How many 8s in 24?

$24 \div 8 =$ ☐

c How many 2s in 24?

$24 \div 2 =$ ☐

d How many 3s in 24?

$24 \div 3 =$ ☐

e How many 6s in 24?

$24 \div 6 =$ ☐

f How many 12s in 24?

$24 \div 12 =$ ☐

3 Use this number line to find the answers.

0 2 4 6 8 10 12 14 16 18 20 22

a How many 5s in 15?

$15 \div 5 =$ ☐

b How many 6s in 18?

$18 \div 6 =$ ☐

c How many 1s in 18?

$18 \div 1 =$ ☐

d How many 3s in 15?

$15 \div 3 =$ ☐

e How many 4s in 16?

$16 \div 4 =$ ☐

f How many 8s in 16?

$16 \div 8 =$ ☐

4 Write a number sentence for each sharing problem.

a 20 stickers, 4 students

☐ =

☐ each

b 16 bones, 8 dogs

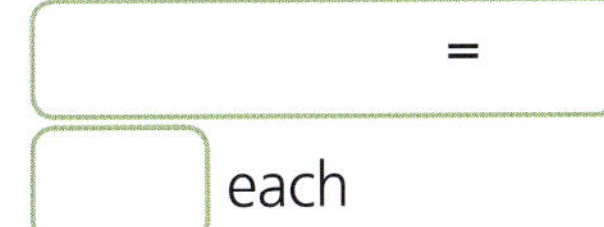

☐ =

☐ each

c 20 toys, 2 children

☐ =

☐ each

 • *AUSTRALIAN SIGNPOST MATHS NSW 4* • ISBN 9780655709053

Division facts

4 × 8 = 32
so
32 ÷ 8 = ☐ or 32 ÷ 4 = ☐

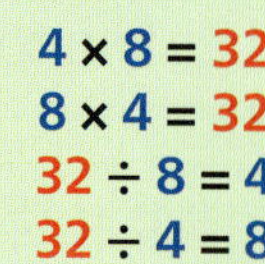

4 × 8 = 32
8 × 4 = 32
32 ÷ 8 = 4
32 ÷ 4 = 8

8 × 4 = 32

$4\overline{)32}$ = 8 $8\overline{)32}$ = 4

Division is related to multiplication.

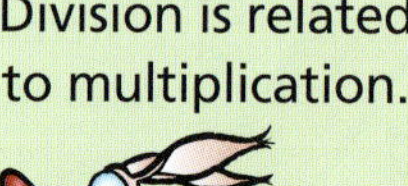

1 **a** 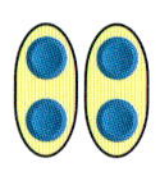
2 × 2 = ☐
4 ÷ 2 = ☐

b 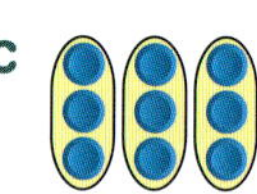
5 × 2 = ☐
10 ÷ 5 = ☐

c
3 × 3 = ☐
9 ÷ 3 = ☐

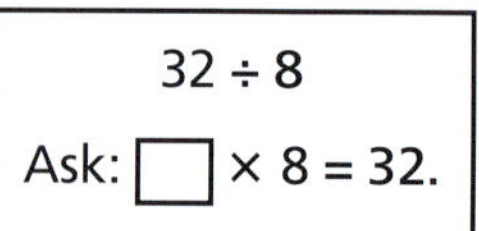

32 ÷ 8
Ask: ☐ × 8 = 32.

2 **a** 3 × 4 = ☐
so 12 ÷ 3 = ☐

b 2 × 8 = ☐
so 16 ÷ 2 = ☐

c 7 × 4 = ☐
so 28 ÷ 7 = ☐

d 9 × 3 = ☐
so 27 ÷ 9 = ☐

e 6 × 5 = ☐
so 30 ÷ 6 = ☐

f 5 × 3 = ☐
so 15 ÷ 5 = ☐

3 Use the multiplication table to answer the division questions.

a 3 × 4 = 12
$4\overline{)12}$ $3\overline{)12}$

b 8 × 5 = 40
$5\overline{)40}$ $8\overline{)40}$

c 10 × 9 = 90
$9\overline{)90}$ $10\overline{)90}$

d 6 × 10 = 60
$10\overline{)60}$ $6\overline{)60}$

e 7 × 8 = 56
$8\overline{)56}$ $7\overline{)56}$

f 5 × 9 = 45
$9\overline{)45}$ $5\overline{)45}$

4 **a** 12 ÷ 6 = ☐ or ☐ × 6 = 12
b 18 ÷ 3 = ☐ or ☐ × 3 = 18
c 35 ÷ 5 = ☐ or ☐ × 5 = 35
d 30 ÷ 5 = ☐ or ☐ × 5 = 30
e 20 ÷ 2 = ☐ or ☐ × 2 = 20
f 24 ÷ 8 = ☐ or ☐ × 8 = 24

5 **a** We bought 80 oranges and put the same number in each of 8 buckets. How many did we put in each bucket? ☐

b We decided to give 4 toys to each girl. If we gave out 32 toys, how many girls were there? ☐

c Four boys shared 28 keys. How many did each boy get? ☐

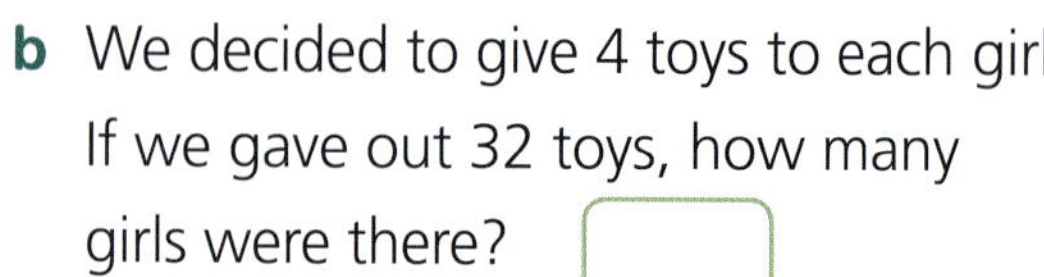

6 Share $136 among 4 people. What is the value of one share? Show your method below. (Estimate your answer first.)

Is the answer close to your estimate?

 • *AUSTRALIAN SIGNPOST MATHS NSW 4* • ISBN 9780655709053

Division facts

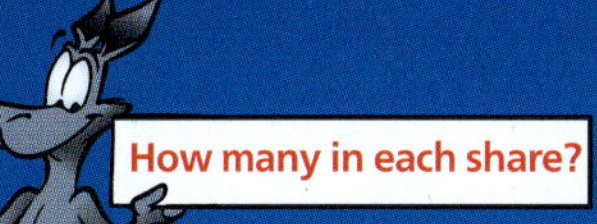

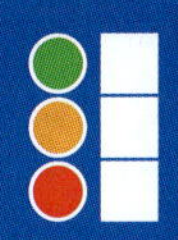

CONCEPT

- Six friends shared $42. How much did each receive?

Find: How much did each receive?

Number sentence: 42 ÷ 6 = ☐

Ask: ☐ × 6 = 42

Answer: Each received $7.

4 × 8 = 32

so

32 ÷ 8 = 4 or 32 ÷ 4 = 8

1 Use the first number sentence to fill in the other two.

a 8 × 3 = 24	b 4 × 9 = 36	c 5 × 6 = 30
24 ÷ 3 = ☐	36 ÷ 4 = ☐	30 ÷ 6 = ☐
24 ÷ 8 = ☐	36 ÷ 9 = ☐	30 ÷ 5 = ☐

(Triangle: 30; 5, 6)

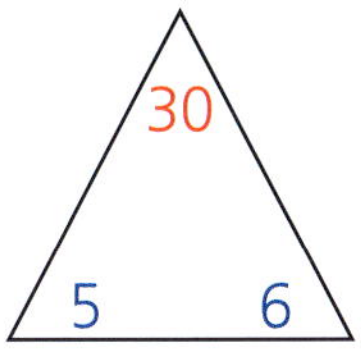

2

a ☐ × 9 = 18	b ☐ × 10 = 20	c ☐ × 3 = 21
d ☐ × 5 = 25	e ☐ × 3 = 9	f ☐ × 6 = 12
g 3 × ☐ = 6	h 2 × ☐ = 10	i 7 × ☐ = 14

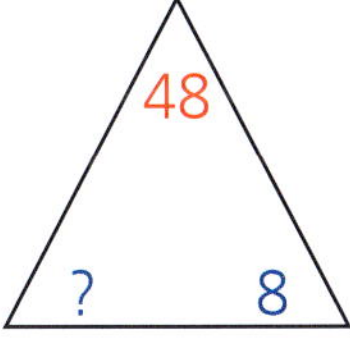

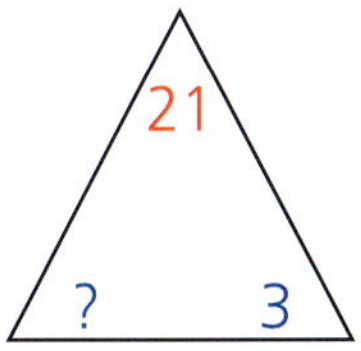

3

a 40 ÷ 5 = ☐	b 63 ÷ 9 = ☐	c 48 ÷ 8 = ☐
d 32 ÷ 4 = ☐	e 3 ÷ 3 = ☐	f 90 ÷ 10 = ☐
g 54 ÷ 9 = ☐	h 35 ÷ 5 = ☐	i 16 ÷ 4 = ☐
j 27 ÷ 3 = ☐	k 72 ÷ 8 = ☐	l 40 ÷ 8 = ☐

(Triangle: 48; ?, 8)

4

a

18	÷ 2	=	
	÷ 3	=	
	÷ 6	=	
	÷ 9	=	

b

24	÷ 3	=	
	÷ 4	=	
	÷ 6	=	
	÷ 8	=	

c

30	÷ 3	=	
	÷ 5	=	
	÷ 6	=	
	÷ 10	=	

5 Use a calculator to check all your answers.

ACTIVITY

Find the number sentences

- One person draws a number line which shows several equal jumps, starting at zero.
- The other person writes multiplication and division number sentences to match the picture.

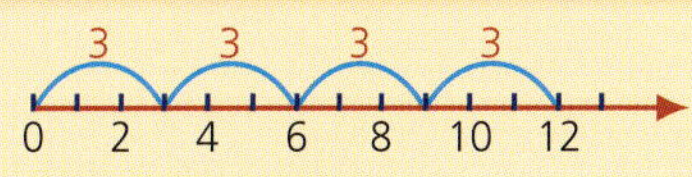

This shows:

4 × 3 = 12

so 12 ÷ 3 = 4

and 12 ÷ 4 = 3.

 • *AUSTRALIAN SIGNPOST MATHS NSW 4* • ISBN 9780655709053

2:43 Odd and even numbers

Is the total even or odd?

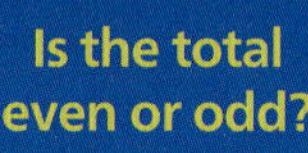

CONCEPT

- Odd numbers end in 1, 3, 5, 7 or 9. 87 is an odd number.
- Even numbers end in 2, 4, 6, 8 or 0. 34 is an even number.

An odd number of items can't be drawn in pairs.
Examples:
569, 12721, 1163

An even number of items can be drawn in pairs.
Examples:
1690, 724, 6928

1 Colour the odd numbers red and the even numbers blue.

83 100 109 111 118 120 125 127 130 3005 6112

2 Why are numbers ending in 1, 3, 5, 7 or 9 odd numbers?

3 Circle the even numbers. Underline the odd numbers.

38 53 75 14 87 92 66 36 29 41 50 35 74 100

482 764 2221 3106 988 3825 24 000

4
a What is the largest even number less than 80?
b What is the largest odd number less than 67?
c What is the largest even number less than 95?
d What is the largest odd number less than 100?

61	62	63	64	65	66	67	68	69	70
71	72	73	74	75	76	77	78	79	80
81	82	83	84	85	86	87	88	89	90
91	92	93	94	95	96	97	98	99	100

5 Find the rules for operating with two even numbers. Try to use mental strategies.

a

6 + 14		10 + 8		100 + 84	
16 + 12		32 + 16		104 + 58	
28 + 4		92 + 20		94 + 94	

even number plus even number =

b

44 – 42		56 – 56		36 – 8	
28 – 16		86 – 20		958 – 602	
32 – 14		198 – 8		600 – 2	

even number minus even number =

Odd and even

Odd numbers end in 1, 3, 5, 7 or 9
Even numbers end in 2, 4, 6, 8 or 0

1 Find the rules for operating with two odd or two even numbers.

a

7 + 7		11 + 3		75 + 25	
1 + 99		17 + 17		133 + 27	
5 + 83		87 + 21		77 + 33	

odd number plus odd number = ____

b

9 – 3		11 – 5		15 – 9	
21 – 11		33 – 19		17 – 15	
65 – 43		73 – 15		49 – 37	

odd number minus odd number = ____

c

12 × 2		8 × 6		4 × 2	
8 × 4		2 × 20		6 × 6	
6 × 4		4 × 10		2 × 8	

even number times even number = ____

d

48 ÷ 2		10 ÷ 10		80 ÷ 2	
40 ÷ 4		24 ÷ 4		40 ÷ 8	
18 ÷ 6		24 ÷ 8		36 ÷ 6	

even number divided by even number = odd or even

Use other pairs of numbers to check these rules.

2 Use many different examples of each case to complete this table. In each case write whether the answer would be odd or even.

Number Types	+	–	×	÷
Even and Even				odd or even
Odd and Odd				
Odd and Even				

Flow chart

Start with a number → Does it end in 1, 3, 5, 7 or 9? — Yes → the number is odd

↓

Does it end in 2, 4, 6, 8 or 0? — Yes → the number is even

3 Use the rules above to cross (✗) the answers that must be wrong.

6248 + 396 = 6645		8104 – 7998 = 106		366 × 47 = 17 201	
6107 ÷ 31 = 196		7319 + 2997 = 10 313		2817 – 199 = 2617	
283 × 654 = 28 353		173 × 881 = 152 416		68 019 ÷ 79 = 862	

2:45 Division using a grid

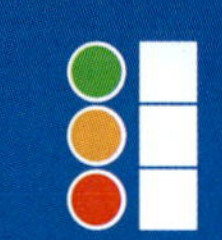

CONCEPT

35
7 5

×	0	1	2	3	4	5	6	7	8	9	10
0	0	0	0	0	0	0	0	0	0	0	0
1	0	1	2	3	4	5	6	7	8	9	10
2	0	2	4	6	8	10	12	14	16	18	20
3	0	3	6	9	12	15	18	21	24	27	30
4	0	4	8	12	16	20	24	28	32	36	40
5	0	5	10	15	20	25	30	35	40	45	50
6	0	6	12	18	24	30	36	42	48	54	60
7	0	7	14	21	28	35	42	49	56	63	70
8	0	8	16	24	32	40	48	56	64	72	80
9	0	9	18	27	36	45	54	63	72	81	90
10	0	10	20	30	40	50	60	70	80	90	100

$5\overline{)35}$ means 35 divided by 5.

7 ← Answer
$5\overline{)35}$

Use the multiplication grid above to answer these division questions.

1

a 15 ÷ 3 = ☐	**b** 20 ÷ 5 = ☐	**c** 16 ÷ 8 = ☐	**d** 90 ÷ 10 = ☐
e 42 ÷ 6 = ☐	**f** 10 ÷ 10 = ☐	**g** 24 ÷ 6 = ☐	**h** 24 ÷ 4 = ☐
i 64 ÷ 8 = ☐	**j** 45 ÷ 5 = ☐	**k** 36 ÷ 6 = ☐	**l** 25 ÷ 5 = ☐
m 72 ÷ 9 = ☐	**n** 16 ÷ 4 = ☐	**o** 10 ÷ 5 = ☐	**p** 81 ÷ 9 = ☐
q 18 ÷ 6 = ☐	**r** 54 ÷ 9 = ☐	**s** 40 ÷ 8 = ☐	**t** 36 ÷ 4 = ☐
u 40 ÷ 8 = ☐	**v** 50 ÷ 10 = ☐	**w** 48 ÷ 6 = ☐	**x** 21 ÷ 3 = ☐

2

a $2\overline{)8}$	**b** $5\overline{)5}$	**c** $2\overline{)6}$	**d** $10\overline{)30}$	**e** $6\overline{)12}$
f $4\overline{)12}$	**g** $10\overline{)80}$	**h** $3\overline{)9}$	**i** $9\overline{)45}$	**j** $8\overline{)32}$
k $5\overline{)30}$	**l** $5\overline{)15}$	**m** $5\overline{)40}$	**n** $3\overline{)24}$	**o** $9\overline{)27}$

3 Follow this track, putting an answer in every empty place.

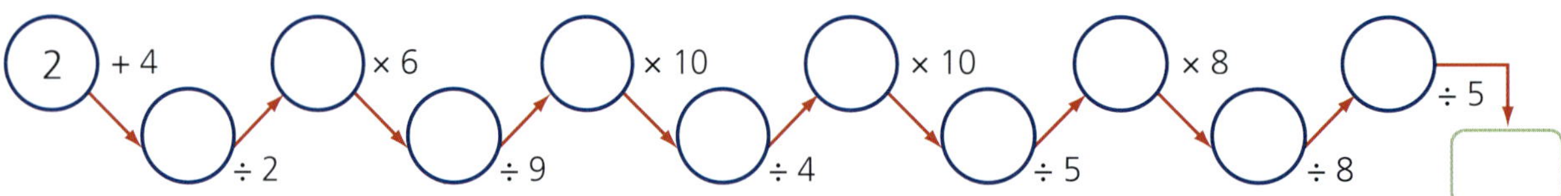

 • *AUSTRALIAN SIGNPOST MATHS NSW 4* • ISBN 9780655709053

× and ÷ tables (by 2, 4, 8)

4 × 8 = 32 so
32 ÷ 4 = 8
and 32 ÷ 8 = 4.

CONCEPT

If 8 x 4 = 32 then
- 32 ÷ 4 (How many 4s in 32?) = 8
- 32 ÷ 8 (32 shared by 8) = 4 (each)

32 ÷ 4 = ☐
- We can ask ☐ × 4 = 32
- We can ask 8 × 4 = 32 so ☐ = 8.

1 Join each question to its answer using a pencil and ruler.

a

× 2	
3 × 2	8
4 × 2	6
7 × 2	12
6 × 2	14
8 × 2	18
9 × 2	16
5 × 2	20
10 × 2	10

÷ 2	
8 ÷ 2	6
6 ÷ 2	9
12 ÷ 2	10
14 ÷ 2	4
18 ÷ 2	3
16 ÷ 2	7
20 ÷ 2	5
10 ÷ 2	8

b

× 4	
3 × 4	16
4 × 4	28
7 × 4	12
6 × 4	32
8 × 4	24
9 × 4	20
5 × 4	40
10 × 4	36

÷ 4	
16 ÷ 4	7
28 ÷ 4	3
12 ÷ 4	6
32 ÷ 4	4
24 ÷ 4	8
20 ÷ 4	10
40 ÷ 4	9
36 ÷ 4	5

c

× 8	
3 × 8	32
4 × 8	24
7 × 8	56
6 × 8	48
8 × 8	64
9 × 8	72
5 × 8	80
10 × 8	40

÷ 8	
32 ÷ 8	7
24 ÷ 8	6
56 ÷ 8	4
48 ÷ 8	9
64 ÷ 8	3
72 ÷ 8	10
80 ÷ 8	5
40 ÷ 8	8

d

×	
3 × 4	28
4 × 8	32
7 × 4	12
6 × 8	64
8 × 8	48
9 × 4	80
5 × 8	40
10 × 8	36

÷	
28 ÷ 4	3
32 ÷ 8	4
12 ÷ 4	8
64 ÷ 8	10
48 ÷ 8	7
80 ÷ 8	9
40 ÷ 8	6
36 ÷ 4	5

e

×	
3 × 8	8
4 × 2	24
7 × 8	56
6 × 8	48
8 × 8	18
9 × 2	64
5 × 8	80
10 × 8	40

÷	
8 ÷ 2	3
24 ÷ 8	8
56 ÷ 8	4
48 ÷ 8	9
18 ÷ 2	6
64 ÷ 8	7
80 ÷ 8	5
40 ÷ 8	10

f

×	
9 × 2	28
7 × 4	48
6 × 8	18
4 × 4	24
3 × 8	16
11 × 2	64
10 × 4	22
8 × 8	40

÷	
28 ÷ 4	6
48 ÷ 8	3
18 ÷ 2	7
24 ÷ 8	11
16 ÷ 4	9
64 ÷ 8	10
22 ÷ 2	4
40 ÷ 4	8

Mental strategies, × and ÷

18 × 3
= (10 × 3) + (8 × 3)
= 30 + 24 = 54

These are some of the strategies that can be used to solve problems.
Look at the question and ask, 'Is there a strategy I can use?'

A	Using × to answer ÷	6 × 4 = 24	so 24 ÷ 6 = 4	and 24 ÷ 4 = 6	
B	Extending known facts	12 × 7	= 11 × 7 + 7	= 77 + 7	= 84
C	Break up a number	5 × 18	= 5 × 2 × 9	= 10 × 9	= 90
D	Multiply in parts	16 × 4	= (10 × 4) + (6 × 4)	= 40 + 24	= 64
E	Multiplying 10s	7 × 40	= 7 × 4 × 10	= 28 × 10	= 280
F	Multiplying 100s	3 × 800	= 3 × 8 × 100	= 24 × 100	= 2400
G	Halve twice to divide by 4.	128 ÷ 4 Halve 128, then halve again. (128 ÷ 2) ÷ 2 = 32			

1 (**A**) Use 7 × 9 = 63, 8 × 4 = 32 and 8 × 6 = 48 to answer:

a 63 ÷ 7 ☐ **b** 63 ÷ 9 ☐ **c** 32 ÷ 8 ☐
d 32 ÷ 4 ☐ **e** 48 ÷ 6 ☐ **f** 48 ÷ 8 ☐

2 (**B**) Use 11 × 6 = 66, 11 × 4 = 44 and 11 × 8 = 88 to answer **a** to **c**.

a 12 × 6 ☐ **b** 12 × 4 ☐ **c** 12 × 8 ☐
d 20 × 4 = 80, 21 × 4 = ☐ **e** 40 × 3 = 120, 41 × 3 = ☐

3 (**C**) Break up a number into one number times another.

a 5 × 16 ☐ **b** 5 × 14 ☐ **c** 5 × 18 ☐
d 18 × 50 ☐ **e** 14 × 50 ☐ **f** 40 × 25 ☐

4 (**D**) Multiply in two easier parts.

a 14 × 4 ☐ **b** 16 × 6 ☐ **c** 15 × 6 ☐
d 12 × 14 ☐ **e** 13 × 15 ☐ **f** 11 × 21 ☐

5 (**E**) Multipy tens numbers.

a 8 × 20 ☐ **b** 7 × 30 ☐ **c** 8 × 40 ☐
d 60 × 7 ☐ **e** 20 × 9 ☐ **f** 70 × 4 ☐

6 (**F**) Multiply hundreds numbers.

a 7 × 200 ☐ **b** 4 × 400 ☐ **c** 7 × 500 ☐
d 600 × 3 ☐ **e** 900 × 6 ☐ **f** 800 × 9 ☐

7 (**G**) Halve and halve again to divide by 4. Halve three times to divide by 8.

a 64 ÷ 4 ☐ **b** 148 ÷ 4 ☐ **c** 160 ÷ 4 ☐
d 160 ÷ 8 ☐ **e** 808 ÷ 8 ☐ **f** 240 ÷ 8 ☐

Multiply in parts

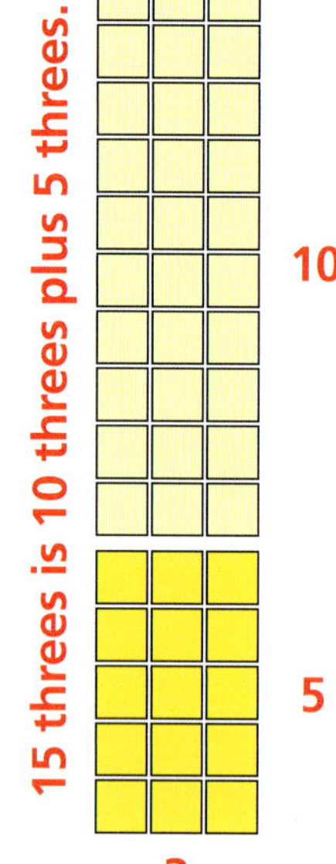

16 × 3 = (10 × 3) + (6 × 3)
= 30 + 18
= 48

2:48 Working with numbers

An estimate is a good guess.

1. Estimate the number of stickers to the nearest ten. [ ]

2. What two multiplication tables are shown by this array?

   [ ] × [ ] = [ ] and [ ] × [ ] = [ ]

3. What two division tables are shown by this array?

   42 ÷ [ ] = [ ] and 42 ÷ [ ] = [ ]

4. How many children could be given 5 stickers? [ ]

5. How many more stickers are needed to make 60? [ ]

6. Halve the number and keep halving for as long as you can.

   a 400 [ ] [ ] [ ] [ ] [ ] **b** 160 [ ] [ ] [ ] [ ] [ ]

   c 256 [ ] [ ] [ ] [ ] [ ] [ ] [ ] [ ] [ ] [ ]

   Double the number and keep doubling until you have filled the boxes.

   d 3 [ ] [ ] [ ] [ ] [ ] [ ]

   e 9 [ ] [ ] [ ] [ ] [ ] [ ]

INVESTIGATION

True or false?

= (2 × 70) + (2 × 2)

2 × 72 [ ]

7. Use doubling and the fact given to answer the questions.

   a 2 × 12 = 24 4 × 12 = [ ], 8 × 12 = [ ], 16 × 12 = [ ]

   b 6 × 3 = 18 12 × 3 = [ ], 24 × 3 = [ ], 48 × 3 = [ ]

   c 7 × 9 = 63 14 × 9 = [ ], 28 × 9 = [ ], 56 × 9 = [ ]

8. You have to design a box that holds 48 chocolates.
   There can be one or two layers, and on each layer the chocolates are arranged in equal rows.
   How many ways could you arrange the chocolates in a box? [ ]

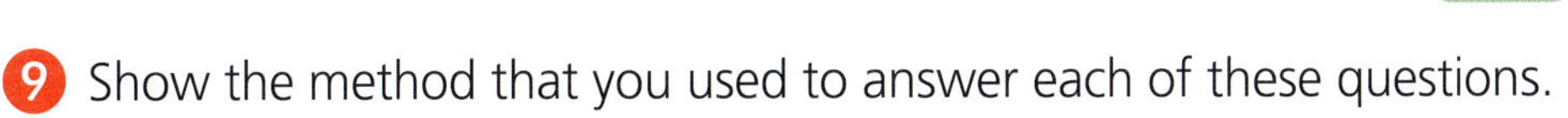

9. Show the method that you used to answer each of these questions.

a

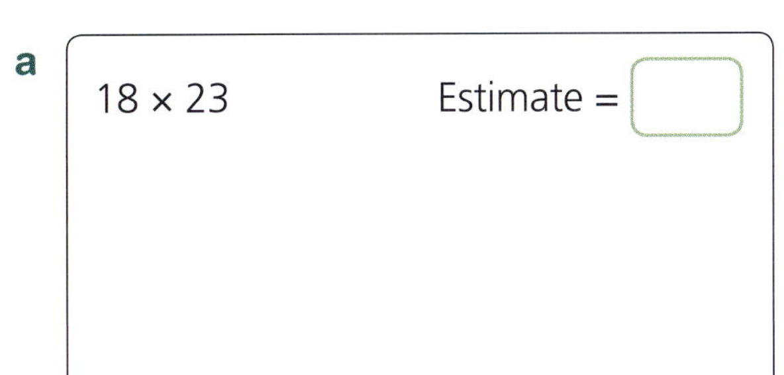

18 × 23 Estimate = [ ]

b

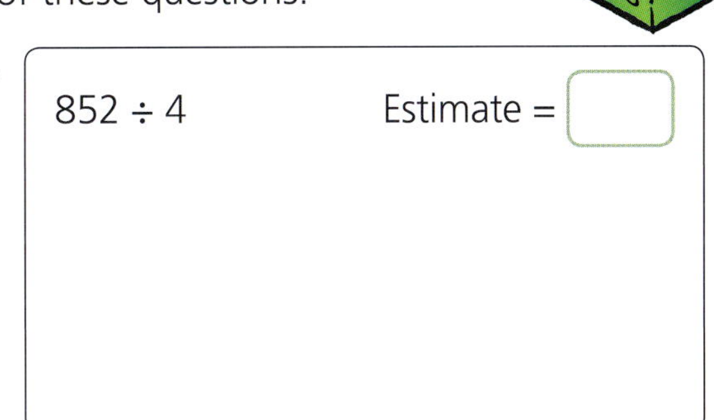

852 ÷ 4 Estimate = [ ]

 • *AUSTRALIAN SIGNPOST MATHS NSW 4* • ISBN 9780655709053

2:49 × and ÷ tables (by 3, 6, 9)

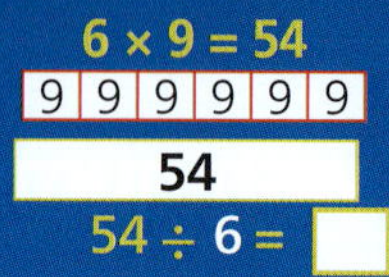

1 Join each question to its answer using a pencil and ruler.

a

× 3	
3 × 3	12
4 × 3	9
7 × 3	18
6 × 3	21
8 × 3	27
9 × 3	24
5 × 3	30
10 × 3	15

÷ 3	
12 ÷ 3	6
9 ÷ 3	9
18 ÷ 3	10
21 ÷ 3	4
27 ÷ 3	3
24 ÷ 3	7
30 ÷ 3	5
15 ÷ 3	8

b

× 6	
3 × 6	24
4 × 6	42
7 × 6	18
6 × 6	48
8 × 6	36
9 × 6	30
5 × 6	60
10 × 6	54

÷ 6	
24 ÷ 6	7
42 ÷ 6	3
18 ÷ 6	6
48 ÷ 6	4
36 ÷ 6	8
30 ÷ 6	10
60 ÷ 6	9
54 ÷ 6	5

c

× 9	
5 × 9	90
10 × 9	45
4 × 9	72
8 × 9	36
3 × 9	54
6 × 9	27
7 × 9	81
9 × 9	63

÷ 9	
90 ÷ 9	4
45 ÷ 9	8
72 ÷ 9	10
36 ÷ 9	3
54 ÷ 9	5
27 ÷ 9	9
81 ÷ 9	7
63 ÷ 9	6

d

× 6	
6 × 6	54
5 × 6	30
9 × 6	36
3 × 6	42
7 × 6	18
8 × 6	12
4 × 6	48
2 × 6	24

÷ 6	
54 ÷ 6	6
30 ÷ 6	5
36 ÷ 6	7
42 ÷ 6	2
18 ÷ 6	9
12 ÷ 6	4
48 ÷ 6	3
24 ÷ 6	8

e

× 9	
8 × 9	72
3 × 9	27
5 × 9	45
7 × 9	63
9 × 9	54
6 × 9	81
4 × 9	18
2 × 9	36

÷ 9	
72 ÷ 9	3
27 ÷ 9	9
45 ÷ 9	8
63 ÷ 9	6
54 ÷ 9	7
81 ÷ 9	5
18 ÷ 9	4
36 ÷ 9	2

f

×	
3 × 5	80
8 × 10	25
5 × 5	15
4 × 10	45
9 × 5	40
6 × 10	20
7 × 5	60
2 × 10	35

÷	
80 ÷ 10	5
25 ÷ 5	9
15 ÷ 5	8
45 ÷ 5	6
40 ÷ 10	3
20 ÷ 10	7
60 ÷ 10	4
35 ÷ 5	2

Division facts

2 kangaroos shared 12 balls.
$6 \times 2 = 12$ so $12 \div 2 = 6$

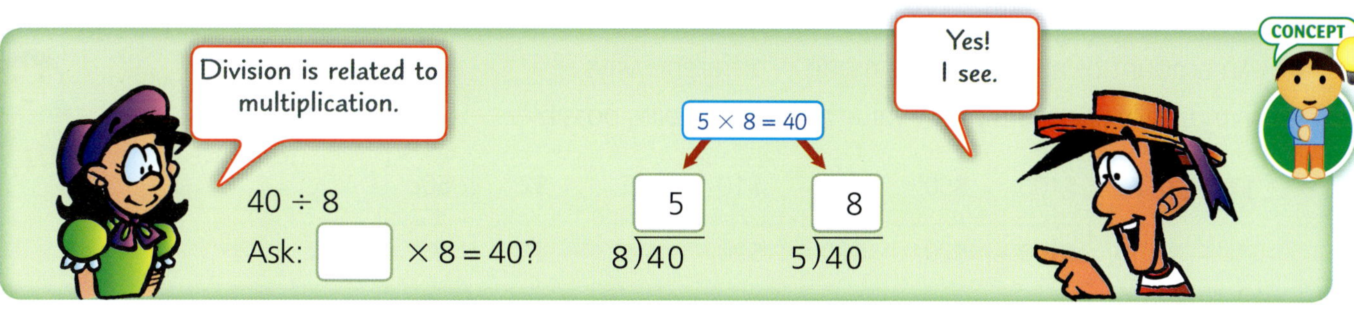

1. Use a multiplication table to answer the division questions.

a $6 \times 10 = 60$ $\quad 6\overline{)60} \quad 10\overline{)60}$

b $5 \times 8 = 40$ $\quad 8\overline{)40} \quad 5\overline{)40}$

c $6 \times 9 = 54$ $\quad 9\overline{)54} \quad 6\overline{)54}$

d $9 \times 8 = 72$ $\quad 8\overline{)72} \quad 9\overline{)72}$

e $7 \times 6 = 42$ $\quad 6\overline{)42} \quad 7\overline{)42}$

f $4 \times 9 = 36$ $\quad 9\overline{)36} \quad 4\overline{)36}$

2.
a ☐ × 2 = 12 **b** 6 × ☐ = 18 **c** ☐ × 4 = 20 **d** 5 × ☐ = 10
e ☐ × 3 = 18 **f** 7 × ☐ = 56 **g** ☐ × 9 = 9 **h** 6 × ☐ = 36
i ☐ × 5 = 35 **j** 4 × ☐ = 32 **k** ☐ × 4 = 16 **l** 3 × ☐ = 27

3.
a 16 ÷ 2 = ☐ **b** 25 ÷ 5 = ☐ **c** 30 ÷ 6 = ☐ **d** 24 ÷ 6 = ☐
e 30 ÷ 3 = ☐ **f** 24 ÷ 4 = ☐ **g** 35 ÷ 7 = ☐ **h** 90 ÷ 9 = ☐
i 24 ÷ 8 = ☐ **j** 48 ÷ 6 = ☐ **k** 64 ÷ 8 = ☐ **l** 36 ÷ 6 = ☐
m 27 ÷ 3 = ☐ **n** 50 ÷ 5 = ☐ **o** 63 ÷ 9 = ☐ **p** 30 ÷ 5 = ☐
q 45 ÷ 5 = ☐ **r** 72 ÷ 9 = ☐ **s** 54 ÷ 6 = ☐ **t** 90 ÷ 10 = ☐
u 81 ÷ 9 = ☐ **v** 48 ÷ 8 = ☐ **w** 16 ÷ 8 = ☐ **x** 30 ÷ 5 = ☐

For **81** ÷ 9 **ask**, 'What times 9 gives **81**?'

ACTIVITY

Dice multiplication

×	1	2	3	4	5	6
1						
2						
3						
4						
5						
6						

- Take turns to throw two dice.
- Multiply the numbers showing.
- Write the answer in the table (each player uses a different colour).
- The first to get 3 answers in a line wins.

Note: Both 3 × 1 and 1 × 3 are made by ⚀ ⚂ .

 • *AUSTRALIAN SIGNPOST MATHS NSW 4* • ISBN 9780655709053

Money

Use 20c and 10c coins to make 70c. in two ways

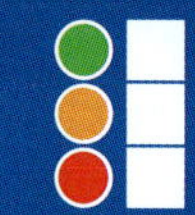

- An amount of money can be made in different ways.
- We usually use the highest value notes and coins possible.

The white boxes stand for coins.

$187.50 = | $100 | $50 | $20 | $10 | $5 | $2 | 50c

or | $100 | $20 | $20 | $20 | $20 | $5 | $2 | 50c

1 Make each amount using the highest value of notes and coins possible.

a $57

b $51.50

c $23

d $60.30

e $188.60

f $96.95

g $133.80

h $165.75

i $65.35

j $153.35

k $275.40

l $212.80

m $107.25

n $422.20

o $301.65

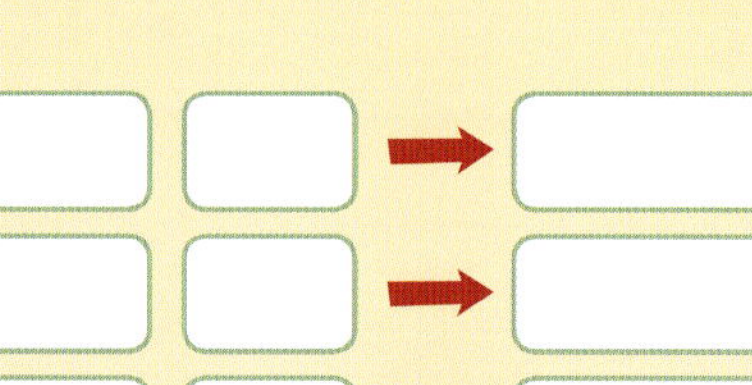

From a collection of coins, choose 8. Write the value of each coin and the total.
Repeat the process each time.

 • *AUSTRALIAN SIGNPOST MATHS NSW 4* • ISBN 9780655709053

Rounding off money

If we pay cash, the cost is rounded to the nearest 5 cents.

When paying by cash, the price is rounded to the nearest 5 cents.

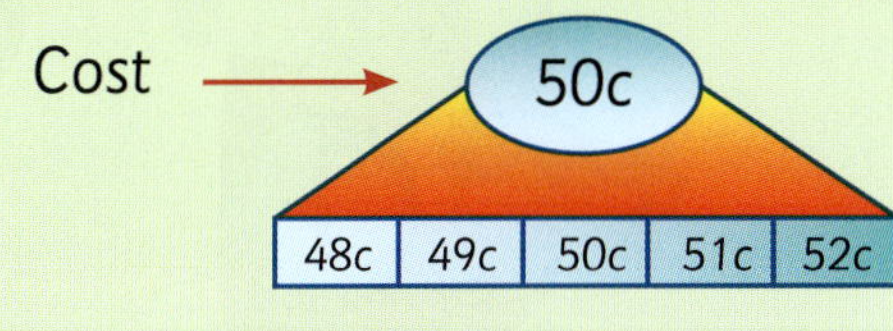

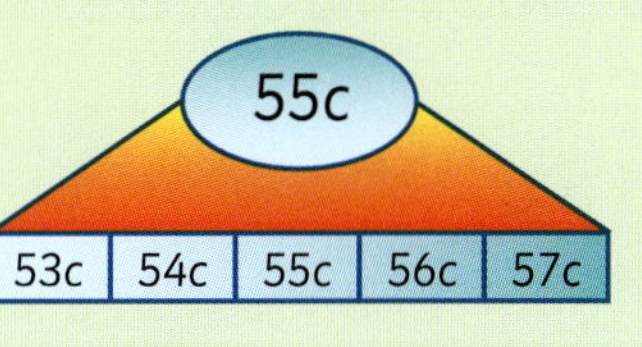

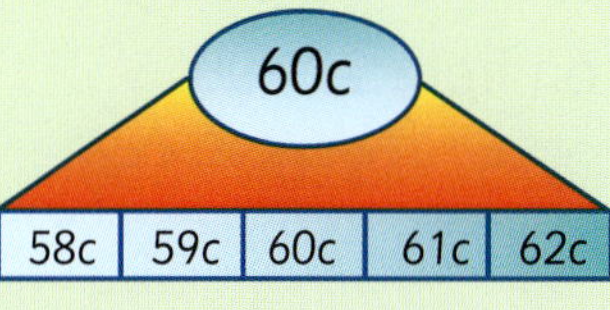

1 Round these amounts to the nearest 5 cents.

a	87c		**b**	$0.87		**c**	$1.52	
d	$6.88		**e**	$3.26		**f**	$9.45	
g	$8.90		**h**	$4.51		**i**	$7.43	
j	$5.04		**k**	$0.59		**l**	$8.74	
m	$7.13		**n**	$4.88		**o**	$0.42	
p	$8.77		**q**	$3.56		**r**	$8.04	

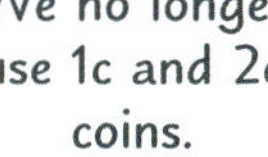

2 Find the total cost of the items then round to the nearest 5c.

a ice cream ($5.86), milk ($2.33), chocolate ($3.58)

b biscuits ($3.35), nuts ($12.48), raisins ($3.96)

c tea ($12.47), scissors ($2.42), calculator ($45.11)

d pens ($3.71), paper ($6.15), cereal ($7.32)

To find the change, follow these steps:

Step 1 Find the total cost using a calculator.
Step 2 Round to the nearest 5 cents.
Step 3 Count on, to work out the change.
Step 4 Write the amount of change.

3 Complete the table.

	Cost of items	Total	Total rounded	Amount given	Count on to give change	Change
a	$1.14, $6.35, $4.17	$11.66	$11.65	$50	5c, $11.70 30c, $12 $8, $20 $30	$38.35
b	$0.98, $7.93, $11.42			$50		
c	$12.56, $5.99, $3.04			$50		
d	$1.78, $4.29, $3.95			$20		
e	$0.75, $0.89, $1.13			$20		
f	$8.46, $12.18, $9.87			$100		
g	$37.54, $9.45, $6.69			$100		

 • *AUSTRALIAN SIGNPOST MATHS NSW 4* • ISBN 9780655709053

2:53 Counting change

Cost = $6
Paid with $20.
Change: $4 and $10

CONCEPT

To give change, we count on from the price paid.

Example: What is the change from $100 if the cost is $23.90?

- Count on from $23.90.

$24… $25… $30… $50… $100

10c	$1	$5	$20	$50

Change = $76.10

1. Count on and write the change given in coins and notes.

	Cost	Money given	Count on → Coins and notes given as change	Total change
a	$6.50	$50	$7 → $8 → $10 → $30 → $50	
b	$1.20	$10	$1.30 → $1.50 → $2 → $3 → $5 → $10	
c	$8.70	$50	$8.80 → $9 → $10 → $30 → $50	
d	$3.00	$100	$5 → $10 → $30 → $50 → $100	
e	$36.40	$50		
f	$67.20	$100		

2. Find the change from $50 using only the boxes you need.

a $36.50 Change =

b $9.20 Change =

c $18.30 Change =

INVESTIGATION

3. Show three different ways of giving change from $50 if the cost is $41.95.

a

b

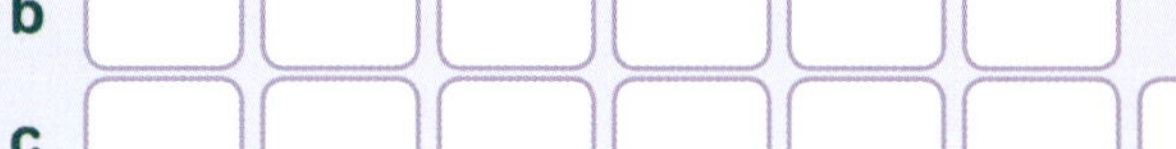

c

Practise giving change using play money.

 • *AUSTRALIAN SIGNPOST MATHS NSW 4* • ISBN 9780655709053

2:54 Multiplying by 10, 100, 1000

7876
If there are only 4 digits, there is no space after the thousands place.

CONCEPT

- 37 tens is 37 × 10. This is written as 370, so to multiply by 10, add one zero.
- 37 hundreds means 37 × 100. This is written 3700, so to multiply by 100, add two zeros.
- 37 thousands means 37 × 1000. This is written 37 000, so to multiply by 1000, add three zeros.

526 × 10
The 5 in the hundreds place becomes a 5 in the thousands place.
The 2 in the tens place becomes a 2 in the hundreds place.

526 × 10
= 5260

For × 10, × 100 and × 1000 move the digits 1, 2 and 3 places to the left.

1

a 56 × 10		**b** 91 × 10		**c** 33 × 10	
d 620 × 10		**e** 2917 × 10		**f** 44 188 × 10	
g 78 × 100		**h** 15 × 100		**i** 48 × 100	
j 913 × 100		**k** 4054 × 100		**l** 7500 × 100	
m 79 × 1000		**n** 98 × 1000		**o** 80 × 1000	
p 300 × 1000		**q** 5835 × 100		**r** 6000 × 100	

85 × 10 = 850, so there are 85 tens in 850.

85 × 100 = 8500, so there are 85 hundreds in 8500.

85 × 1000 = 85 000, so there are 85 thousands in 85 000.

853 has 85 tens.
8567 has 85 hundreds.
85 453 has 85 thousands.

2 How many tens can be taken from these numbers?

a 460 ☐ **b** 427 ☐ **c** 3263 ☐ **d** 9473 ☐

3 How many hundreds can be taken from these numbers?

a 4200 ☐ **b** 9372 ☐ **c** 5839 ☐ **d** 2034 ☐

4 How many thousands can be taken from these numbers?

a 67 000 ☐ **b** 37 830 ☐ **c** 19 472 ☐ **d** 35 075 ☐

5 This place-value house shows 287 481.

Thousands					
H	T	O	H	T	O
2	8	7	4	8	1

a How many thousands can be taken? ☐

b How many hundreds can be taken? ☐

c How many tens can be taken? ☐

2:55 Dividing by 10, 100, 1000

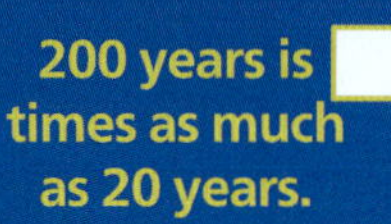

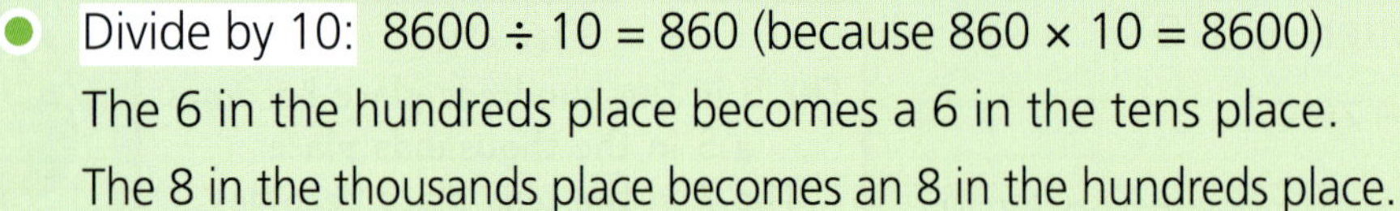

- Divide by 10: 8600 ÷ 10 = 860 (because 860 × 10 = 8600)
  The 6 in the hundreds place becomes a 6 in the tens place.
  The 8 in the thousands place becomes an 8 in the hundreds place.
- Divide by 100: 8600 ÷ 100 = 86 (because 86 × 100 = 8600)
  The 6 in the hundreds place becomes a 6 in the ones place.
  The 8 in the thousands place becomes an 8 in the tens place.
- Divide by 1000: 86 000 ÷ 1000 = 86 (because 86 × 1000 = 86 000)
  The 6 in the thousands place becomes a 6 in the ones place.
  The 8 in the ten-thousands place becomes an 8 in the tens place.

CONCEPT

When dividing numbers that have zeros at the end:
I remove one zero if I'm dividing by ten, 2 if by 100 and 3 if by 1000.

60 000 ÷ 100 = 600

1

a 660 ÷ 10		**b** 200 ÷ 10		**c** 830 ÷ 10	
d 6700 ÷ 10		**e** 85 370 ÷10		**f** 22 000 ÷10	
g 7800 ÷ 100		**h** 48 000 ÷ 100		**i** 41 400 ÷ 100	
j 33 300 ÷ 100		**k** 53 600 ÷ 100		**l** 50 000 ÷ 100	
m 19 000 ÷ 1000		**n** 31 000 ÷ 1000		**o** 80 000 ÷ 1000	
p 300000 ÷ 1000		**q** 104 000 ÷ 1000		**r** 700000 ÷ 1000	

2 How many tens can be taken from these numbers?

a 930   **b** 620   **c** 2578   **d** 493 543

3 How many hundreds can be taken from these numbers?

a 2700   **b** 2467   **c** 65 376   **d** 963 584

4 How many thousands can be taken from these numbers?

a 83 000   **b** 92 456   **c** 73 465   **d** 956 306

5 This place-value house shows 218 547.

Thousands					
H	T	O	H	T	O
2	1	8	5	4	7

a How many thousands can be taken?

b How many hundreds can be taken?

c How many tens can be taken?

23 000 ÷ 10 (or 100 or 1000)

Dividing by 10 moves all digits one place to the right (by removing a zero).
Dividing by 100 moves all digits two places to the right (by removing two zeros).
Dividing by 1000 moves all digits three places to the right (by removing three zeros).

 • *AUSTRALIAN SIGNPOST MATHS NSW 4* • ISBN 9780655709053

Linking ÷ and ×

408 / 17 / 24

17 × 24 = 408
24 × 17 = 408
408 ÷ 17 = 24
408 ÷ 24 = 17

CONCEPT

7 × 4 = 28
so
28 ÷ 7 = 4
and
28 ÷ 4 = 7

17 × 24 = 408
so
408 ÷ 17 = 24
and
408 ÷ 24 = 17

If 17 × ☐ = 408
then 408 ÷ 17 = ☐
and
If ☐ × 24 = 408
then 408 ÷ 24 = ☐

What is each share if $270 is shared among 9?

In each case, use a calculator to find the missing number.

Example

9 × ☐ = $270
Answer = $270 ÷ 9
= $30
Calculator keys used:
270 ÷ 9 =

1 a 8 × ☐ = 168
168 ÷ 8 = ☐

b 5 × ☐ = 225
225 ÷ 5 = ☐

c 7 × ☐ = 245
245 ÷ 7 = ☐

d 4 × ☐ = 504
504 ÷ 4 = ☐

e 3 × ☐ = 435
435 ÷ 3 = ☐

f 9 × ☐ = 351
351 ÷ 9 = ☐

How many $8 hats can I buy with $192?

Example

☐ × $8 = $192
Answer = $192 ÷ $8
= 24 hats
Calculator keys used:
192 ÷ 8 =

2 a ☐ × 7 = 476
476 ÷ 7 = ☐

b ☐ × 3 = 486
486 ÷ 3 = ☐

c ☐ × 5 = 835
835 ÷ 5 = ☐

d ☐ × 8 = 296
296 ÷ 8 = ☐

e ☐ × 9 = 504
504 ÷ 9 = ☐

f ☐ × 6 = 648
648 ÷ 6 = ☐

3 a 14 × ☐ = 224
Answer = ☐

b 17 × ☐ = 884
Answer = ☐

c 24 × ☐ = 1632
Answer = ☐

d ☐ × 35 = 4410
Answer = ☐

e ☐ × 62 = 1550
Answer = ☐

f ☐ × 27 = 729
Answer = ☐

g 38 × ☐ = 988
Answer = ☐

h 63 × ☐ = 1701
Answer = ☐

i 75 × ☐ = 1875
Answer = ☐

24 times what number gives 1632? We divide 1632 by 24.

 • *AUSTRALIAN SIGNPOST MATHS NSW 4* • ISBN 9780655709053

2:57 Missing number strategies

True or false?
$13 + 5 = 9 + 9$

1 Linking addition and subtraction.

a 8 – ☐ = 1 **b** 9 – ☐ = 0 **c** 15 – ☐ = 10 **d** 10 – ☐ = 10

e ☐ – 3 = 7 **f** ☐ – 10 = 10 **g** ☐ – 7 = 8 **h** ☐ – 5 = 4

2 Finding the difference.

Write the missing numbers.

a ☐ + 8 = 10 **b** ☐ + 3 = 7 **c** ☐ + 8 = 15

d 9 + ☐ = 12 **e** 8 + ☐ = 17 **f** 10 + ☐ = 10

g ☐ + 11 = 15 **h** ☐ + 9 = 14 **i** ☐ + 12 = 12

j 14 + ☐ = 20 **k** 18 + ☐ = 23 **l** 17 + ☐ = 19

m ☐ + 9 = 20 **n** ☐ + 15 = 25 **o** ☐ + 11 = 40

3 Each side of an = sign has the same value. Find the missing numbers.

a 10 – ☐ = 10 – 7 **b** 18 + ☐ = 15 + 8 **c** 21 – ☐ = 19 – 7

d 16 – 7 = ☐ + 6 **e** 24 + ☐ = 35 – 6 **f** 30 – 15 = 6 + ☐

4 Compensation strategy.

a 887 + 96 = 887 + 100 – ☐ = ☐ **b** 416 + 49 = 416 + 50 – ☐ = ☐

c 1076 + 97 = 1076 + 100 – ☐ = ☐ **d** 253 + 89 = 476 + 90 – ☐ = ☐

5 Linking multiplication and division.

a ☐ × 6 = 18 **b** ☐ × 5 = 35 **c** ☐ × 4 = 24 **d** ☐ × 3 = 27

e 4 × ☐ = 20 **f** 7 × ☐ = 21 **g** 9 × ☐ = 90 **h** 8 × ☐ = 40

i ☐ × 10 = 80 **j** ☐ × 6 = 36 **k** ☐ × 4 = 28 **l** ☐ × 5 = 35

m ☐ ÷ 2 = 8 **n** ☐ ÷ 4 = 3 **o** ☐ ÷ 5 = 8

p 24 ÷ ☐ = 3 **q** 24 ÷ ☐ = 4 **r** 24 ÷ ☐ = 8

24 ÷ ☐ = 8.
Ask, '24 divided by what number gives 8?'

6 Mixed operations

a 6 + 7 + ☐ = 15 **b** 3 – 1 + ☐ = 12 **c** 8 + 7 + ☐ = 20

d 4 × 2 + ☐ = 10 **e** 6 × 5 – ☐ = 26 **f** 21 ÷ 3 + ☐ = 13

g 2 × ☐ + 1 = 9 **h** 3 × ☐ + 2 = 17 **i** 2 × ☐ + 1 = 7

 • *AUSTRALIAN SIGNPOST MATHS NSW 4* • ISBN 9780655709053

Partitioning, + and –

These strategies help you work it out in your head.

CONCEPT

When we partition, adding larger numbers is easier.

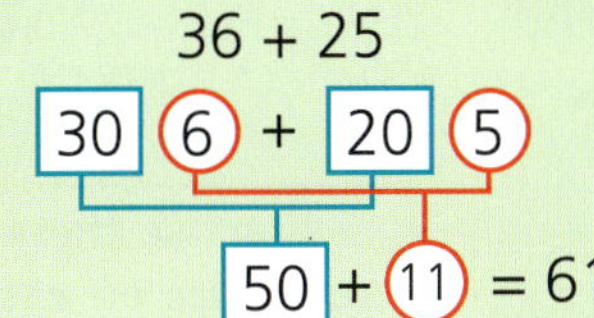

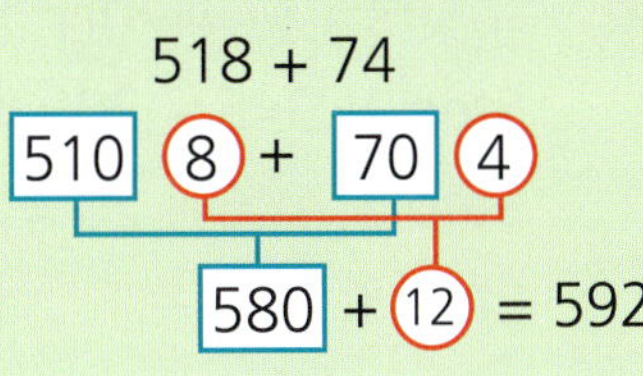

1 Use partitioning to add these numbers.

a 47 + 36

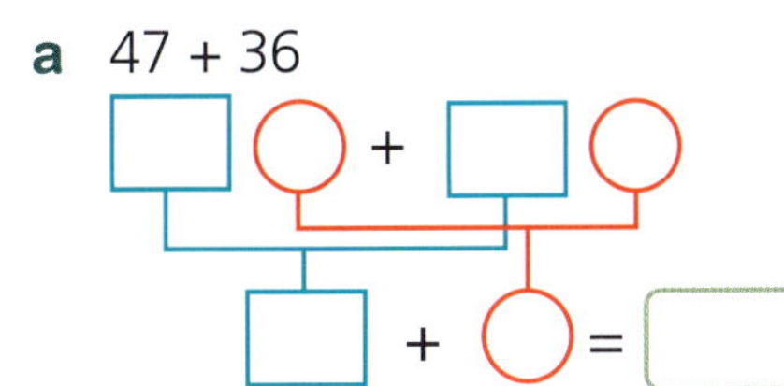

b 25 + 29

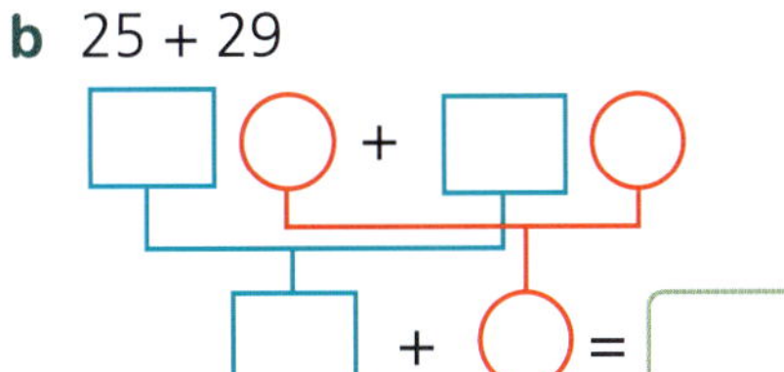

c 648 + 45

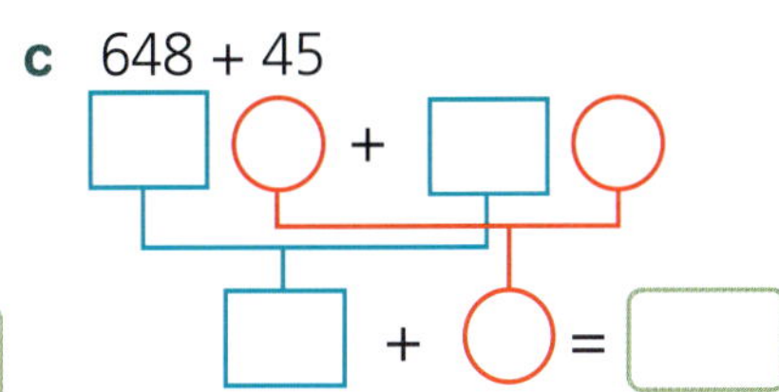

d 67 + 49

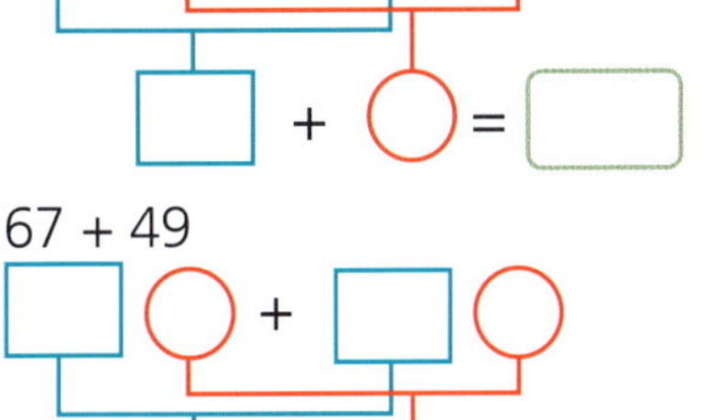

e 437 + 35

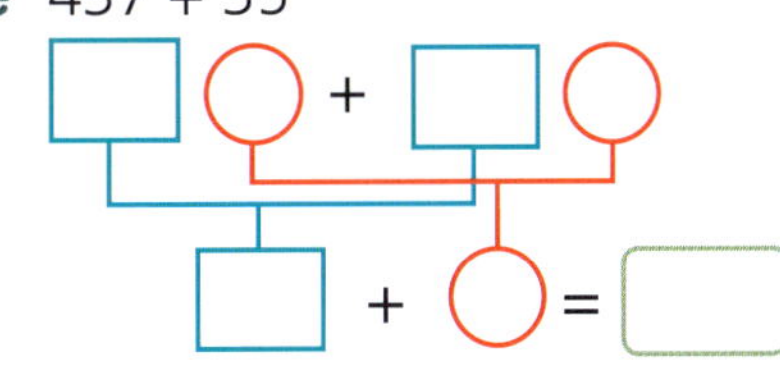

f Try these in your head.

86 + 37 =

639 + 25 =

427 + 37 =

CONCEPT

When we partition to subtract we must make sure we can subtract the second number.

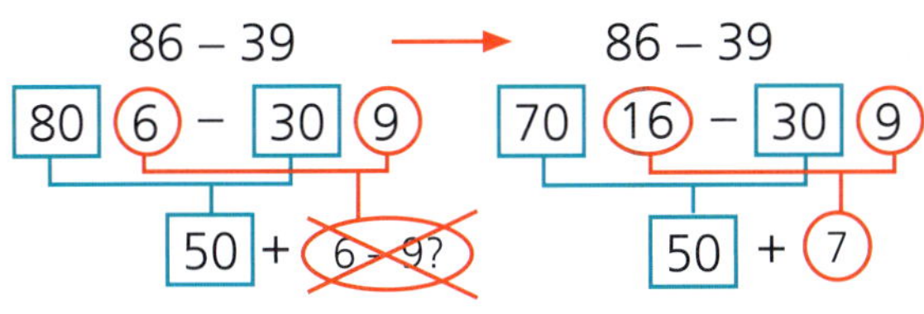

We cannot subtract 9 from 6 so we break up 86 into 70 + 16.

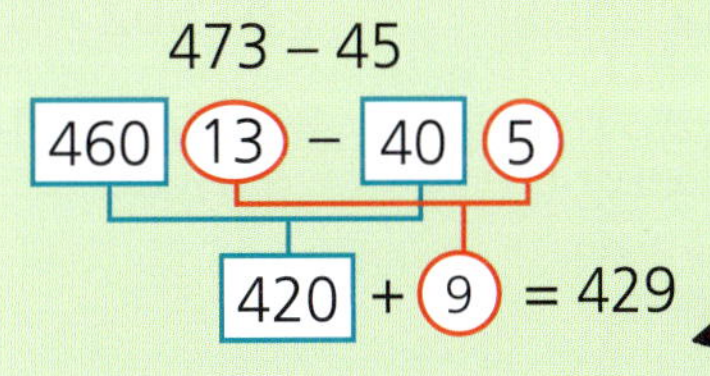

We must add the two parts we have subtracted.

2 Use partitioning to subtract these numbers.

a 52 – 28

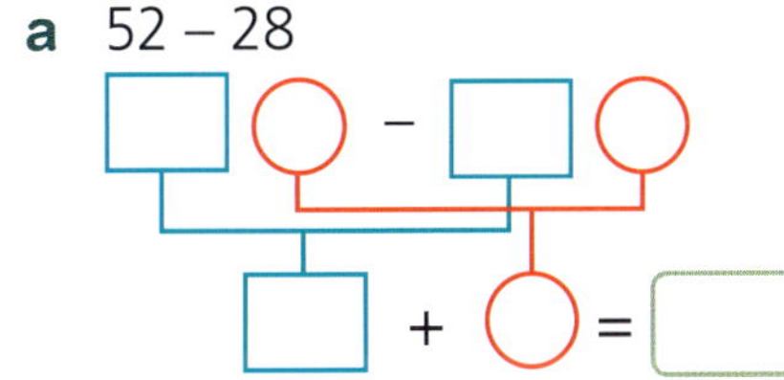

b 73 – 46

c 273 – 46

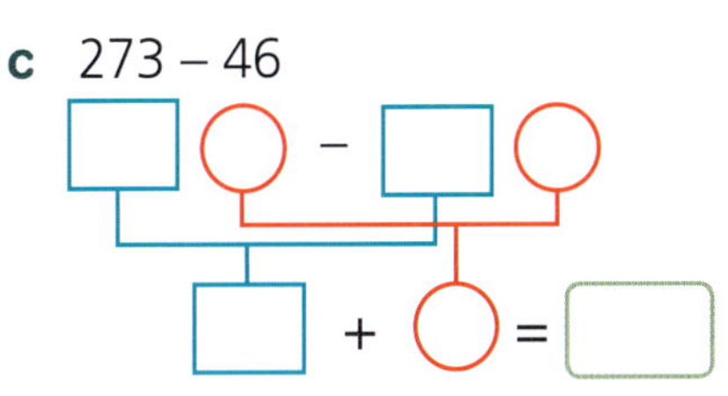

d 114 – 37

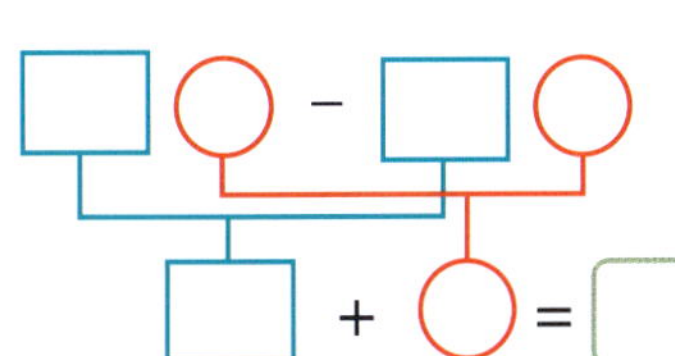

e 313 – 47

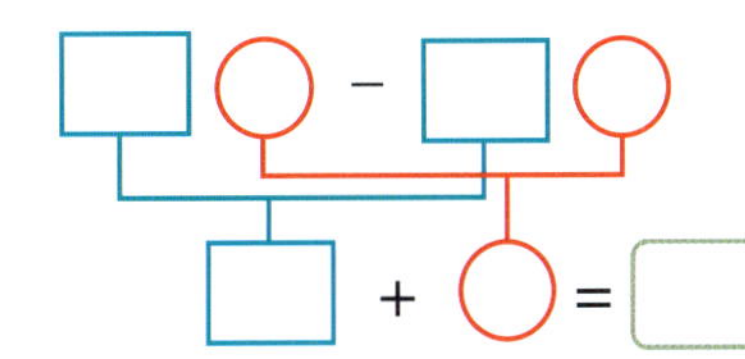

f Try these in your head.

245 – 27 =

461 – 58 =

314 – 45 =

 • *AUSTRALIAN SIGNPOST MATHS NSW 4* • ISBN 9780655709053

2:59 Mental strategies, + and –

Choose a strategy that makes it easier.

CONCEPT

Practise using these mental strategies.

A	Bridging to 10s	338 + 23	= 338 + (2 + 20 + 1)	= 361
B	Break up the number	346 – 227	Step 1: 346 – 200 = 146 Step 2: 146 – 20 = 126 Step 3: 126 – 7	= 119
C	Constant difference	18 – 11 (–1, –1)	=17 – 10	= 7
		623 – 398 (+2, +2)	= 625 – 400	= 225
D	Levelling	6 + 19 (–1, +1)	= 5 + 20	= 25
		143 + 36 (–3, +3)	= 140 + 39	= 179

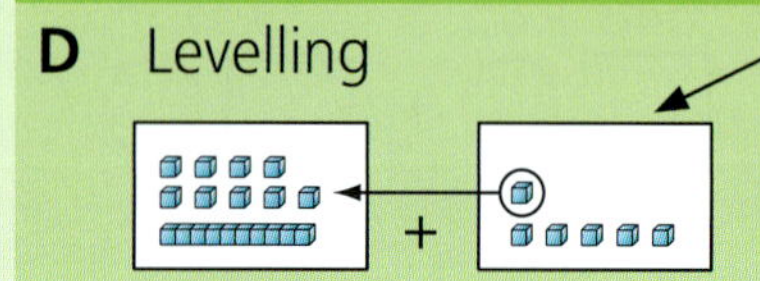

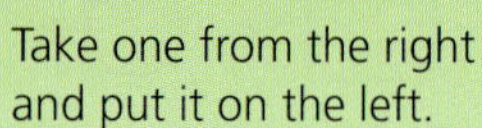

Take one from the right and put it on the left.

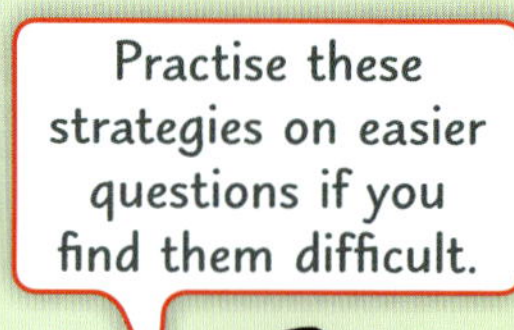

1 Bridge to 10s. (**A**)

a 26 + 35 ☐ b 48 + 24 ☐ c 55 + 38 ☐

d 336 + 56 ☐ e 237 + 47 ☐ f 618 + 67 ☐

2 Use place value to break up the number. (**B**)

a 356 – 127
356 – 100 =
256 – 20 =
236 – 7 =

b 562 – 134
562 – 100 =
– 30 =
– 4 =

c 472 – 145
☐
☐
☐

3 Rewrite the question. Add or subtract from both numbers. Keep the difference constant. (**C**)

a 51 – 25 — 56 – 30 =
b 62 – 37 — .... – 40 =
c 71 – 38 — .... – 40 =
d 381 – 202 — .... – 200 =
e 562 – 397 ☐
f 467 – 304 ☐
g 531 – 496 ☐
h 671 – 404 ☐

4 Rewrite the question. Take from one number and add to the other to make the question easier. (**D**)

a 23 + 38 — 21 + 40 =
b 69 + 32 — 70 +
c 58 + 43 ☐
d 158 + 25 — 160 +
e 245 + 38 ☐
f 459 + 34 ☐
g 347 + 96 ☐
h 461 + 195 ☐

 • *AUSTRALIAN SIGNPOST MATHS NSW 4* • ISBN 9780655709053

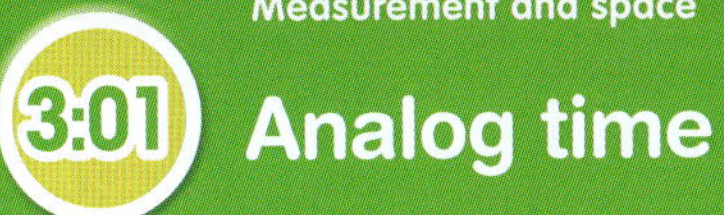

3:01 Analog time

30 minutes after 20 past the hour, would be ... ______ to the next hour.

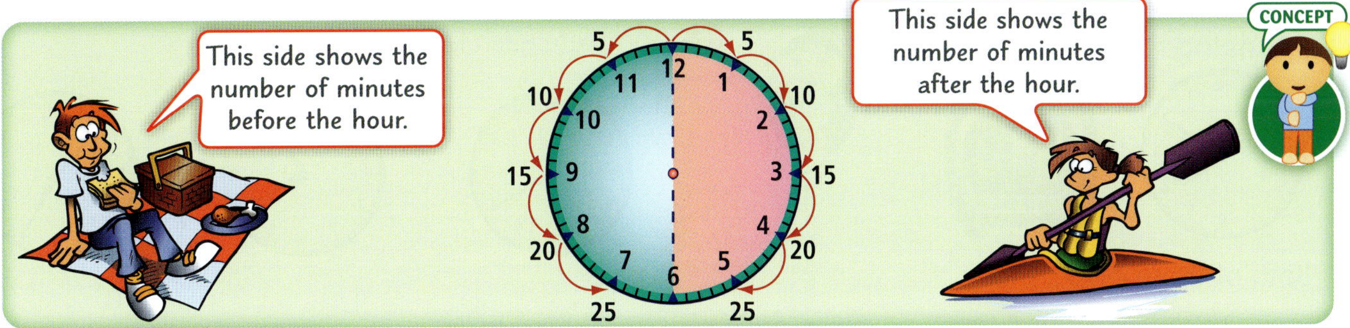

1 Complete the label for each time shown.

2 Complete the clocks to show the given times.

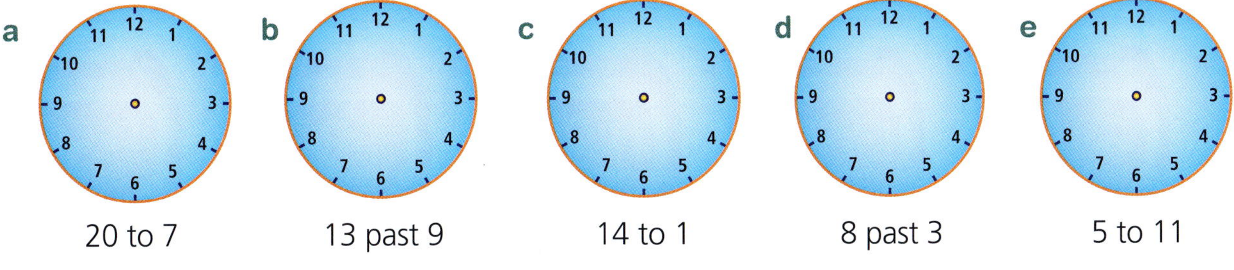

a 20 to 7

b 13 past 9

c 14 to 1

d 8 past 3

e 5 to 11

3 Write the time that is five minutes after:

a	8 past 9		**b**	21 past 4		**c**	8 to 12	
d	19 past 3		**e**	12 to 6		**f**	18 to 1	
g	25 past 11		**h**	29 past 3		**i**	5 to 10	

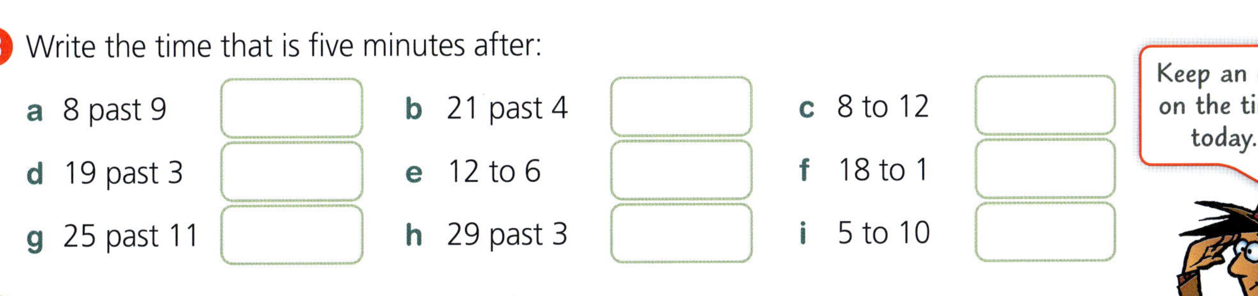

4 Write the time that is five minutes before:

a	23 past 6		**b**	26 past 9		**c**	29 to 10	
d	13 to 7		**e**	14 to 5		**f**	4 to 2	
g	18 past 11		**h**	5 to 8		**i**	3 past 2	

 • *AUSTRALIAN SIGNPOST MATHS NSW 4* • ISBN 9780655709053

3:02 Analog and digital time

These clocks show 8 o'clock or 0 minutes past 8.

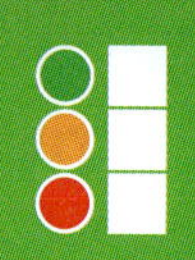

CONCEPT

Both of these clocks show ten minutes past 4 or 4 ten.

1 Complete each label.

a 12 : ☐ ☐ past 12

b 4 : ☐ ☐ past 4

c 10 : ☐ ☐ past 10

d 4:35 ☐ to ☐

e 2:40 ☐ to ☐

f 8:25 ☐ past ☐

g 3:45 ☐ to ☐

h 5:05 ☐ past ☐

i 2 : ☐ ☐ to 3

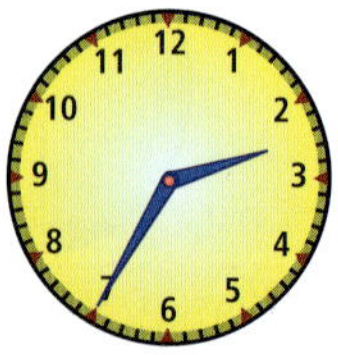

j 11 : ☐ ☐ to 12

k 8 : ☐ ☐ to 9

l 3 : ☐ ☐ to 4

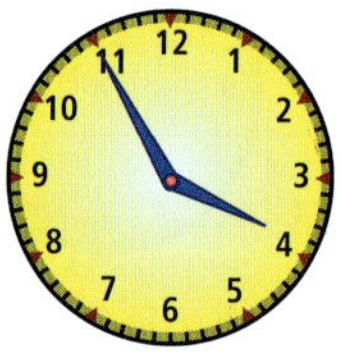

m 4 : ☐ ☐ to 5

n 6:10 ☐ past ☐

o 12:35 ☐ to ☐

p 11:50 ☐ to ☐

q 7:05 ☐ past ☐

r 9:55 ☐ to ☐

ACTIVITY

Join the clocks that show the same time.

© PEARSON AUSTRALIA 2024 • *AUSTRALIAN SIGNPOST MATHS NSW 4* • ISBN 9780655709053

3:03 Analog and digital time

Digital time shows how many minutes past the hour.

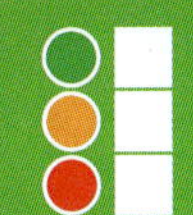

CONCEPT

1 Complete the labels for each time shown.

a 11 : ___ ___ past ___

b 7 : ___ ___ past ___

c 4 : ___ ___ to ___

d 5 : ___ ___ past ___

e 3 : ___ ___ to ___

f 12 : ___ ___ to ___

g 9 : ___ ___ past ___

h 6 : ___ ___ to ___

i 10 : ___ ___ past ___

j 8 : ___ ___ to ___

k 2:42 ___ to ___

l 4:58 ___ to ___

m 9:19 ___ past ___

n 7:09 ___ past ___

o 11:38 ___ to ___

2 Write the time that is one minute before:

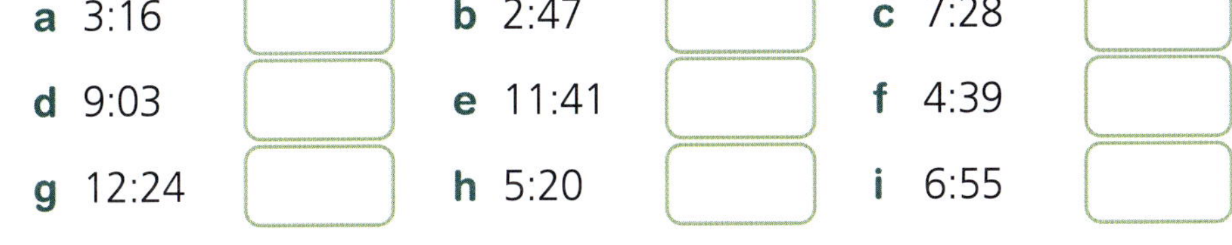

a 3:16		**b** 2:47		**c** 7:28	
d 9:03		**e** 11:41		**f** 4:39	
g 12:24		**h** 5:20		**i** 6:55	

3 Write how many more minutes it would be to the next hour.

a 4:13		**b** 9:41		**c** 7:32	
d 10:54		**e** 8:16		**f** 5:58	

Analog and digital time

4:00 means 4 o'clock.
9:30 means 9 thirty.

1 Complete the label for each time shown.

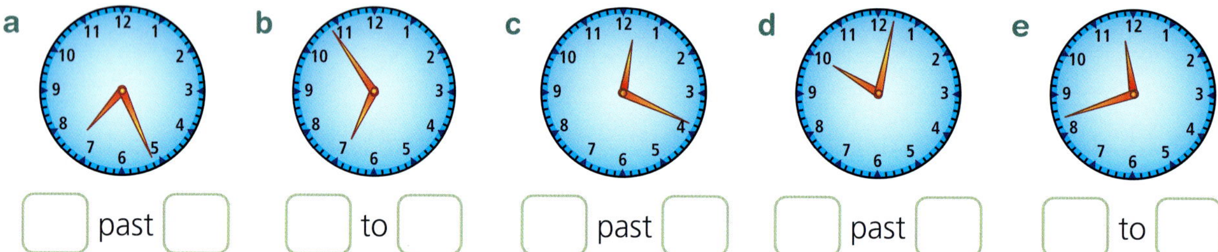

a ☐ past ☐ b ☐ to ☐ c ☐ past ☐ d ☐ past ☐ e ☐ to ☐

2 Complete the label for each time shown.

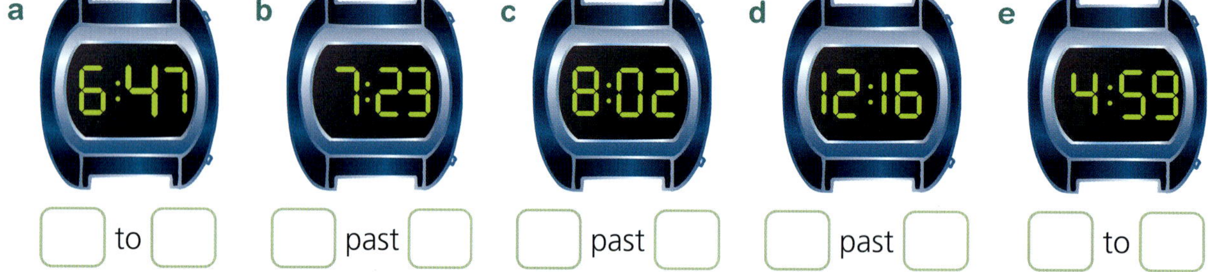

a ☐ to ☐ b ☐ past ☐ c ☐ past ☐ d ☐ past ☐ e ☐ to ☐

3 The race began at 10:25. I finished at 10:46. How long did I take? ☐ min

Ron, who was also in the race, finished at 11:00. How long did he take? ☐ min

The winner of the race finished the run at 10:39. By how much did he beat me? ☐ min

At 1:37, I walked back to school. It took me 9 minutes. When did I reach school? ☐

Ron left at 1:37 and did not reach school until 2:00. How long did it take him? ☐ min

4 We left Griffith at 9:07 and arrived in Hillston at 10:00. How long did we take? ☐

5 Jindi, Jedda and Maali walked from the waterhole to the river to meet their father's boat.

They left at 7:15 and arrived at 8:00. How long did it take them to reach the river? ☐ min

Their father's boat arrived 20 minutes after them. When did the boat arrive? ☐

3:05 Perimeter

1 metre = 100 centimetres
1 m = 100 cm
cm is short for centimetres.

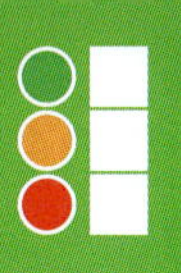

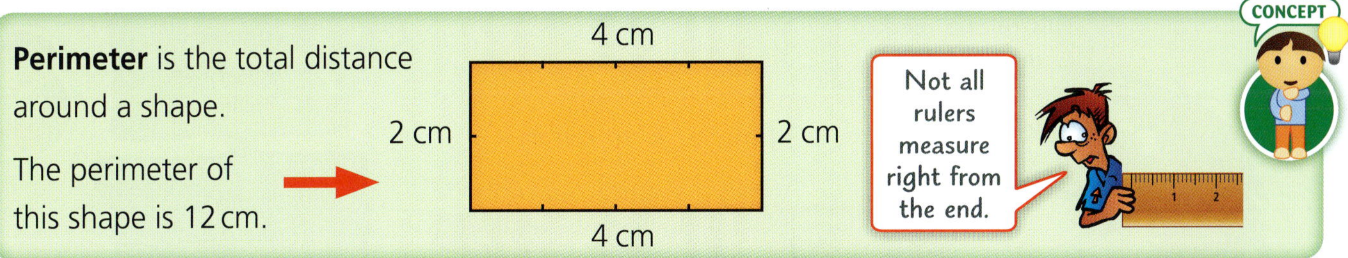

1 Estimate and then measure the perimeter (P) of each shape.

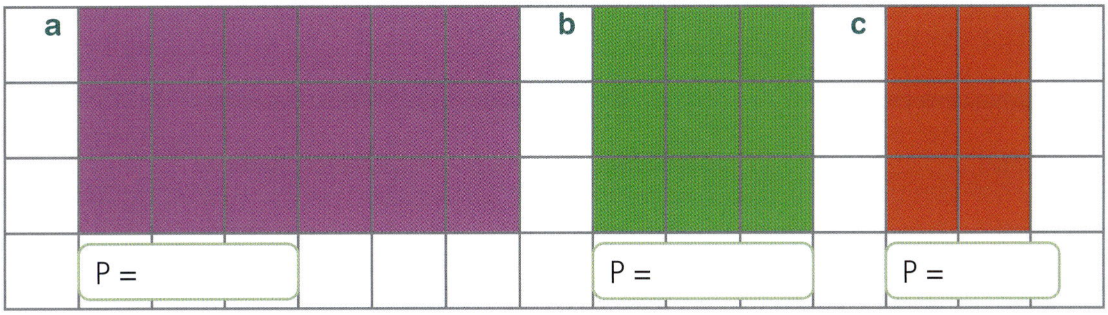

a P =

b P =

c P =

d P =

e P =

f P =

g ☐ cm ☐ cm ☐ cm ☐ cm P =

h ☐ cm ☐ cm ☐ cm P =

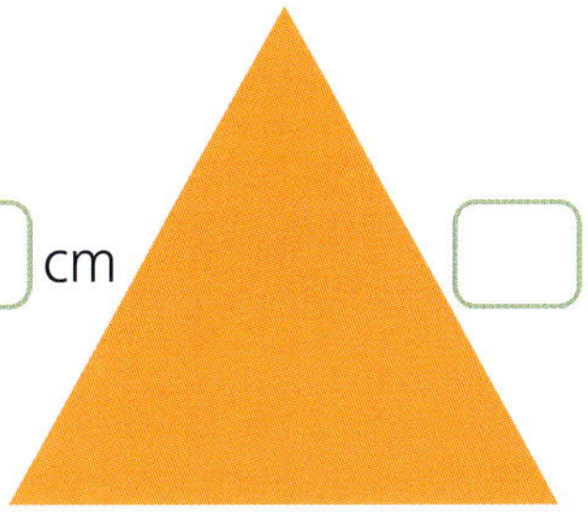

i ☐ cm ☐ cm ☐ cm P =

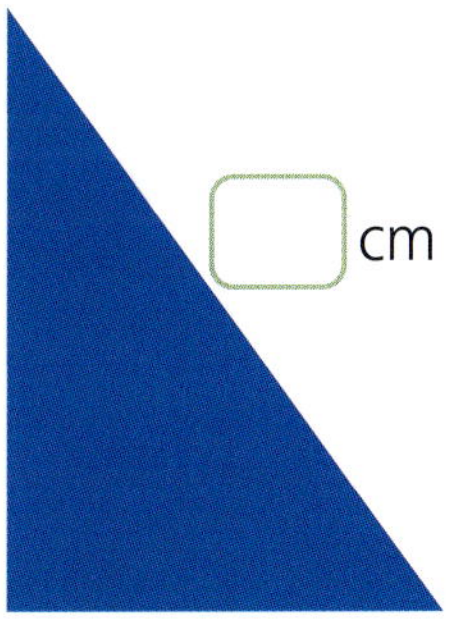

j Order parts **a** to **c** above from shortest to longest perimeter. ☐

2 Write the lengths in centimetres.

a 1 m 26 cm ☐ **b** 1 m 73 cm ☐

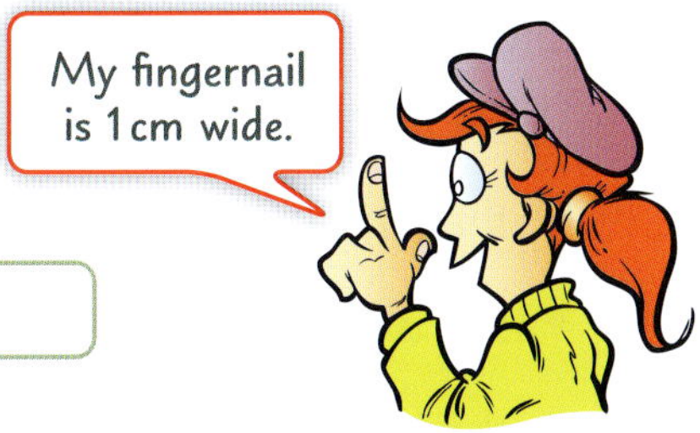

My fingernail is 1 cm wide.

3 Write the lengths as metres and centimetres.

a 238 cm ☐ **b** 213 cm ☐

 • *AUSTRALIAN SIGNPOST MATHS NSW 4* • ISBN 9780655709053

3:06 Centimetres and millimetres

10 mm = 1 cm
100 cm = 1 m
1000 mm = 1 m

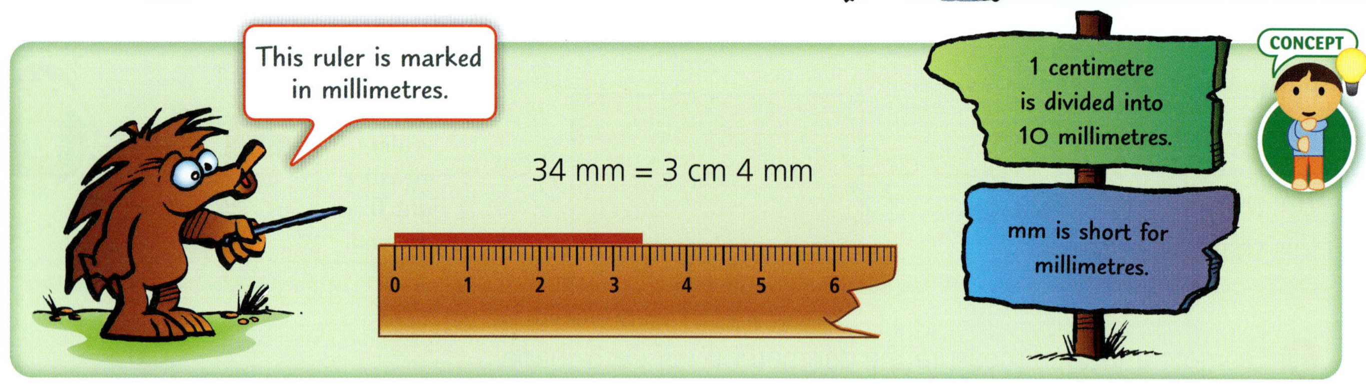

1 Estimate, then measure the length of each bar.

a ______ [ ] mm **b** ______ [ ] mm

c ______ [ ] mm **d** ______ [ ] mm

e ______ [ ] mm **f** ______ [ ] mm

2 Write these as millimetres.

a 1 cm 9 mm	[ ] mm	**b** 4 cm 7 mm	[ ] mm
c 6 cm 1 mm	[ ] mm	**d** 3 cm 6 mm	[ ] mm
e 5 cm 5 mm	[ ] mm	**f** 7 cm 2 mm	[ ] mm

3 Write these as centimetres and millimetres.

a 25 mm [ ] **b** 68 mm [ ] **c** 51 mm [ ]

d 92 mm [ ] **e** 43 mm [ ] **f** 87 mm [ ]

ACTIVITY

- Estimate, then use a ruler to measure these objects to the nearest millimetre.

		Length		Width		Height	
	Object	**Estimate**	**Measure**	**Estimate**	**Measure**	**Estimate**	**Measure**
A	tens block						
B	lunch box						
C	eraser						
D	book						

Order the lengths of A, B, C and D from shortest to longest [ ]

- Use a tape measure to measure these objects to the nearest centimetre.
  - the length of a brick [ ]
  - the width of your desk [ ]
  - the height of your chair [ ]

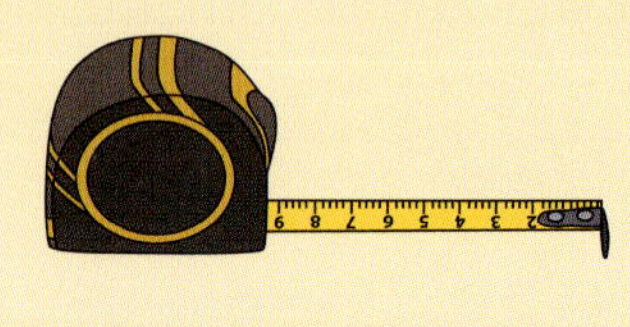

Not all rulers measure right from the end.

3:07 Using millimetres

The width of my thumb is ☐ mm.

The length of my finger is ☐ mm.

1 Record the length of each red bar.

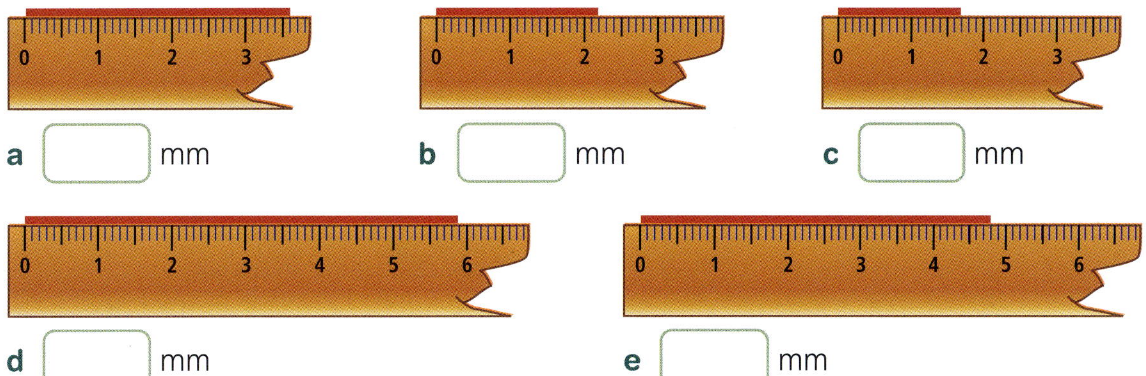

a ☐ mm **b** ☐ mm **c** ☐ mm

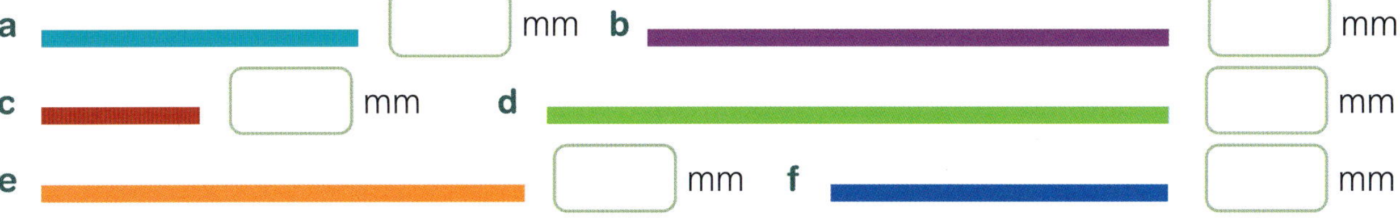

d ☐ mm **e** ☐ mm

2 Estimate, then measure the length of each bar.

a ☐ mm **b** ☐ mm

c ☐ mm **d** ☐ mm

e ☐ mm **f** ☐ mm

3 Write these as millimetres.

a 3 cm 2 mm		**b** 8 cm 1 mm		**c** 1 cm 9 mm	
d 7 cm 4 mm		**e** 2 cm 8 mm		**f** 4 cm 6 mm	
g 5 cm 5 mm		**h** 3 cm 7 mm		**i** 10 cm	

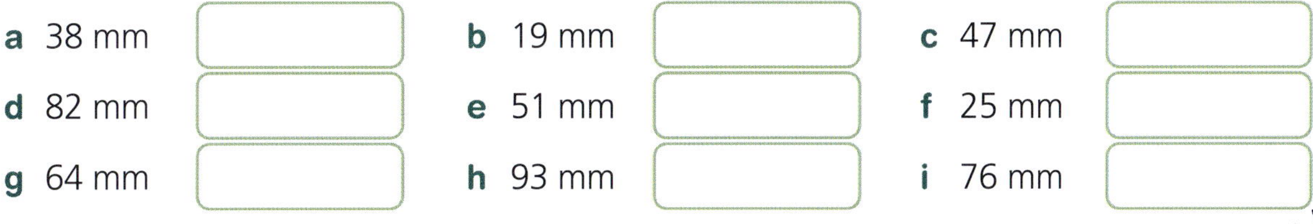

4 Write these as centimetres and millimetres.

a 38 mm		**b** 19 mm		**c** 47 mm	
d 82 mm		**e** 51 mm		**f** 25 mm	
g 64 mm		**h** 93 mm		**i** 76 mm	

5 Estimate, then find the perimeter of each shape.

a

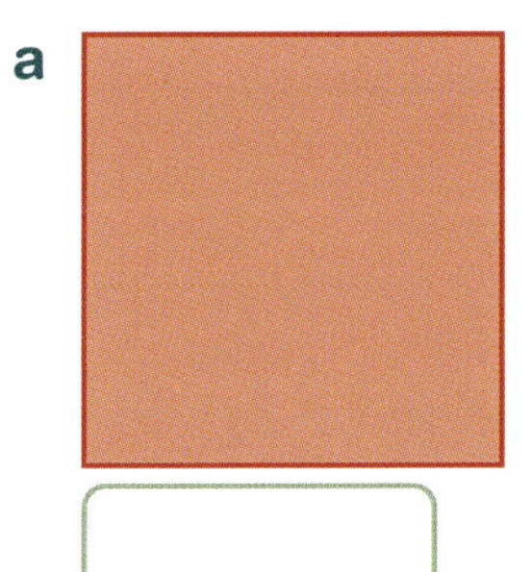

b

c

 • *AUSTRALIAN SIGNPOST MATHS NSW 4* • ISBN 9780655709053

3:08 The square centimetre

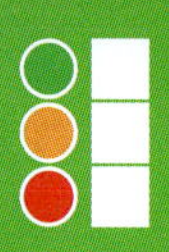

This is 3 rows of 4.
$3 \times 4 = 12$
(12 square units)

INVESTIGATION

- Use a 1 cm grid transparency to measure and compare the areas of different surfaces.
- Discuss ways to find the area when some squares are not fully covered.
- List items that have an area between 20 and 50 square centimetres.

This area is about 15 square centimetres.

1. Estimate the order of areas **a** to **f** in Question 2 from smallest to largest.

2. Use a 1 cm grid transparency to find the area of each shape.

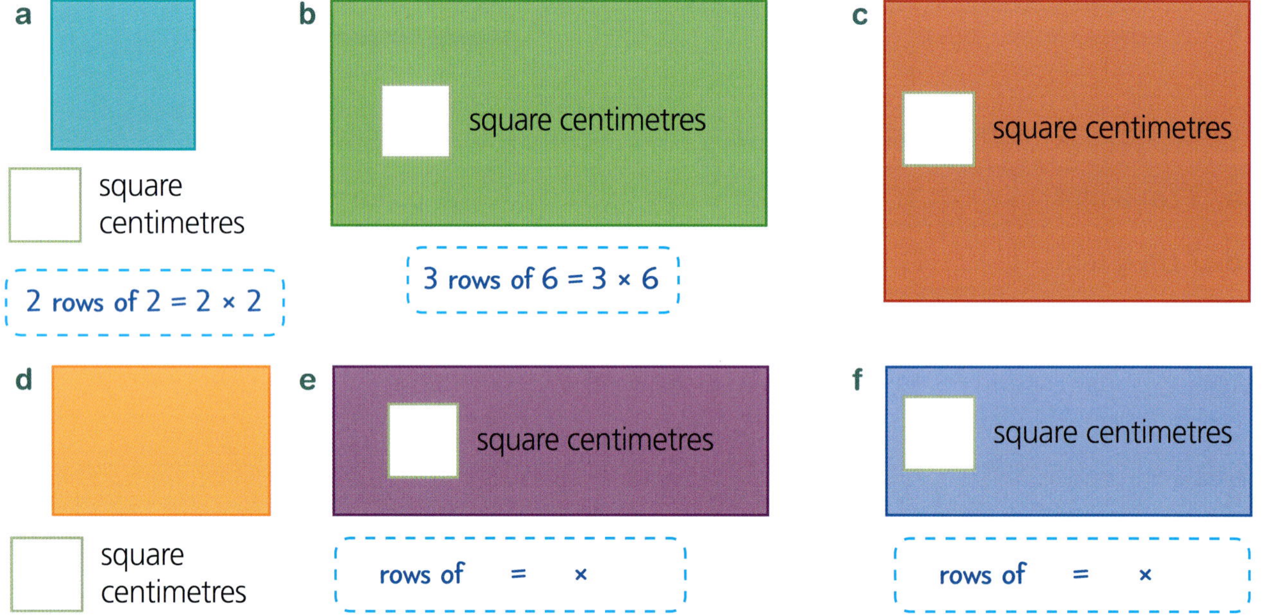

3. Use your answers to Question 2 to write the order of areas **a** to **f** from smallest to largest.

Do these answers match your estimates from Question 1.

4. Draw your own grid to find the area of each shape. Estimate each area first.

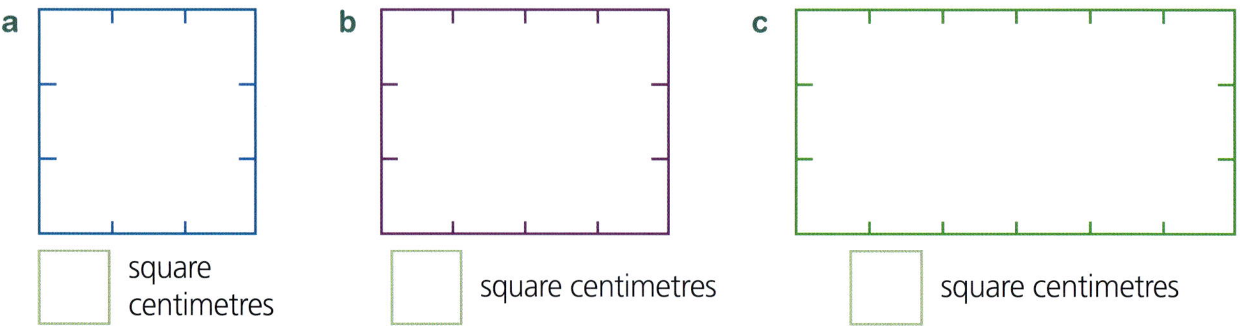

 • *AUSTRALIAN SIGNPOST MATHS NSW 4* • ISBN 9780655709053

The square centimetre

On 1 cm grid paper, trace your hand. Estimate the area by counting squares that are more than half used.

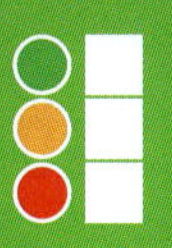

Oscar placed a leaf on 1 cm grid paper to find the area.

How can we measure area more accurately?

- The area of the white grid is 35 square centimetres.
- The area of the leaf is less than 35 square centimetres.
- How many squares are more than half covered by the leaf? ______

1. Draw your own grid and find the area (**A**) and perimeter (**P**) of each shape.

a

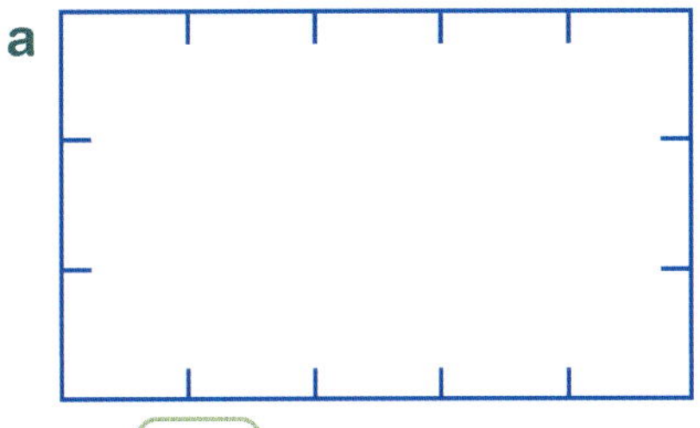

A: ____ square centimetres **P:** ____ cm

b

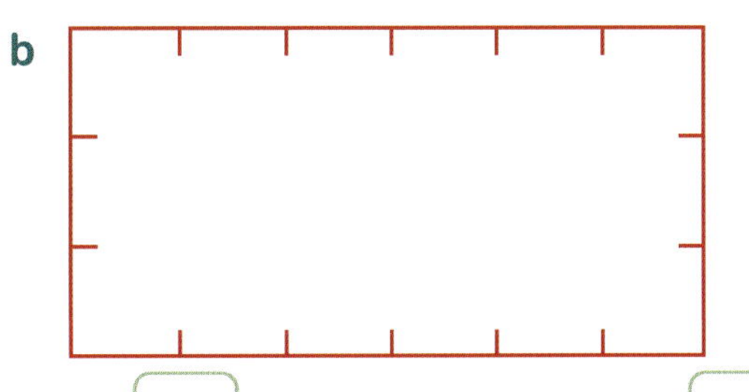

A: ____ square centimetres **P:** ____ cm

c

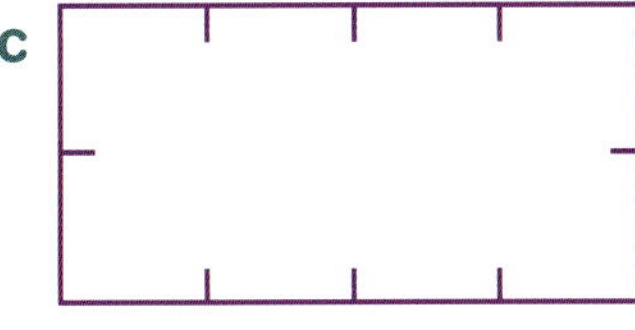

A: ____ square centimetres **P:** ____ cm

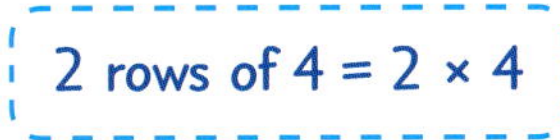

d

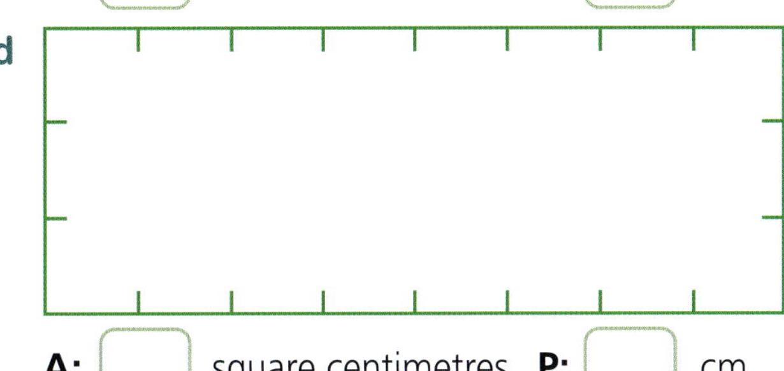

A: ____ square centimetres **P:** ____ cm

ACTIVITY

- Use a 10 cm by 10 cm grid transparency to find an area:
  - less than 100 square centimetres ______
  - about 100 square centimetres ______
  - more than 100 square centimetres ______
- Place a leaf on 1 cm grid paper to estimate the area. What did you discover?

______

100 square centimetres

3:10 The square centimetre

What is the area of your thumbnail? about ☐ square centimetres

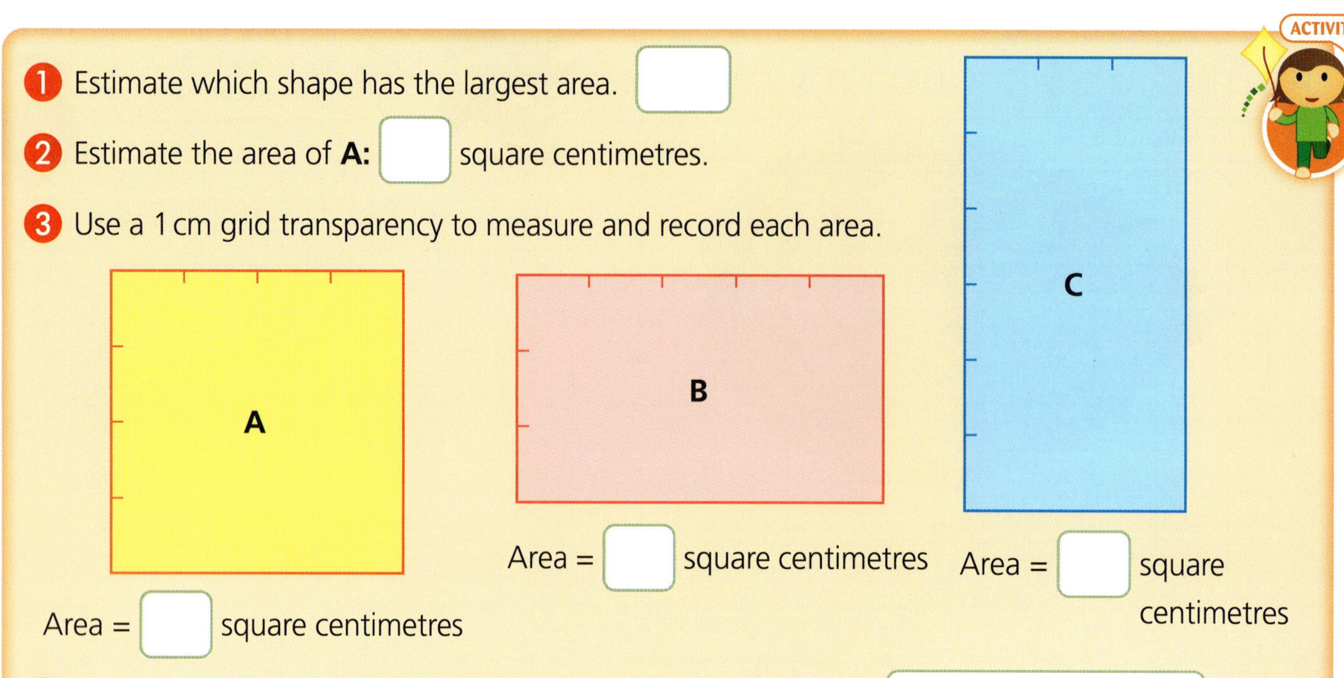

1. Estimate which shape has the largest area. ☐
2. Estimate the area of **A:** ☐ square centimetres.
3. Use a 1 cm grid transparency to measure and record each area.

A — Area = ☐ square centimetres

B — Area = ☐ square centimetres

C — Area = ☐ square centimetres

4. Order the areas in descending order (from largest to smallest). ☐

5. Estimate the area of the top of small rectangular objects. Measure each area to the nearest square centimetre using 1 cm grid paper. Order the areas in ascending order from smallest (1) to largest (4).

Description of area	Estimate	Measurement	Order

Objects you could measure:

- a small book
- a piece of paper
- a matchbox top
- a tissue box top
- a sticky note
- a bus pass

6. Draw two different rectangles that have the same area as the one drawn.

1 row of 12 = 12 square centimetres

Using measurement scales

When we use a measuring instrument, we read the scale to the nearest unit mark.

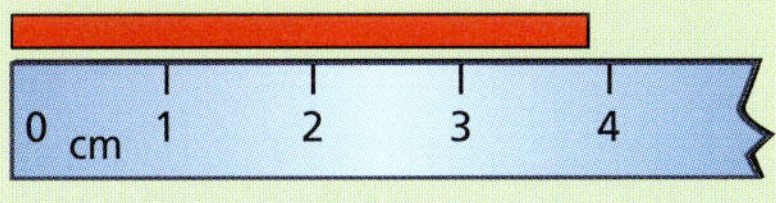

The measured length would be recorded as 4 cm.

1 Record the measure of the bar using each of the rulers.

a 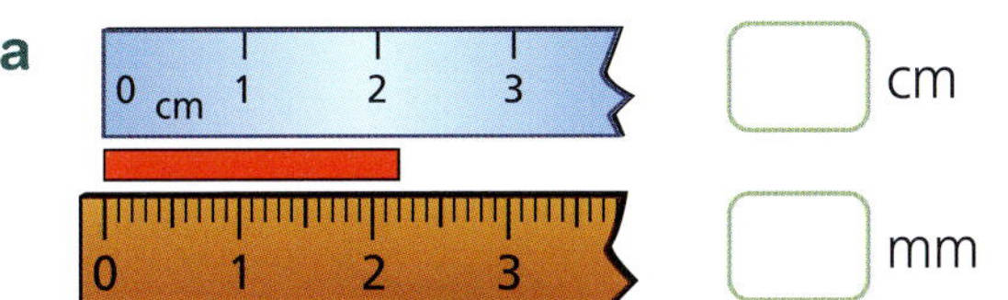

☐ cm

☐ mm

b 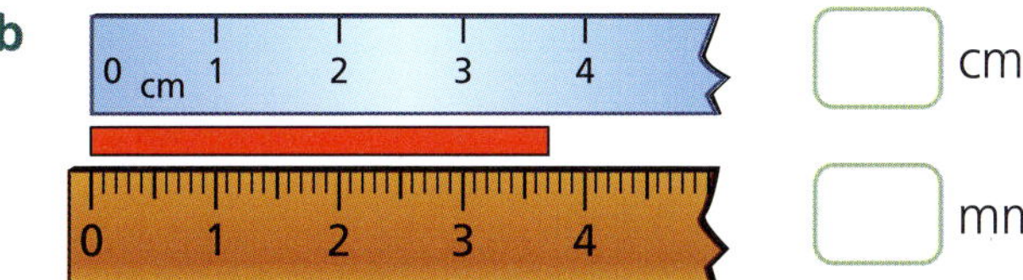

☐ cm

☐ mm

c 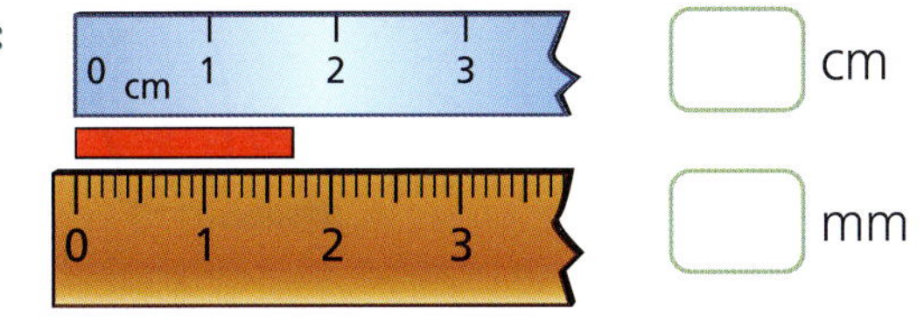

☐ cm

☐ mm

d 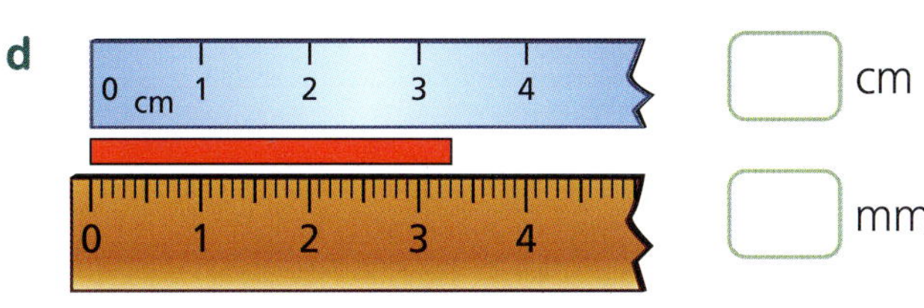

☐ cm

☐ mm

e 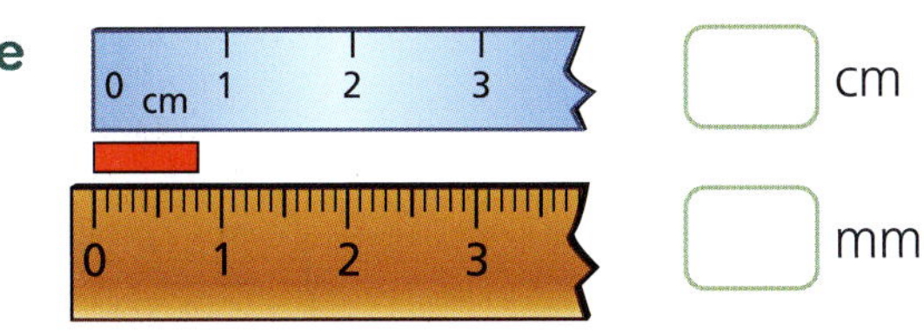

☐ cm

☐ mm

f 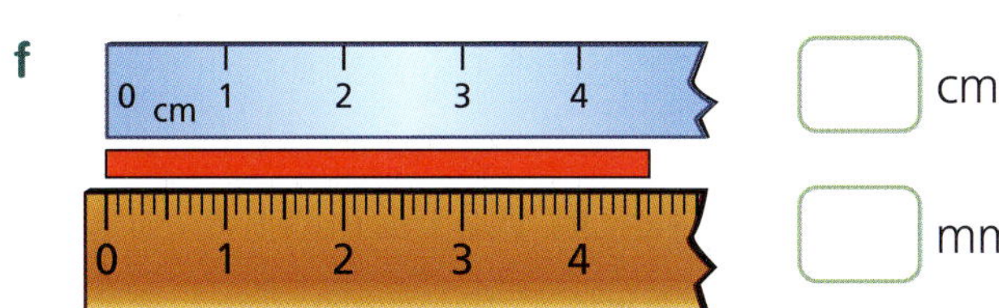

☐ cm

☐ mm

g 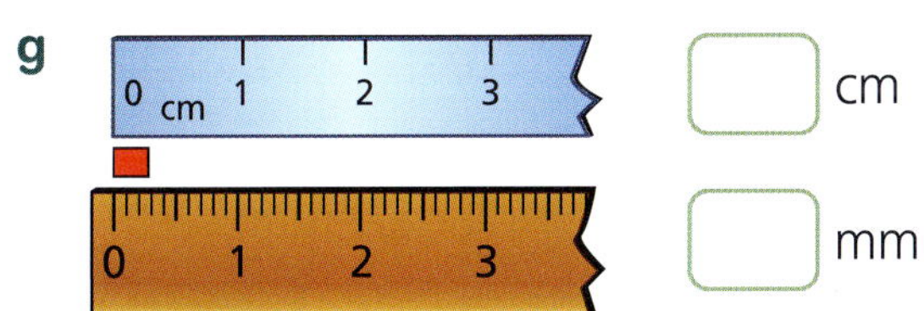

☐ cm

☐ mm

h What does a measurement of 0 cm mean?

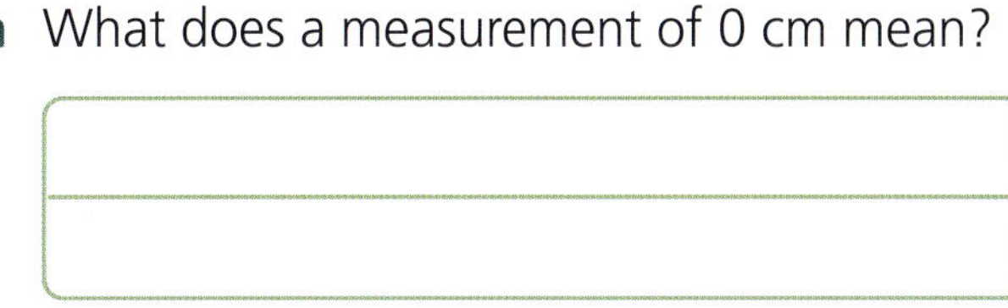

2 Record the measure shown on each scale.

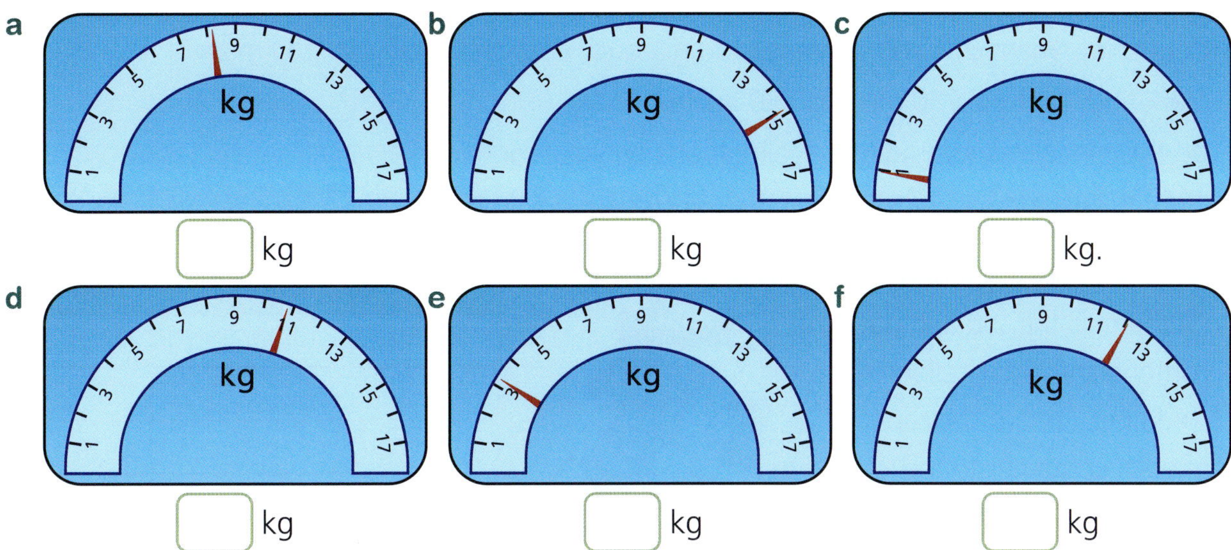

a ☐ kg **b** ☐ kg **c** ☐ kg.

d ☐ kg **e** ☐ kg **f** ☐ kg

See *Extra Support 17* (Temperature) *and 18* (Recording temperature).

 • *AUSTRALIAN SIGNPOST MATHS NSW 4* • ISBN 9780655709053

3:12 The millilitre

We need a smaller unit to measure small capacities.

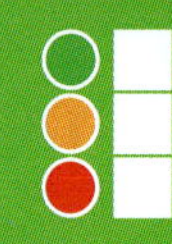

CONCEPT

- Millilitres are used to measure smaller capacites than 1 litre.
- **mL** stands for millilitres.
- One litre is **1000 mL**.
  Half a litre is **500 mL**.
  A quarter of a litre is **250 mL**.

Capacity is the space within a container.

Volume is the space taken up by an object.

ACTIVITY

1. Find or research four containers that have millilitre labels. List them in order of size from smallest to greatest capacity.

Container	Capacity

2. **Make a calibrated container.**

You will need: water, a marker, a funnel, a calibrated measuring cup, a container larger than 1 L (You could use a 1 L milk container.)

Step 1: Pour exactly 100 mL into the container.

Step 2: Mark a line at the water level and label it 100 mL (see picture).

Step 3: Continue to pour 100 mL into the container and mark the water in the same way as the picture.
How many 100 mL measures did you need, to pour in 1 L? ☐

Step 4: Empty the container.

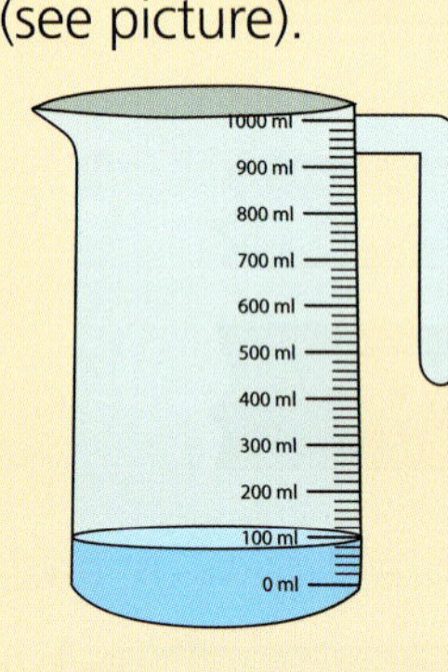

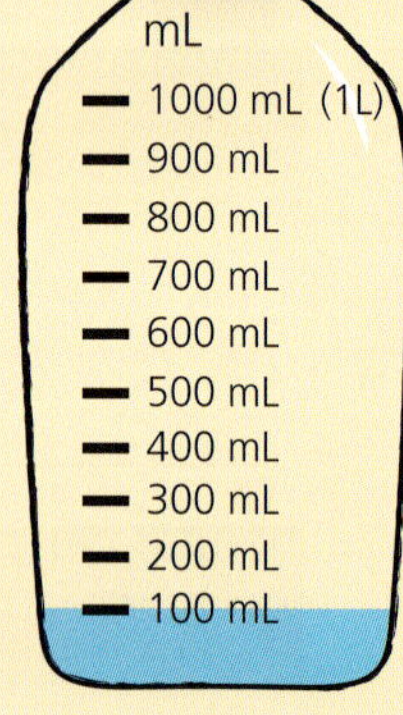

3. **Check the accuracy of your calibrated measure.**

Count how many 250 mL measures you need to reach the 1000 mL (1 L) mark. ☐

Mark and label the 250 mL and 750 mL levels.

Do these new marks match the calibrations on your container? ☐

If not, fill each measure to exactly the right level next time.

4. Find containers that have a capacity less than 1 L. Fill them to the top and pour the contents into your calibrated container. Record the capacity of each container to the nearest calibrated mark.

Container	Capacity

Using millilitres

Half a litre = 500 mL
A quarter of a litre = 250 mL
Three quarters of a litre = 750 mL

ACTIVITY

1. Use a medicine glass to measure the capacity of these small containers. Fill the medicine glass to a mark that you estimate will fill the container. Pour water into the small container until it is full. Calculate how much water you used to fill the container to complete the table.

	Container	Estimate	Capacity	Description of estimate	Difference
A	teaspoon	15 mL	5 mL	too big	10 mL
B	tablespoon				
C	bottle lid				
D	egg cup				

mL 40 30 20 15 10 5 2

1 mL has the same volume as a ones block.

2. Order containers **A** to **D** from smallest to largest capacity. ______

3. **a** Write the closest measuring line for each volume of water.

A
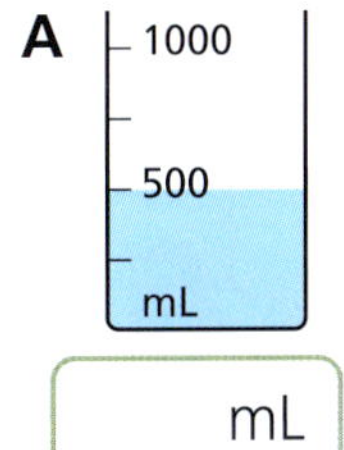

______ mL

B
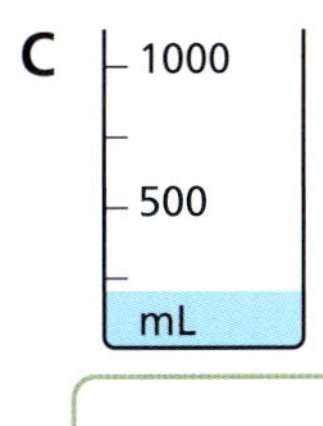

______ mL

C
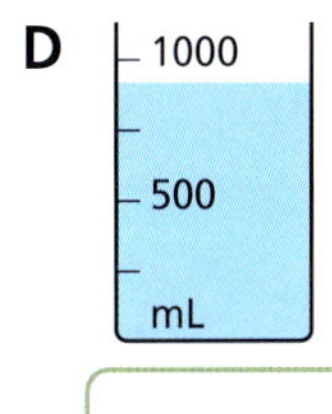

______

D
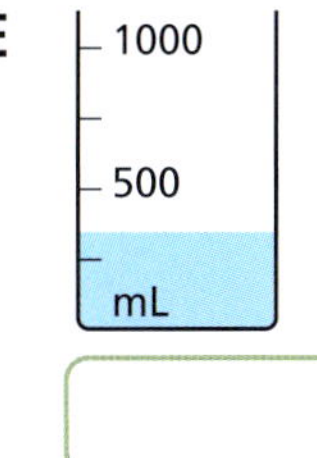

______

E 1000 500 mL
______

b Order these volumes of water, from smallest to largest (**A**, **B**, **C**, **D** and **E**). ______

c On container **C** above, draw a water level of 750 mL.

4. Which measure (**L** or **mL**) has been left off each label?

a

b

c

d

e

f

 • *AUSTRALIAN SIGNPOST MATHS NSW 4* • ISBN 9780655709053

3:14 Using millilitres

A bucket can hold 9 L of water.
9 L = 9000 mL

CONCEPT

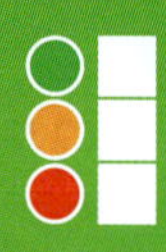

- A quarter of a litre is **250 mL**.
  Half a litre is **500 mL**.
  One litre is **1000 mL**.
  Two litres is **2000 mL**.
  $2\frac{1}{2}$ litres is **2500 mL**.

JUICE

- A teaspoon holds about 5 mL.
  A juice popper holds 200 mL.
  A mug holds about 350 mL.
  A 1 L milk container holds 1 L.

Use these items as benchmarks when you estimate capacity.

1 How many litres are there in:

a 1000 mL? ☐ b 7000 mL? ☐ c 5000 mL? ☐ d 3000 mL? ☐
e 6000 mL? ☐ f 4000 mL? ☐ g 2000 mL? ☐ h 8000 mL? ☐

2 How many millilitres are there in:

a 2 L? ☐ b 7 L? ☐ c 3 L? ☐ d 5 L? ☐
e 8 L? ☐ f 4 L? ☐ g $6\frac{1}{2}$ L? ☐ h $9\frac{1}{2}$ L? ☐

3 Would we use litres (**L**) or millilitres (**mL**) to measure:

a drink in a cup? ☐ b water in a bath? ☐
c medicine in a teaspoon? ☐ d juice in a glass? ☐
e water in a fish pond? ☐ f petrol in our car? ☐
g cream in a small carton? ☐ h ice cream in a large container? ☐

4 Record the measure shown.

a 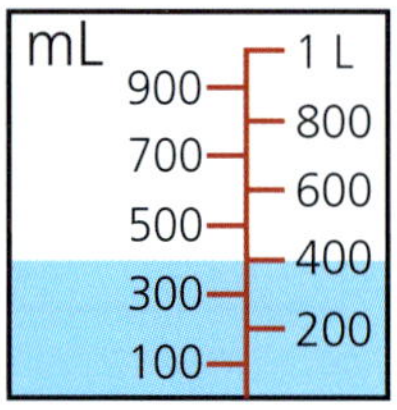

mL
900
700
500
300
100
1 L
800
600
400
200

☐

b 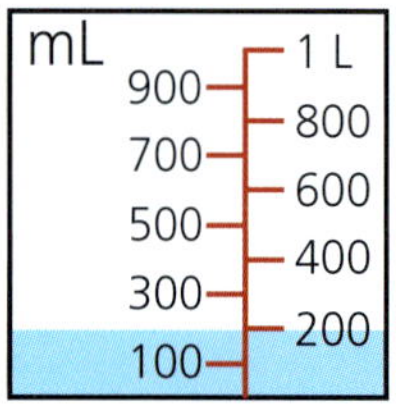

mL
900
700
500
300
100
1 L
800
600
400
200

☐

c 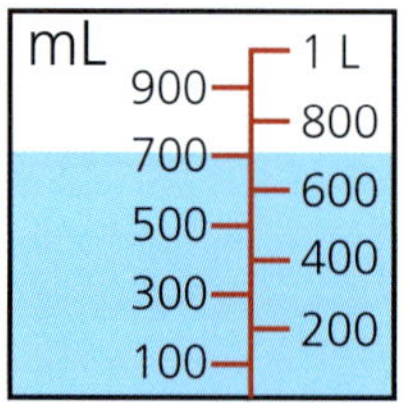

mL
900
700
500
300
100
1 L
800
600
400
200

☐

mL and L are both useful units.

INVESTIGATION

5 How many of these items would you need to reach a total capacity of 1 litre?

a 200 mL apple juice popper ☐ b 250 mL apple juice ☐
c 500 mL water bottle ☐ d 100 mL sauce jar ☐

A teaspoon is about 5 mL.

6 How many teaspoons of water are needed to fill a jar with a capacity of?

a 50 mL? ☐ b 40 mL? ☐ c 30 mL? ☐ d 20 mL? ☐

 • *AUSTRALIAN SIGNPOST MATHS NSW 4* • ISBN 9780655709053

3:15 Using L and mL

How much milk?

CONCEPT

1 What is the total capacity of each set of containers?

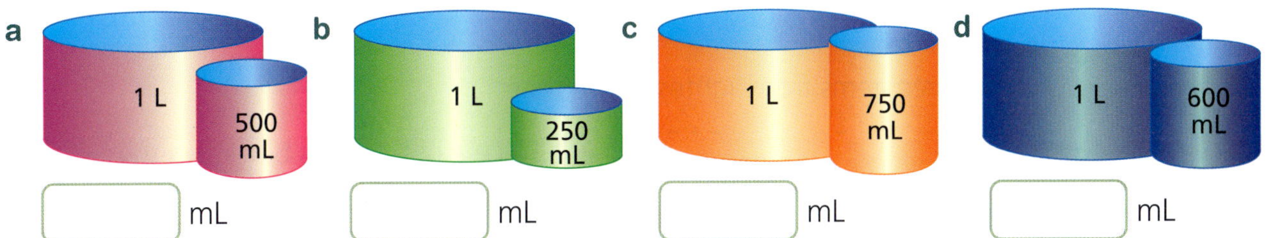

a ______ mL b ______ mL c ______ mL d ______ mL

2 Write these as millilitres.

a 1 L 300 mL ______ **b** 1 L 490 mL ______ **c** 1 L 875 mL ______

d 1 L 625 mL ______ **e** 1 L 750 mL ______ **f** 2 L 500 mL ______

3 Write these as litres and millilitres.

a 1600 mL ______ **b** 1900 mL ______ **c** 1350 mL ______

d 1250 mL ______ **e** 1425 mL ______ **f** 2750 mL ______

4 Would you use litres or millilitres to measure:

a water in a bucket? ______ **b** water in a teacup? ______

c ice cream in a cone? ______ **d** milk in a small carton? ______

e liquid in an egg? ______ **f** petrol in a car? ______

g medicine in a dessertspoon? ______ **h** liquid in an eye-dropper? ______

5 Record the measure shown.

a
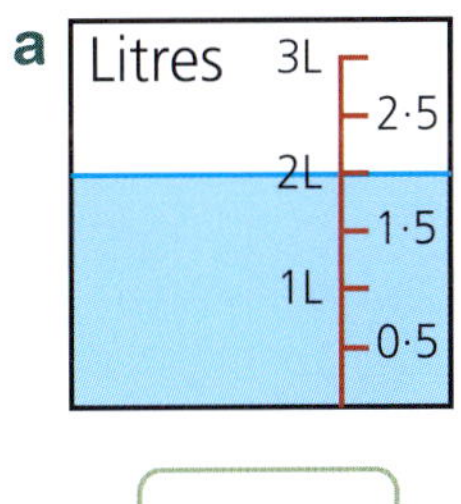

b
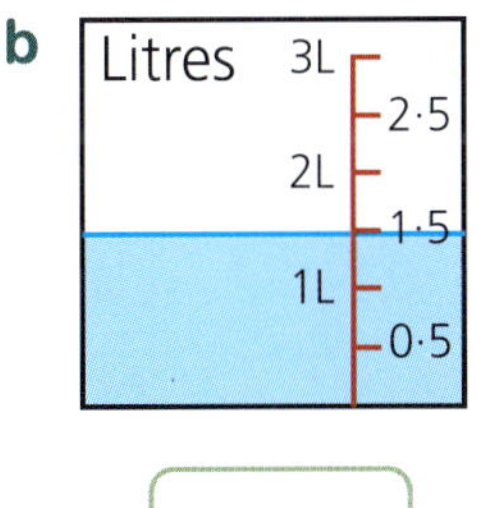

c
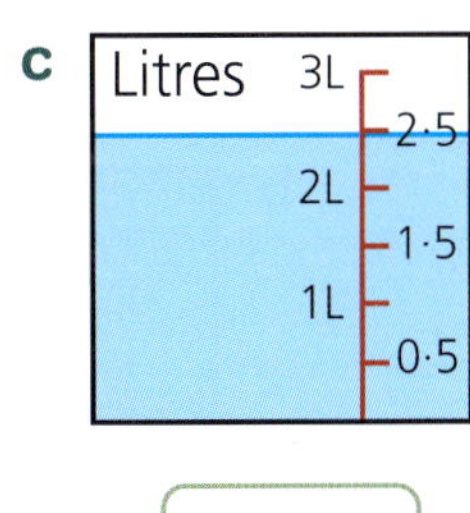

d
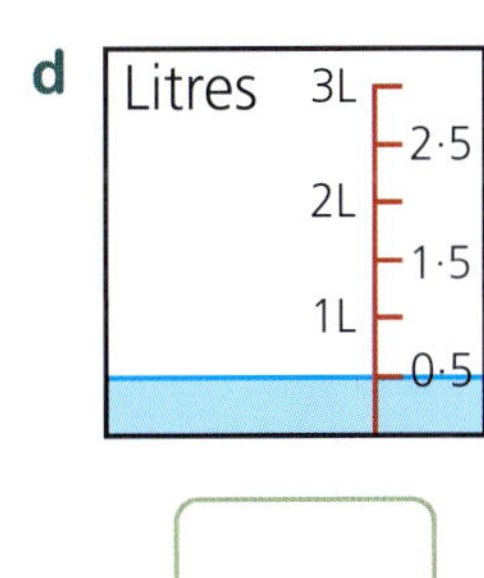

3:16 Using grams

500 grams is half of a kilogram.
250 grams is a quarter of a kilogram.

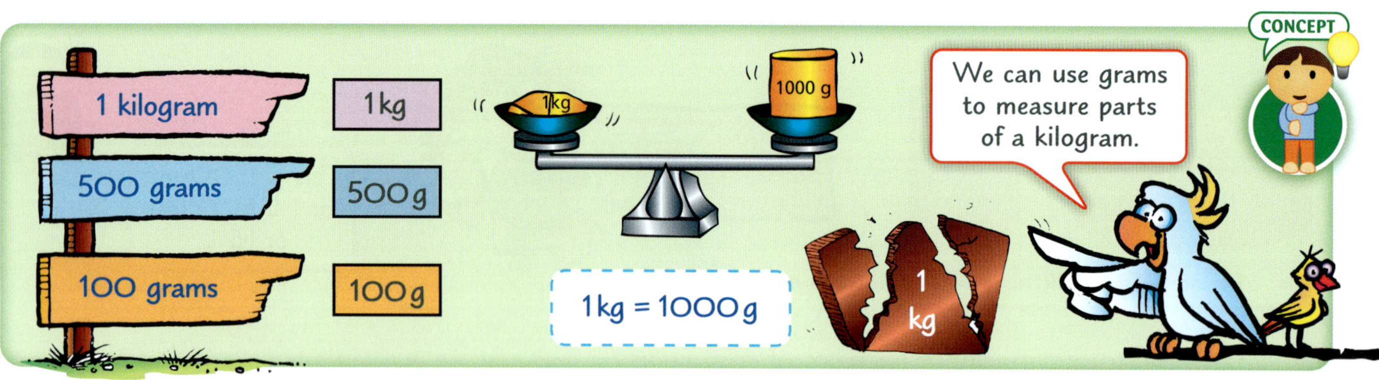

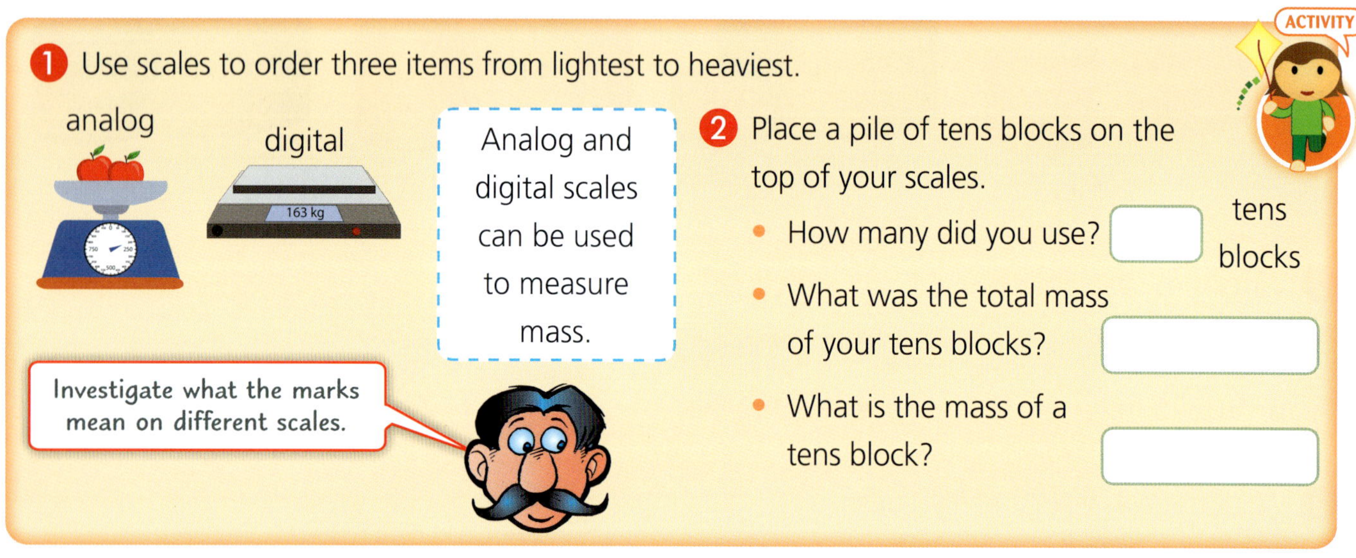

1 Use scales to order three items from lightest to heaviest.

Analog and digital scales can be used to measure mass.

2 Place a pile of tens blocks on the top of your scales.

- How many did you use? ____ tens blocks
- What was the total mass of your tens blocks? ____
- What is the mass of a tens block? ____

3 Write the mass in short form.

a sixty grams ____
b one hundred grams ____
c forty kilograms ____
d thirty grams ____
e nine kilograms ____
f seventy grams ____

4 Which unit of mass (**g** or **kg**) has been left off each package?

a 

b 

c 

d 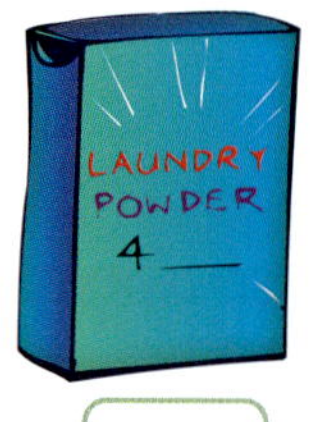

e 

5 Use the marks on the scales to write the mass to the closest mark shown on the scale.

a
0 g, 200, 400, 600, 800, 1 kg

b 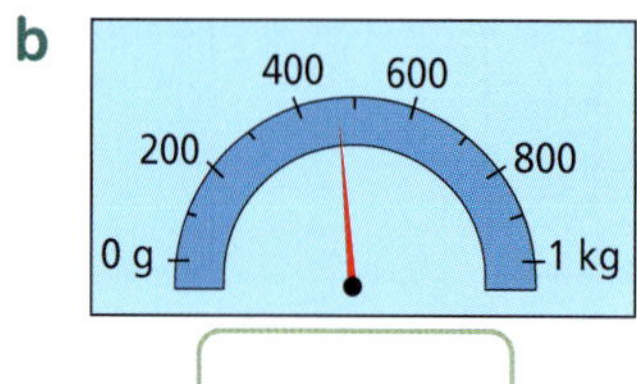

c 

 • *AUSTRALIAN SIGNPOST MATHS NSW 4* • ISBN 9780655709053

3:17 Measuring mass

The one in my right hand feels heavier than one kilogram.

1 Use the short form to write:

a 60 grams
b 1 kilogram
c 350 grams
d 1700 grams
e 1300 grams
f 3 kilograms
g 5 kilograms 300 grams
h 14 kilograms 100 grams

2 Which unit of mass (**g** or **kg**) has been left off each item?

a Jam 350
b Lollies 150
c Cake 2
d Rice Flakes 200
e Chips 100

3 How many grams are there in:

a 1 kilogram 500 grams?
b 5 kilograms 900 grams?

4 How many kilograms are there in:

a 1000 g?
b 4000 g?
c 6000 g?
d 8000 g?

ACTIVITY

- Use scales to measure objects that are heavier than 1 kg (correct to the nearest 100 g). Complete the table.

	Object	Estimated mass	Actual mass
A			
B			
C			
D			
E			

- Order A, B, C, D and E from lightest to heaviest.

 • *AUSTRALIAN SIGNPOST MATHS NSW 4* • ISBN 9780655709053

Telling the time

5:20 means 20 minutes past 5.
5:40 means 40 minutes past 5 or 20 minutes to 6.

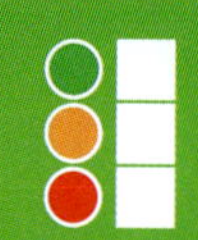

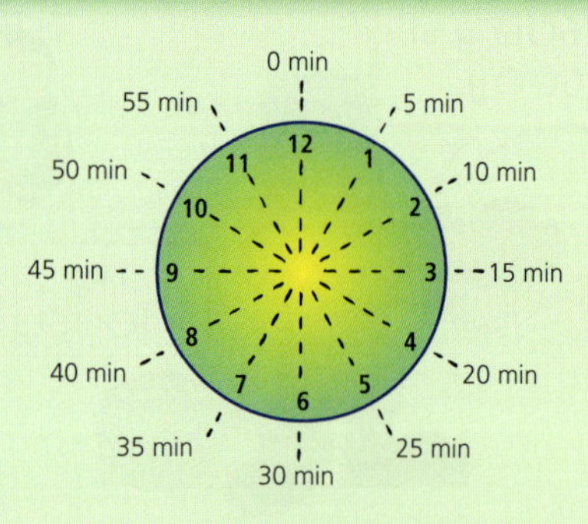

It takes 5 minutes for the minute hand to move from one numeral to the next.

- The hour hand has passed 7.
- The minute hand has moved 5, 10, 15, 20 minutes from 12.
- The time is ______ past ______ or ____ : ____.

- The hour hand has passed 1.
- The minute hand has moved 5, 10, 15, 20, 21, 22 minutes from 12.
- The time is ______.

60 minutes = 1 hour

- The hour hand is approaching 6.
- The minute hand has 5, 10, 11, 12, 13, 14 minutes to go before it reaches 12.
- The time is ______.

60 – 14 = 46 | 5:46

- The hour hand is approaching 11.
- The minute hand has 5, 10, 15, 20, 21, 22, 23 minutes to go before it reaches 12.
- The time is ______.

60 – 23 = 37 | 10:37

1 Write the times for each clock.

a

______ past ______
____ : ____

b

______ to ______
____ : ____

c

______ past ______
____ : ____

d

______ to ______
____ : ____

e

______ to ______
____ : ____

f

______ to ______
____ : ____

3:19 Time

A fortnight is 14 days.
365 days = 1 year
366 days = 1 leap year

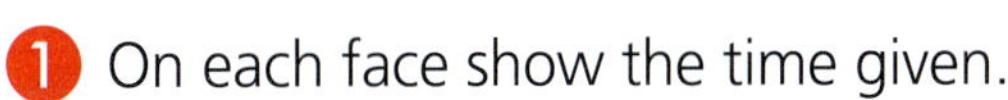

1 On each face show the time given.

a 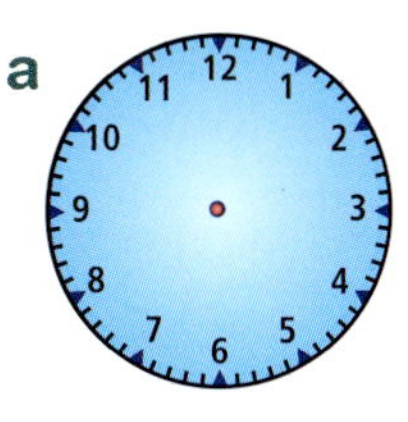
a quarter to 8

b 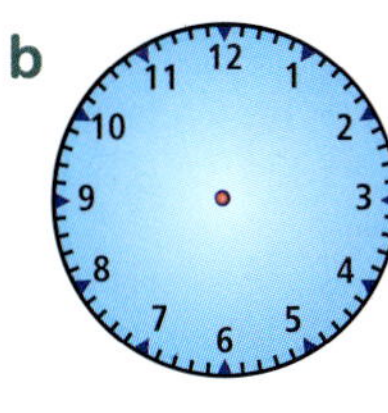
7 past 4

c 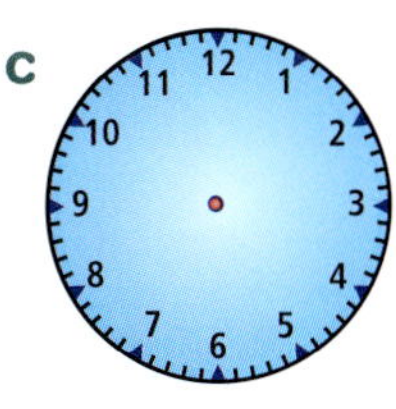
20 to 11

d 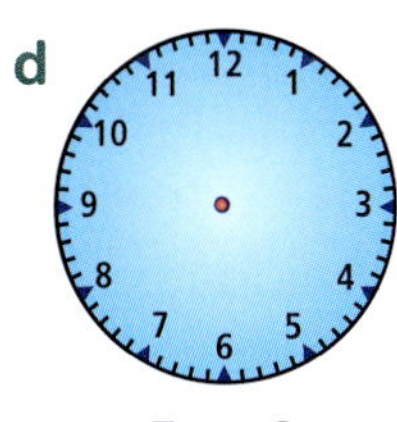
5 to 2

e 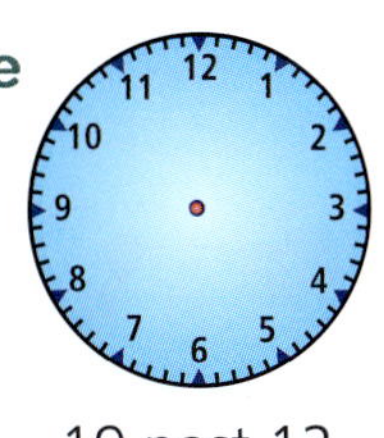
19 past 12

2 Complete the label for each time shown.

a 

☐ to ☐

b 

☐ past ☐

c 

☐ to ☐

d 

☐ past ☐

e 

☐ to ☐

3 How many more minutes will it take for the minute hand to reach the 12?

a 
☐ minutes
The time is: ☐

b 
☐ minutes

The time is: ☐

c 
☐ minutes
The time is: ☐

d
☐ minutes
The time is: ☐

e 
☐ minutes
The time is: ☐

4 Complete:

a 7 weeks = ☐ days
b 3 fortnights = ☐ days
c 28 days = ☐ fortnights
d 3 weeks = ☐ days
e 77 days = ☐ weeks
f 14 weeks = ☐ fortnights
g 21 days = ☐ weeks
h 35 days = ☐ weeks
i 14 days = ☐ weeks

5 Complete:

a 4 consecutive years would include ☐ normal years and ☐ leap year.
b 3 years = ☐ days
c 3 years = ☐ months
d 730 days = ☐ years
e 60 months = ☐ years
f 3 years = ☐ weeks
g 208 weeks = ☐ years

6 I started training at 3:37.1 finished at 4:00. For how long did I train? ☐ min

My friend trained from 3:25 until 4:00. For how long did she train? ☐ min

See *Extra Support 13 and 14* (The calendar).

 • *AUSTRALIAN SIGNPOST MATHS NSW 4* • ISBN 9780655709053

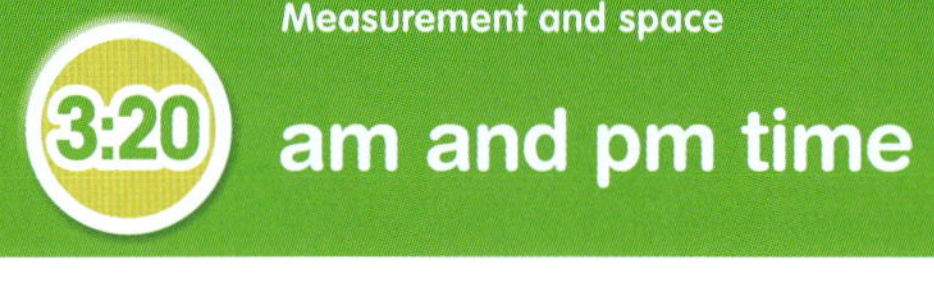

3:20 am and pm time

am: From midnight until noon
pm: From noon until midnight

1 hour 20 minutes is written 1 h 20 min

When we write digital time we usually add **am** or **pm**.

Ante meridiem (am), is Latin for before midday.

Post meridiem (pm), is Latin for after midday.

10:46 pm

1 Write a digital label for each time shown.

a 
afternoon
___ : ___ pm

b 
morning
___ : ___ am

c 
evening
___ : ___ pm

d 
morning
___ : ___

e 
evening
___ : ___

2 For each digital time, write **before** midday or **after** midday.

a 

b 

c 

d 

e 

3 There are 60 minutes in an hour. How long is it from:

a 7:52 am till 8 am? ☐ min **b** 8:35 pm till 9 pm? ☐ min

c 4:29 am till 5 am? ☐ min **d** 5:13 pm till 6 pm? ☐ min

e 11:04 am till 12 noon? ☐ min **f** 11:19 pm till midnight? ☐ min

4 I finished playing soccer at 2:00 pm. How long had I been playing if I started at:

a 1:54 pm ☐ minutes **b** 1:42 pm ☐ minutes **c** 1:36 pm ☐ minutes

d 1:21 pm ☐ minutes **e** 1:17 pm ☐ minutes **f** 1:03 pm ☐ minutes

5 My test was handed in at 10:00 am. How long did I take to complete the test if I started at:

a 9:51 am? ☐ min **b** 9:47 am? ☐ min **c** 9:33 am? ☐ min

d 9:26 am? ☐ min **e** 9:15 am? ☐ min **f** 9:09 am? ☐ min

 • *AUSTRALIAN SIGNPOST MATHS NSW 4* • ISBN 9780655709053

Converting lengths

3 cm 4 mm = 34 mm
4 m 56 cm = 456 cm

CONCEPT

We can write measurements in decimal form.
For example, 3·4 cm or 4·56 m.

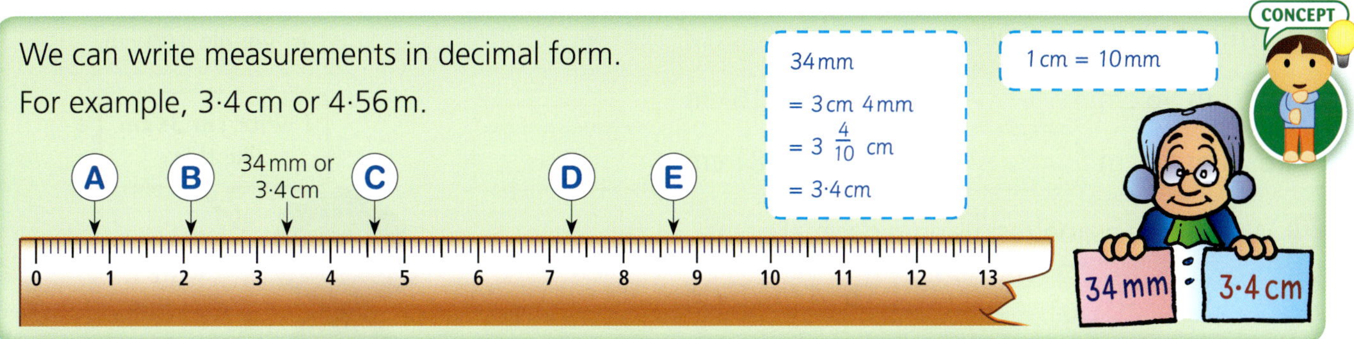

1 Record the lengths from 0 shown on the ruler. Write the cm measurements using a decimal.

A ☐ mm ☐ cm **B** ☐ mm ☐ cm **C** ☐ mm ☐ cm **D** ☐ mm ☐ cm **E** ☐ mm ☐ cm

2 Use the decimal form to write these as centimetres.

a 65 mm ☐ **b** 23 mm ☐ **c** 91 mm ☐ **d** 42 mm ☐
e 34 mm ☐ **f** 87 mm ☐ **g** 112 mm ☐ **h** 139 mm ☐

CONCEPT

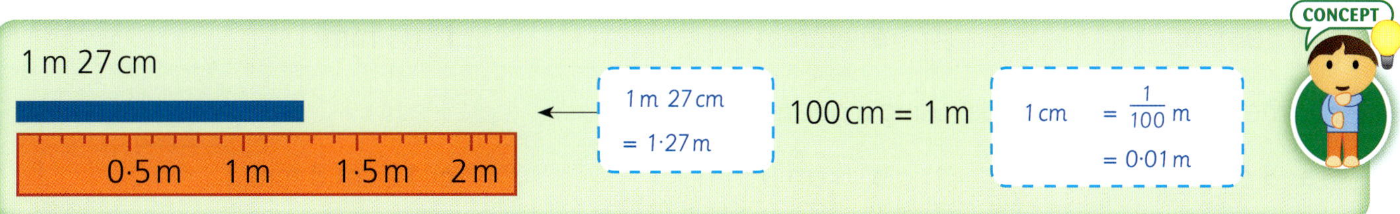

3 Use the decimal form to write these as metres.

a 156 cm ☐ **b** 341 cm ☐ **c** 819 cm ☐ **d** 253 cm ☐
e 594 cm ☐ **f** 473 cm ☐ **g** 1321 cm ☐ **h** 3472 cm ☐

4 Write these as centimetres.

a 1·42 m ☐ **b** 3·65 m ☐ **c** 9·73 m ☐ **d** 2·81 m ☐
e 2·18 m ☐ **f** 4·64 m ☐ **g** 6·07 m ☐ **h** 10·52 m ☐

ACTIVITY

- Find a variety of objects in the classroom to measure.
- Use the best units of measure and complete the table.

Object measurement	mm	cm	m
A book	274 mm	27·4 cm	—

3:22 Length

Estimate, then measure the perimeter of the large blue rectangle below. ______ cm

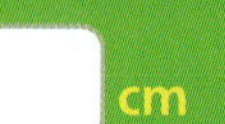

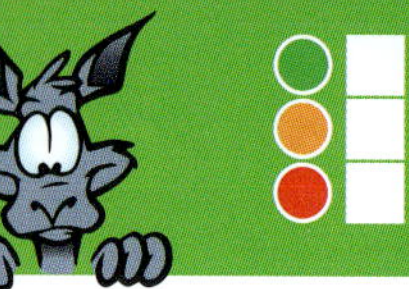

1 m equals 100 cm.

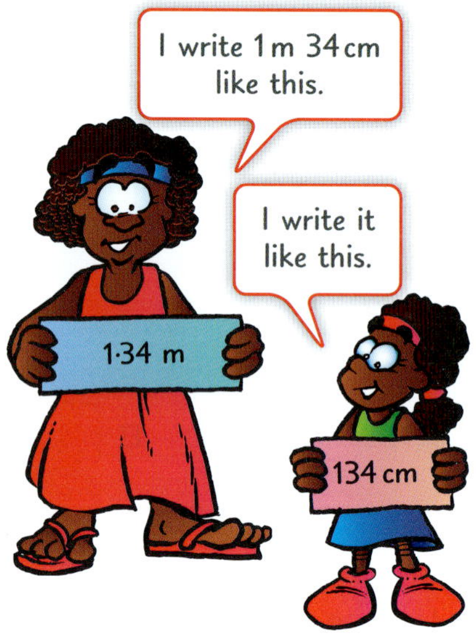
I write 1 m 34 cm like this.
I write it like this.
1·34 m
134 cm

1 Write these as centimetres.

a 2 m 56 cm ______ **b** 3 m 16 cm ______
c 5 m 40 cm ______ **d** 7 m 81 cm ______

2 Write these as metres, using a decimal point.

a 3 m 63 cm ______ **b** 4 m 25 cm ______
c 8 m 47 cm ______ **d** 5 m 87 cm ______

3 Write these as metres and centimetres.

a 119 cm ______ **b** 853 cm ______
c 582 cm ______ **d** 697 cm ______
e 935 cm ______ **f** 374 cm ______

4 Write these as centimetres and millimetres.

a 27 mm ______ **b** 36 mm ______ **c** 51 mm ______
d 19 mm ______ **e** 42 mm ______ **f** 85 mm ______

5 Write these as centimetres, using a decimal point.

a 3 cm 6 mm ______ **b** 6 cm 9 mm ______ **c** 12 cm 8 mm ______

6 Write these as millimetres.

a 5 cm 4 mm ______ **b** 6 cm 9 mm ______ **c** 1 cm 1 mm ______
d 8 cm 7 mm ______ **e** 4 cm 3 mm ______ **f** 2 cm ______

7 Which unit (**m**, **cm** or **mm**) has been left off each measurement of length?

a
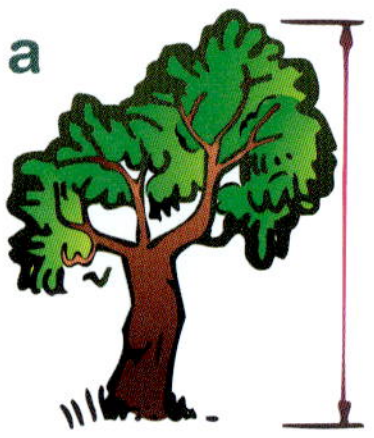
tree **5**

b
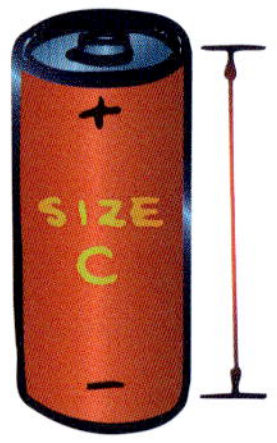
SIZE
C
battery **5**

c
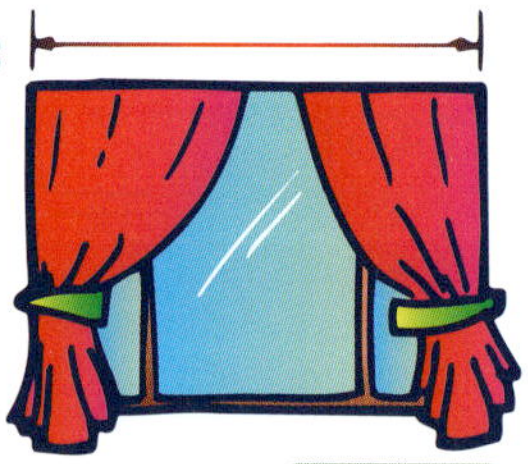
window **3**

d
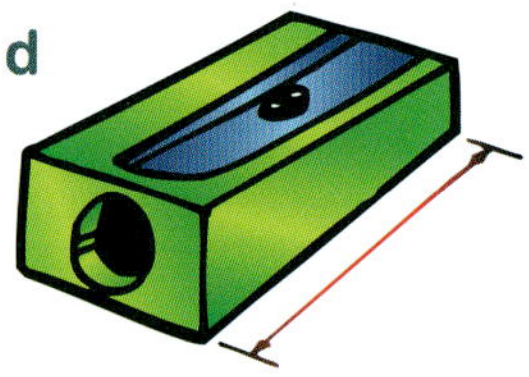
sharpener **25**

e
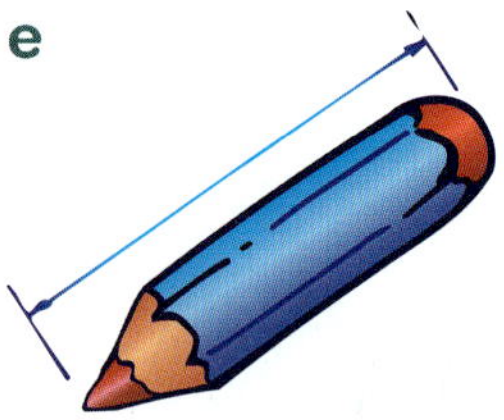
pencil **14·5**

f
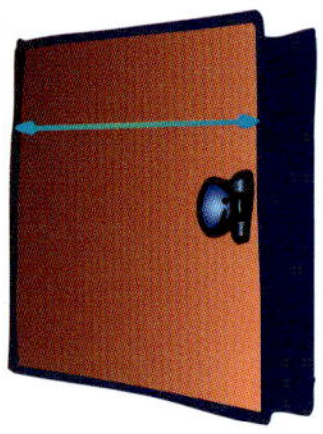
door **1·2**

g
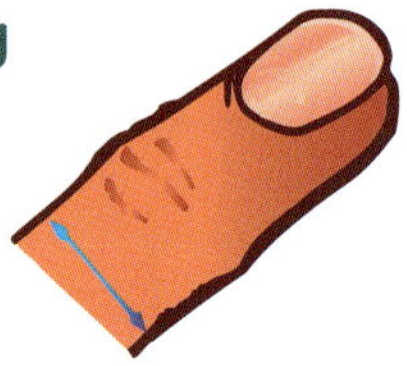
finger **12**

h
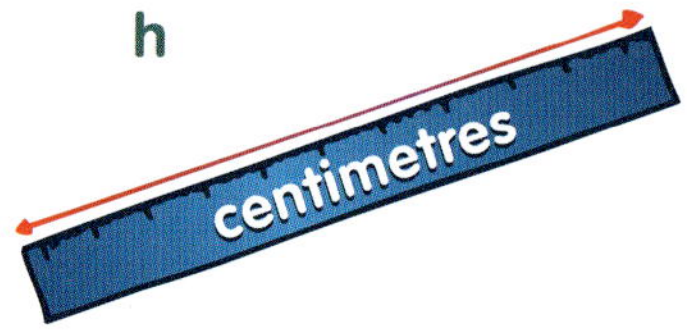
centimetres
ruler **300**

3:23 Length

When rounding to the nearest cm, round up for 5 mm and above, round down for less than 5 mm.

1 Complete this table.

Millimetres	cm and mm	cm as a decimal	Rounded to the nearest cm
39 mm		3·9 cm	
	6 cm 3 mm	6·3 cm	
56 mm			
	7 cm 2 mm		
81 mm			
	4 cm 5 mm		
	9 cm 4 mm		

2 Use a strip of 1 cm grid paper to measure the distance around:

a a pen ______ cm

b drink bottle ______ cm

c a pencil ______ cm

d your head ______ cm

e your arm ______ cm

3 Measure the length of each line correct to the nearest millimetre.

a ______ mm

b ______ mm

c ______ mm

d ______ mm

e ______ mm

f ______ mm

g ______ mm

h ______ mm

4 Estimate, then measure the perimeter of each shape.

A

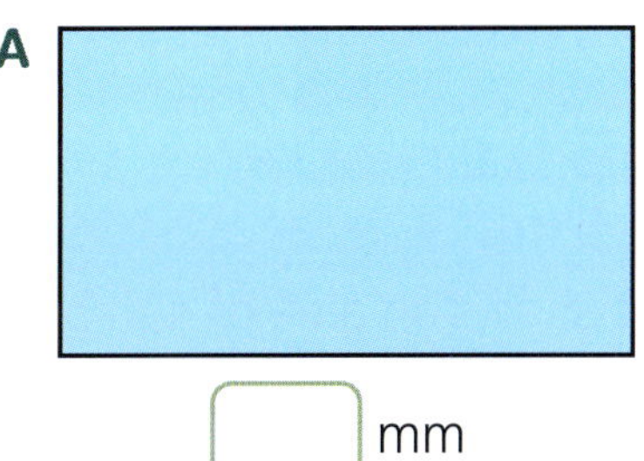

______ mm

B

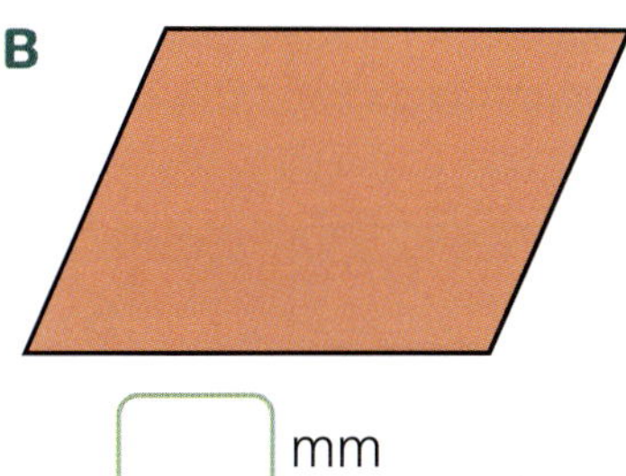

______ mm

C

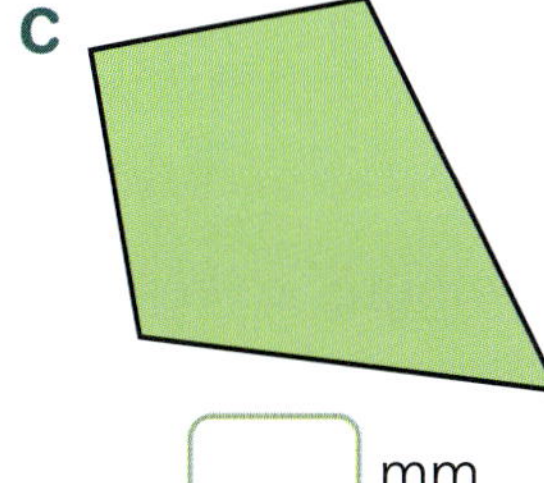

______ mm

Which shape **A**, **B** or **C** has the longest perimeter? ______

ACTIVITY

- Discuss what you would use to measure these lengths. Estimate, then measure each. Record your results on your own paper.
  - the length of a path
  - the length of the classroom
  - the distance around a tree
  - the height of a door
  - the length of a hose
  - the length of a handball court
  - the distance around a bottle
  - the width of a window

Trundle Wheel

 • *AUSTRALIAN SIGNPOST MATHS NSW 4* • ISBN 9780655709053

3:24 The square metre

Estimate the area of a table cloth. ☐ square metres

ACTIVITY

You will need metre rulers, tape measures, chalk and a large concrete area.

1 On a large concrete area, use chalk to draw and label these three shapes.

A A square with sides 3 m.

B A rectangle with sides 2 m and 4 m.

C A rectangle with sides 5 m and 2 m.

It is important to measure accurately.

2 Which area do you think is the largest: **A**, **B** or **C**? ☐

3 **a** Write an estimate of the area of each shape.

b Draw a square metre grid on each shape.

c Record the area of each shape.

d Number the areas 1 to 3, in descending order, with largest (1) to smallest (3).

Area	Estimate	Measurement	Order
A			
B			
C			

4 List areas in your classroom that are:

a larger than a square metre ☐

b smaller than a square metre ☐

5 Would you use square centimetres or square metres to find the area of a:

a basketball court? ☐

b door? ☐

c computer screen? ☐

d classroom floor? ☐

e sticky note? ☐

f matchbox lid? ☐

g pattern block? ☐

h wall? ☐

6 **a** This picture shows an area 2 m by 8 m.

The area is ☐ square metres.

2 m

8 m

b This picture shows an area of 4 m by 4 m.

The area is ☐ square metres.

4 m

c What do you notice about these two areas? ☐

7 Explain the difference between area and perimeter.

☐

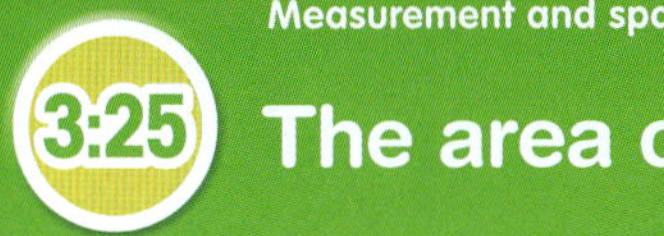

The area of a triangle

Use a grid overlay to measure the area of the rectangles in the Concept box.

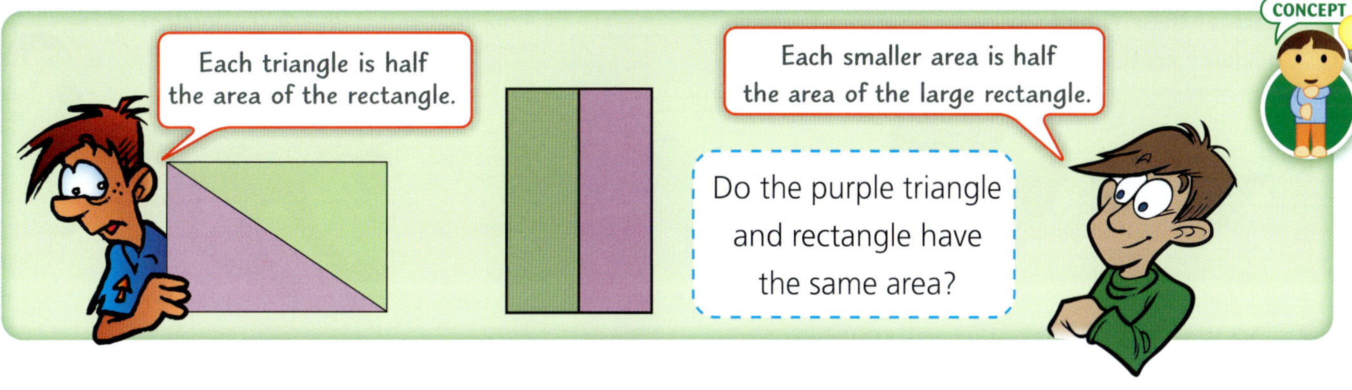

1 Use the grid to find the area of each rectangle and triangle.

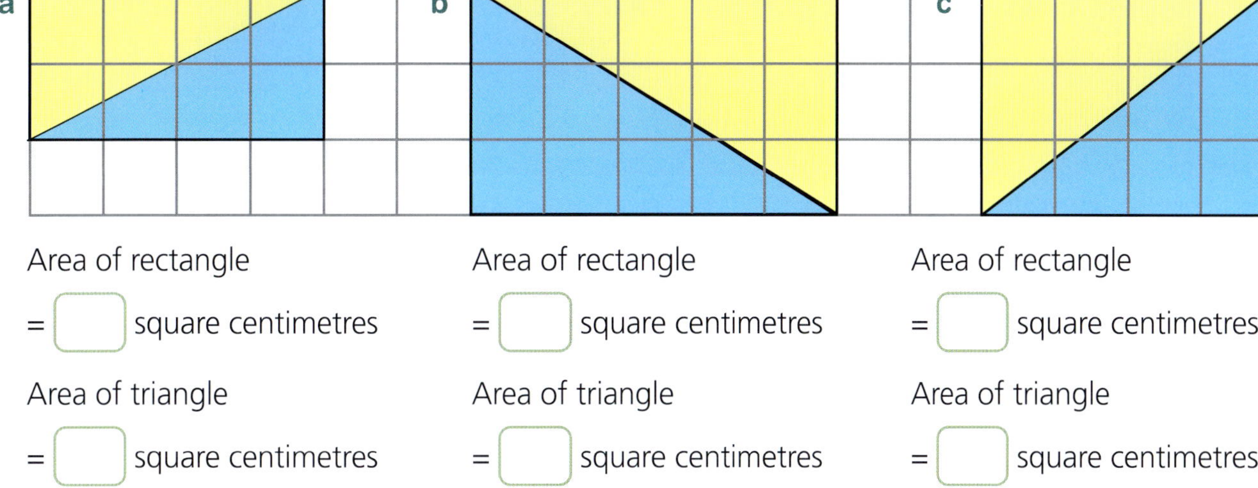

a Area of rectangle = ☐ square centimetres

Area of triangle = ☐ square centimetres

b Area of rectangle = ☐ square centimetres

Area of triangle = ☐ square centimetres

c Area of rectangle = ☐ square centimetres

Area of triangle = ☐ square centimetres

2 Before calculating the areas below, estimate which is the smallest rectangle? ☐

Use a 1 cm grid transparency, or draw a grid, to find the area of each rectangle.

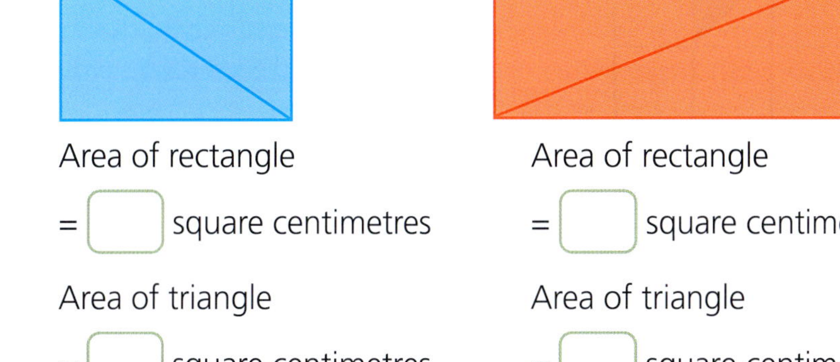

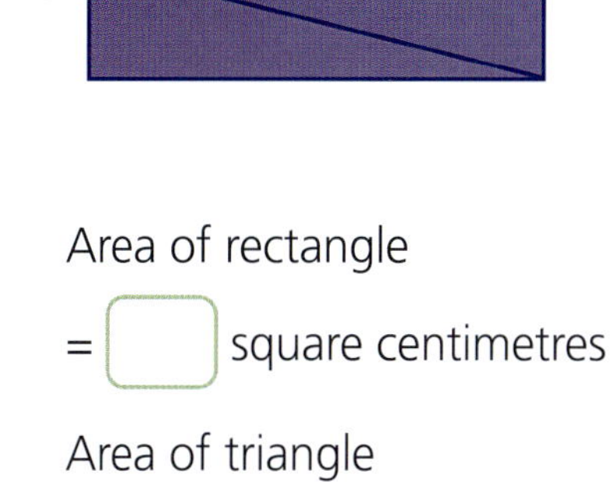

a Area of rectangle = ☐ square centimetres

Area of triangle = ☐ square centimetres

b Area of rectangle = ☐ square centimetres

Area of triangle = ☐ square centimetres

c Area of rectangle = ☐ square centimetres

Area of triangle = ☐ square centimetres

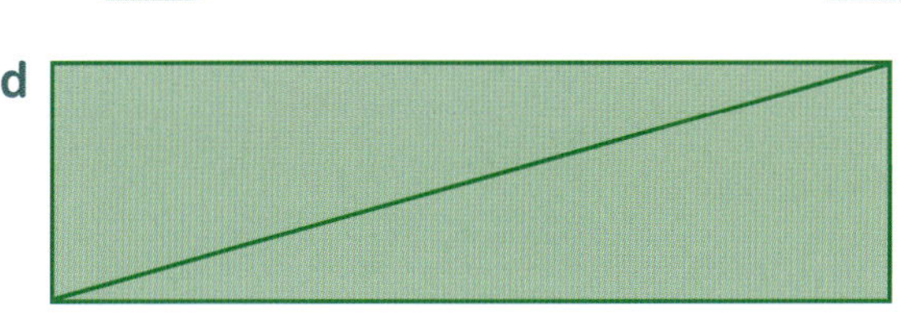

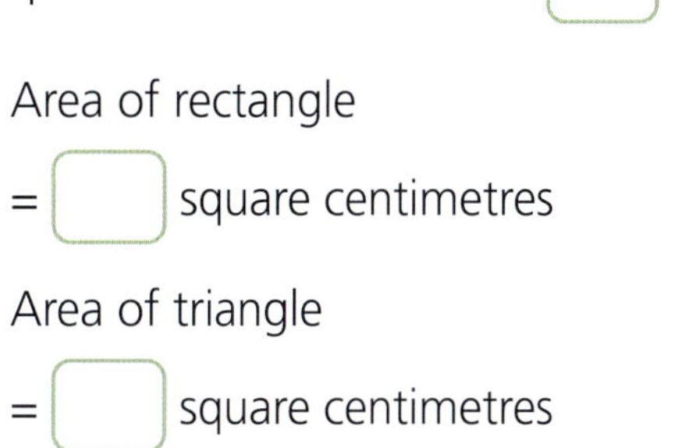

d Area of rectangle = ☐ square centimetres

Area of triangle = ☐ square centimetres

 • *AUSTRALIAN SIGNPOST MATHS NSW 4* • ISBN 9780655709053

3:26 The area of a triangle

We can cut squares into half squares.

1 Find the area of each grid and triangle.

a

Area of grid = ☐ square centimetres

Area of triangle = ☐ square centimetres

b

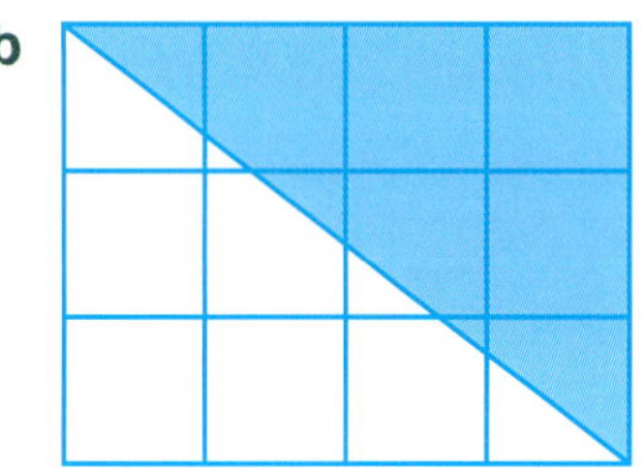

Area of grid = ☐ square centimetres

Area of triangle = ☐ square centimetres

c

Area of grid = ☐ square centimetres

Area of triangle = ☐ square centimetres

2 Find the area of each triangle. Think carefully about how you could find the area of part c.

a

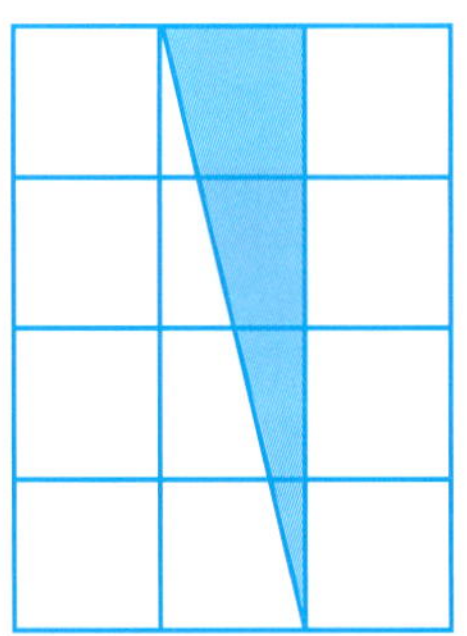

Area of triangle = ☐ square centimetres

b

Area of triangle = ☐ square centimetres

c

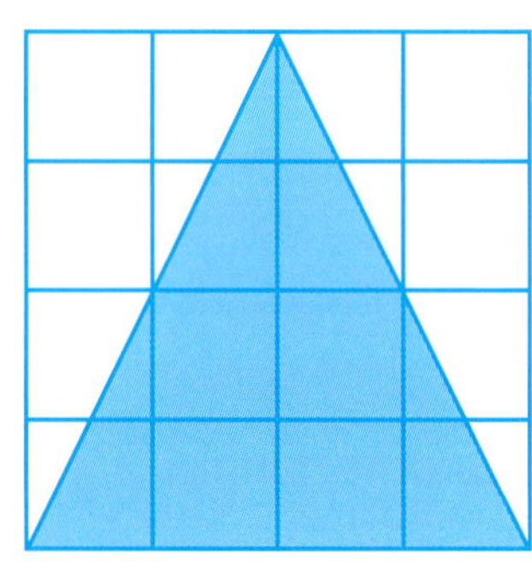

Area of triangle = ☐ square centimetres

Cut and find area

- Cut a square with 4 cm sides from 1 cm grid paper. Find its area.
- Draw in the diagonals and cut along them to form four triangles.
- Rearrange them to make a rectangle (as shown) and find its area.

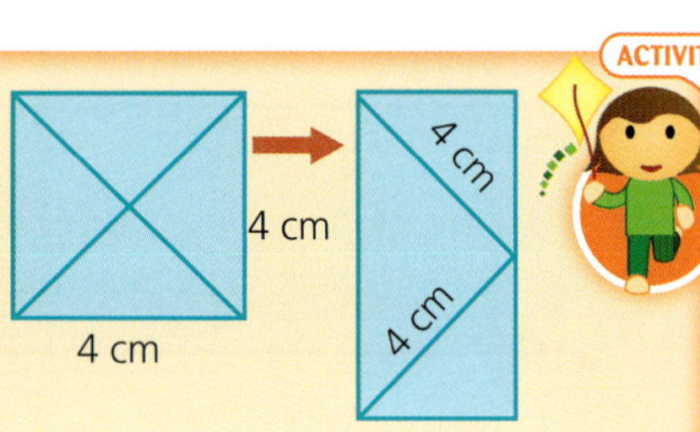

 • *AUSTRALIAN SIGNPOST MATHS NSW 4* • ISBN 9780655709053

3:27 Using grams

The mass of 1 mL of water is very close to 1 gram.

Use scales to find an object that is:

About $\frac{1}{4}$ kg	
About $\frac{1}{2}$ kg	
About $\frac{3}{4}$ kg	
About 1 kg	

1 Write the short form for:

a 100 grams ☐ **b** 600 grams ☐ **c** 1 kilogram ☐
d 500 grams ☐ **e** 3 kilograms ☐ **f** 1300 grams ☐
g 10 kilograms ☐ **h** 956 grams ☐ **i** 875 grams ☐

2 How many kilograms are there in:

a 3000 g? ☐ **b** 7000 g? ☐ **c** 2000 g? ☐
d 5000 g? ☐ **e** 9000 g? ☐ **f** 4000 g? ☐

3 How many grams are there in:

a 2 kg? ☐ **b** 1 kg 200 g? ☐ **c** 3 kg? ☐
d 1 kg 600 g? ☐ **e** 5 kg? ☐ **f** 1 kg 450 g? ☐
g 1 kg 980 g? ☐ **h** 1 kg 500 g? ☐ **i** 7 kg? ☐

4 How many grams are there in:

a $\frac{1}{2}$ kg? ☐ **b** $\frac{3}{4}$ kg? ☐ **c** $\frac{1}{4}$ kg? ☐ **d** $1\frac{1}{2}$ kg? ☐
e $1\frac{3}{4}$ kg? ☐ **f** $1\frac{1}{4}$ kg? ☐ **g** $2\frac{1}{2}$ kg? ☐ **h** $3\frac{1}{2}$ kg? ☐

5 Order these objects from least mass to greatest mass.

A 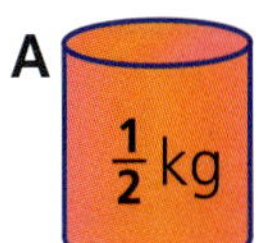

B 

C 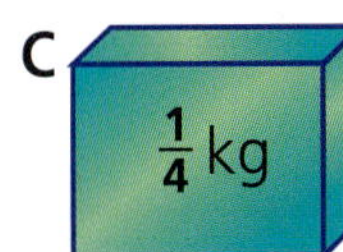

D 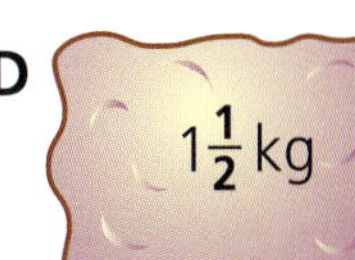

☐

 • *AUSTRALIAN SIGNPOST MATHS NSW 4* • ISBN 9780655709053

3:28 Measuring mass

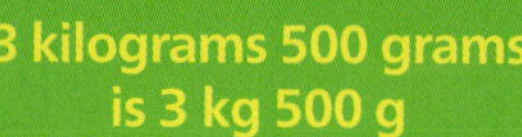

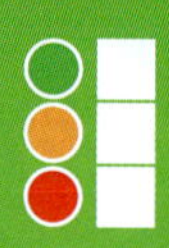

1 Use the short form to write:

a 1 kilogram ☐ b 450 grams ☐ c 3 kilograms ☐

d 1 kilogram 560 grams ☐ e 2 kilograms 125 grams ☐

2 How many grams are in:

a 3 kilograms? ☐ b 5 kilograms? ☐ c 9 kilograms? ☐

d 7 kilograms? ☐ e 4 kilograms? ☐ f 6 kilograms? ☐

3 How many kilograms are in:

a 1000 grams? ☐ b 8000 grams? ☐ c 2000 grams? ☐

d 4000 grams? ☐ e 6000 grams? ☐ f 5000 grams? ☐

4 Write each measurement as kilograms (kg) using one decimal place.

a 100 g ☐ b 300 g ☐ c 900 g ☐

d 500 g ☐ e 700 g ☐ f 1400 g ☐

Digital scales

700 g

0·7 kg

Analog scales

0 kg 1 2 3 4

The measure next to the blue dot is 4 kg 750 g.

5 Write each measurement as grams (g). 0·4 kg = 400 g

a 0·5 kg ☐ b 0·2 kg ☐

c 0·8 kg ☐ d 0·6 kg ☐

6 There are three marks between 0 and 1 on these analog scales. These stand for 250 g, 500 g and 750 g. Write the measure that is next to the:

a white dot ☐ b black dot ☐

c yellow dot ☐ d green dot ☐

ACTIVITY

● Use scales and standard masses to complete this table.

Mass	Objects found
Less than 100 g	
About 500 g	
About 1 kg	
More than 1 kg	

1 litre of water weighs about 1 kilogram.

1 L 1.0 L 0.5 L

1 kg

Using am and pm time

Sometimes the am and pm are left out on timetables.

Use the timetable to answer the following questions.
The train leaves Ironbark at 6:10 am.

Add am or pm for each time in the timetable.

Mulga line timetable		am or pm
Arriving		
Ironbark	6:10	
Christmas Ck	7:25	
Mt Gordon	7:50	
Richmond	8:45	
Wandong	10:05	
Carbor	11:40	
Black Hill	12:30	
Mulga	1:15	

1 At what time does the train arrive in:

a Ironbark? ☐ b Richmond? ☐
c Carbor? ☐ d Mt Gordon? ☐
e Wandong? ☐ f Mulga? ☐

2 At which station does the train arrive at:

a 8:45 am ☐ b 7:25 am ☐
c 12:30 pm ☐ d 6:10 am ☐
e 1:15 pm ☐ f 10:05 am ☐

3 If the train is two hours late, at what time does it arrive in:

a Ironbark? ☐ b Carbor? ☐
c Mulga? ☐ d Wandong? ☐
e Black Hill? ☐ f Richmond? ☐

am means 'before noon' (from midnight until noon).

pm means 'after noon' (from noon until midnight).

4 If the train is half an hour early, at what time does it arrive in:

a Black Hill? ☐ b Richmond? ☐ c Carbor? ☐
d Mulga? ☐ e Ironbark? ☐ f Wandong? ☐

5 At which station does the train arrive at:

a half past 12? ☐ b a quarter past 1? ☐
c a quarter to 9? ☐ d 5 past 10? ☐
e 20 to 12? ☐ f 10 to 8? ☐

6 Complete the time line for the Mulga Line train.

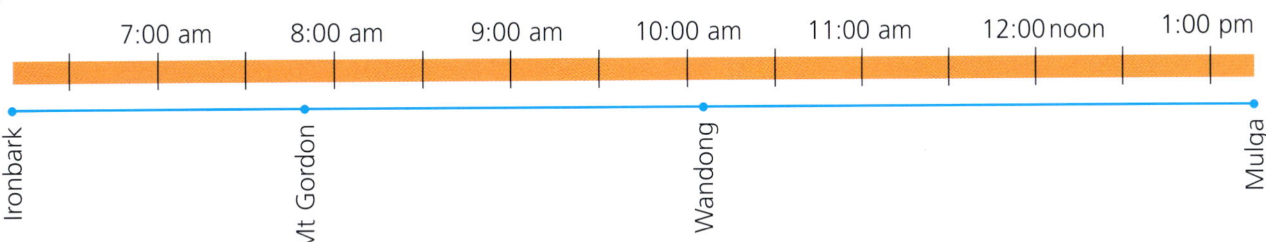

See *Extra Support 15* (Timelines).

Seconds

60 seconds = 1 minute
60 minutes = 1 hour
24 hours = 1 day

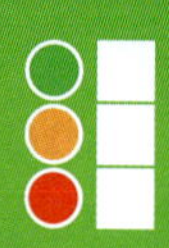

CONCEPT

Clocks sometimes have a second hand.
This clock, shows 21 minutes, 29 seconds past 1.
The time shown here can be writen as

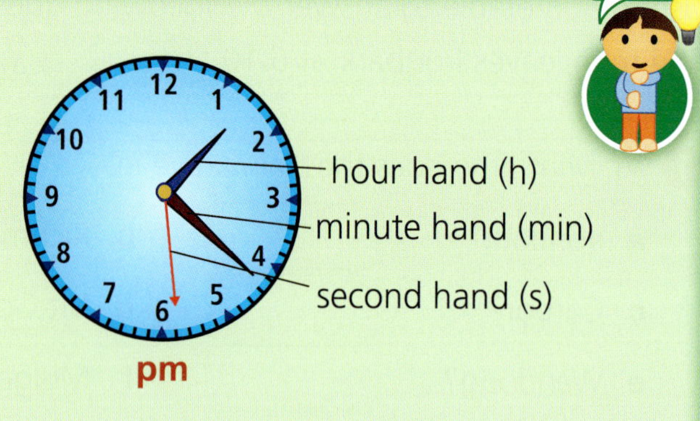

- While the **second hand** moves one full turn around the clock (60 s), the **minute hand** moves one small unit (1 min).

1 Write the time on each clock using hours, minutes and seconds.

A

B

C

D

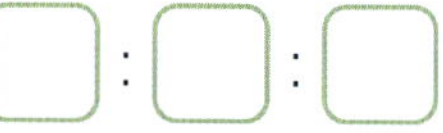

a How many seconds have past since the last minute was reached?

A: B: C: D:

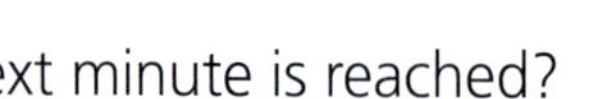

b How many seconds will it be until the next minute is reached?

A: B: C: D:

c Which clocks show an afternoon time?

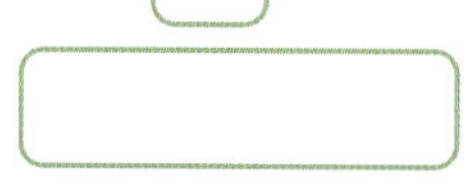

2 List events that would be measured using seconds.

INVESTIGATION

3 Set a timer for 60 seconds. In that time, see how many number sentences you can write that are equal to 30 (for example, $25 + 5 = 30$).

4 Have a partner use a stopwatch to time you. Record your time in minutes and seconds.

	minutes	seconds
write your full name		
sing a song		
jump 10 times		

	minutes	seconds
say your 5 × tables		
read a page of a book		
count to 200		

 • *AUSTRALIAN SIGNPOST MATHS NSW 4* • ISBN 9780655709053

3:31 The stopwatch

minutes
seconds

We round the time to the nearest second.

Stopwatches measure the time an activity takes.

This **analog stopwatch** shows 3 minutes and 50 seconds to the nearest second.

This **digital stopwatch** shows 12 minutes and 21 seconds to the nearest second.

CONCEPT

1 **a** Estimate how long it would take for the whole class to do each activity.
Have a student record the time taken for each activity.

	Estimated time	Actual time	Shortest (1) to longest (4)
write their name			
line up at the door			
walk to the ____________ and back			
walk into the room and sit at a desk			

b Choose another activity to measure (e.g. time taken to tie your shoelaces). Estimate, then use a countdown timer to check if the activity can be completed in the estimated time.

Activity	Estimated time	Actual time

2 Circle the faster time in each pair. The faster time is the lower time.

a 01:29 15 / 01:31 39

b 04:58 06 / 04:39 19

c 19:02 06 / 16:15 38

d 00:34 92 / 00:28 35

e 02:21 08 / 02:21 00

3 Write the slower times from Question **2** parts **a** and **b** in full to the nearest second (e.g. for 03:23 46 write 3 minutes and 23 seconds).

a ____________ **b** ____________

ACTIVITY

Use a timer to record the duration of an event in your day. Record what you found.

Event: ____________ Time: ____________

See *Extra Support 16* (Comparing decimal measurements).

3:32 Comparing lengths

25 mm	
18 mm	?

What's the difference?

- We can compare measurements using subtraction.

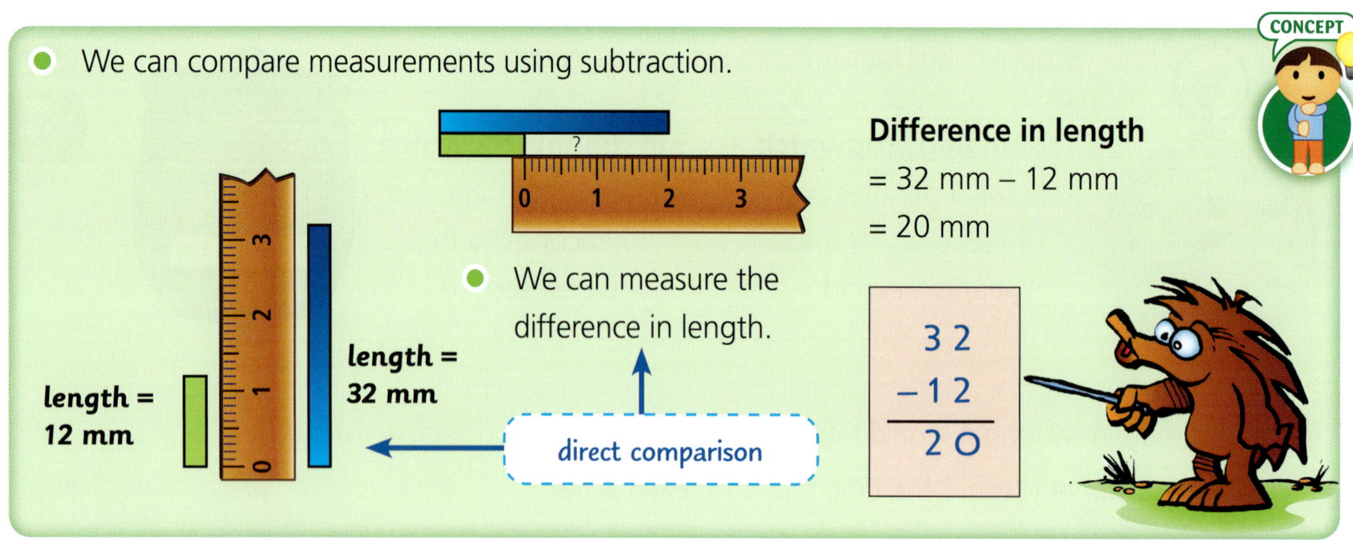

1. What is the difference in length of the rectangles:

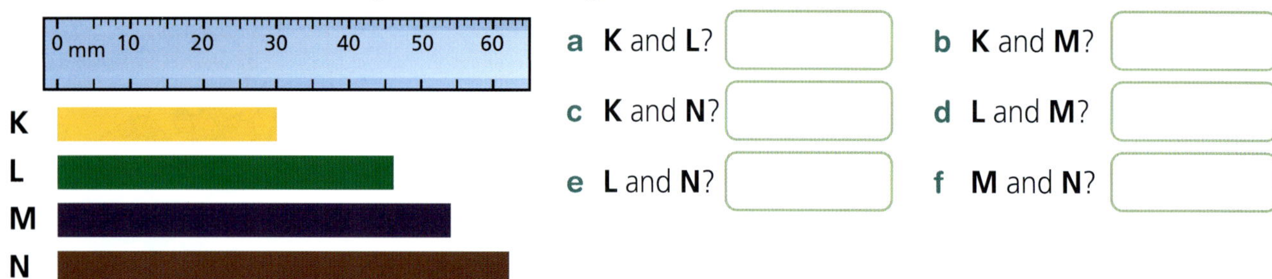

a K and L? ______ b K and M? ______
c K and N? ______ d L and M? ______
e L and N? ______ f M and N? ______

2. Measure the length of each rod in millimetres.

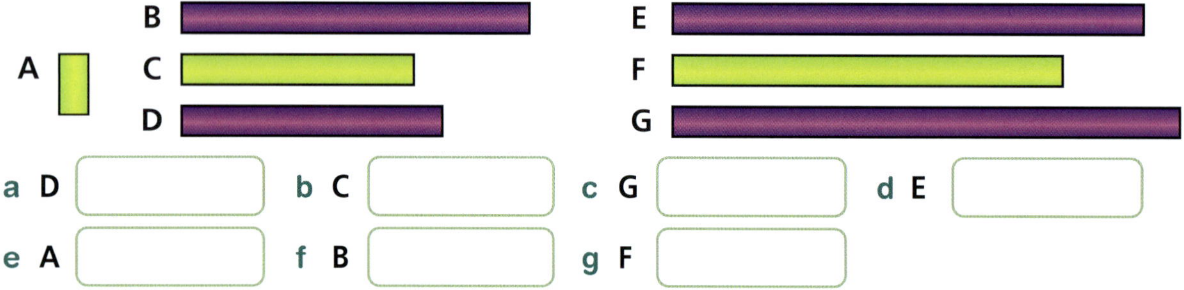

a D ______ b C ______ c G ______ d E ______
e A ______ f B ______ g F ______

3. On your own paper, calculate the difference in length of:

a A and B ______ b C and D ______ c E and F ______
d G and A ______ e E and C ______ f D and G ______
g C and A ______ h D and E ______ i B and C ______

INVESTIGATION

- Explain how you would find the difference between the distance around a tree and the thickness of the tree.

© PEARSON AUSTRALIA 2024 • *AUSTRALIAN SIGNPOST MATHS NSW 4* • ISBN 9780655709053

3:33 Using mm when building

The measurements shown on building plans are in millimetres.

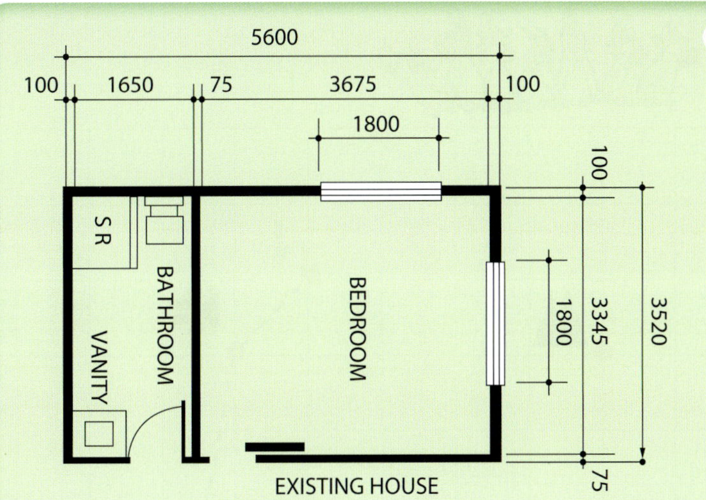

CONCEPT

- This is the building plan for an extension to Tom's house.
  - All measurements are in millimetres.
  - S R stands for shower recess. Vanity stands for a sink.
  - There are two windows and a sliding door in the bedroom.
  - Even the thickness of the walls is given, so the correct thickness of wood will be used for the walls.

1 Write the length of the longer side of the extension in:

a millimetres ______ mm **b** metres and millimetres ______ m ______ mm

2 Write the length of the shorter side of the extension in:

a millimetres ______ mm **b** metres and millimetres ______ m ______ mm

3 What is the measurement given for the shorter wall in the:

a bathroom? ______ mm **b** bedroom? ______ m ______ mm

4 True or false?

a The longer wall of the bathroom is the same length as the shorter wall of the bedroom. ______

b The width of the shower recess is about 940 mm. ______

c The thickness of the outer walls is greater than the thickness of the wall joining the existing house. ______

d The vanity is wider than the shower recess. ______

e The width of each window is the same. ______

INVESTIGATION

- Use a tape measure to find 3 objects that are longer than a metre. Write the length of each of these objects in millimetres.

______ ______ ______

Length on a map

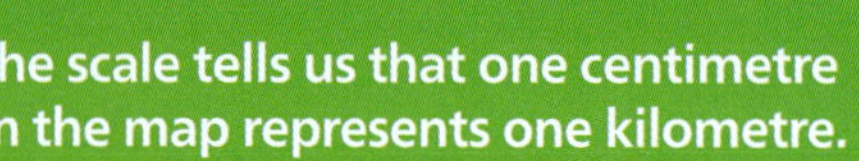

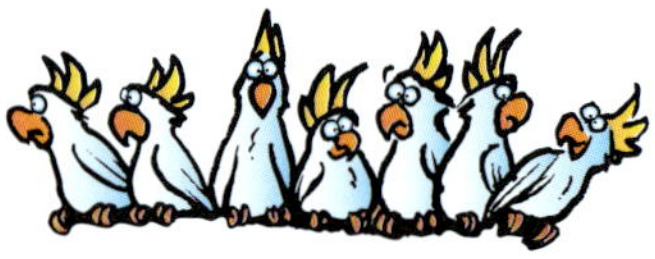

Country map

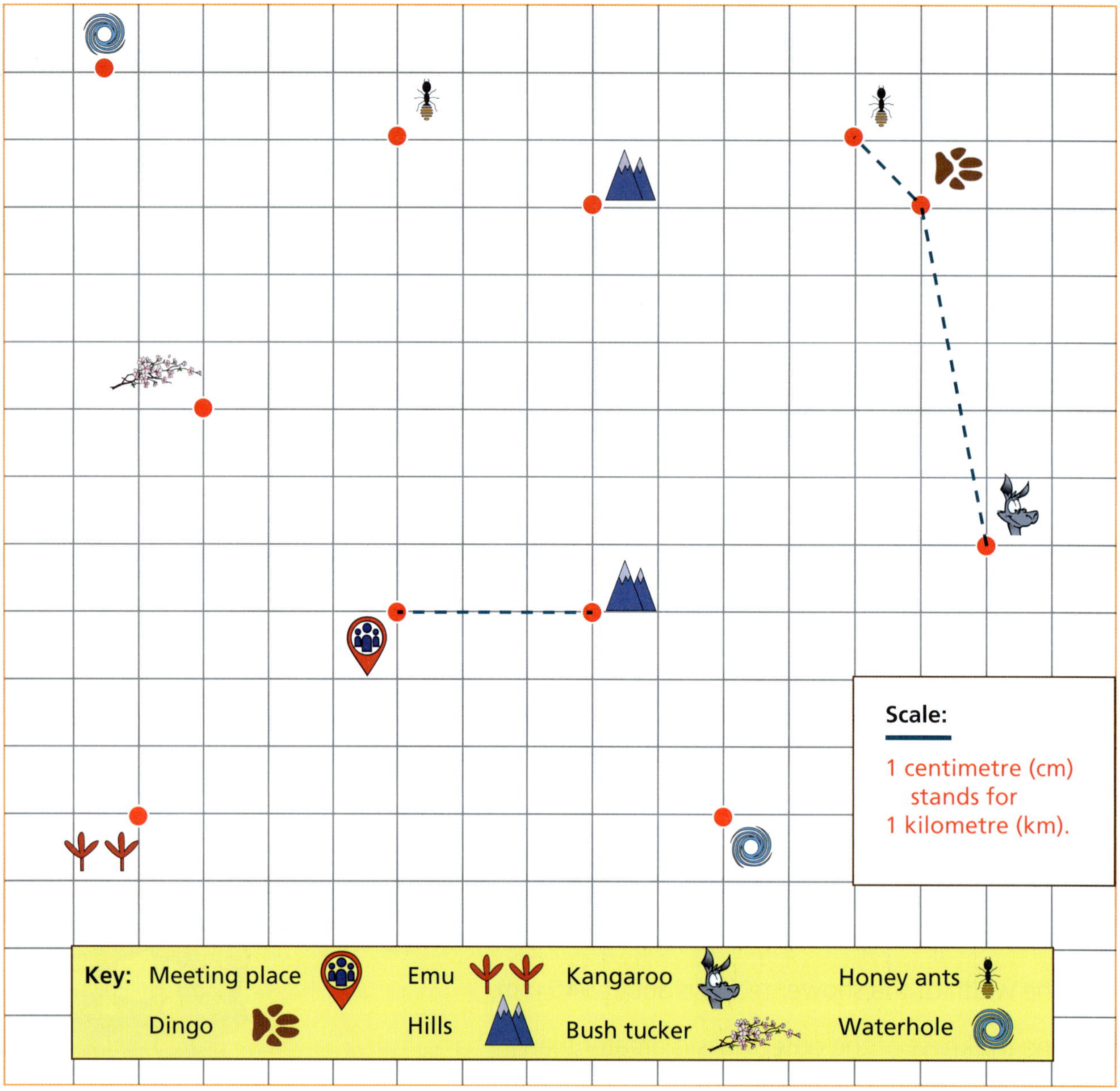

The centres of the red dots show the position of the places.

1 Find the distance to the nearest kilometre (km) between the meeting place and the nearest:

a hills ______ b honey ants ______ c waterhole ______

d emu ______ e dingo ______ f kangaroo ______

2 Each millimetre on the map stands for 100 metres. Find the distance between the dingo and:

a the kangaroo ______ m b the nearest honey ant ______ m

3:35 Problem solving

Don't forget to include units of measurement in your answer.

- Underline the important information.
  On your own paper write what you have to find and a number sentence to show how you will find it. Do your calculations, then write the answer.

1. The length of the tree's shadow was half of its real height. If the height of the tree was 36 m, how long was the shadow? ______

   Use the cartoon to estimate the width of:

   a the house. ______ **b** the truck. ______

2. The temperature at 5 pm on Monday was 27°C. On Tuesday at 5 pm the temperature was 6°C higher. On Wednesday at 5 pm the temperature was 13°C less than Tuesday's. What was Wednesday's temperature at 5 pm? ______

3. The jug held one litre of water. It was full before I poured out 275 mL. How much water still remained in the jug? ______

4. The jar of jam I bought weighed 350 g, the rice flakes weighed 200 g, the tissues 150 g and the cake 750 g. What was the total weight of these items? ______

5. **a** I arrive at 6:42 pm. How long do I wait for the show to begin if it starts at 7 pm? ______

   b I left at 9:12 pm, and arrived home at 10 pm. How long was my trip? ______

6. I left on January 27 and returned home on February 2. What was the total number of days that I was away or travelling? ______

7. **a** My bag weighs 1 kg 500 g. After it was put on the scales with my other luggage, the total was 4 kg. How much does my other luggage weigh? ______

   b When I returned from my trip, my luggage weighed 7 kg 365 g. How much heavier was my luggage on the return trip? ______

8. The width of the wall is 3345 mm. Of this, the door takes up 1800 mm. How much width of the wall is left to hang up my photos? ______

9. My goal is to swim 800 m each day.

   a One lap of the pool is 50 m. How many laps should I swim each day? ______

   b I swam only 550 m on the first day. How far should I swim on the second day to make up for this short fall? ______

 • *AUSTRALIAN SIGNPOST MATHS NSW 4* • ISBN 9780655709053

Problem solving

20 – 19 + 18 – 17 + 16 – 15 + 14
= (1) + (1) + (1) + 14
= 17

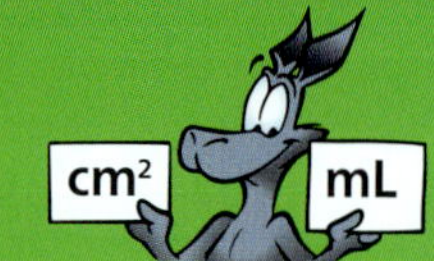

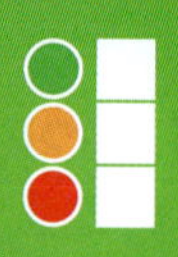

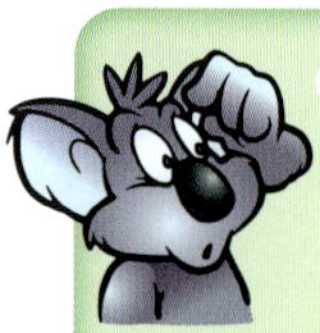

cm²
mL

List the pairs of numbers that make this algorithm true.

□□
– □
―――
2

Clues:
One number has 2 digits.
The other one has 1 digit.
Their difference is 2.

The answers are:
------ and ------
or ------ and ------

CONCEPT

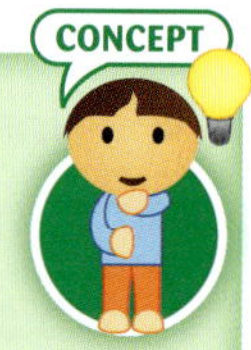

1 List the pairs of numbers that have the difference given.

a
□□□
– □□
―――
3

----

b
□□□□
– □□□
―――
2

----

2 30 – 29 + 28 – 27 + 26 – 25 + 24 – 23 + 22 – 21 + 20 – 19 + 18 – 17 + 16 – 15

3 **a** Soft drink was for sale in 300 mL, 600 mL and 2000 mL plastic bottles. I bought one of each. How many mL of soft drink did I buy?

b Write the answer to part **a** using litres and millilitres (L and mL).

c If each millilitre of soft drink has a mass of one gram and the three drink containers have a mass of 20 g altogether, what was the total mass?

4 I worked from 9:17 am until 10 am. Then I worked from 10:21 am to 11 am. For how long did I work altogether?

5 **a** I was walking along a path which was 850 m long. After travelling 247 m, I saw a snake. How far from the end of the path was the snake?

b 100 m before the end of the path I saw a bull-ant nest. How far was the nest from the start of the path?

c How far was the nest from the snake?

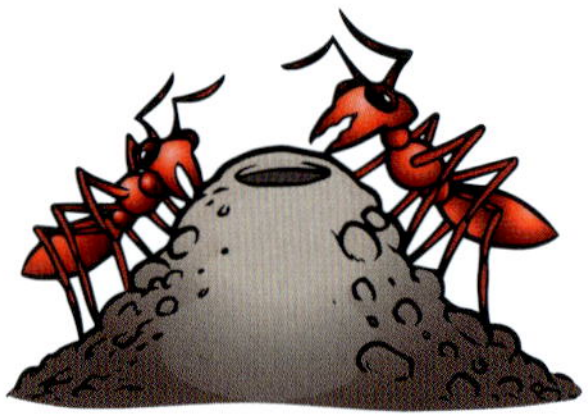

6 The area of the book is 600 square centimetres. My notepad was covering 238 square centimetres of this area. What area of my book was not covered by my notepad?

7 My table is 3 m 25 cm long and 2 m wide. My desk is 150 cm long and 45 cm wide.

a How much longer is my table than my desk?

b How much wider is the table than my desk?

8 I built a bird breeding box. All four sides are 10 cm wide and 20 cm long. The two square ends are 10 cm wide and 10 cm long. What was the total surface area of the box before I made a hole for the entrance?

10 cm
10 cm
20 cm
10 cm

 ISBN 9780655709053

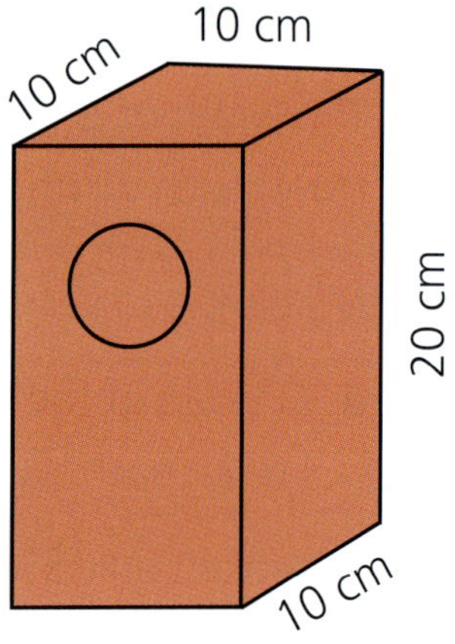

3:37 Calculating volume

2 layers of 4
= 4 + 4 = 8

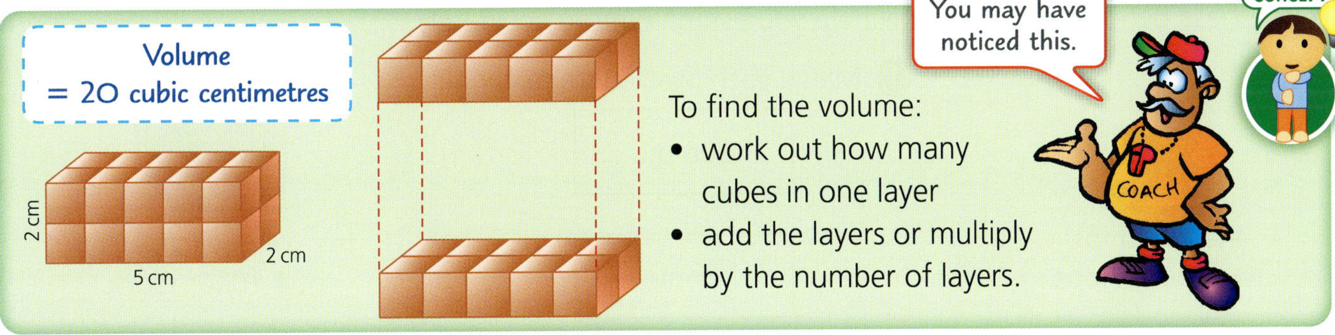

To find the volume:
- work out how many cubes in one layer
- add the layers or multiply by the number of layers.

1 John built prisms like the one above having a base 5 cm long and 2 cm wide. What would be the volume if the prism built has:

a 1 layer? ______ **b** 3 layers? ______ **c** 4 layers? ______

2 Find the volume of each prism.

a

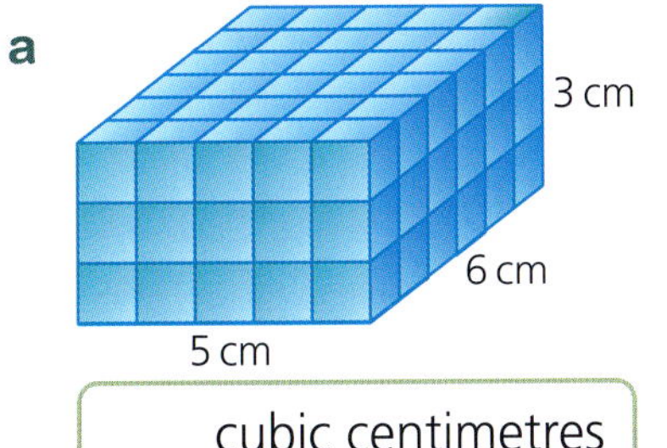

______ cubic centimetres

b 2 cm, 7 cm, 5 cm

______ cubic centimetres

c

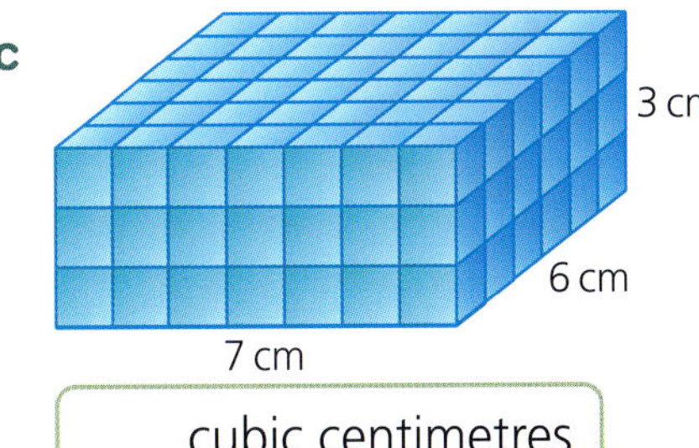

______ cubic centimetres

d 2 cm, 3 cm, 12 cm

______ cubic centimetres

e

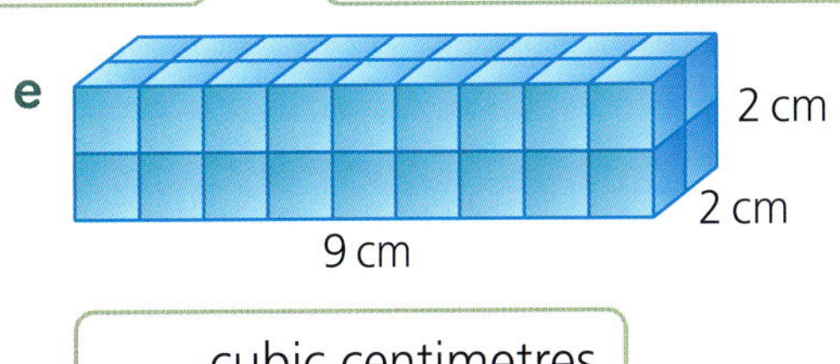

______ cubic centimetres

3 Use 1 cm blocks to make two rectangular prisms, **A** and **B**. Complete the table.

	Container	Description	Volume
A	cubic centimetres	layers of	cubic centimetres
B	cubic centimetres	layers of	cubic centimetres

4 Use interlocking cubic centimetre blocks (or ones blocks) to estimate the capacity of small rectangular containers. Place blocks on the top to find the volume of one layer, then place blocks along the side to find the number of layers. Calculate the volume.

Container	Estimate	Volume
matchbox	cubic centimetres	cubic centimetres
popper	cubic centimetres	cubic centimetres

 • *AUSTRALIAN SIGNPOST MATHS NSW 4* • ISBN 9780655709053

3:38 Personal benchmarks

My weight (mass) ______

My height ______

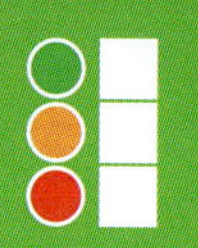

Learn these benchmarks. They will help you estimate more accurately.

1 Match each oval with a rectangle.

the length of two of my steps

the length of a full-sized pool

the capacity of a bucket

the capacity of a small bottle of water

the capacity of this milk container

the mass of 1 L of milk

temperature of a hot day

600 mL
1 m
50 m
the same as 1 L of water
100 square centimetres
1 square centimetre
11 L
2 L
10 cm
5°C
1 kg
600 cm^2
1 cm
35°C

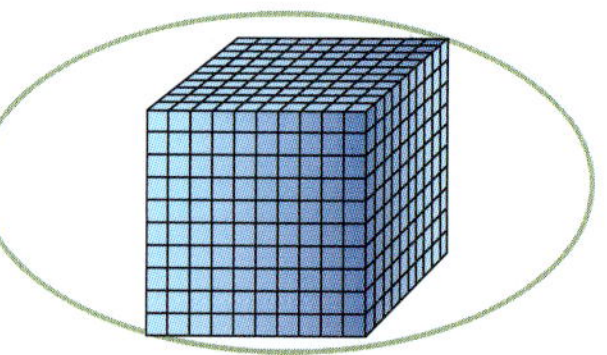

the volume (capacity) of a 1000s block

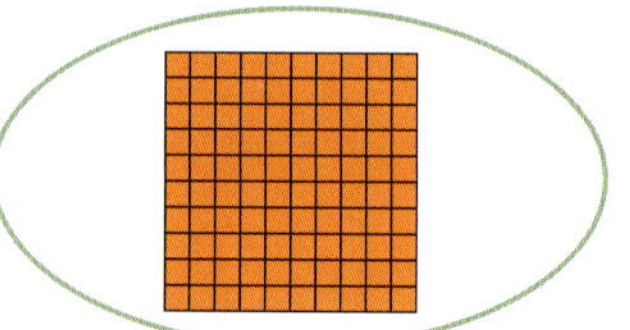

the area of the front of a 100s block

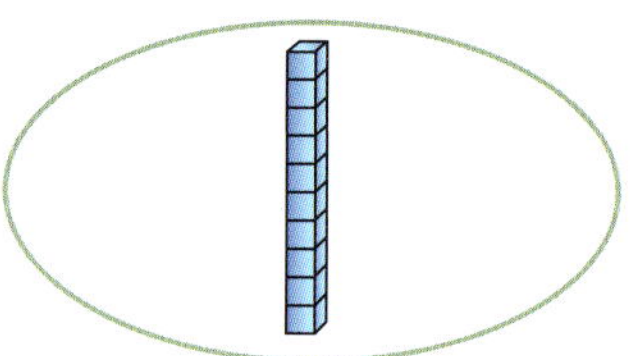

the height of a tens block

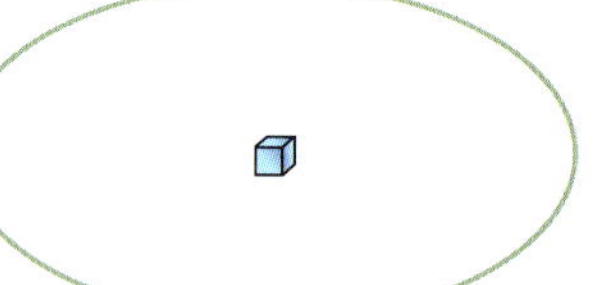

the front area of a ones block

the area of a page of this textbook

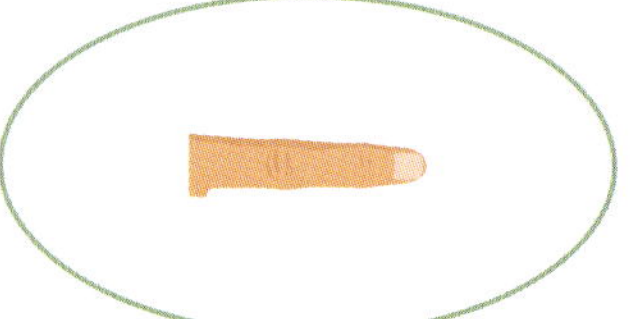

the width of my finger

temperature on a cold day

See *Extra Support 17* (Temperature) and *Extra Support 18* (Recording temperature).

Flip, slide and turn

If you fold along a line of symmetry, the two halves will match.

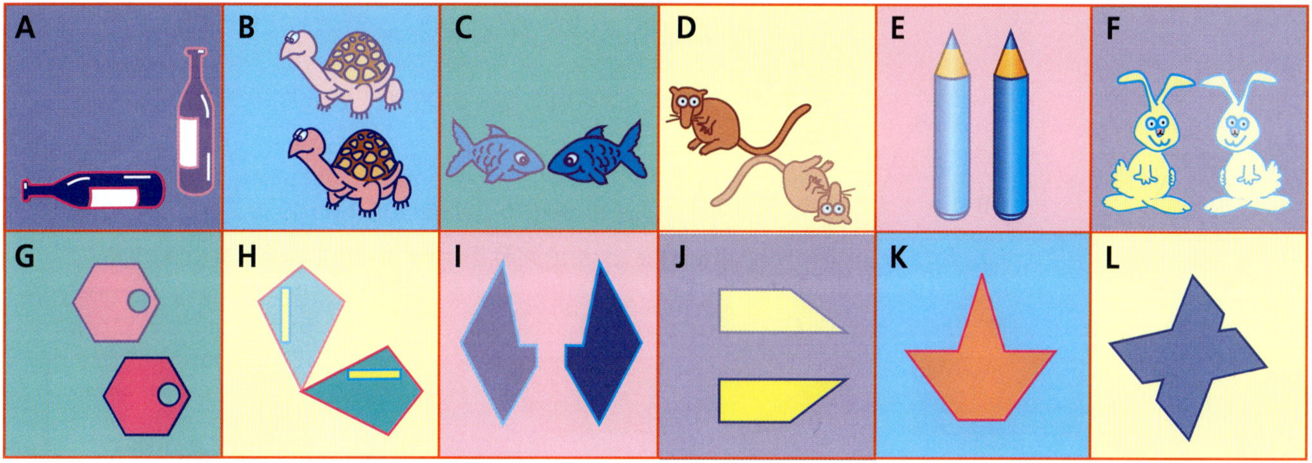

1 Which pictures (**A** to **J**) are samples of:

a flip (reflection)? ______ **b** slide (translation)? ______

c turn (rotation)? ______

2 Which picture could be an example of a flip or a slide? ______

3 How many axes of symmetry has picture:

a **K**? ______ **b** **L**? ______ **c** **C**? ______

d **D**? ______ **e** **E**? ______ **f** **F**? ______

g **G**? ______ **h** **H**? ______ **i** **I**? ______

Try to draw pictures of your own that show flip, slide or turn.

Turning patterns (rotational symmetry)

ACTIVITY

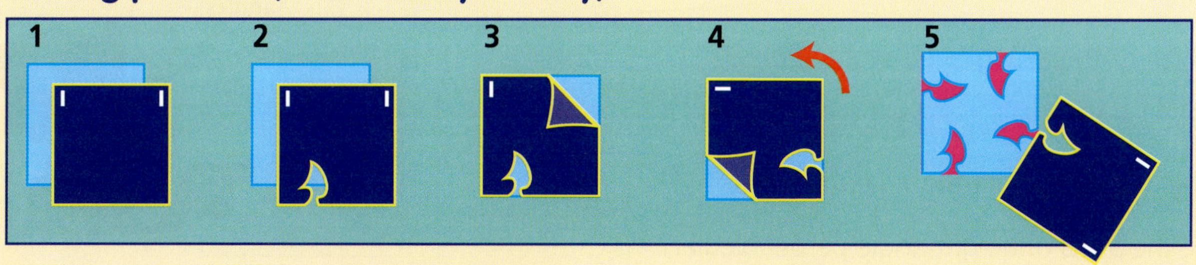

1 Use two identical cardboard squares.
2 From one side of square 1, cut out an interesting shape.
3 Put square 1 on top of the other square and trace the shape you have made.
4 Turn square 1 and trace the shape onto each side of the other square.
5 Colour the pattern you have made.
Make other patterns starting with:
a two regular hexagons **b** two regular octagons

See *Extra Support 3* (Tangrams) and *Extra Support 4* (Flip, slide, turn).

4:02 Angles and 2D shapes

The size of an angle is the amount of turn from one arm to the other.

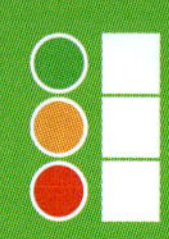

1

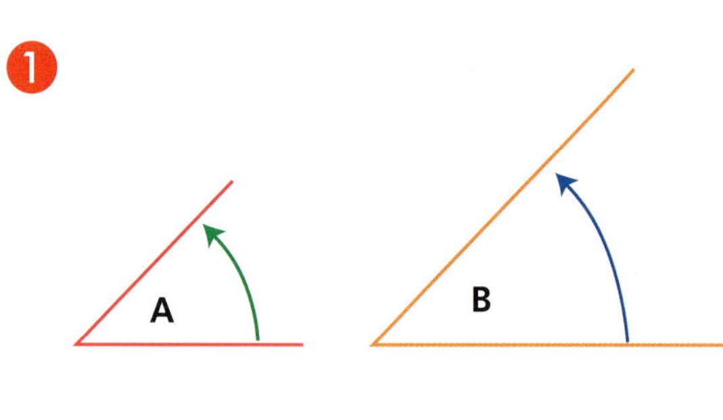

a Are these angles the same size?

b Does an angle get bigger if you make its arms longer?

c The angle at the corner of a page is called a **right angle**. Is angle **B** bigger than a right angle?

2

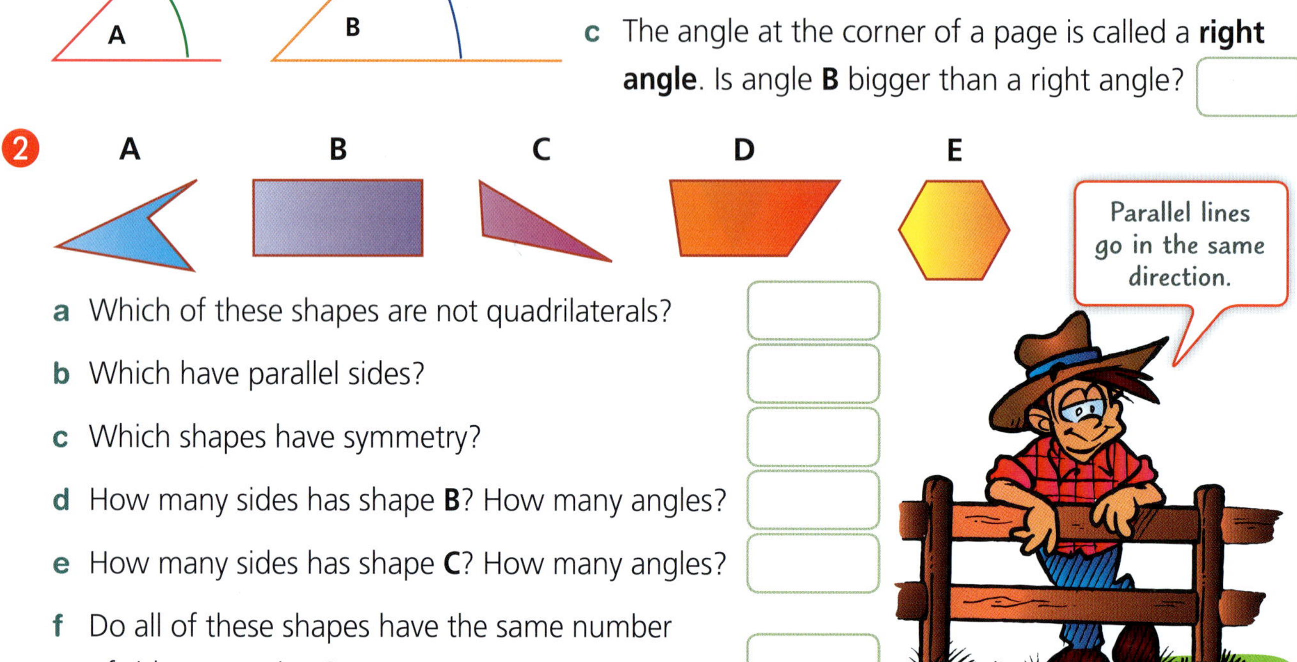

a Which of these shapes are not quadrilaterals?

b Which have parallel sides?

c Which shapes have symmetry?

d How many sides has shape **B**? How many angles?

e How many sides has shape **C**? How many angles?

f Do all of these shapes have the same number of sides as vertices?

3 Use the corner of a sheet of paper to test these angles.

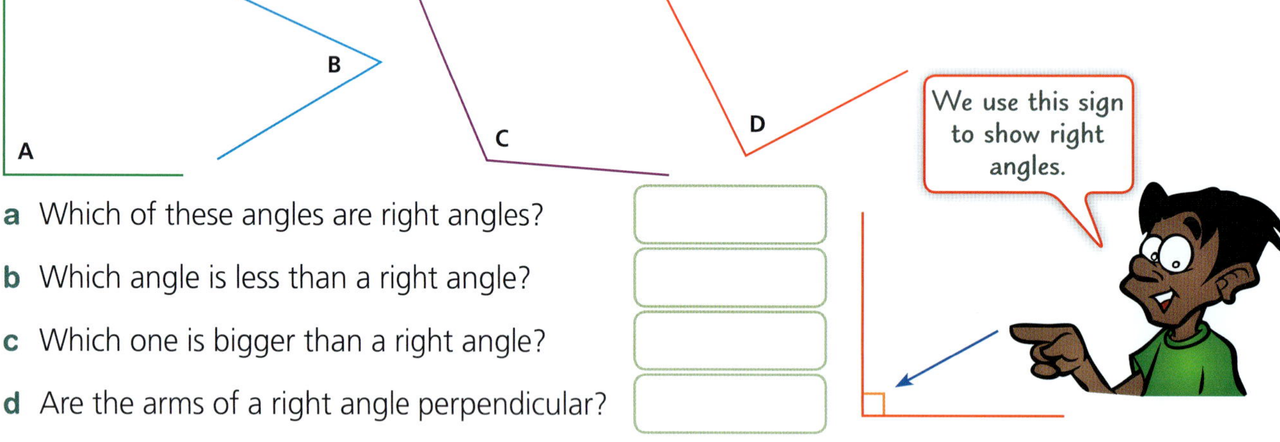

a Which of these angles are right angles?

b Which angle is less than a right angle?

c Which one is bigger than a right angle?

d Are the arms of a right angle perpendicular?

4 On your own paper, use a pencil and ruler to draw or trace:

a a square **b** a rectangle **c** a pentagon **d** a trapezium

e a right angle **f** an angle smaller than a right angle

5 Which triangle has:

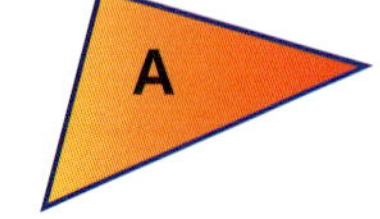

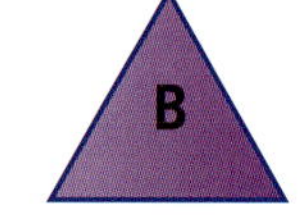

a all sides equal?

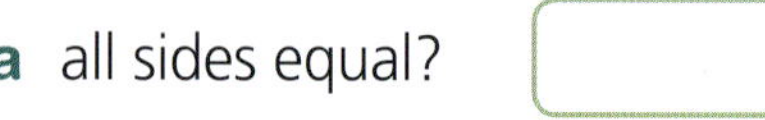

b two sides equal?

c no sides equal?

d a right angle?

 • *AUSTRALIAN SIGNPOST MATHS NSW 4* • ISBN 9780655709053

4:03 Comparing angles

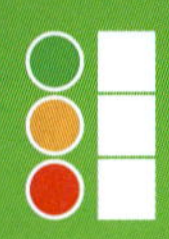

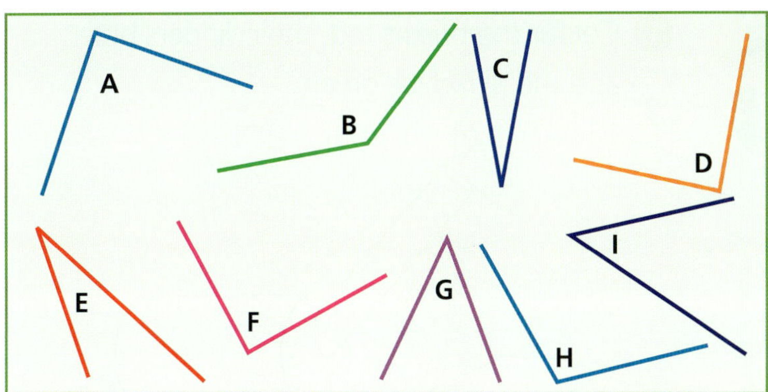

1 Use the corner of a page to test the angles above.
Put the letter of each angle in the correct column.

My angle (right angle)	Smaller	The same	Larger

2 Which angle is smaller:

a **A** or **B**? ☐ **b** **C** or **D**? ☐ **c** **E** or **F**? ☐ **d** **G** or **H**? ☐

3 Fold your paper right angle to make half a right angle. Use this new angle to test the angles at the top of the page. Put the letter of each angle in the correct column.

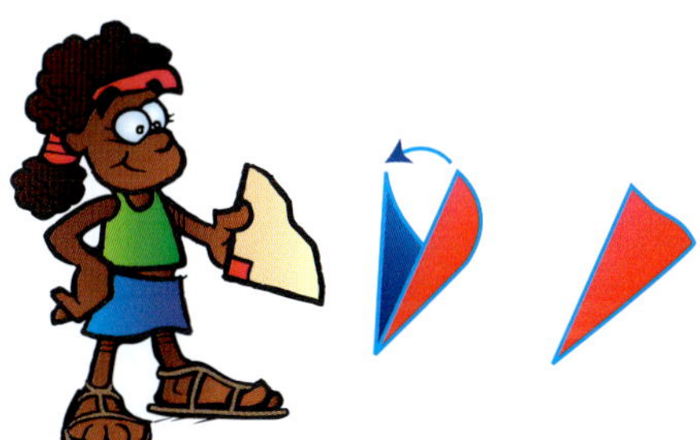

Half of a right angle	Smaller	The same	Larger

4 Draw each angle showing both arms and the vertex.

a the opening of a gate

vertex

b the slope of a road

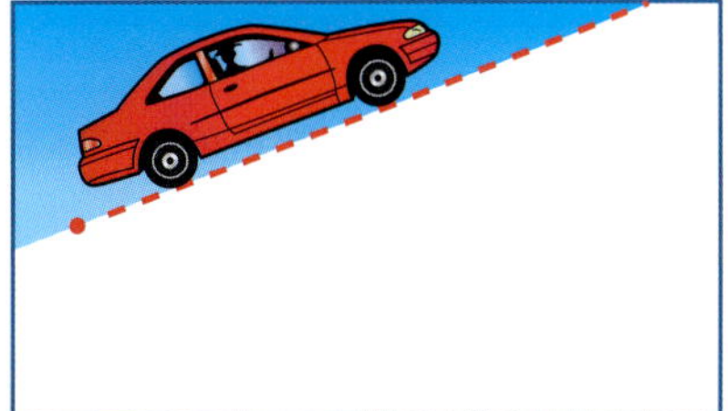

c the swing of a bat

ACTIVITY

Name an angle in your classroom that is:

- smaller than a right angle ______
- greater than a right angle ______

Use computer software to create simple shapes that involve direction and angles.

 ISBN 9780655709053

4:04 3D objects

Are the cross-sections that are parallel to the base, the same size and shape as the base?

Prisms have:
- ends that are the same shape
- sides that are rectangles.

Cylinders have:
- ends that are circles
- one curved surface.

1 Colour the prisms red, the cylinders blue and the pyramids green.

- What shapes are the surfaces of the objects in Question 1? Discuss.

2

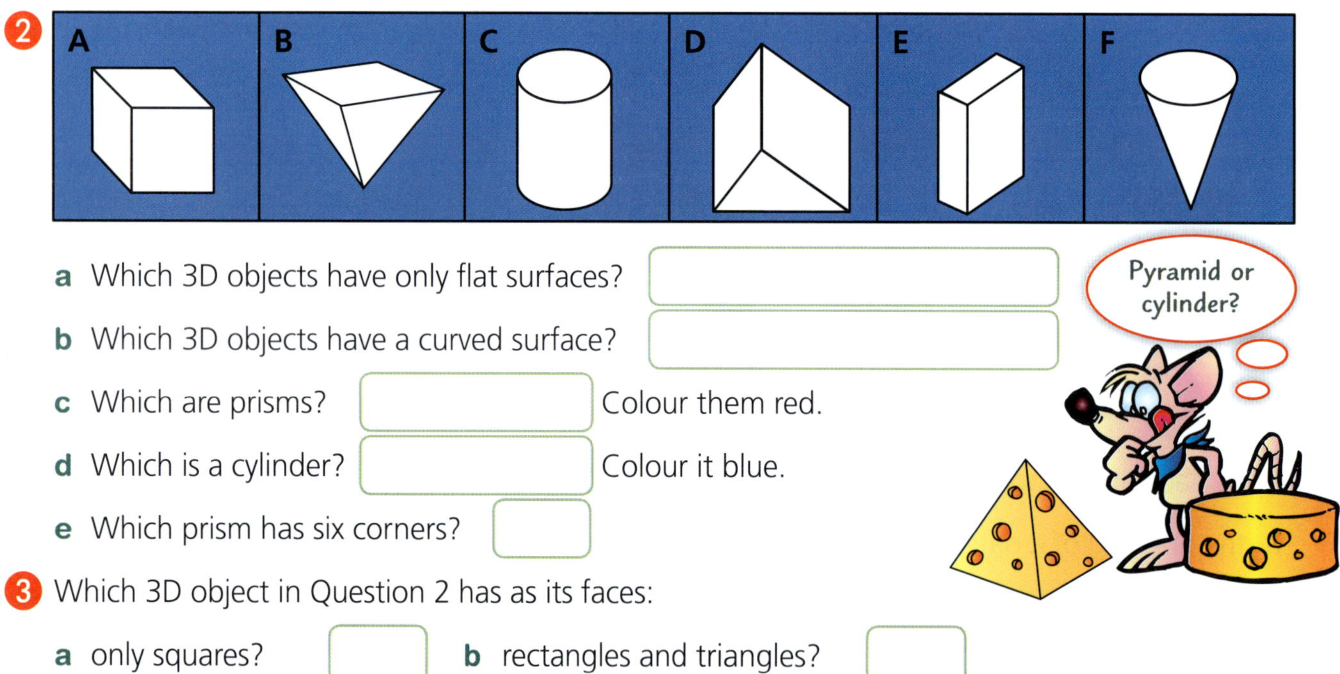

a Which 3D objects have only flat surfaces?

b Which 3D objects have a curved surface?

c Which are prisms? Colour them red.

d Which is a cylinder? Colour it blue.

e Which prism has six corners?

3 Which 3D object in Question 2 has as its faces:

a only squares?

b rectangles and triangles?

c only rectangles?

d triangles and a square?

INVESTIGATION

Make a list of real-life objects that are prisms.

4:05 Prisms and pyramids

A face is a flat surface that has straight sides.

1 Which of these 3D objects are:

a prisms?

b pyramids?

Which shapes have:

c a square base?

d a rectangular base?

e a triangular base?

f a hexagonal base?

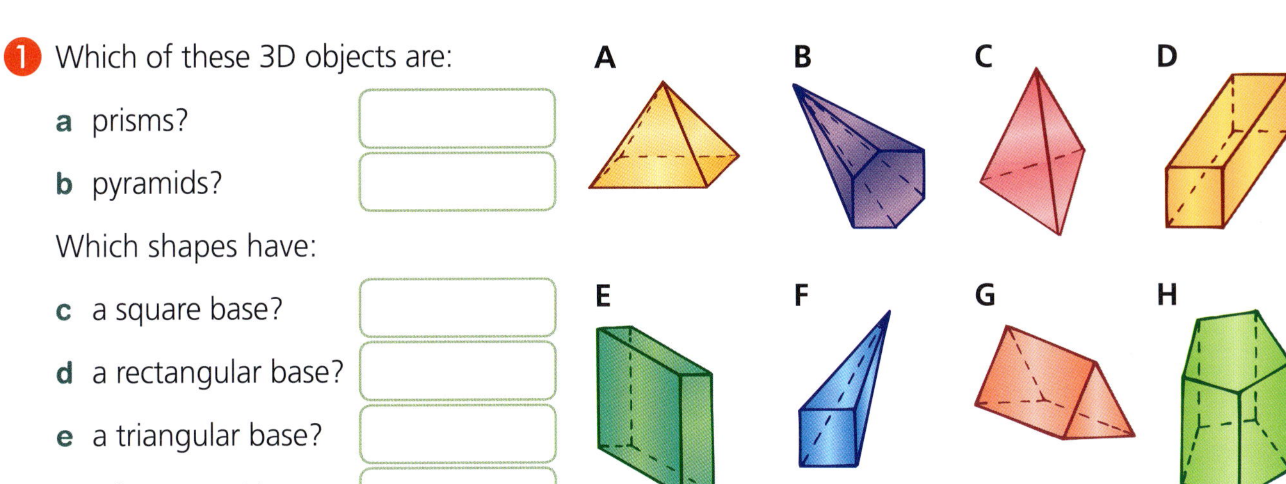

2 These models have been made by class 4B.

A

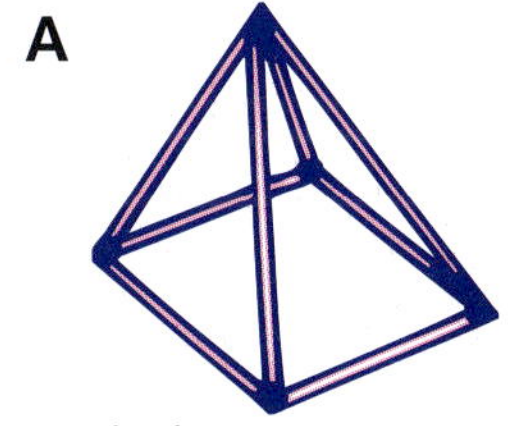

A skeleton made of straws and Plasticine.

B

Plasticine modelled to make the solid.

C

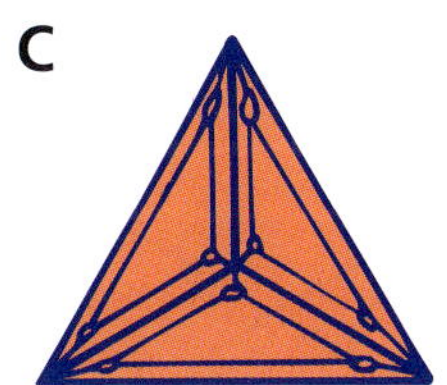

Cardboard shapes joined by elastic bands.

D

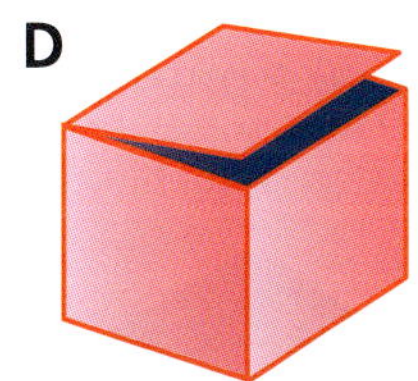

A folded net made of paper.

E

Plastic shapes fitted together.

Name the 3D object modelled in:

a A

b B

c C

d D

e E

ACTIVITY

- Choose at least two of the methods above to model:
  - a cube
  - a pyramid
  - a prism
- Try to make more prisms and pyramids using these methods.

ICT

Use 2D and 3D shapes from a computer program to make a poster.

Faces of prisms and pyramids

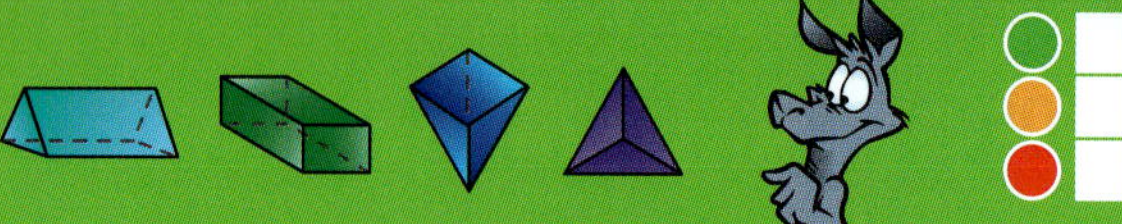

1 Would these faces make a prism (**A**) or a pyramid (**B**)?

a

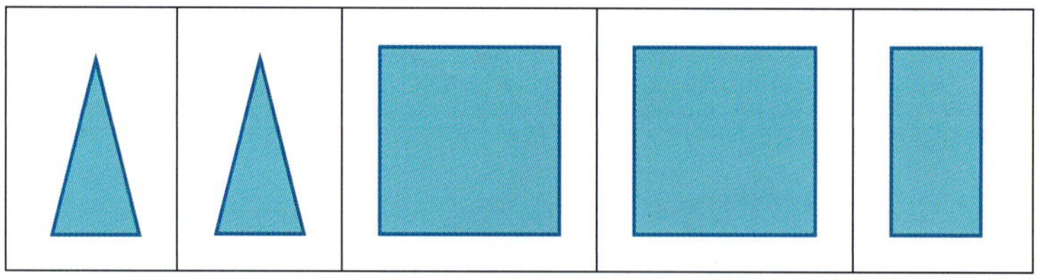

b

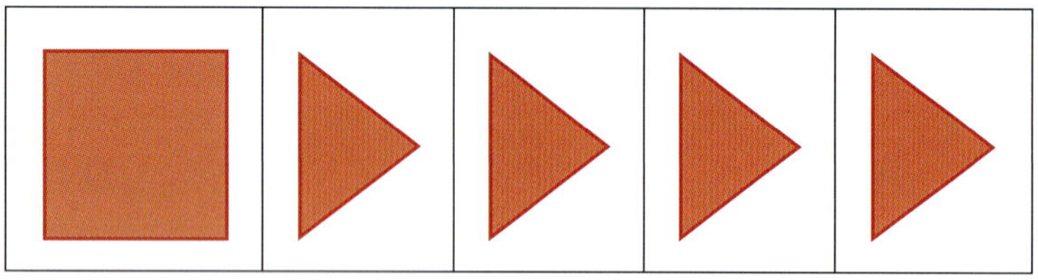

c

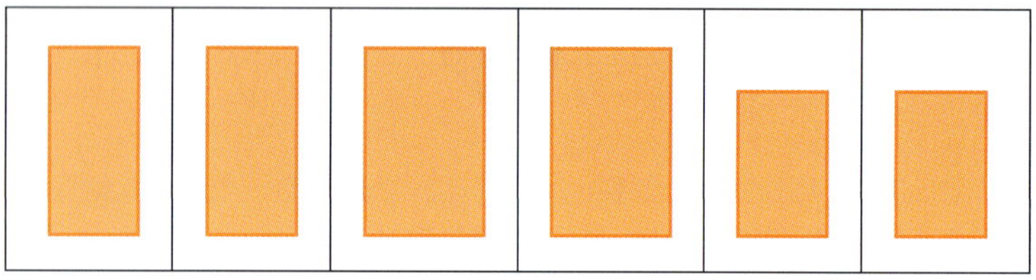

d

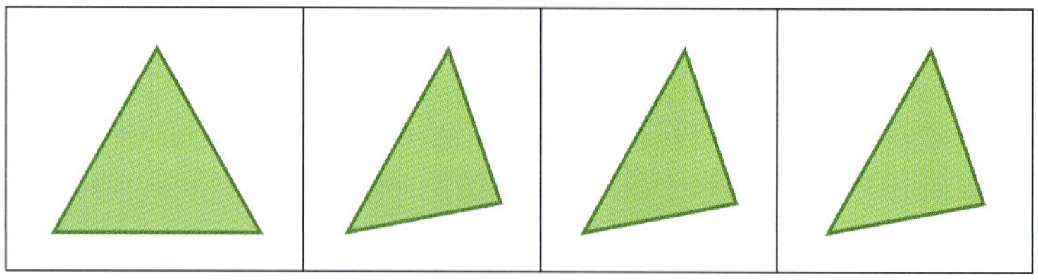

- The ends of a prism are the same shape and size. They are called bases. The other faces are rectangles.
- A pyramid has one base. The other faces are triangles.

We like pyramids and prisms.

2 Would these nets make prisms or pyramids? Discuss the reasons for your answers.

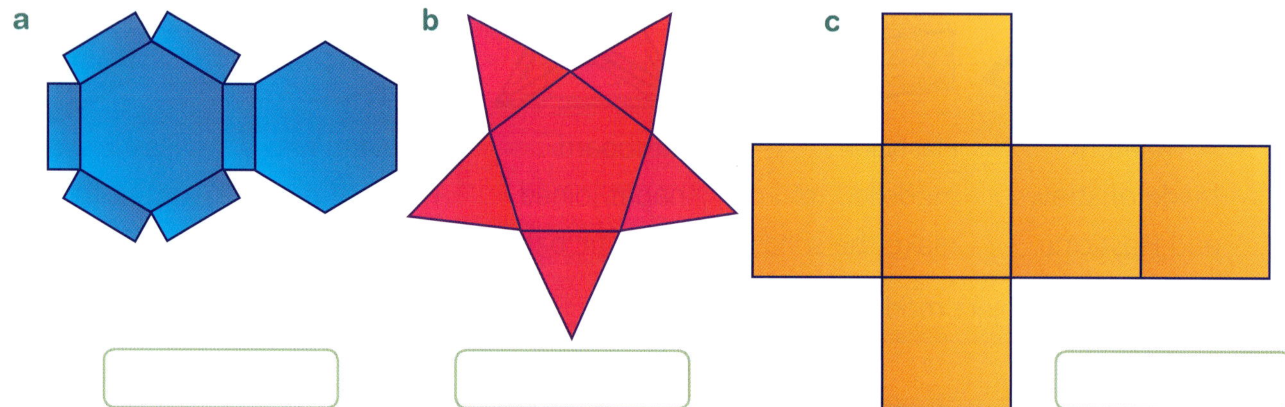

ACTIVITY

- Use cardboard nets or plastic interlocking shapes to make a model of:
  - a prism
  - a cube
  - a pyramid.

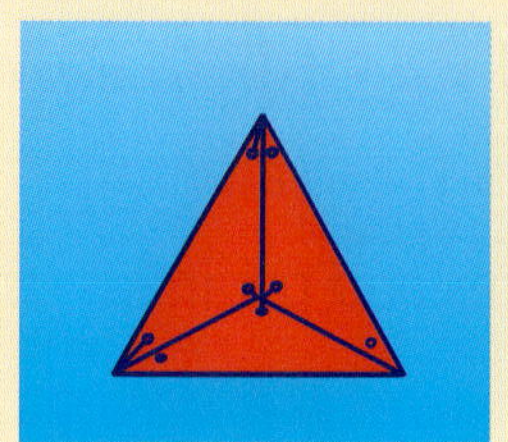

Prisms and pyramids

Is my cash register a prism?

A

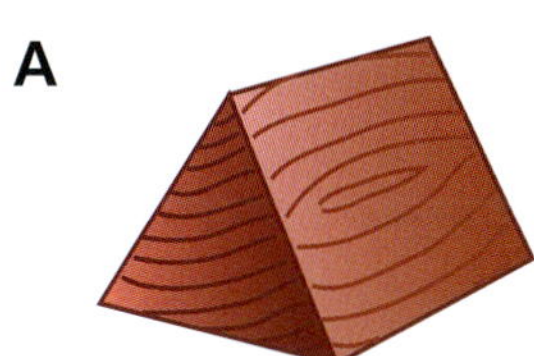

B

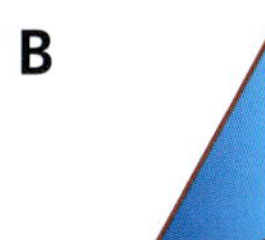

C

D

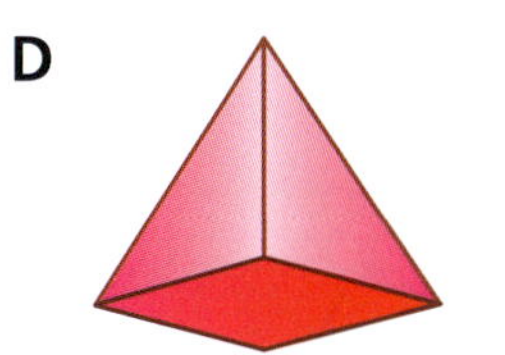

E

F

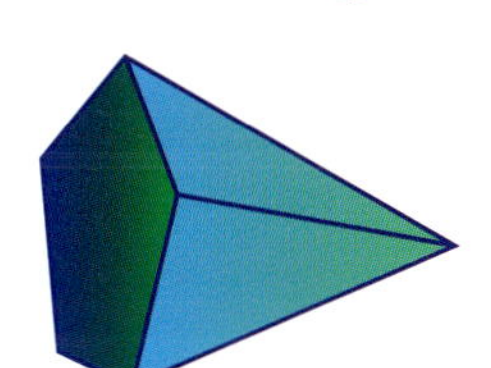

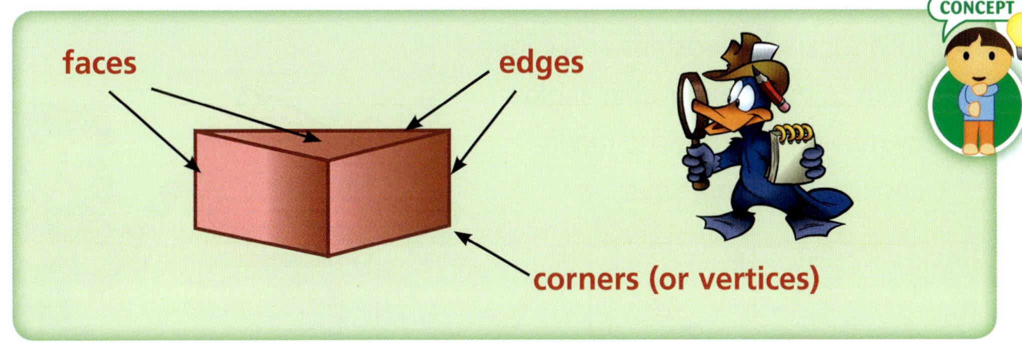

1 Complete the table to describe these 3D objects.

	Name of the object	Number of faces	Number of corners	Number of edges
A				
B				
C				
D				
E				
F				

2 Use this grid paper to complete the drawings of these 3D objects.

pyramid prism prism

ACTIVITY

- Some prisms and pyramids can be drawn using parallel lines.

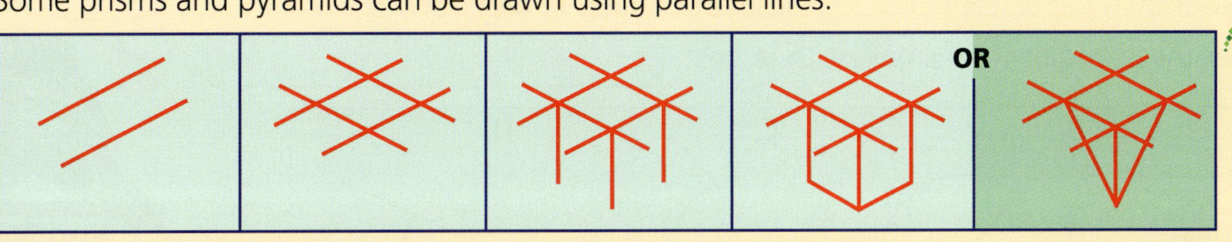

Step 1 Draw two pairs of parallel lines which cross.

Step 2 Draw three lines of equal length straight down from the corners. Join the ends to get a prism.

OR Choose a point in the middle below (or above) the figure. Draw lines from three corners to this point to get the pyramid.

- Use this method to draw: • five prisms • five pyramids

 • *AUSTRALIAN SIGNPOST MATHS NSW 4* • ISBN 9780655709053

4:08 Drawing angles

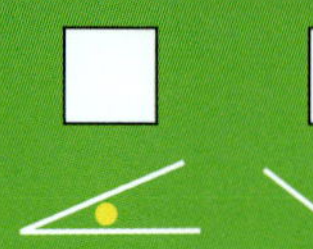
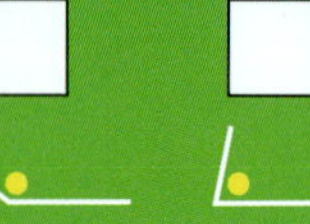

Write 1, 2, 3 for smallest to largest.

CONCEPT

- Julia took two geostrips and joined them to make a movable angle.
- By moving its arms, she made angles of different sizes.

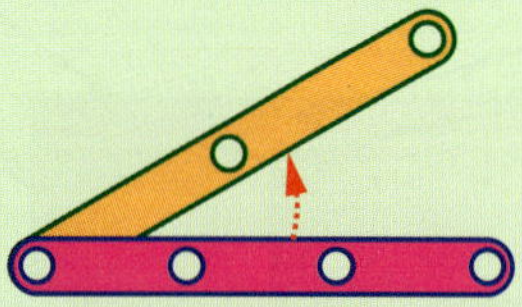

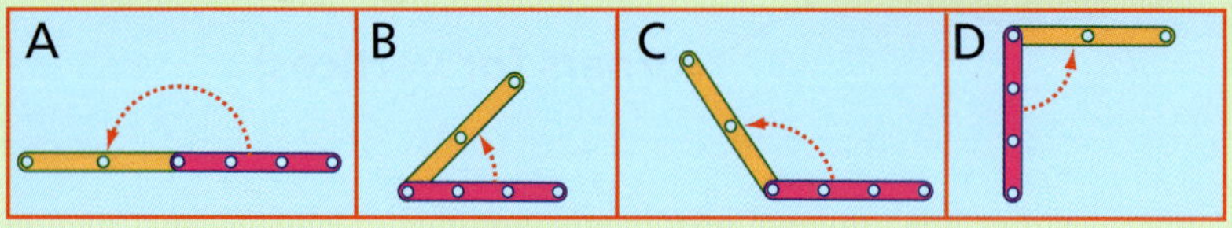

A B C D

This is a right angle.

A right angle is a square corner.

1. Geostrips were used to make the angles in **A**, **B**, **C** and **D** above. Which is the larger angle:

   a **A** or **B**? ______ **b** **B** or **C**? ______

   c **C** or **D**? ______ **d** **A** or **C**? ______

   e Which angle is a right angle? ______

The size of an angle is the amount of turning between its arms.

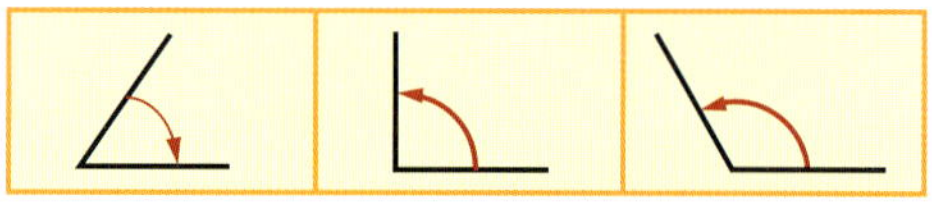

2. Trace these angles.

   a the corner of a book **b** blades of scissors **c** your choice

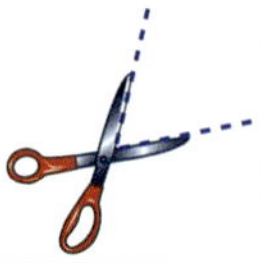

3. What is a right angle? ______

The angle made by my open book is a straight angle.

4. On your own paper, copy or trace these four angles in order of size.
   Order these angles from smallest to largest. ______

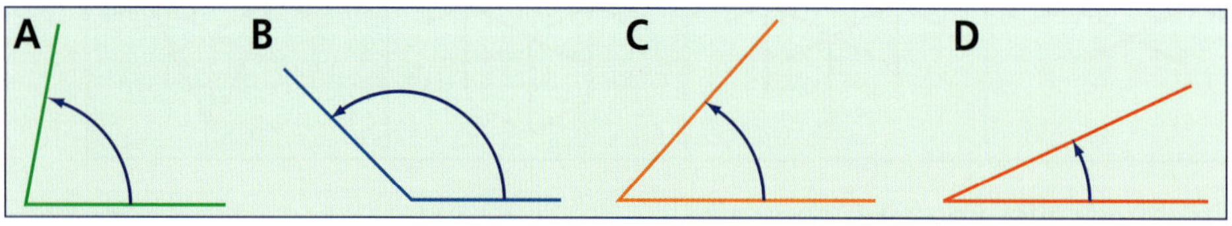

   A B C D

ACTIVITY

- Describe two angles in the room. Identify the smallest and the largest.

 • *AUSTRALIAN SIGNPOST MATHS NSW 4* • ISBN 9780655709053

Angles as quarter and half turns

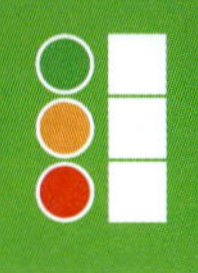

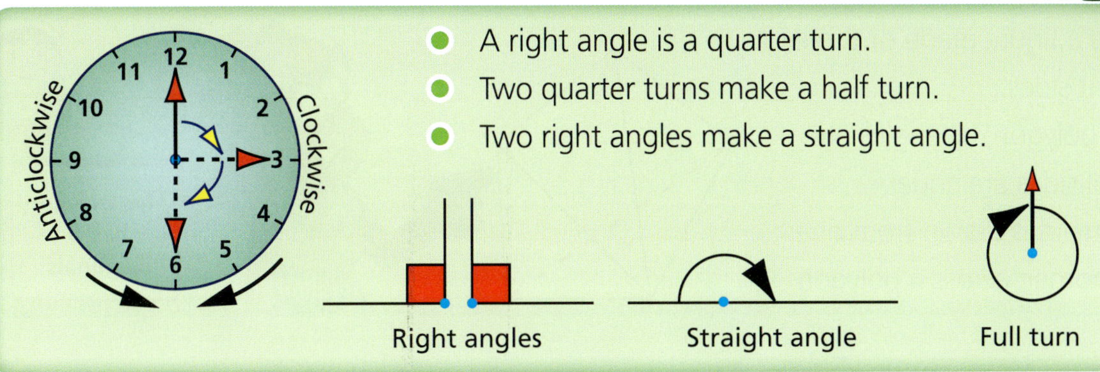

- A right angle is a quarter turn.
- Two quarter turns make a half turn.
- Two right angles make a straight angle.

1 Draw an angle that represents:

a quarter turn	a half turn	a full turn
•	•	•

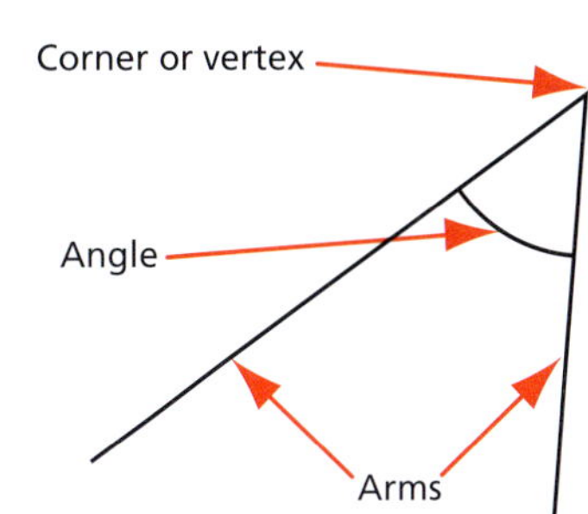

2 When turning the minute hand on a clock:

a a half turn anticlockwise is the same as ______ clockwise.

b a three-quarter turn anticlockwise is the same as ______ clockwise.

c two quarter turns clockwise is the same as ______ anticlockwise.

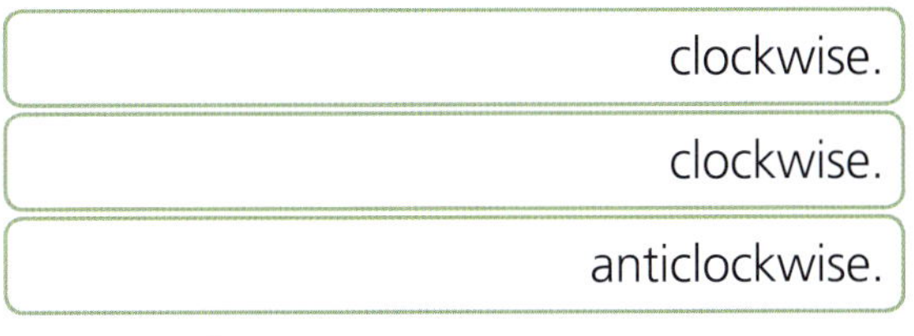

3 a How many quarter turns make a full turn? ______

b How many right angles make a full turn? ______

c How many right angles make a straight angle? ______

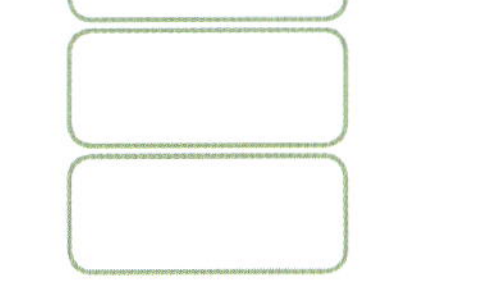

4

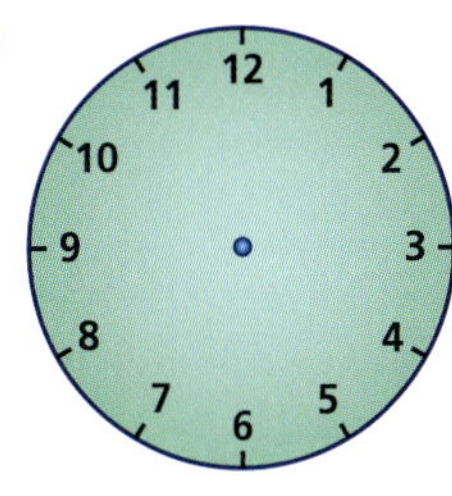

a Using the centre of the clock as the vertex of the angles, how many right angles can you draw at one time that do not overlap or share an arm? ______

b If each arm must point to a number on the clock, how many different right angles could be drawn? ______

- List places in real life that show:
  - right angles ______
  - straight angles ______
  - full turns. ______

 • *AUSTRALIAN SIGNPOST MATHS NSW 4* • ISBN 9780655709053

4:10 Investigating polygons

Polygon is a Greek word meaning 'many sides'.

- A polygon is a figure made of three or more straight sides.
- In a regular polygon, all angles are equal and all sides are equal.
- Diagonals are lines drawn from one corner to another, across a polygon.

1 **a** Draw all of the diagonals that can be drawn from the red dot in each shape.

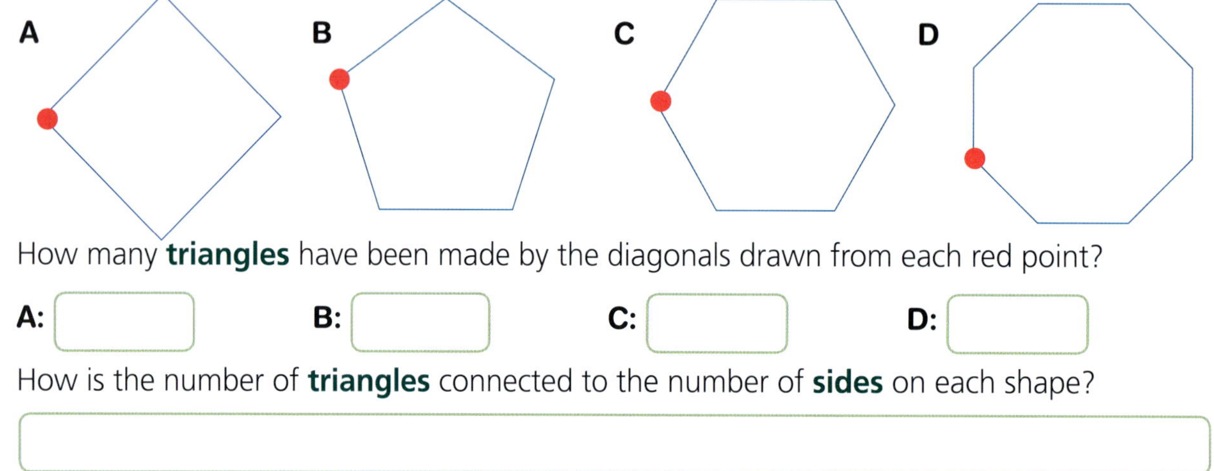

How many **triangles** have been made by the diagonals drawn from each red point?

A: ______ B: ______ C: ______ D: ______

How is the number of **triangles** connected to the number of **sides** on each shape?

______

b Draw all of the lines of symmetry on each regular shape. Use a ruler and pencil.

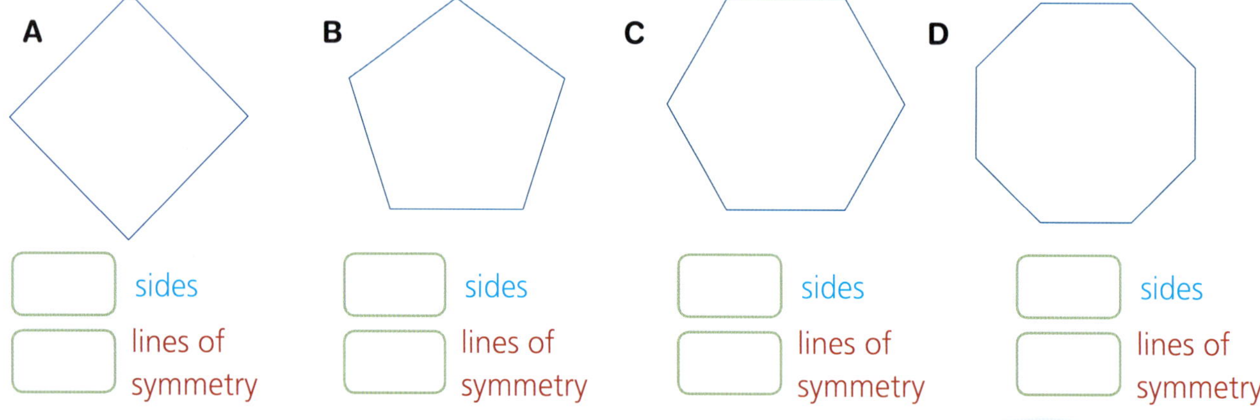

A	B	C	D
______ sides	______ sides	______ sides	______ sides
______ lines of symmetry	______ lines of symmetry	______ lines of symmetry	______ lines of symmetry

2 Complete this table for the regular shapes above.

Regular shape	Number of sides	Number of angles	Number of lines of symmetry
square			
pentagon			
hexagon			
octagon			

 • *AUSTRALIAN SIGNPOST MATHS NSW 4* • ISBN 9780655709053

4:11 Visualising shapes

These shapes are the same. I've turned one to get the other.

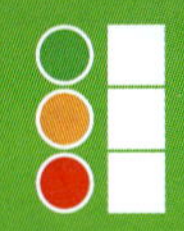

We can combine shapes in different ways.
Here a square and two triangles have been used.

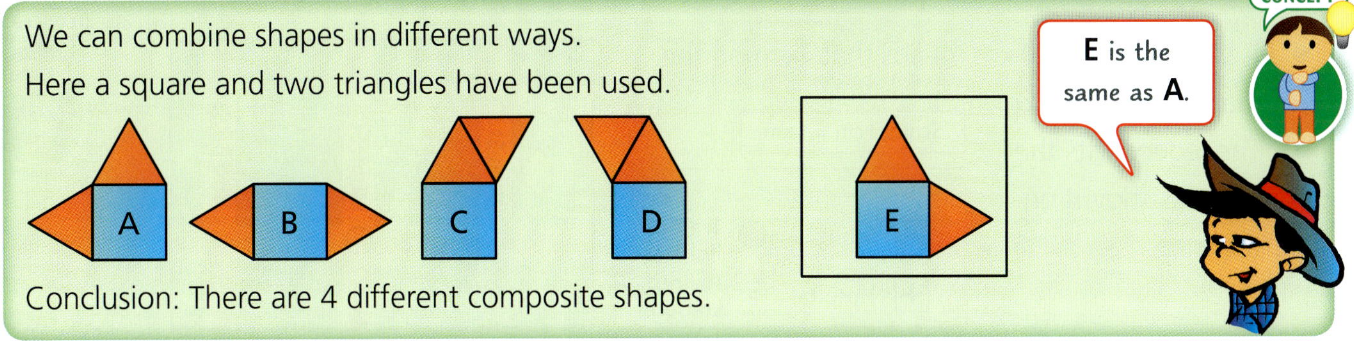

Conclusion: There are 4 different composite shapes.

1 **a** Draw as many different composite shapes (combinations) as you can using the two squares and the triangle. A combination is not different if it is turned.

b How many different combinations are possible using just three of the squares?

2

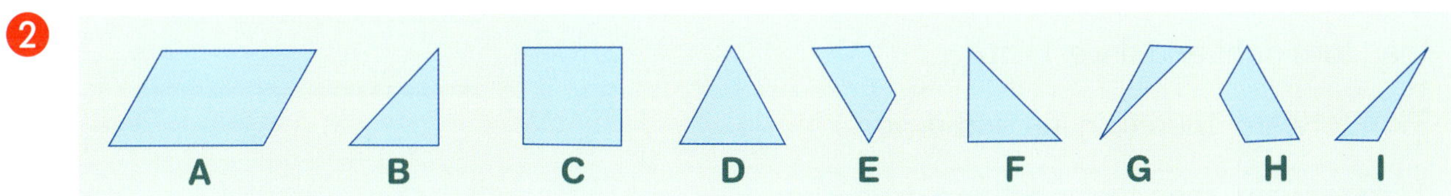

Two of these shapes have been used to make each shape below. Which shapes have been used?

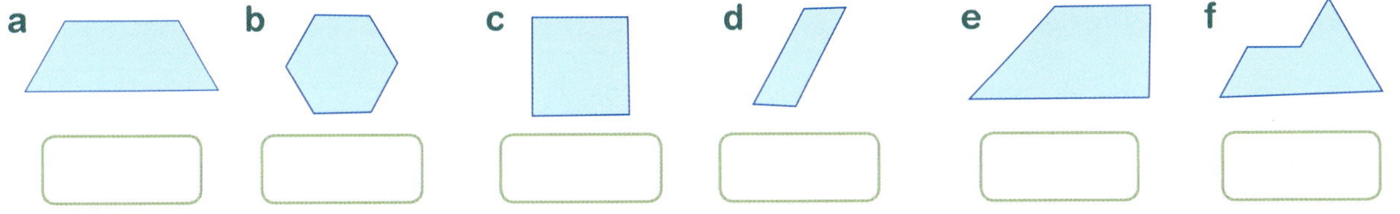

ACTIVITY

- Luna used pattern blocks to make these designs. Use pattern blocks to copy these designs, then make some of your own.
- Use isometric dot paper to copy the designs below.

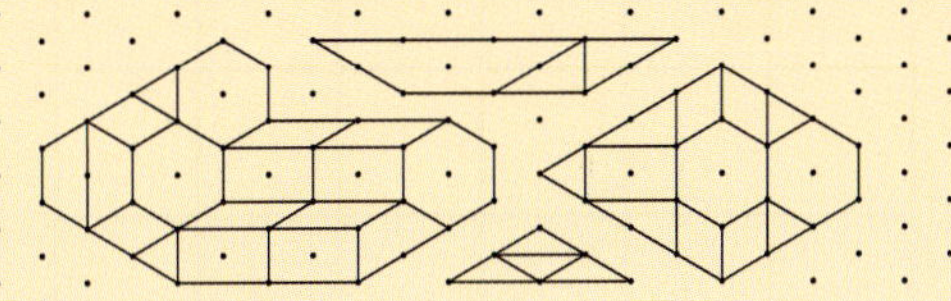

- Discuss: What shapes make the hexagon?

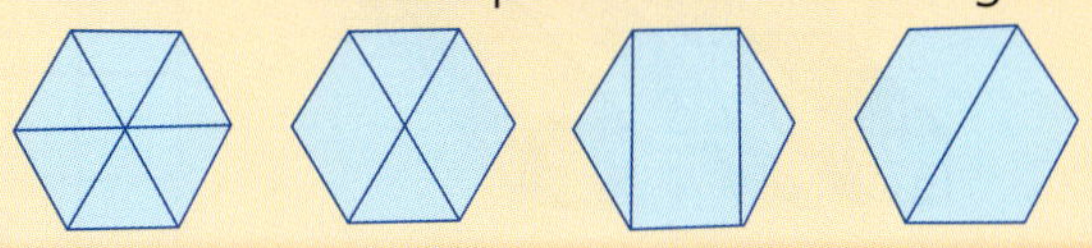

See *Extra Support 3* (Tangrams) and *Extra Support 4* (Flip, slide, turn).

4:12 Maps

When we look at a map we have a 'bird's-eye view'.

CONCEPT

- A scale of 1 cm = 1 km means that 1 cm on the map represents 1 km.
- The legend lists the features shown on the map.

Scale: 1 cm = 1 km

Legend
- School
- Traffic lights
- Hospital
- Police station

N

Meg St, Warn St, Munn St, Joseph St, March St

1 On which street on the map above would you find the:

a school? ______ **b** traffic lights? ______

c hospital? ______ **d** police station? ______

What special feature would you find on:

e Warn St? ______ **f** Joseph St? ______

g Meg St? ______ **h** March St? ______

2 Starting at the red arrow position, where will you be if you drive:

a 1 km forward, then turn left and drive 2 km, then turn right and drive 1 km? ______

b 3 km forward, then turn left and drive 1 km? ______

c 1 km forward, then turn right and drive 2 km, then turn left and drive 2 km? ______

3 Where are the traffic lights? ______

4 **a** How far is it from the school to the police station? ______

b How far is it from the school to the hospital? ______

ACTIVITY

- Draw a map of the picture below using the scale 1 cm = 10 m and a legend.

SCHOOL
SHOPS
GYM

1cm = 10m

Scale

Legend

	School
	Gym
	Shops

 • *AUSTRALIAN SIGNPOST MATHS NSW 4* • ISBN 9780655709053

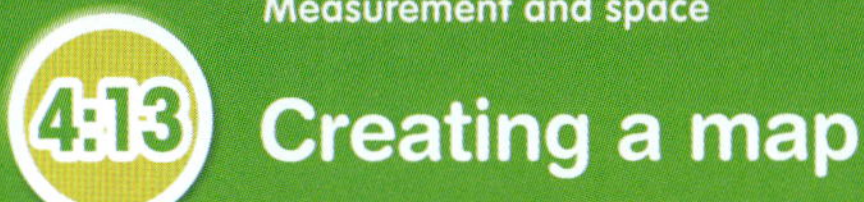

Measurement and space

4:13 Creating a map

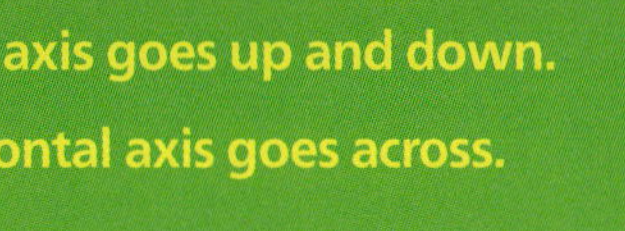

1. Use the scale 2 cm = 1 m to draw a map of your room. Make up your own legend and icons to represent the features of the room. First record the dimensions of the room.

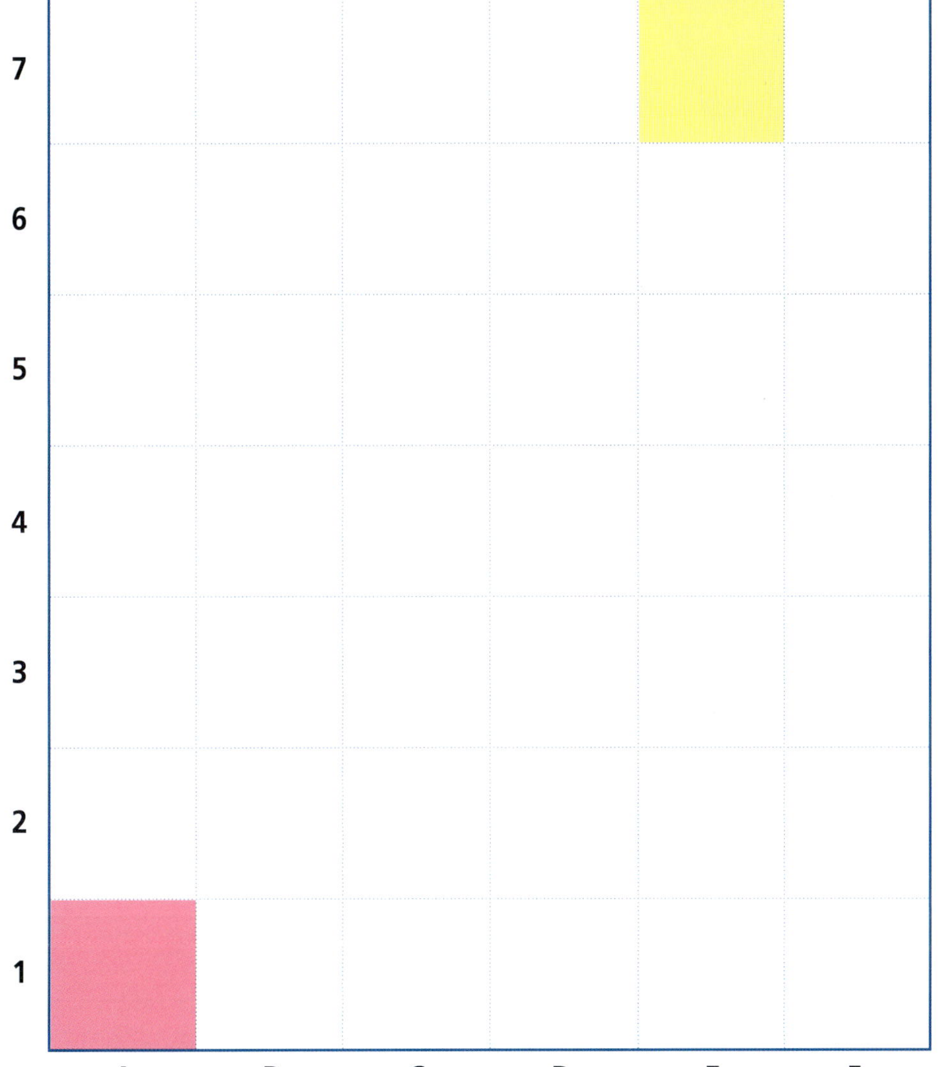

Scale

2 cm = 1 m

Legend

☒ desk

Grid references

- We call the yellow square E7.
- We call the pink square A1.

2. List the features in your room using grid references to describe where each feature is found.

4:14 Cones, cylinders and spheres

Why is the base of a cone not a face?

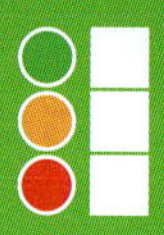

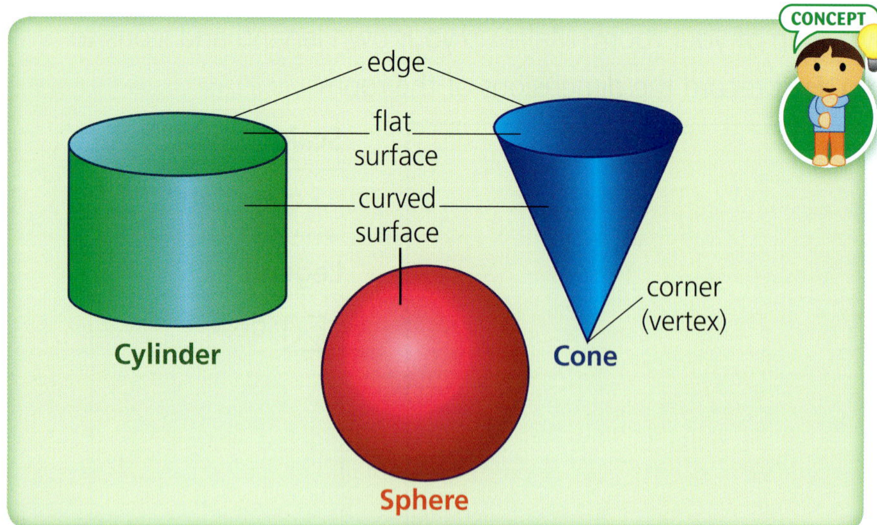

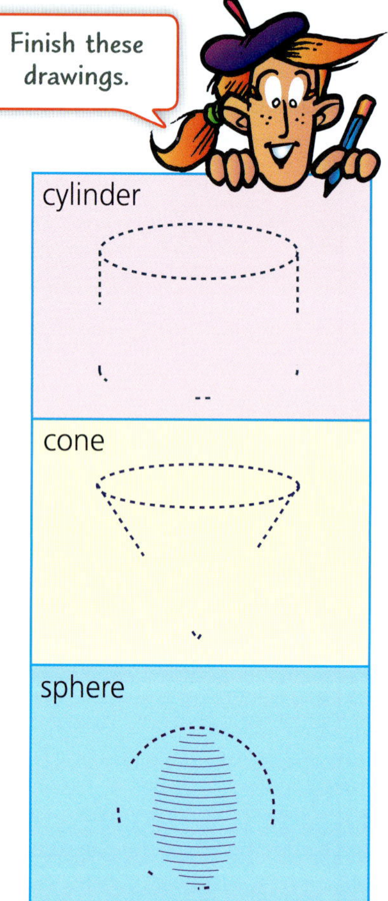

1 Use the pictures above to complete this table.

Shape	Number of surfaces	Number of corners	Number of edges
cylinder			
cone			
sphere			

2 What are some things that look like cylinders? List as many as you can.

3 What are some things that look like cones?

4 What are some things that look like spheres?

5 Write the name of each 3D object under its picture.

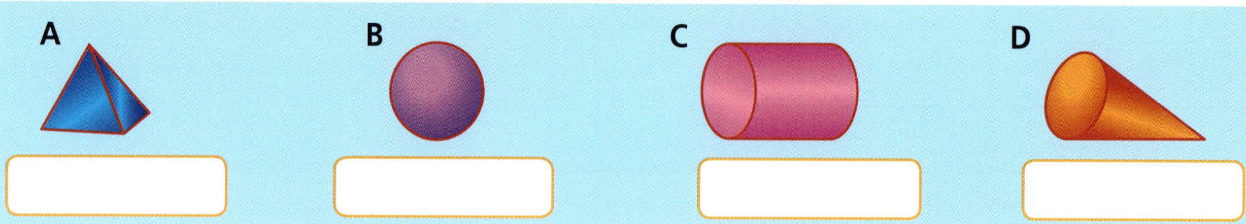

When we cut each 3D object parallel to its base, which of these have:

a uniform cross-sections (always the same)?

b cross-sections that are the same shape but different sizes?

 • *AUSTRALIAN SIGNPOST MATHS NSW 4* • ISBN 9780655709053

4:15 Views of 3D objects

Can you name the shapes made by each view in Question 2?

1 Draw the table and chair from the front, top and side.

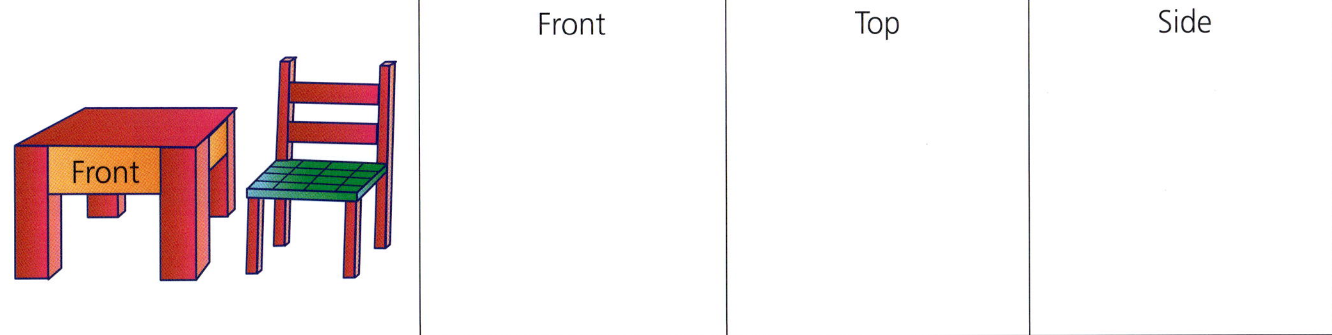

2 Join each set of pictures on the left to its 3D object on the right. Name each 3D object.

Top view	Front view	Side view		3D object	Name

3 Use blocks to make models of these prisms. Write down the number of blocks used in each model.

ACTIVITY

4 Use blocks to make the model in the picture. Study the model and:

a draw it from the top.

b draw it from the side.

side

front

How many blocks in the model show:

c 3 faces?

d 2 faces?

e 1 face?

f 4 faces?

4:16 Compasss directions

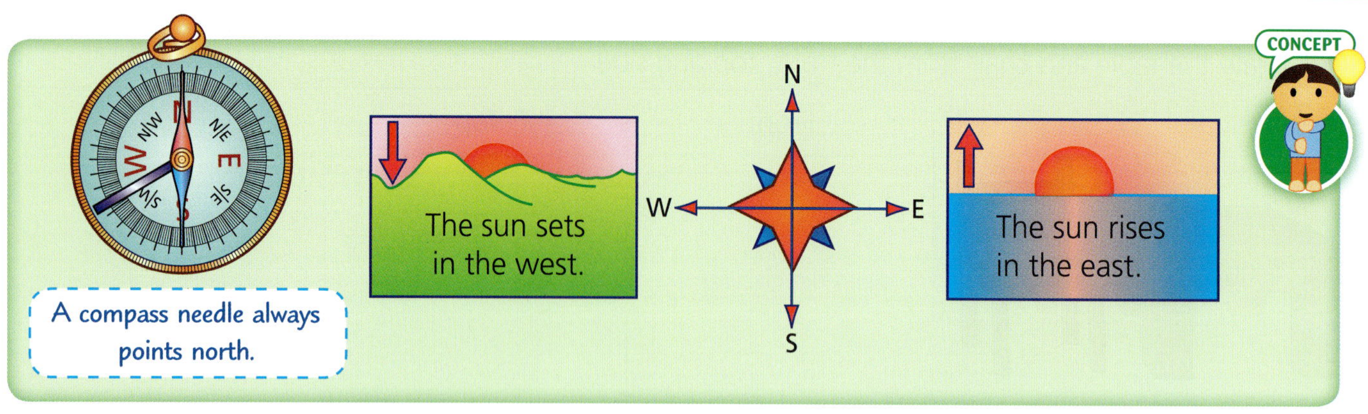

1. Write **north**, **south**, **east** and **west** around the map.

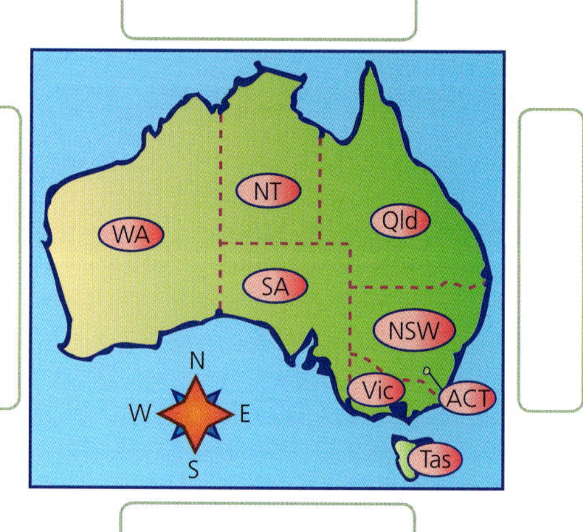

2. Write the full name for:
   - **a** WA
   - **b** NT
   - **c** SA

3. Write the names of the two largest states in the east.

4. Which landmark is:
   - **a** north of Bart's Cave?
   - **b** west of Queen Hill?
   - **c** south of Black Rock?
   - **d** west of Red Cove?
   - **e** south of Jake's Grave?
   - **f** east of Bart's Cave?
   - **g** north of Queen Hill?

5. Use the map in Question 4 to answer these questions.
   - **a** The treasure is buried east of Land's End and south of Queen Hill. Mark this spot on the map with an **X**.
   - **b** Our ship sank north of Land's End and west of Jake's Grave. Mark this spot on the map with an **S**.
   - **c** The captain broke his leg south of Bart's Cave and east of Land's End. Mark this spot on the map with a **C**.

4:17 Compass directions

We turn the compass until arrow is pointing to N (north).

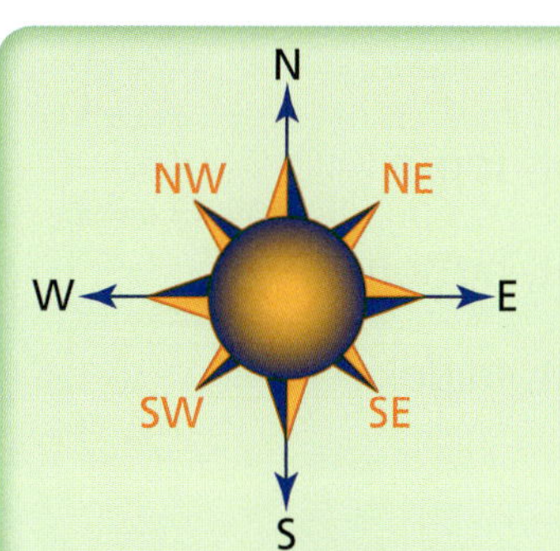

- North-east is halfway between north and east.
- North-west is halfway between north and west.
- South-east is halfway between south and east.
- South-west is halfway between south and west.

The needle of a compass points towards north.

West is a quarter turn to the left from north.

CONCEPT

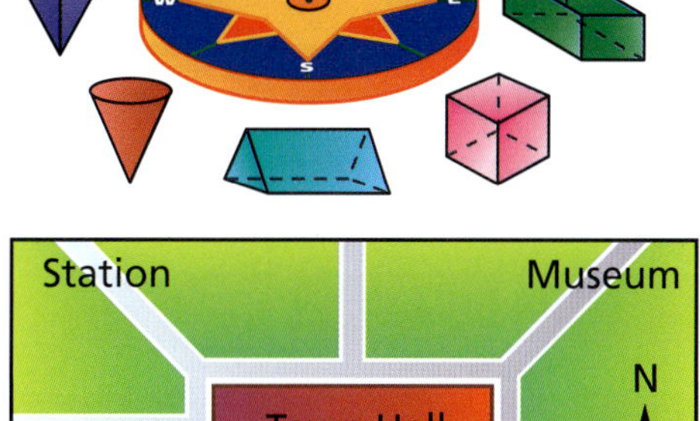

1 Around this compass, find which 3D object is:

- **a** east
- **b** west
- **c** south
- **d** north
- **e** north-east
- **f** south-west
- **g** south-east
- **h** north-west

2 On the map above, what place is:

- **a** north-east of Town Hall?
- **b** south-east of Town Hall?
- **c** south-west of Town Hall?
- **d** north-west of Town Hall?

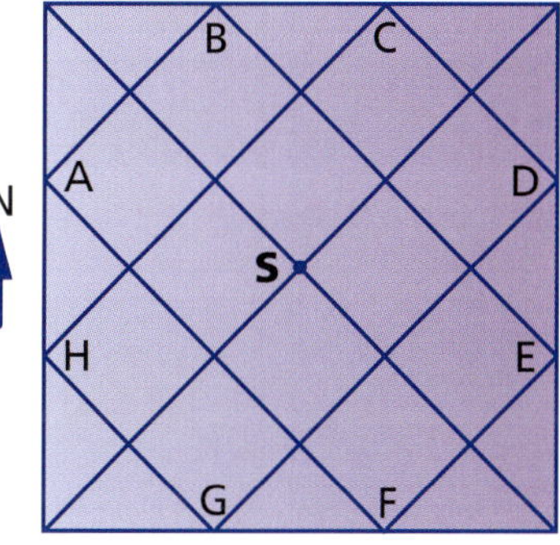

North, East, West, South = NEWS

3 Starting at **S**, where do you finish, if you travel:

- **a** 2 units north-west, then 1 unit south-west?
- **b** 1 unit south-east, then 2 units south-west?
- **c** 2 units north-east, then 1 unit south-east?
- **d** 1 unit south-west, then 2 units north-west?

4 Write directions to go from **S** to **E**.

 • *AUSTRALIAN SIGNPOST MATHS NSW 4* • ISBN 9780655709053

4:18 Describing position

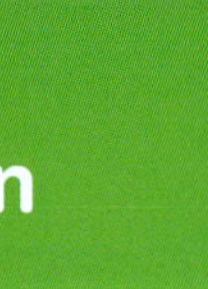

We usually give the column name first. 'Left, top row' gives 'pear'.

	left	right
top row	pear	carrot
middle row	apple	strawberry
bottom row	cherries	banana

1 Name the food in the box that is:

a left, bottom ______ b right, top ______
c left, middle ______ d right, bottom ______
e left, top ______ f right, middle ______

Write down the position of the:

g apple ______ h strawberry ______
i cherries ______ j pear ______
k carrot ______ l banana ______

2 These are desks in a classroom.
Name the person in:

	1	2	3	4
blue	Tom	Sophie	Rex	Peter
red	Ruby	Kate	Ethan	Chris
green	Georgia	Rocco	Ben	Oscar

a column one, red row ______
b column three, blue row ______
c column one, blue row ______
d column four, red row ______
e 2, blue ______ f 3, red ______ g 1, green ______ h 4, green ______

3 Write down the column number and row letter for the:

a rectangle ______
b square ______
c hexagon ______
d triangle ______
e circle ______
f prism ______
g pyramid ______
h cone ______
i net ______
j pentagon ______
k rhombus ______
l trapezium ______
m right angle ______ n parallel lines ______

	1	2	3	4	5
D					
C					
B					
A					

4:19 Using position in maps

One grid reference could contain a part of both states.

1 What town can be found in:

a column 2, 5th row?

b column 6, 2nd row?

c column 4, 5th row?

d column 2, 1st row?

e column 2, 3rd row?

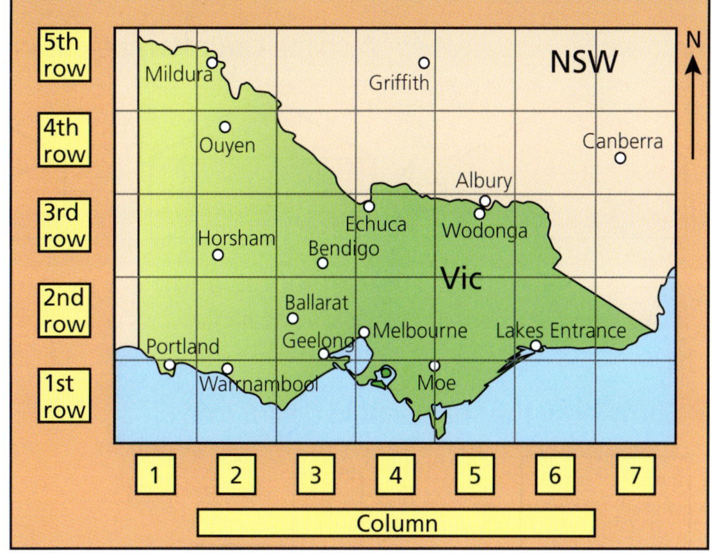

f Which town is north of Melbourne?

2 Using the map in Question 1, give the position of the box where you find:

a Melbourne

b Echuca

c Geelong

d Ballarat

e Portland

f Wodonga

g Bendigo

h Ouyen

i Which boxes show part of Moe?

j Which town is west of Wodonga and north of Melbourne?

k Which town is east of Echuca and in New South Wales?

l Which town is west of Griffith but in Victoria?

3 On the grid to the right draw:

a a rectangle in C2

b an oval in A3

c a square in A1

d a triangle in C3

e a rhombus in B2

f an octagon in B1

g a trapezium in A2

h a parallelogram in B3

i a pentagon in C1

3			
2			
1			
	A	B	C

 • *AUSTRALIAN SIGNPOST MATHS NSW 4* • ISBN 9780655709053

4:20 Visualising shapes

Use a ruler and a pencil to show how each shape can be cut.

CONCEPT

A shape can often be cut into other shapes.

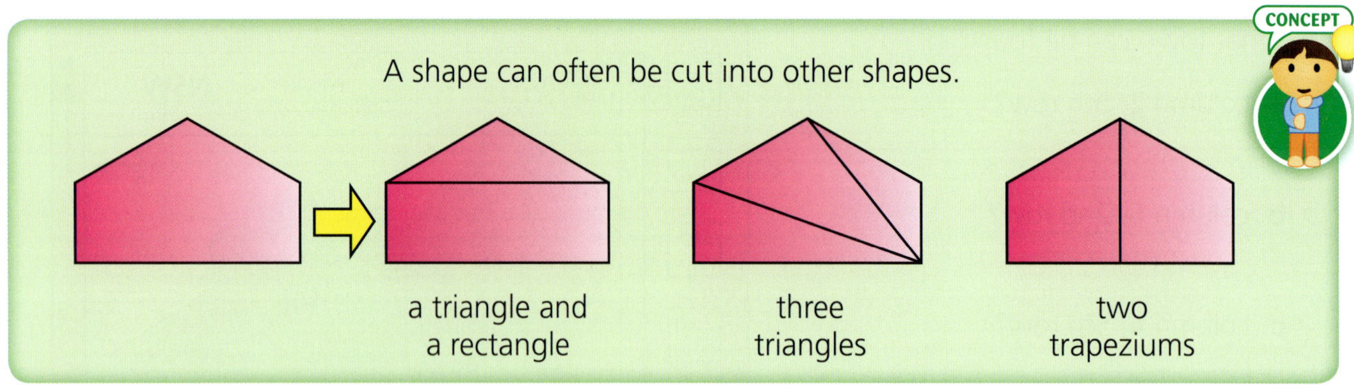

a triangle and a rectangle | three triangles | two trapeziums

1. Show how the shape could be cut into:

2 triangles

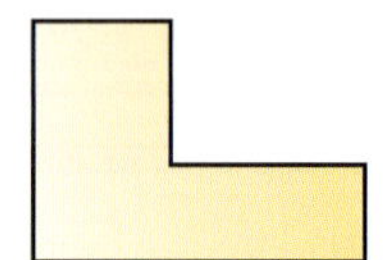
a square and a rectangle

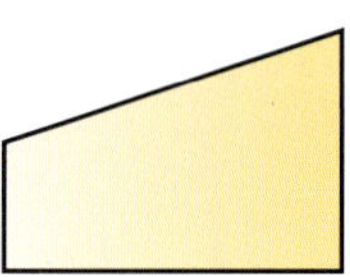
a triangle and a rectangle

5 squares

2. Draw lines only from the vertices (corners) to make 3 triangles.

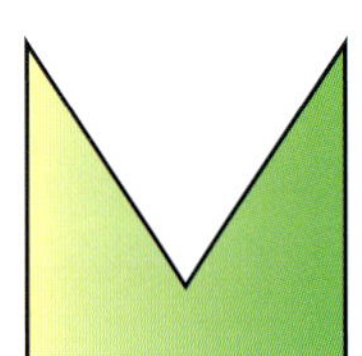

3. Show how the shape could be cut into:

4 triangles and a square

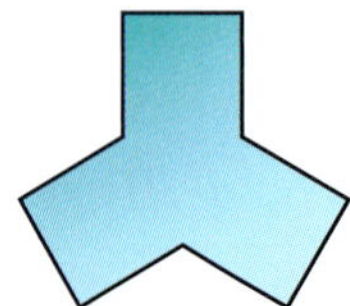
a triangle and 3 squares

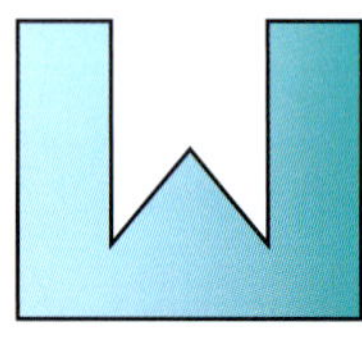
3 rectangles and a triangle

4. Circle all of the shapes in Questions 1 and 2 that have line symmetry.
On square dot paper, draw three shapes that have line symmetry.

ACTIVITY

- Use the grids to draw symmetrical patterns using dots like the picture on the left.

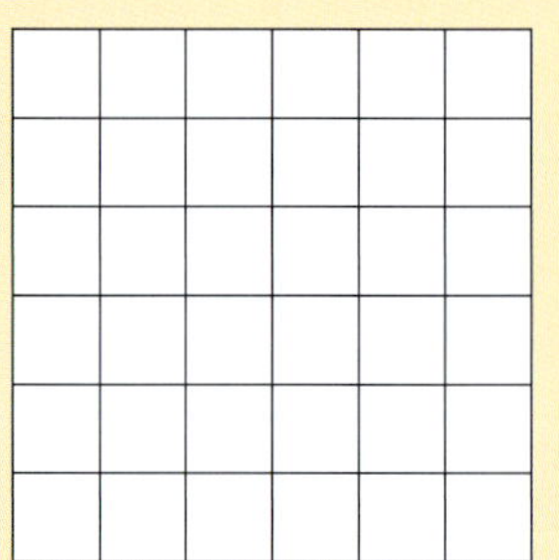

See *Extra Support 3* (Tangrams) and *Extra Support 4* (Flip, slide, turn).

Acute and obtuse angles

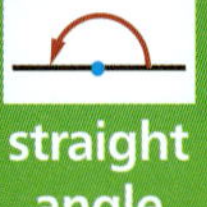
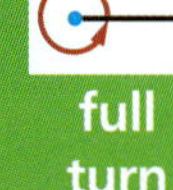
right angle · straight angle · full turn

acute

obtuse

- An angle that is less than a right angle is called an **acute angle**.
- An angle that is larger than a right angle but smaller than a straight angle is called an **obtuse angle**.

1 Which of these angles are:

a right angles?

b acute angles?

c obtuse angles?

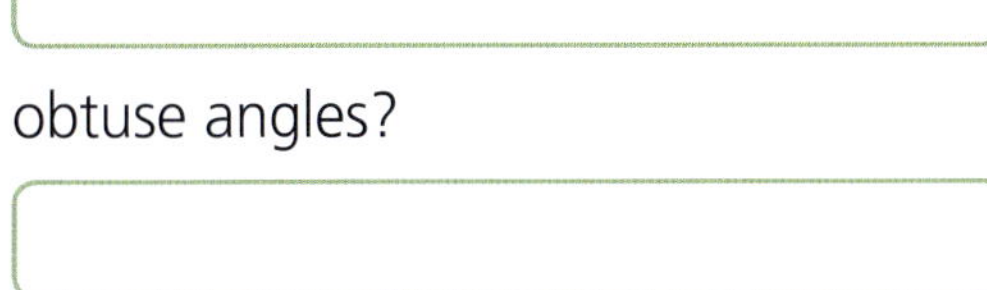
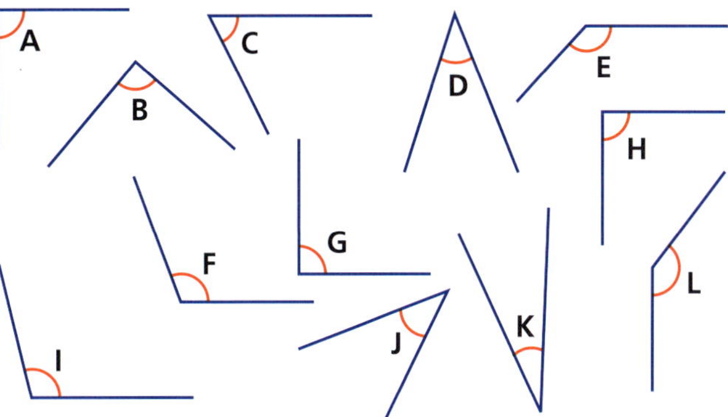

2 Place in order from smallest angle to largest angle:

a **A**, **C** and **D**
b **D**, **E** and **G**
c **F**, **J** and **H**
d **B**, **K** and **L**
e **C**, **G** and **K**
f **G**, **F** and **L**

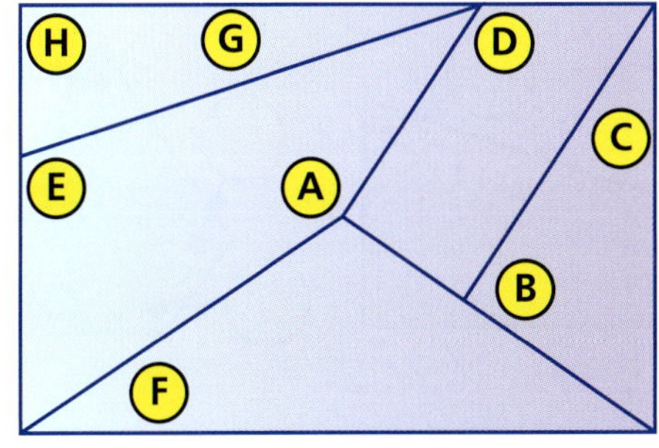

3 Name each angle as acute, right or obtuse.

a A
b B
c C
d D
e E
f F
g G
h H

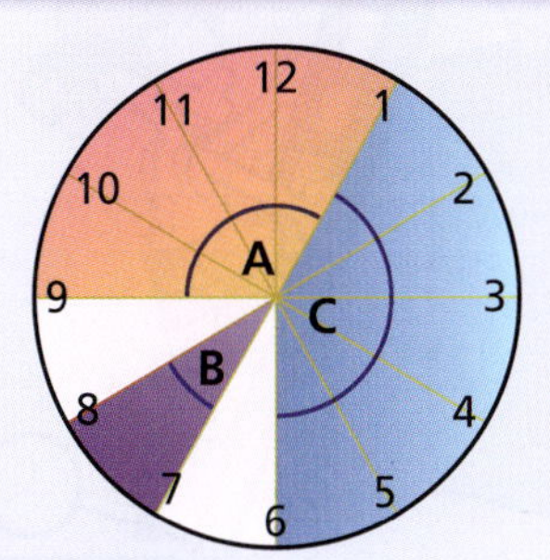

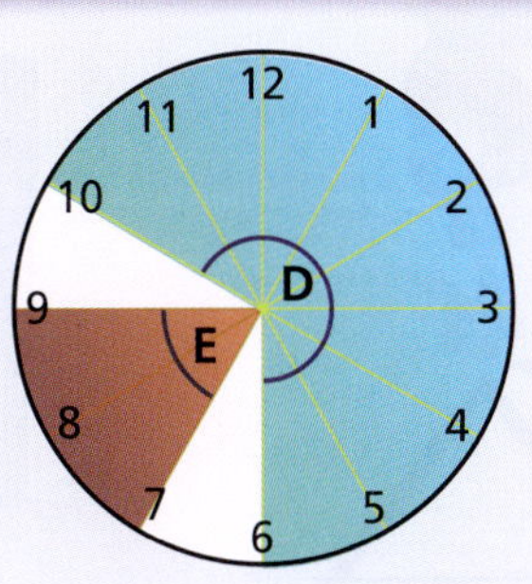

4 Which two angles have a total size equal to:

a a right angle?

b a straight angle?

c a full turn?

4:22 Angles of any size

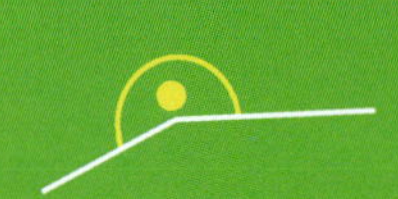
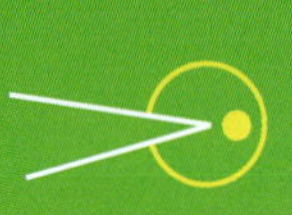

Picture						
Type	acute	right	obtuse	straight	reflex	revolution
Size	less than a right angle	a square corner	between right and straight	like a straight line	between straight and full turn	a full turn

1 Name each type of angle.

a 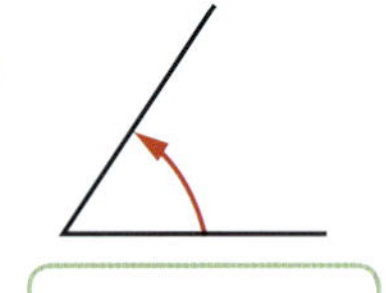

b 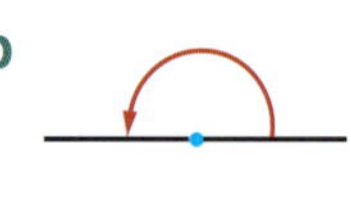

c 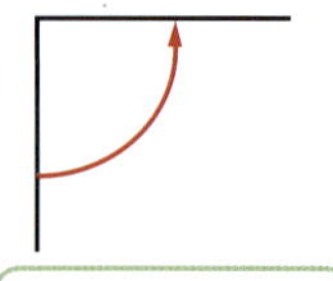

d 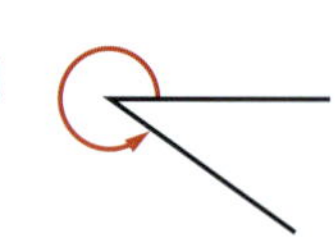

e **f** **g** 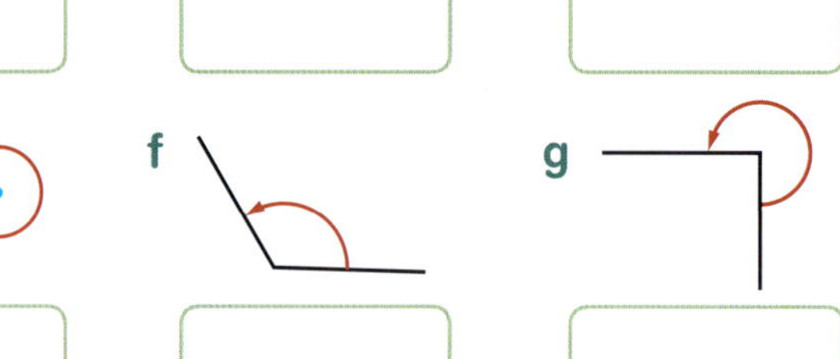

h 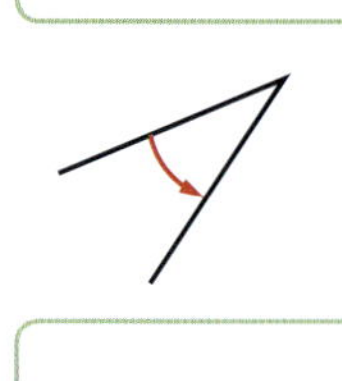

2 In each circle write (A) for acute angle, (O) for obtuse angle or (R) for reflex angle.

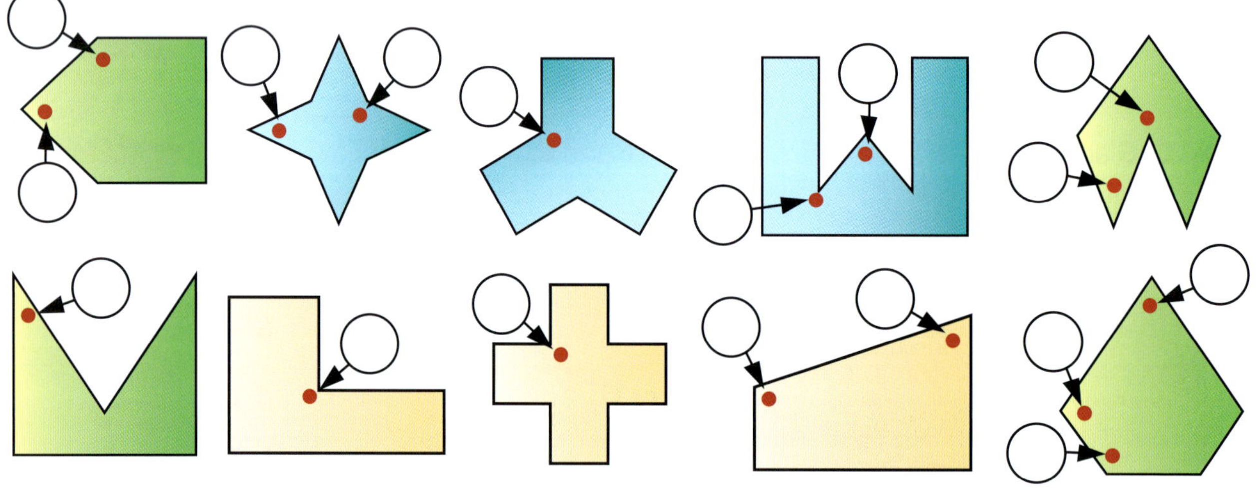

 ISBN 9780655709053

4:23

Horizontal and vertical

Without measuring, it is hard to know if a shape is regular.

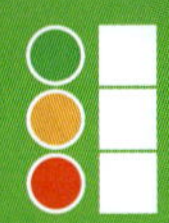

CONCEPT

Surfaces that go straight up and down are **vertical**.
Surfaces that go straight across are called **horizontal**.

1. Isla and Oliver were building a birdcage.
   - Some pipes had to be horizontal, and others vertical. To test these they used a spirit level.

   - When the bubble is in the middle of the glass tube, the spirit level is horizontal (or vertical).
     Which pipes in this cage are:

   a horizontal?

   b vertical? **c** sloping?

2. **a** Why would triangles be used in the cage?

   b Which three pipes are parallel to **H**?

   c Which three are parallel to **J**?

   d Which three are parallel to **A**?

   e List examples of parallel lines in our community.

3. Which pipes have been used to make:

   a triangles?

   b rectangles?

4. **a** Are any of the shapes used in the birdcage regular?

   b List the pipes that are perpendicular to pipe **G**.

ACTIVITY

- Write down the way you would test a surface to see if it is:
  - horizontal
  - vertical

Test as many surfaces as you can.

  ISBN 9780655709053

4:24 Tessellating designs

A tessellation!

1 Complete the tessellations within the rectangles.

G

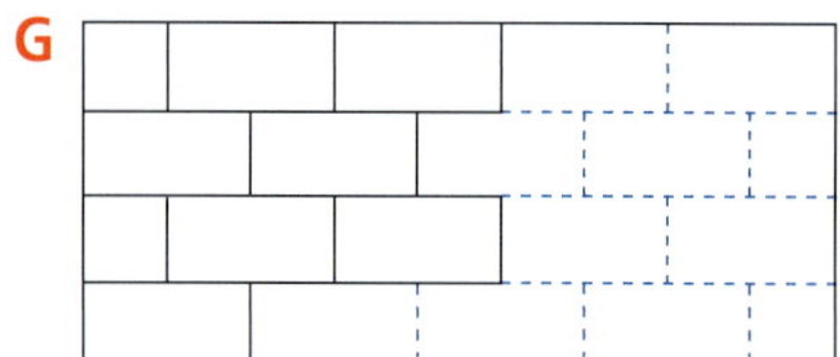

H

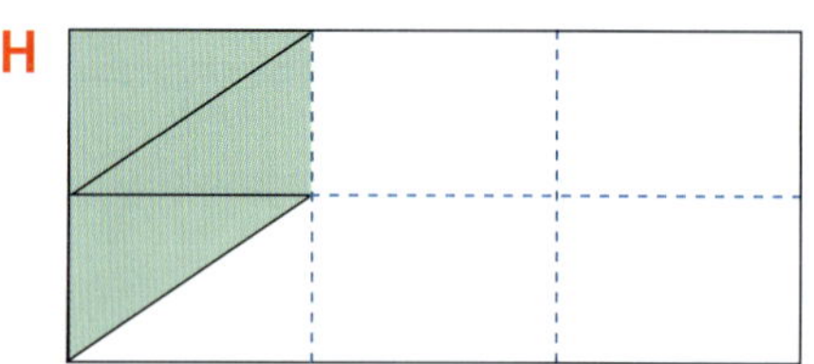

a Which of these designs could involve only slides (translations)?

b Which of these designs involves turns (rotations) as well as slides or flips (reflections)?

2

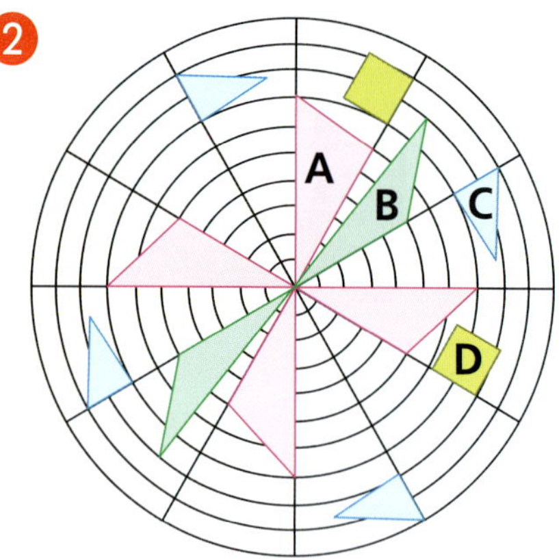

K: a quarter-turn clockwise

L: a half-turn clockwise

M: a three-quarter-turn clockwise

Which of the rotations above has been used to move the lettered shape to its other positions?

a A

b B

c C

d D

3

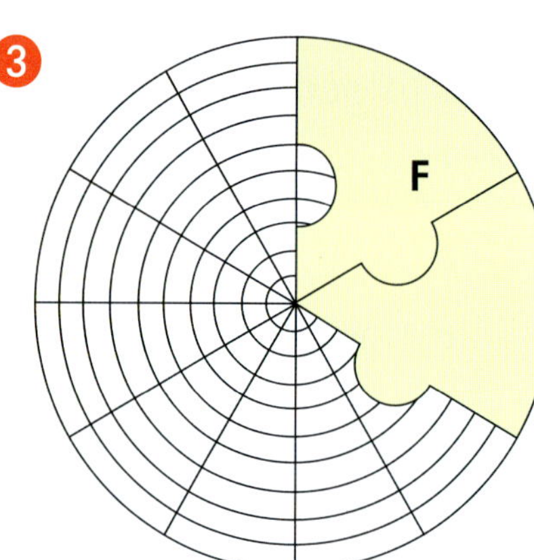

a Sam has begun a design. He started with one-sixth of a circle, cut half of a smaller circle from one side and stuck it on the other side.

Will shape F turn to cover the circle?

b Draw the rest of the design.

4 Draw a tessellation of your own within each rectangle.

5 Use rotation to draw your own design within this polar grid. You could use a different colour for each part.

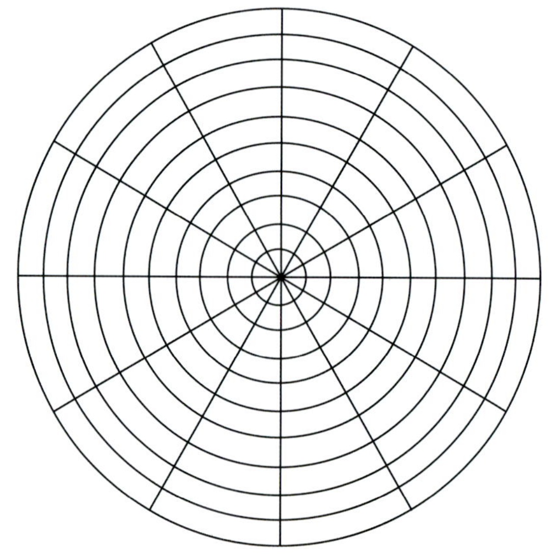

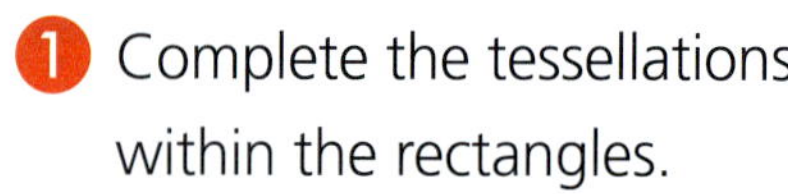
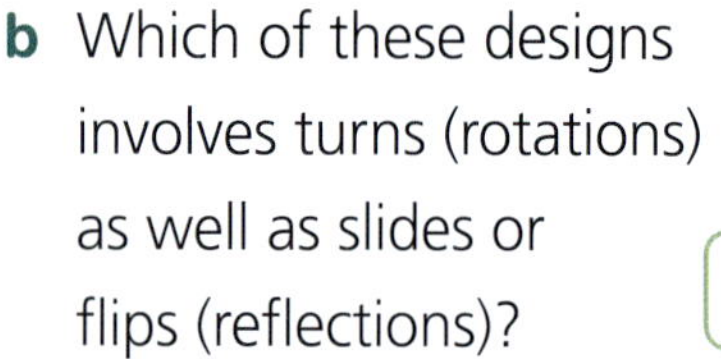

See *Extra Support 3* (Tangrams) and *Extra Support 4* (Flip, slide, turn).

4:25 Tessellations

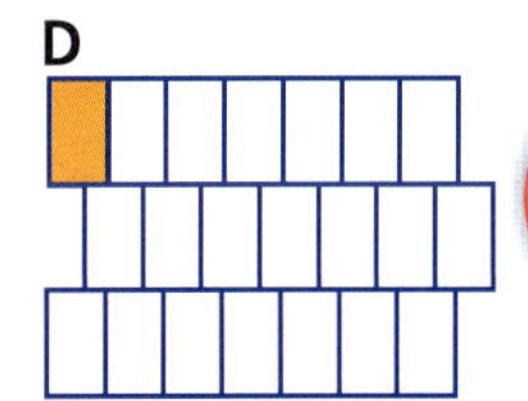

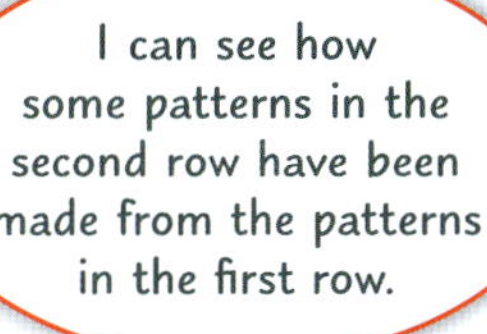

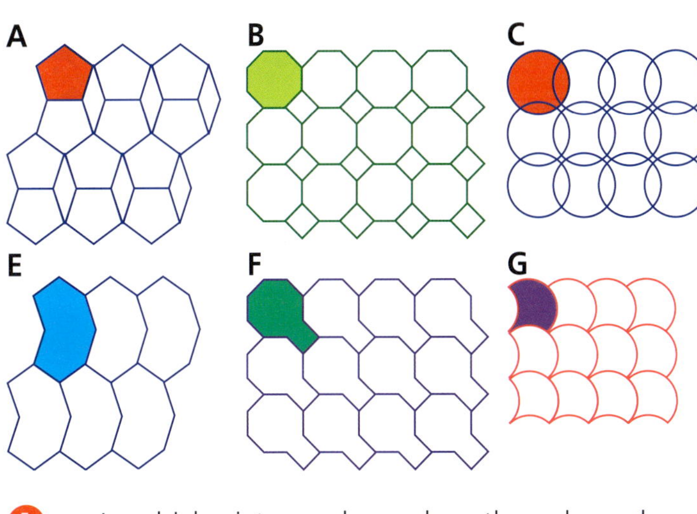

1 a In which pictures above does the coloured shape tessellate? ______

b In **A**, **B** and **C**, colour any gaps or overlaps black.

Identical shapes tessellate if they fit together without gaps or overlaps.

2 Peter wanted to tile his parents' bathroom. He used dot paper to draw the two tile patterns below.

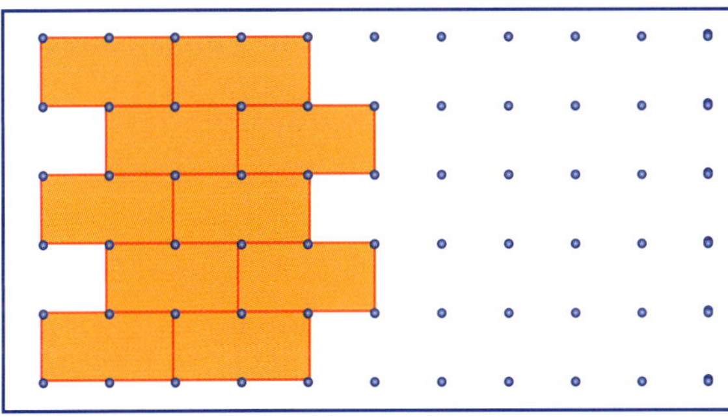

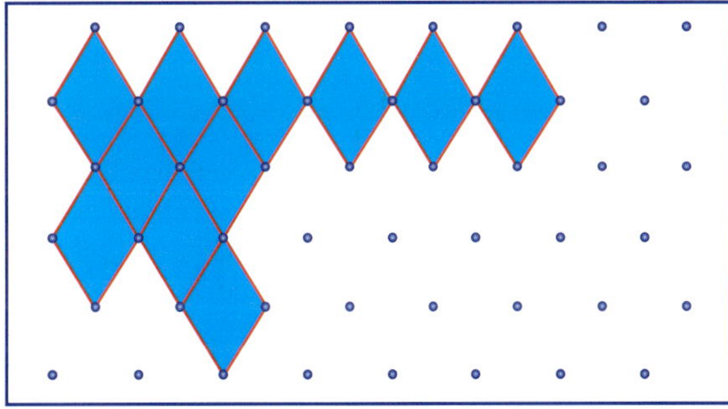

a Draw ten more tiles on each pattern.

b Do the tiles tessellate? ______

ICT

- Grace used this pattern to draw a tessellating bird.
- Complete the tessellation by drawing more birds. Dots have been drawn to help you.
- Use computer drawing tools to create a tessellating design by copying, pasting and rotating regular shapes.

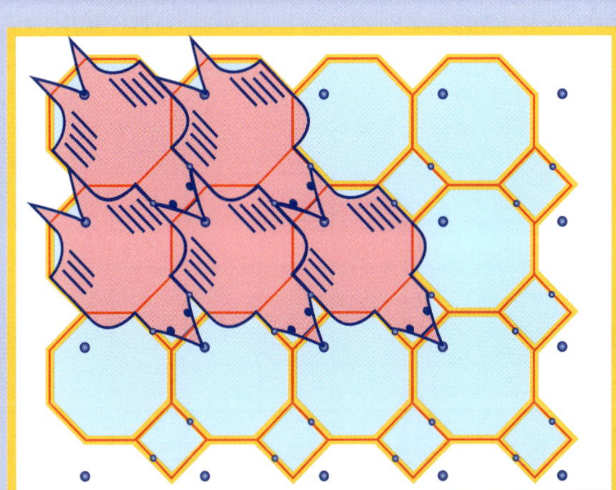

  ISBN 9780655709053

Spreadsheets

- We say the column, then the row.
- B14 and C14 have been joined (merged).

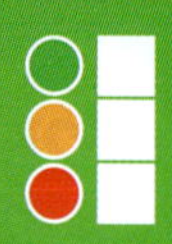

CONCEPT

- Susan and Alan were tested on the x 4 and x 5 tables.
- The answers to the x 4 tables are in Column B.
- Discuss the test results of Susan and Alan.

× 4 and × 5 tables facts (title)

	A	B	C	D	E	F	G	H
1	× 4 tables				× 5 tables			
2	1	4			1	5		
3	2	8			2	10		
4	3	12			3	15		
5	4	16			4	20		
6	5	20			5	25		
7	6	24			6	30		
8	7	28			7	35		
9	8	32			8	40		
10	9	26			9	45		
11	10	40			10	50		
12	11	44			11	55		
13	12	48			12	60		
14		Test results				Test results		
15	Susan	8	11		Susan	10	12	
16	Alan	7	10		Alan	12	12	

- **This cell is called C15.**
- **This cell is called F13.**

1 Put a tick in:

a C2 ☐ **b** A14 ☐ **c** D7 ☐ **d** G10 ☐ **e** H3 ☐

2 What number is in:

a B8 ☐ **b** F4 ☐ **c** C16 ☐ **d** F15 ☐ **e** A9 ☐

3 **a** Write K in D14. ☐ **b** Write L in H2. ☐ **c** Write M in C7. ☐

	A	B	C	D	E	F
1	**Pets kept**					
2	**Birds**	5				
3	**Mice**	6				
4	**Turtles**	1				
5						
6	**Athletics**					
7	**Name**	Amy	Holly	Sam	Yong	Luke
8	**Attendance**	4	5	3	7	6

4 **a** How many birds were kept as pets? ☐

b What was the total number of pets? ☐

c Who attended athletics most? ☐

d What are the coordinates of the cell that has been highlighted in red? ☐

e What are the coordinates of 'Pets kept'? ☐

4:27 Drawing views of objects

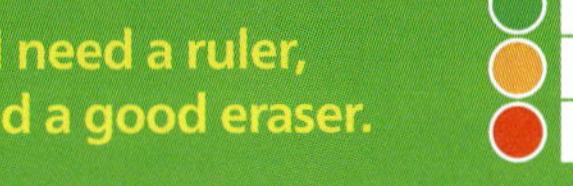

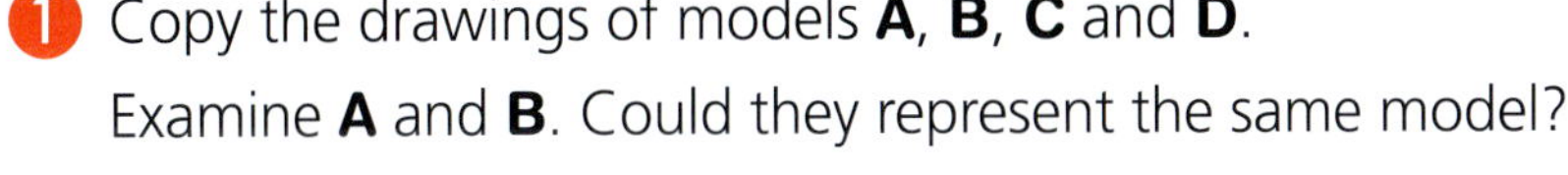

1. Copy the drawings of models **A**, **B**, **C** and **D**.
   Examine **A** and **B**. Could they represent the same model? [ ]

   Examine **C** and **D**. Could they represent the same model? [ ]

2. Construct two 3D models using six connecting cubes.
   Draw two different views of each of your models.

A

B

C

D

Model 1

Model 2

5:01 Drawing tables

This table has 6 different categories.
One is 'small blue' button.

1 Use the picture to fill in the two-way table.

Buttons			
	Red	Blue	Green
Large			
Small			

2 Use the table above to fill in this simpler table.

Buttons		
Red	Blue	Green

3 Use the table above to fill in this simpler table.

Buttons	
Large	
Small	

4 Show the data from Question 2 on a graph.

5 Fill in this table using data about your family and friends.

Name	Age	Male or Female
Me		

6 Use the dice to complete the table.

Number of times thrown					
⚀	⚁	⚂	⚃	⚄	⚅

Graphing the weather

ACTIVITY

- For the next month record the weather like this.
- At the end of the month cut up the calendar. Glue the pieces to make a graph like this.
- Use the graph to describe the month's weather.

5:02 Chance

'Even chance' means that an outcome is as likely to happen as not to happen.

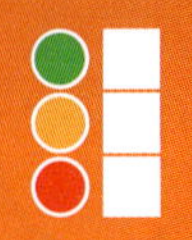

1 Without looking, Min must choose one card.

a Is she more likely to choose red or black? ______

b Is she certain to choose an ace? ______

c Is there an even chance to choose red? ______

d The chance of choosing black is 1 out of ______.

e The chance of choosing red is 2 out of ______.

2 List all possible outcomes of this spinner.

a Which colour is it most likely to land on? ______

b Which colour is it least likely to land on? ______

c Which colour has an even chance of occurring? ______

d What is the chance of spinning pink? ______

e The chance of landing on red is ______ out of 8.

f The chance of landing on blue is ______ out of 8.

g The chance of landing on yellow is ______ out of 8.

There is also an even chance that red will not be spun.

3 Order these events from 1 (least likely) to 4 (most likely).

- The principal will visit our classroom tomorrow. ______
- It will be sunny tomorrow. ______
- Our class will use books tomorrow. ______
- The next person to visit our room will be female. ______

4 Write three things that might happen tomorrow.

Order each event from 1 (least likely) to 3 (most likely).

______ ______

______ ______

______ ______

Heads or tails?

head tail

Toss a coin 50 times and keep a tally of the number of heads and tails.

How many heads are most likely to occur in 50 tosses: 15, 25 or 35? ______

5:03 Chance

If all outcomes are just as likely to happen, we say they have an 'equal chance' of happening.

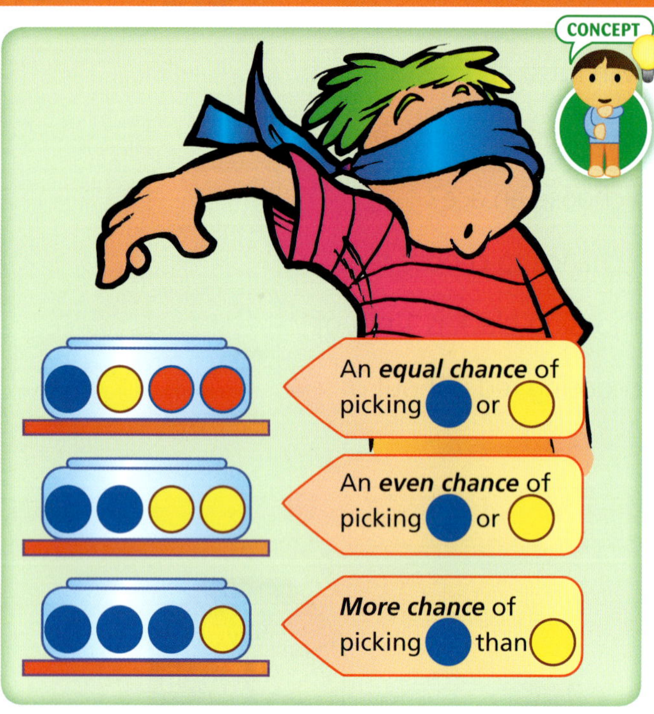

1 Write these events in order from least likely to most likely.

least likely ○ ○ ○ ○ ○ most likely

A The principal will come to school on Monday with no shoes on.

B If I throw a normal dice I will get a 4.

C If I drop a glass onto a rock it will break.

D If I toss a coin it will be a head.

E Our next teacher will be from Mars.

2

Rachel 1 | Alan 2 | Alf 3 | Mia 4 | Emma 5 | Aria 6

To decide who works together, **two counters** at a time are taken from the jar.

Numbers 1 to 6

Who will work together if the numbers chosen are:

a 3 and 5 ? ______ **b** 2 and 4? ______

c 1 and 6? ______

d Does each number have the same chance of being chosen? ______

In a random selection, each number has the same chance of being chosen. You could carry out this experiment in your classroom.

3 Choose a label to answer each question.
In Question 2, what is the chance that:

a the numbers 6 and 7 are picked? ______

b the numbers 1 and 2 are picked? ______

c two numbers less than 10 are picked? ______

d when Alf is chosen, he will be working with a girl? ______

e at least one of the pairs will be two girls? ______

impossible | **not likely** | **even chance** | **very likely** | **certain**

Using graphs

Column graphs need a title, categories and a scale.

1. Rhonda graphed the number of calls made each day last week by her family.

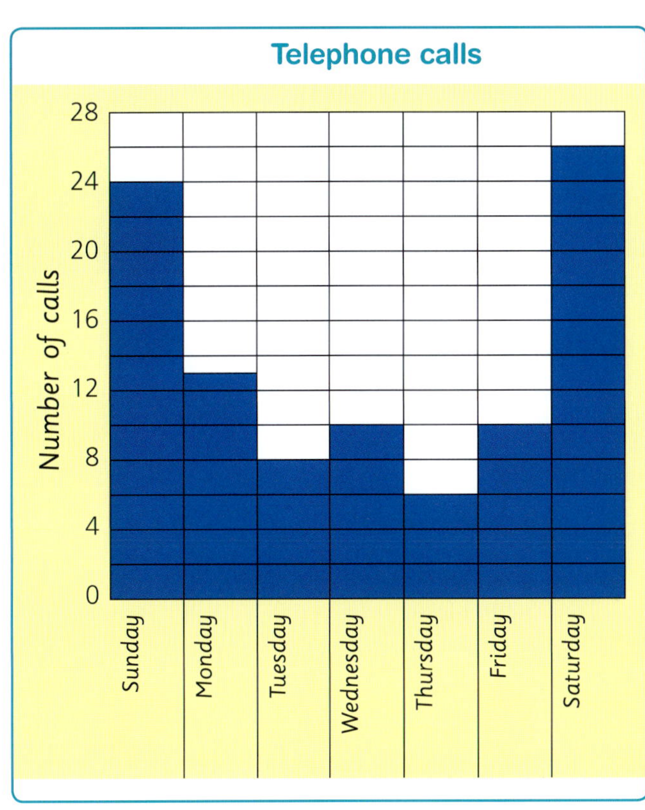

   a How many calls were made on Monday? [ ]

   b On what day was the greatest number of calls made? [ ]

   c On what day was the least number made? [ ]

   d What is the difference between the number of calls made on Saturday and the number made on Thursday? [ ]

   e What is the total number of calls made for the week? [ ]

   f Why do you think more calls were made on Sunday and Saturday? [ ]

2. Rhonda kept this tally of calls made by her children. Use the tally to draw the graph.

Name	Number of calls
Alana	𝍸 𝍸 𝍸 𝍸 𝍸 𝍸
Rachel	𝍸 𝍸 𝍸 𝍸 𝍸
Naomi	𝍸 ||||
Luke	𝍸 𝍸 |||
Heather	𝍸 𝍸 𝍸 ||

Calls made

Alana
Rachel
Naomi
Luke
Heather

0 4 8 12 16 20 24 28 32

Number of calls

When columns are drawn across, it is called a bar graph.

3. Complete this column graph to represent the data in this table.

Income last week

Kai	$300
Tye	$500
Mia	$450
Woo	$250

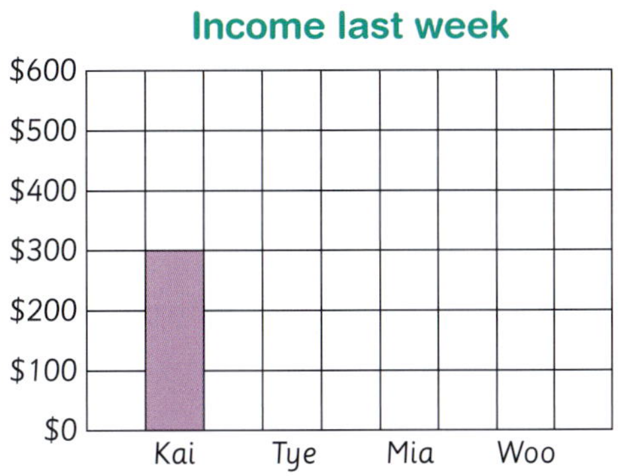

4. Tim is 15 and Sue is 10. Complete the graph's scale.

Reading graphs

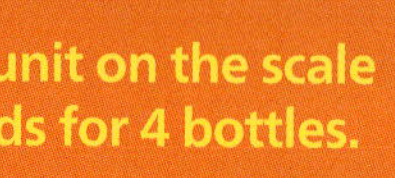

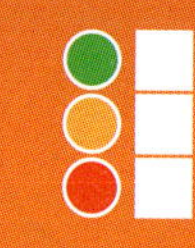

1

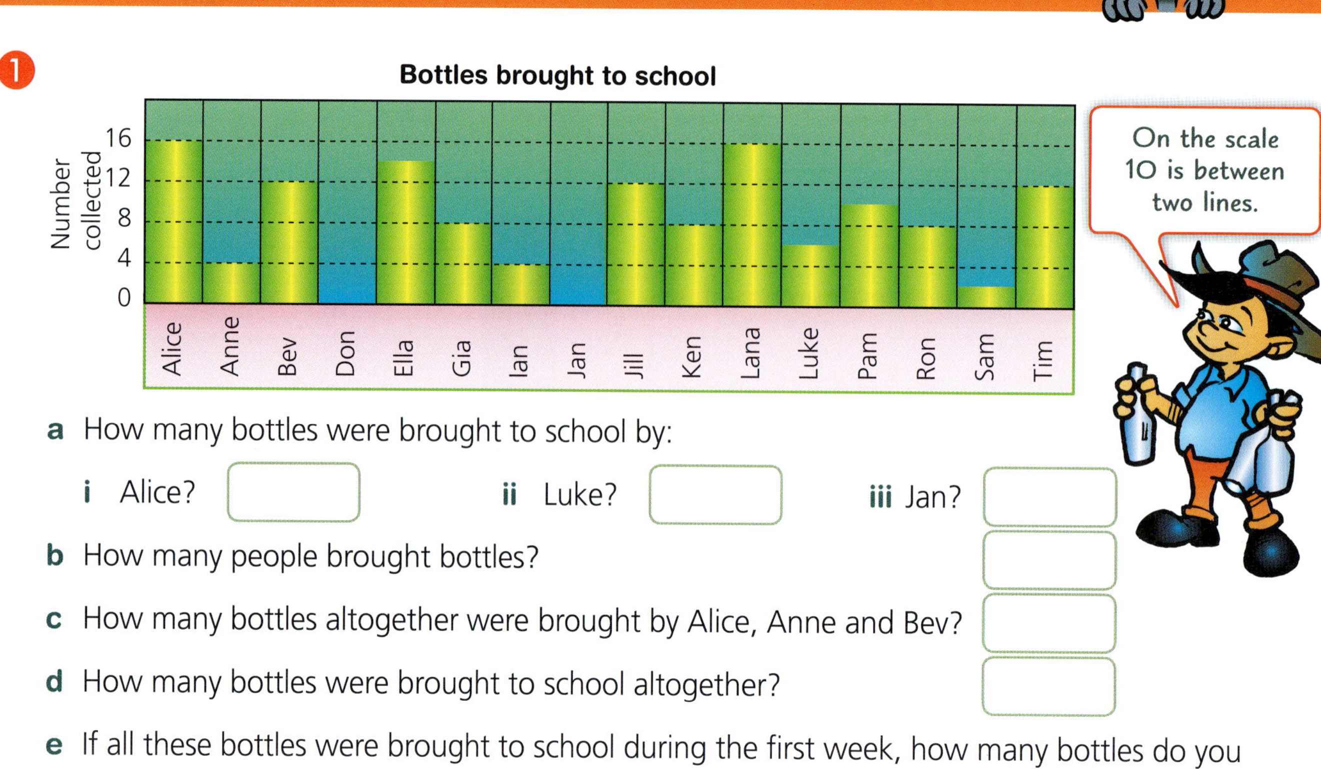

a How many bottles were brought to school by:

i Alice? ___ ii Luke? ___ iii Jan? ___

b How many people brought bottles? ___

c How many bottles altogether were brought by Alice, Anne and Bev? ___

d How many bottles were brought to school altogether? ___

e If all these bottles were brought to school during the first week, how many bottles do you think would be brought during the first two weeks? How did you get your answer?

___

2

Sport chosen by class 4R

Volleyball
Basketball
Tennis

SPORT

0 8 16 20 32 40 48

Number of students

a Which was the most popular sport? ___

b How many students chose basketball? ___

c How many students chose volleyball? ___

d How many students made a choice? ___

Tally marks

ACTIVITY

Tally marks used in South America and Asia also have five lines.
With a partner, create your own five-line tally marks.

	1	2	3	4	5
South America	|	⌐	⊓	□	⊠
Asia	一	丅	下	止	正

Discuss: When would tally marks be useful?

 • *AUSTRALIAN SIGNPOST MATHS NSW 4* • ISBN 9780655709053

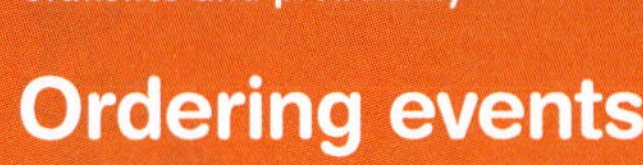

5:06 Ordering events

'Fifty-fifty' is another way of saying 'even chance'.

1 Choose the label you think best for each part below.

impossible | unlikely | even chance | very likely | certain

a My first throw of the dice will be a one. ____________

b I will throw a zero on a dice. ____________

c When I throw a dice the number will be greater than one. ____________

In this jar are 3 red and 3 yellow marbles. Blindfolded, I draw one out.

Which label from above is best for each of these statements?

d I will draw out a coloured marble. ____________

e I will draw out a blue marble. ____________

f I will draw out a yellow marble. ____________

2 Ms Adams placed two yellow and two blue counters in a hat. She had two more yellow and two more blue counters. Which two counters must she put into the hat so that she would be:

a more likely to draw out a yellow than a blue counter? ____________

b more likely to draw out a blue than a yellow counter? ____________

c equally likely to draw out a blue or a yellow counter? ____________

3 A B C D E F

The spinners above stop on either red or yellow.

a Which spinners are equally likely to stop on red as on yellow? ____________

b Which spinners are more likely to stop on red than on yellow? ____________

c Which spinners are more likely to stop on yellow than on red? ____________

4 Here is the head and tail of an old Australian penny.

a If I toss a coin in the air, would a head be more likely to show than a tail? ____________

b If two coins are tossed, what outcomes could result?

____

5 heads have been tossed in a row. What is likely to happen if I toss the coin again? Discuss.

 • *AUSTRALIAN SIGNPOST MATHS NSW 4* • ISBN 9780655709053

Chance used in games

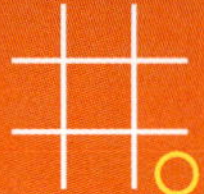

Is it best to start at a corner when playing *Noughts and Crosses?*

1 Caroline tossed a coin many times. She kept this tally of the results.

Tossing a coin		
Tossed	**Tally**	**Total**
Heads	𝍸 ||||	
Tails	𝍸 𝍸 |	

a How many times did she toss the coin? [ ]

b What fraction of the time did she toss:

i a head? [ ] **ii** a tail? [ ]

2 When playing cricket, we toss a coin to see who will bat first. How would you describe the chance that our team will win the toss? [ ]

3 100 tickets were sold in a raffle. John bought 70 of the tickets, Peta bought 25, Jeremy bought 2 and Danika bought none.
Choose a label that describes the chance that the winner will be:

a John [ ] **b** Peta [ ]

c Danika [ ] **d** Jeremy [ ]

e none of the four people mentioned [ ]

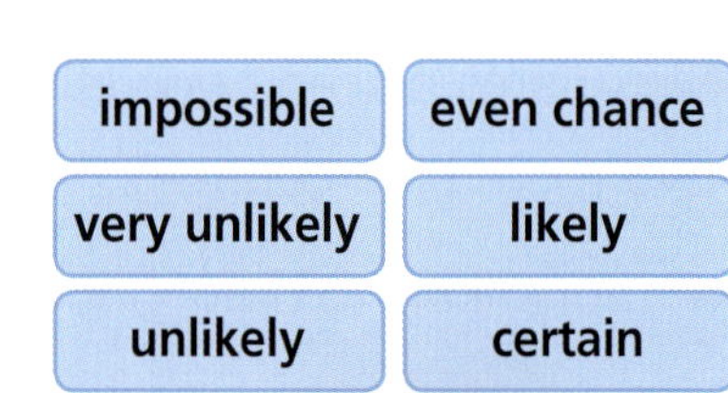

4 Two dice are rolled. **Jack** wins if his two rolls add to an odd number. **Emma** wins if her rolls add to 6. and **Luke** wins if his rolls add to 2 or 4.

a Write their names in order from most likely to win, to least likely to win.

[ ]

b Which person has an even chance of winning? [ ]

What's my age?

- Ask friends to write the month in which they were born. (1 for January, 2 for February, 3 for March, etc.)
- Tell them to multiply this number by 5, then add 2, then multiply by 20, then add their age in years, then subtract 40.
- Ask the person their answer.

Solution

- The last two digits of the answer give you the age. The other digits give you the month of birth. For example, 714 means the person is 14 and was born in July (the 7th month).

 • *AUSTRALIAN SIGNPOST MATHS NSW 4* • ISBN 9780655709053

5:08 Tally marks

Why do we use tally marks?
Why do we use groups of 5?

Tally the colours

ACTIVITY

- Start on any white square.
- Throw a dice and move that many spaces clockwise.
- Each time record the colour you land on, as a tally mark.
- Throw the dice 50 times.

Colour	Tally	Total
White		
Blue		
Red		
Green		
Yellow		
Orange		

Before you start, try to guess which colour will appear the most.

Green	Red	Blue	White
Yellow			Orange
Red			Yellow
White	Blue	Red	Green

Use squared paper to graph your results.

1. Erica asked 300 people to name their favourite sport. She made this tally of their answers.

Sport	Tally	Total
Tennis	𝍸 𝍸 𝍸 𝍸 𝍸 𝍸 𝍸 𝍸 𝍸	
Athletics	𝍸 𝍸 𝍸 𝍸 𝍸 𝍸 𝍸	
Swimming	𝍸 𝍸 𝍸 𝍸 𝍸 𝍸 𝍸 𝍸 |||	
Hockey	𝍸 𝍸 𝍸 𝍸 𝍸 |||	
Basketball	𝍸 𝍸 𝍸 𝍸 𝍸 𝍸 𝍸 |||	
Cricket	𝍸 𝍸 𝍸 𝍸 𝍸 𝍸 𝍸 𝍸 ||	
Football	𝍸 𝍸 𝍸 𝍸 𝍸 𝍸 𝍸 𝍸 𝍸		
Other	𝍸 𝍸 𝍸 𝍸 ||||	

a Complete the **Total** column.

b What was the most popular sport? ______

c How many more people chose swimming than athletics? ______

d Altogether, how many chose athletics and tennis? ______

e Name two sports which might have been included in *Other*. ______

INVESTIGATION

- To conduct a survey, we decide how many categories we will use.
- Ask 10 people for their favourite sport. Choose 5 sports to put in your survey.
- Ask 20 people which of these sports they like most. Keep a tally and then graph the data on a column graph.

 • • ISBN 9780655709053

5:09 Collecting information

A prediction is your best guess.

INVESTIGATION

You are to measure the hand length of 12 boys and 12 girls, in centimetres (to the nearest cm).

Compare your results with the results of others.

1 Who will you measure?

2 How will you measure hand length?

I will use

3 Make some predictions.
Who will have the longest hand, a boy or a girl?
Who will have the shortest hand, a boy or a girl?

4 Measure a few hands before you decide which measurements you will use in the left column.

5 Use tallies to record your results below.

Hand lengths of boys and girls

Measurement in centimetres	Boys' tally	Total	Girls' tally	Total

6 **Results**

The longest hand belonged to a ______. The shortest hand belonged to a ______.

7 Make a strip of paper that has the same length as:

a the shortest male hand
b the shortest female hand
c the longest male hand
d the longest female hand

8 **Your comments**

5:10 Using spinners

I wonder which spinner would give more red outcomes.

Aim: To compare the chances of spinning *red* on different spinners.

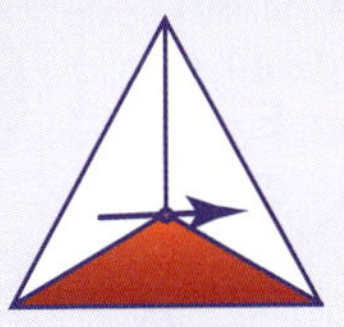

A

B

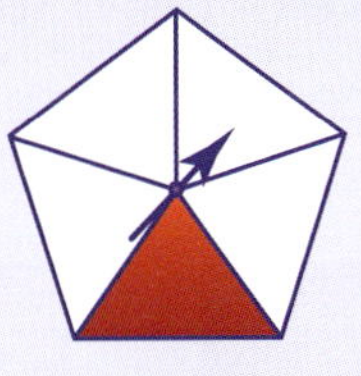

C

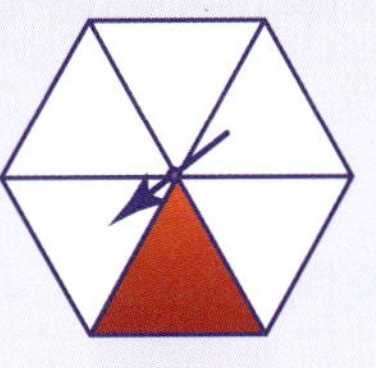

D

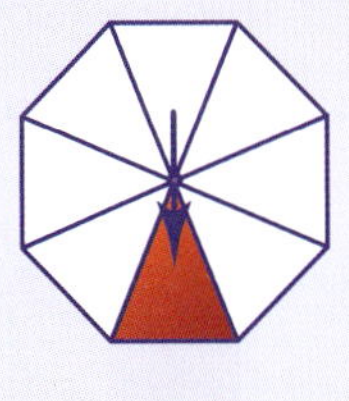

E

1 Experiment

- Find or make spinners like these.
- One student will spin each spinner 20 times while another student records the tally of red outcomes in the table below.

a Which spinner do you think will have most red spins?

b Which spinner do you think will have least red spins?

c Carry out the experiments.

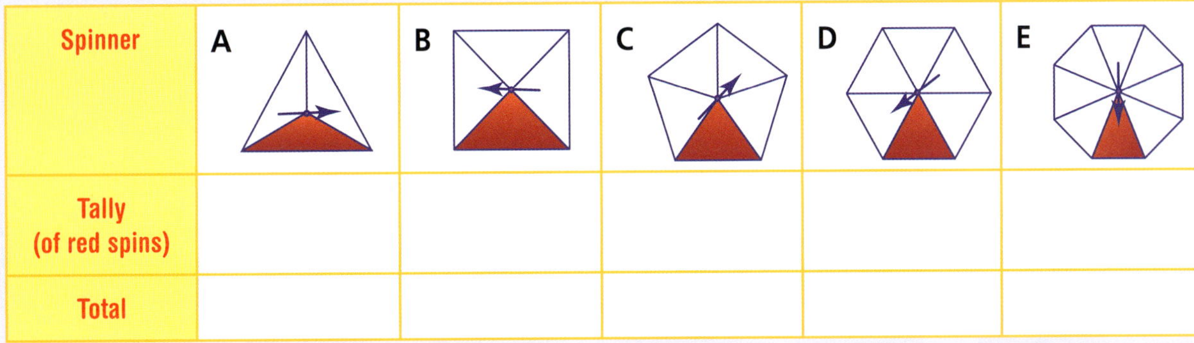

Spinner	A	B	C	D	E
Tally (of red spins)					
Total					

d Which spinner had most red spins?

e Which spinner had least red spins?

From your results, on which spinner is red:

f most likely to be spun?

g least likely to be spun?

h If we combined the results of many students, would we have a better idea of the answers to parts **f** and **g**? Why or why not?

i Put **A** to **E** in order, from most likely to spin red to least likely.

 • *AUSTRALIAN SIGNPOST MATHS NSW 4* • ISBN 9780655709053

5:11 Unequal outcomes

An 'even' or 'fifty-fifty' chance means the outcome is as likely to happen as not happen.

CONCEPT

- Each side of these squares has the same chance of being spun.
- The two colours usually have a different chance of being spun.

There is no chance of spinning red on spinner **E**.

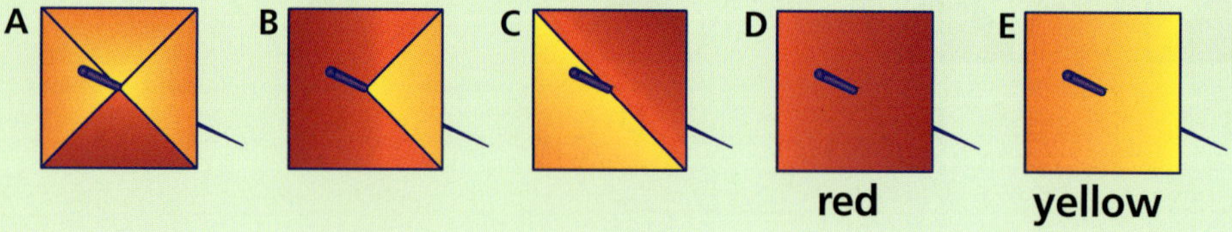

A B C D E

red yellow

1 For which of the spinners above is the chance of spinning red:

a impossible? ______ **b** certain? ______ **c** an even chance? ______

d unlikely? ______ **e** likely? ______

2 Put the spinners above in order, least likely to most likely of spinning red. Discuss your answer. ______

3 Put the spinners in order, least likely to most likely of spinning red.

a 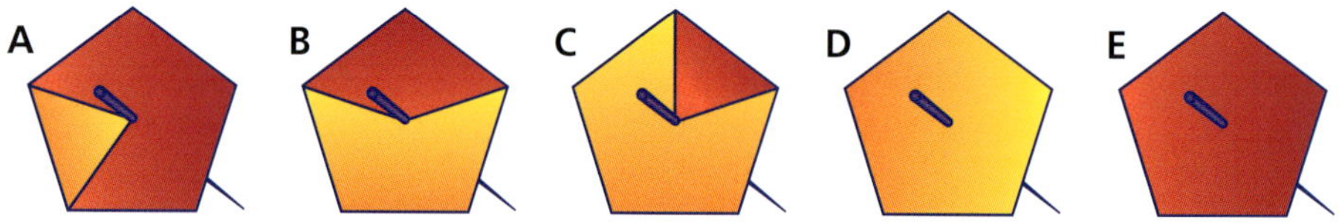 A B C D E ______

b 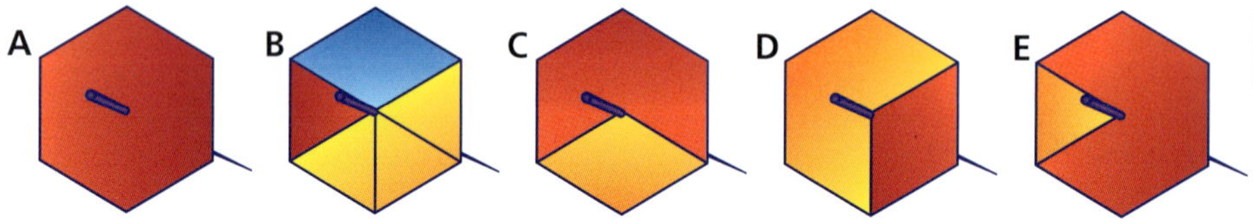 A B C D E ______

c A B C D E ______

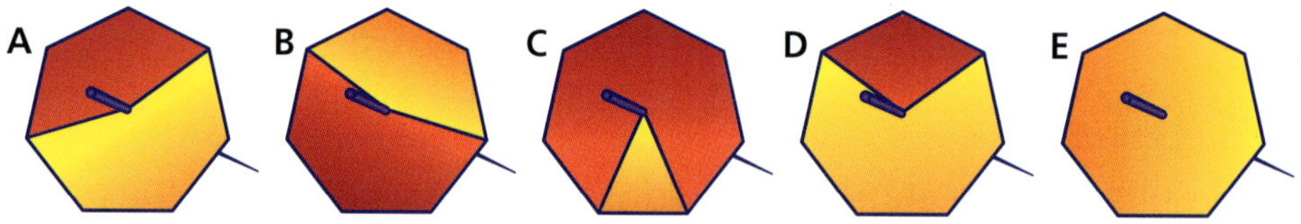

INVESTIGATION

4 Put the numbers 1 to 6 on the faces of a matchbox.
Are the faces equally likely to land face up when the box is tossed? ______
Carry out this experiment 50 times, keeping a tally of the results.
What did you discover? ______

Tally					
1	2	3	4	5	6

 • *AUSTRALIAN SIGNPOST MATHS NSW 4* • ISBN 9780655709053

5:12 Surveys

- **Surveys** are used to discover information, to give us a general view of a situation or to check predictions.
- If everyone is surveyed from the group we wish to study, we have carried out a **census**.
- We can use a spreadsheet to graph the data we collect.
- These graphs were made by a spreadsheet to show ***When my classmates go to bed***.

1 Abbie conducted a survey of the students in her class. This, of course included herself. Her topic was: ***How many children are in your family?*** Complete the **Number** column below.

Abbie's survey — Children in families

Tick the box next to the number of children in your family.

- ☐ 1 child
- ☐ 2 children
- ☐ 3 children
- ☐ 4 children
- ☐ 5 children
- ☐ 6 children
- ☐ more than 6

Abbie's survey — Children in families

Category	Tally	Number
1 child	𝍸 I	
2 children	𝍸 𝍸	
3 children	𝍸 II	
4 children	III	
5 children	II	
6 children		
more than 6	I	

Enter this data into a spreadsheet. Use this to create a horizontal column graph.

2 Conduct the survey below and use the results to complete the table.

Children in families

Tick the box next to the number of children in your family.

- ☐ 1 child
- ☐ 2 children
- ☐ 3 children
- ☐ 4 children
- ☐ 5 children
- ☐ 6 children
- ☐ more than 6

Children in families

Category	Tally	Number
1 child		
2 children		
3 children		
4 children		
5 children		
6 children		
more than 6		

5:13 Graphing data

How much does each picture stand for?

1 a How many trains were sold on Monday?

b On which day were the most trains sold?

c How many trains were sold altogether?

d If there were 200 trains for sale, how many trains were not sold?

e Why do you think no trains were sold on Thursday?

f If the trains were sold in boxes of 10, how many boxes were sold?

Toy trains sold	= 10 toy trains
Monday	
Tuesday	
Wednesday	
Thursday	
Friday	

2 Katie surveyed students at her school to find out how they travelled to school. She recorded her results (to the nearest 10).

Bus	30
Walk	60
Car	70
Bike	40

a Which option was most common?

b How many students use a bus or car?

c Approximately how many students did she survey?

d Should Katie expect the same results every day?

e Complete the picture graph to display her results.

f Why is it useful to make = 10 students? Discuss.

Key: = 10 students	
Bus	
Walk	
Car	
Bike	

INVESTIGATION

3 Eva rolled two dice 25 times and found each total. She used a column graph to record her results.

a Carry out this activity and record your results.

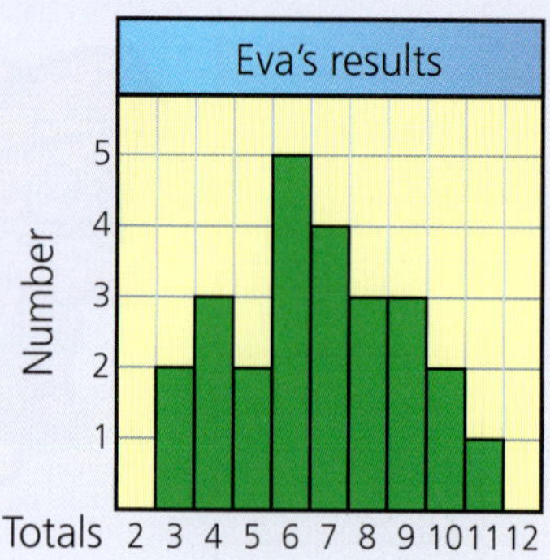

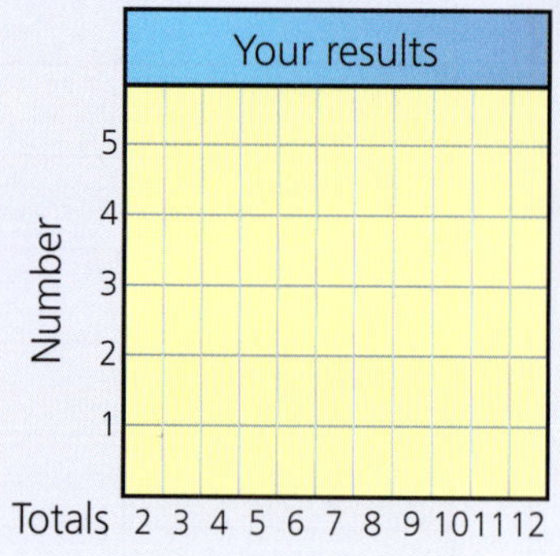

b Compare your results with Eva's results.

5:14 Chance experiments

I will not return the counter.

1 We begin with 4 green counters and 3 red counters. We will choose 3 counters.

One counter will be taken at random as each choice is made, and it is **not replaced**.

Use *likely*, *equally likely* or *unlikely* to give the chance of choosing a **red counter** each time.

a 1st choice: Chance of choosing a red counter is ______.

b 2nd choice: Chance of choosing a red counter if a green counter was chosen as the first choice is ______.

c 3rd choice: Chance of choosing a red counter if two green counters have been chosen as the first two choices is ______.

Conclusion: In this experiment, what happens in the first choice affects the chances in the second choice. When tossing a coin, this is not the case.

d If the counter is replaced after each choice, would the chance of choosing a red counter on the second choice be the same as it was for the first choice? ______

2 Put the same number of red and green counters in a container. One counter will be drawn out and then replaced.

a How many red counters would you expect to get in 10 turns? ______

b Give a reason for your answer. ______

c Carry out this experiment. The number of red counters chosen = ______. Discuss.

d Carry out this experiment a second time. Were your results the same?

3

- Take a counter at random from a bag containing 5 red, 3 blue and 1 yellow counter. Record a tally mark for that colour.
- Return the counter to the bag.
- Repeat the experiment 50 times.

	Tally	
Red		
Blue		
Yellow		

4 Write **equally likely** (**E**) or **not equally likely** (**N**) in each case.

a It will land on 1, 2 or 3. ______

b The drawing pin will land face up or face down. ______

c The next child born will be a girl or a boy. ______

 • *AUSTRALIAN SIGNPOST MATHS NSW 4* • ISBN 9780655709053

5:15 Carry out your own survey

Choose your question carefully.

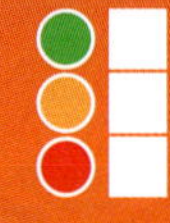

INVESTIGATION

Step 1: Choose a topic you are interested in for your survey.

Topic:

Step 2: Write a question to ask people about your topic.

Question:

Step 3: Decide how you will collect and record the answers (data).

Step 4: Predict what the data will show.

I think

Step 5: Represent your result using tables and graphs. (You could use technology to do this.)

Step 6: Reflect and write what you have learnt from your data.

I found

Step 7: Share your results.

Reflection: Was using a survey useful? What did you do well and what could you do better next time? What other topics could you research using a survey?

 ISBN 9780655709053

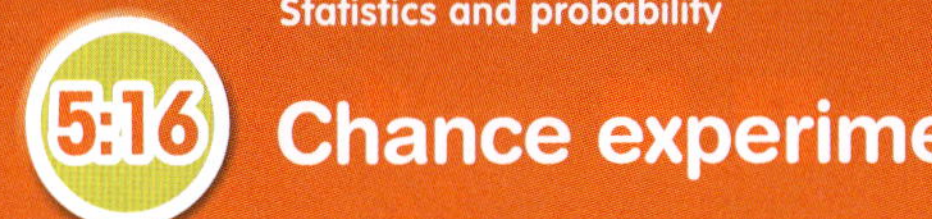

5:16 Chance experiments

A head was tossed more than twice as much.

1 Matt tossed a coin 10 times and made this graph.

Heads							
Tails							

a Which outcome occurred more often?

b Do these results mean that heads is more likely to be tossed than tails?

Why or why not?

2 **a** If you tossed a coin 10 times, how many heads would you predict?

b Toss a coin 10 times. Colour a circle after each toss.

Heads										
Tails										

c Do you think heads or tails is more likely, or are they equally likely?

d If many students combined their results would we have a better idea of whether heads and tails are equally likely?

e Why or why not?

3 **a** If we toss two coins we could toss **2 heads**, **2 tails** or **1 head and 1 tail**. Which of these do you think is most likely?

b Toss two coins 50 times and make a tally of the results.

c Which outcome occurred most often?

d Did this agree with your prediction?

e Compare your results with others in the class.

f What do you think is the likelihood of the three results occurring? Report your findings here.

Tally		
2 heads	**1 head 1 tail**	**2 tails**

Addition and subtraction facts

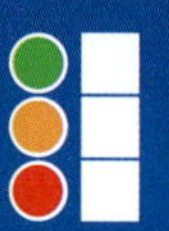

Make sure you know your addition and subtraction facts.

Once you learn your addition tables, use them for subtraction.

- If **6 + 7 = 13**, then 13 – 6 = 7 and 13 – 7 = 6.
- If **8 + 9 = 17**, then 17 – 8 = 9 and 17 – 9 = 8.

1 Join each question to the correct answer using a ruler and pencil. You could practise your addition and subtraction facts by rubbing out your answers and doing them again.

a +

Question	Answer
2 + 6	1
4 + 6	7
0 + 1	8
5 + 7	9
5 + 6	10
0 + 7	11
4 + 5	12
7 + 10	15
8 + 7	17
10 + 10	18
9 + 9	20

Speed:

b +

Question	Answer
2 + 3	4
4 + 3	5
2 + 2	7
5 + 4	9
8 + 5	8
8 + 0	10
7 + 5	11
1 + 9	12
10 + 5	13
6 + 5	15
10 + 9	19

Speed:

c +

Question	Answer
3 + 6	6
2 + 8	7
4 + 2	8
5 + 2	9
4 + 7	10
3 + 5	11
9 + 6	12
6 + 6	13
8 + 8	14
7 + 6	15
10 + 4	16

Speed:

d +

Question	Answer
3 + 4	5
6 + 2	6
4 + 5	7
3 + 2	8
2 + 4	9
8 + 4	10
4 + 9	11
5 + 5	12
4 + 7	13
7 + 8	14
5 + 9	15

Speed:

e –

Question	Answer
8 – 6	1
10 – 4	0
1 – 0	2
12 – 5	4
11 – 6	6
7 – 7	5
9 – 5	7
17 – 7	8
15 – 7	10
11 – 8	9
18 – 9	3

Speed:

f –

Question	Answer
5 – 2	2
7 – 3	3
4 – 2	4
9 – 4	5
13 – 5	0
8 – 8	1
12 – 5	6
10 – 9	7
15 – 5	8
11 – 5	10
19 – 10	9

Speed:

g –

Question	Answer
6 – 4	0
5 – 2	1
10 – 9	2
7 – 7	3
9 – 3	4
7 – 3	5
10 – 3	6
14 – 5	7
9 – 4	8
18 – 8	9
10 – 2	10

Speed:

h –

Question	Answer
6 – 5	0
9 – 9	1
6 – 3	2
8 – 6	3
8 – 4	4
16 – 9	5
9 – 4	6
16 – 7	7
17 – 7	8
10 – 4	9
17 – 9	10

Speed:

See 2:05 (Addition, no trading), 2:06 (Addition and subtraction, no trading) and 2:07 and 2:08 (Addition to 99 with trading).

Building to the next 10

$8 + 7 = 8 + 2 + 5 = 10 + 5$
$38 + 7 = 38 + 2 + 5 = 40 + 5$
$78 + 7 = 78 + 2 + 5 = 80 + 5$

- When adding a single-digit number to a 2-digit number, build to the **next 10** and then add the part of the single-digit number that you have not used.

$28 + 8 = 28 + 2 + 6$
$= 30 + 6$
$= 36$

Build to the next 10 to find the answer.

1
- **a** 7 + 5 = 7 + 3 + ☐
  = ☐
- **b** 8 + 4 = ☐
- **c** 19 + 7 = ☐
- **d** 18 + 9 = ☐
- **e** 17 + 4 = ☐
- **f** 19 + 8 = ☐
- **g** 17 + 5 = ☐
- **h** 18 + 3 = ☐
- **i** 19 + 5 = ☐
- **j** 17 + 6 = ☐
- **k** 18 + 8 = ☐
- **l** 19 + 6 = ☐
- **m** 19 + 9 = ☐
- **n** 18 + 5 = ☐
- **o** 19 + 4 = ☐

2
- **a** 29 + 5 = 29 + 1 + ☐
  = ☐
- **b** 29 + 3 = ☐
- **c** 27 + 4 = ☐
- **d** 28 + 7 = ☐
- **e** 27+ 5 = ☐
- **f** 28 + 2 = ☐
- **g** 29 + 4 = ☐
- **h** 37 + 6 = ☐
- **i** 39 + 5 = ☐
- **j** 38 + 5 = ☐
- **k** 37 + 4 = ☐
- **l** 39 + 6 = ☐
- **m** 38 + 4 = ☐
- **n** 39 + 3 = ☐
- **o** 37 + 5 = ☐

3
- **a** 48 + 4 = 48 + 2 + ☐
  = ☐
- **b** 47 + 5 = ☐
- **c** 49 + 6 = ☐
- **d** 47 + 6 = ☐
- **e** 48 + 5 = ☐
- **f** 47 + 4 = ☐
- **g** 49 +4 = ☐
- **h** 57 + 4 = ☐
- **i** 59 + 3 = ☐
- **j** 58 + 3 = ☐
- **k** 57 + 5 = ☐
- **l** 59 + 4 = ☐
- **m** 58 + 4 = ☐
- **n** 57 + 6 = ☐
- **o** 58 + 5 = ☐

See 2:09 (Jump strategy, +) and 2:35 (Mental strategies, +).

Tangrams

7-piece tangrams were invented in China 4000 years ago.

1

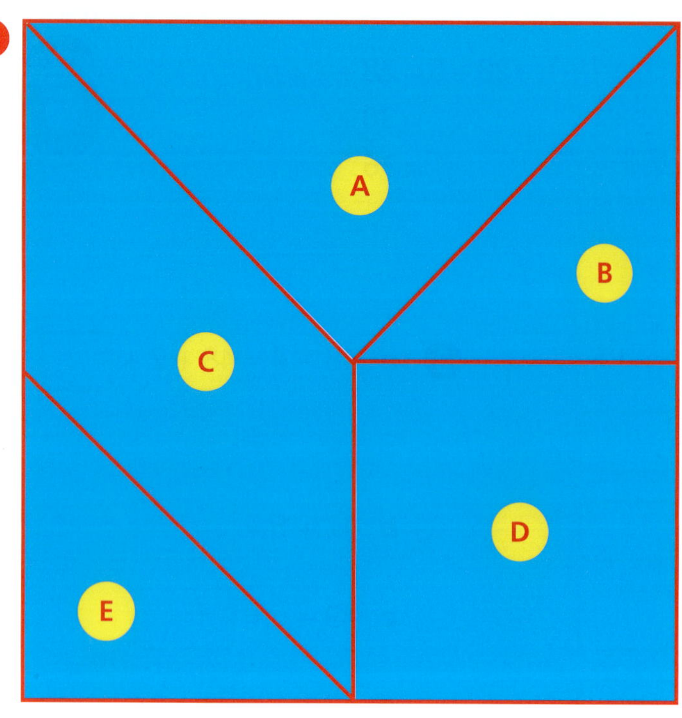

a Trace this tangram onto paper, cut it into 5 pieces and label them **A** to **E**.

b Without looking at this page, arrange your 5 pieces to make a square.

c Use your 5 pieces to make these pictures.

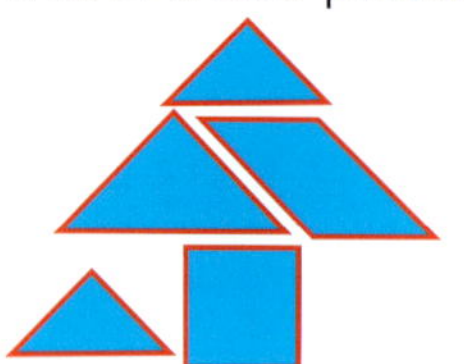

d Make patterns of your own.

e Paste your best pattern onto cardboard or coloured paper.

2

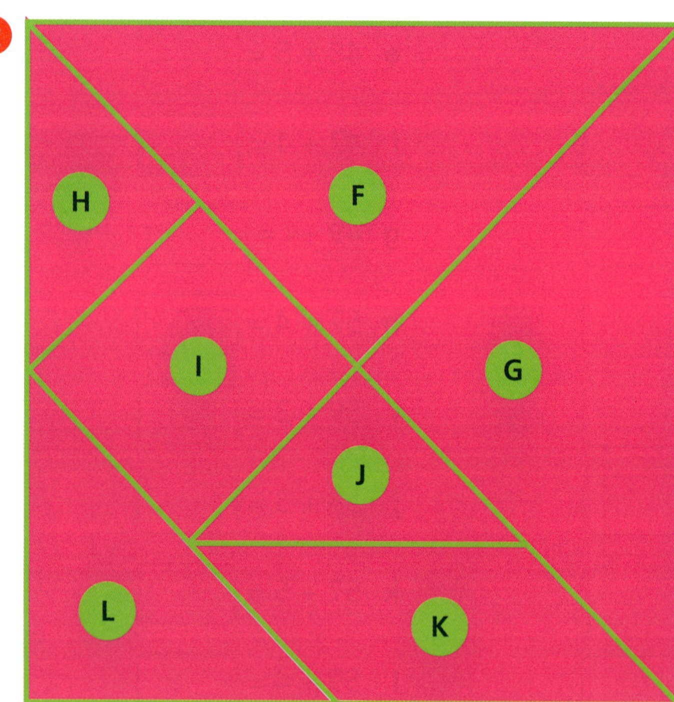

a Trace this tangram onto paper, cut it into 7 pieces and label them **F** to **L**.

b Without looking at this page, arrange your 7 pieces to make a square.

c Use your 7 pieces to make these pictures.

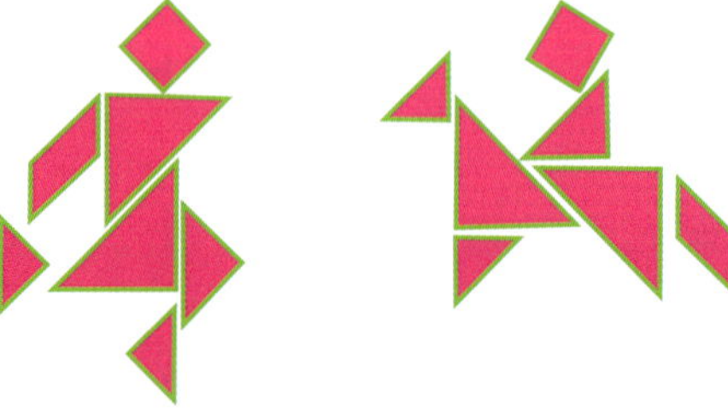

d Make a square using pieces **F** and **G**.

e Using pieces **H**, **I** and **J**, make these shapes:

e Use the seven pieces to make these pictures

f Copy two of the pictures here.

See 4:01 (Flip, slide and turn), 4:11 and 4:20 (Visualising shapes), 4:24 (Tessellating designs) and 4:25 (Tessellations).

Flip, slide, turn

A shape has symmetry if one side is the reflection of the other.

There are 3 ways to repeat a shape:
A flip the shape (reflect it)
B slide the shape (translate it)
C turn the shape (rotate it).

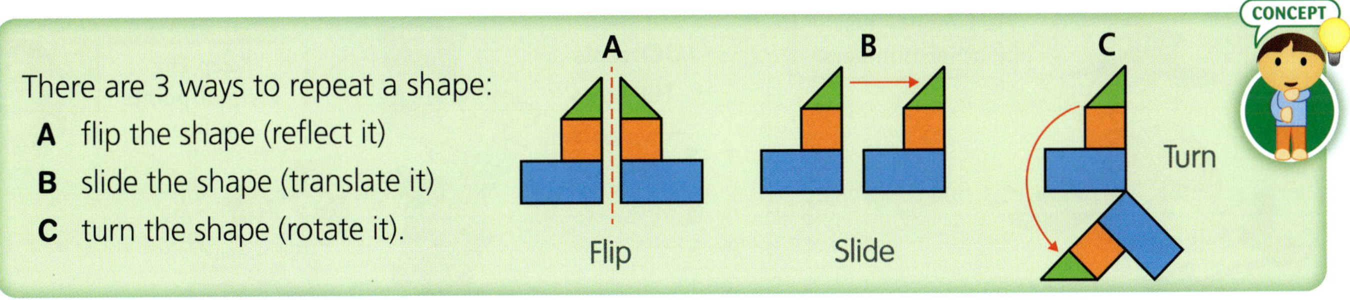

1 Is the coloured shape made by a **flip** (reflection), **slide** (translation) or **turn** (rotation)?

a

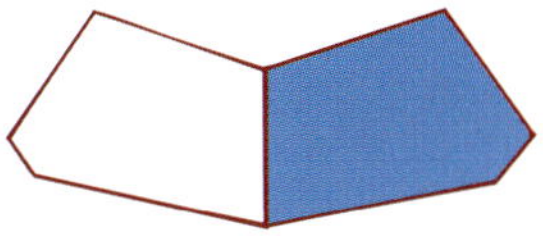

b

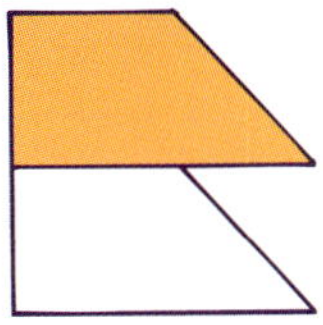

c

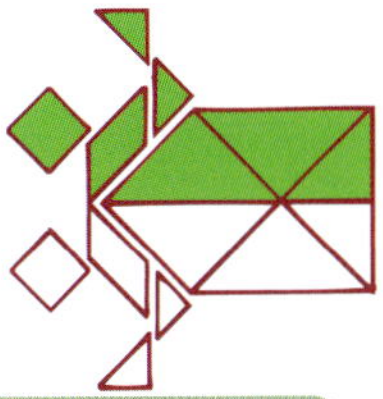

d

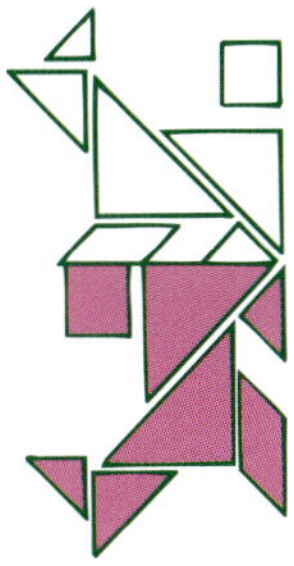

e

f

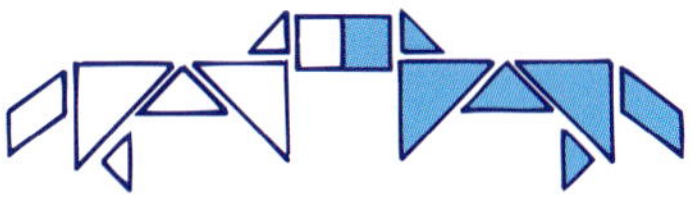

g

h

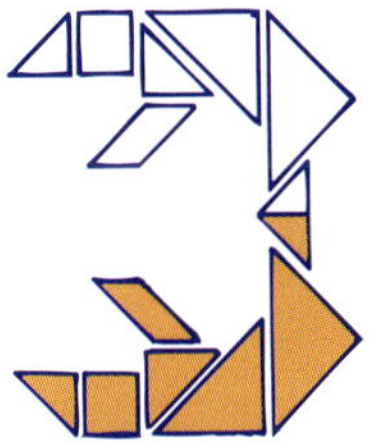

i

j

k Which of these shapes are symmetrical?

2 Draw all lines of symmetry. Is the coloured shape made by a flip, a slide or a turn?

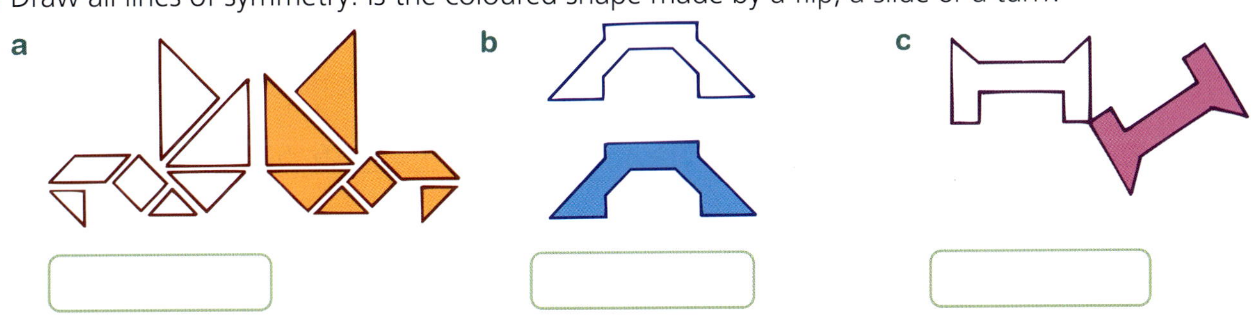

See 4:01 (Flip, slide and turn), 4:11 and 4:20 (Visualising shapes), 4:24 (Tessellating designs) and 4:25 (Tessellations).

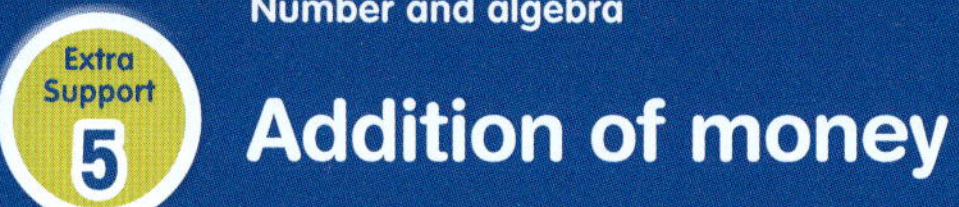

Addition of money

A decimal point (or full stop) separates the dollars and cents.
10 lots of 10 cents make 1 dollar.

1

a $0.41 + $0.37	**b** $0.64 + $0.88	**c** $1.26 + $3.47	**d** $2.24 + $3.07	**e** $3.75 + $2.94
f $4.69 + $3.56	**g** $2.63 + $2.07	**h** $5.83 + $2.68	**i** $4.96 + $1.47	**j** $2.79 + $4.32
k $2.41 + $3.67	**l** $4.06 + $2.91	**m** $3.77 + $1.63	**n** $1.92 + $4.37	**o** $5.16 + $1.98

2 Write each as an algorithm or use a mental strategy to find your answer.

a $1.56 + $2.23 ______ **b** $4.01 + $1.76 ______

c $3.51 + $2.17 ______ **d** $5.03 + $3.65 ______

e $2.37 + $4.12 ______ **f** $6.45 + $2.03 ______

3 Find the total if I bought:

a a cake for $5.50 and a drink for $4.05. ______

b a dessert for $4.95 and a drink for $3.25. ______

c a sandwich for $7.30 and a drink for $1.55. ______

d a biscuit for $3.75 and a drink for $4.95. ______

4

a $2.21	**b** $1.61	**c** $4.68	**d** $5.91
$0.85	$3.17	$1.83	$1.45
+ $1.82	+ $4.05	+ $2.86	+ $1.65

See 2:23 and 2:24 (Addition to 999) and 2:25 (Writing algorithms).

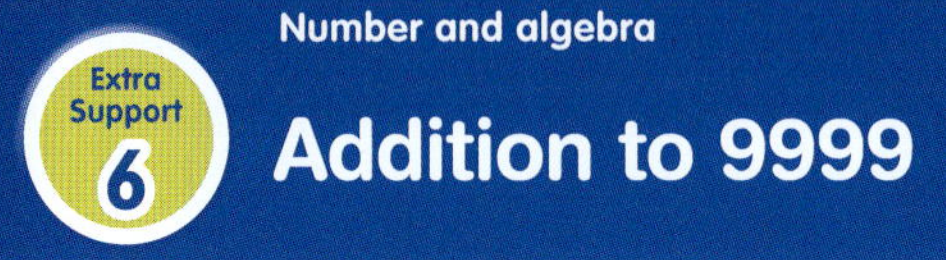

Addition to 9999

Th means thousands.
H means hundreds.

T means tens.
U means ones.

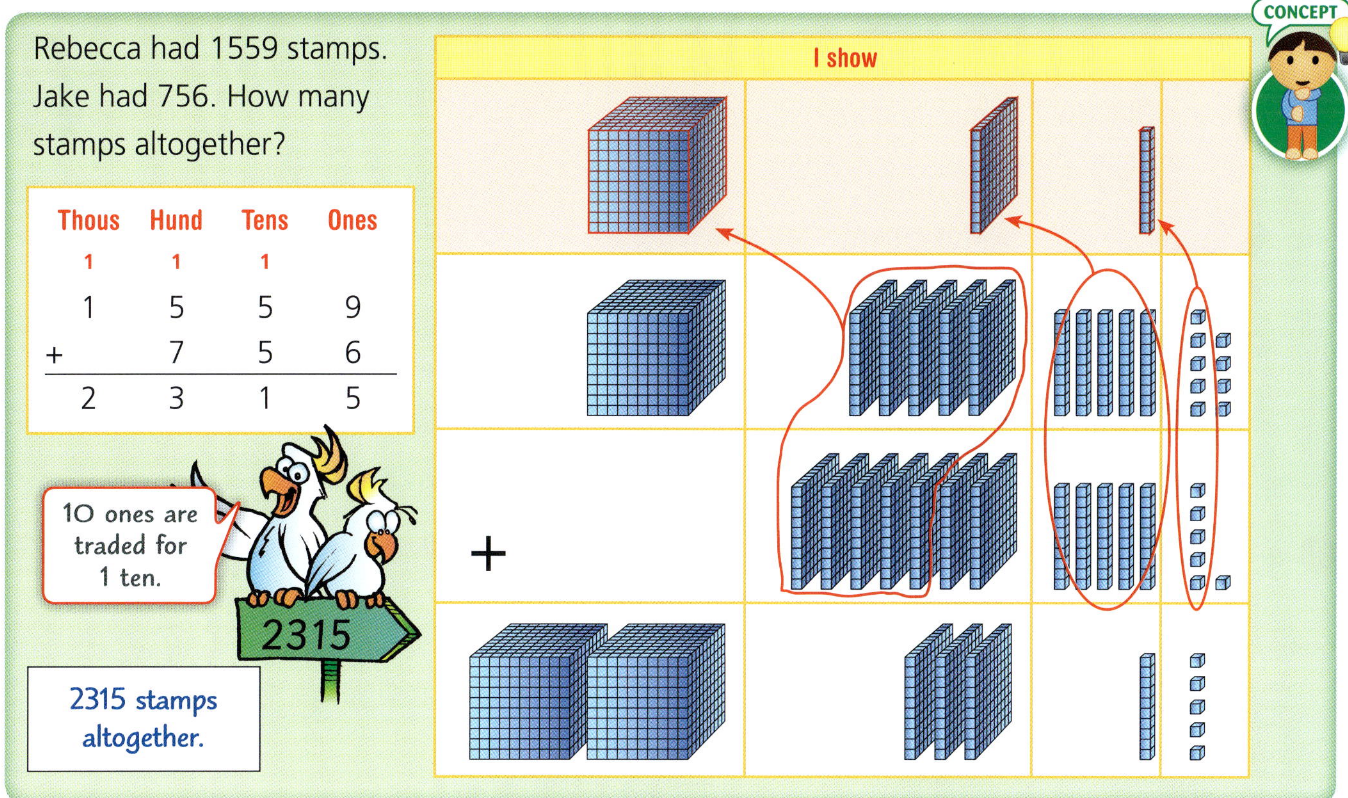

Rebecca had 1559 stamps. Jake had 756. How many stamps altogether?

Thous	Hund	Tens	Ones
1	1	1	
1	5	5	9
+	7	5	6
2	3	1	5

2315 stamps altogether.

1

	a	b	c	d	e
	Th H T U	Th H T U	Th H T U	Th H T U	Th H T U
	3 4 1 6	8 1 0 4	6 3 1 8	3 9 2	3 5
	+ 2 0 5 2	+ 8 7 1	+ 1 2 7 0	+ 3 4 0 6	+ 7 9 3 2

f	g	h	i	j
3 4 1 8	7 9 5 0	6 0 8 7	9 4 6	6 4 9 2
+ 2 9 0 6	+ 6 5 0	+ 1 1 6 4	+ 2 6 2 7	+ 1 7 4 8

2

a	b	c	d	e
5 0 7 1	3 8 3 1	2 5 1 6	3 1 9 5	7 0 4 1
+ 2 1 2 4	+ 1 0 5 4	+ 1 8 2 7	+ 5 7 3 0	+ 9 7 8

f	g	h	i	j
4 6 9 2	7 4 7 2	4 7 9	1 7 9 3	6 0 9 7
+ 2 8 1 3	+ 1 8 0 9	+ 3 8 6 0	+ 5 8 2 4	+ 1 8 3 5

3

a	b	c	d	e
$ 7 5 4 2	$ 6 5 4 9	$ 3 5 8 1	$ 2 5 9 1	$ 7 0 5 9
+ $ 1 6 0 7	+ $ 1 7 4 2	+ $ 4 3 2 8	+ $ 3 7 0 6	+ $ 2 3 7 1

See 2:23 and 2:24 (Addition to 999) and 2:25 (Writing algorithms).

 • *AUSTRALIAN SIGNPOST MATHS NSW 4* • ISBN 9780655709053

Addition to 9999

13 hundreds
= 1 thousand + 3 hundreds

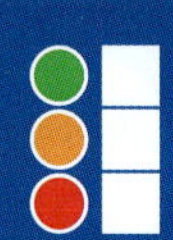

CONCEPT

I have three stamp albums. In the first is 3087 stamps, in the second 1872 stamps and in the third 4378. How many stamps have I got altogether?

How many stamps?

3087 + 1872 + 4378 = ☐

Answer

I have 9337 stamps.

	Thous	Hund	Tens	Ones
	1	2	1	
	3	0	8	7
	1	8	7	2
+	4	3	7	8
	9	3	3	7

1

a

	Th	H	T	U
	1	8	3	5
		4	0	8
+	5	3	1	8

b

	Th	H	T	U
		9	9	9
	4	2	5	6
+	1	6	8	0

c

	Th	H	T	U
	8	4	1	8
		6	4	7
+		7	5	3

d

	Th	H	T	U
	3	8	4	2
		7	0	6
+	2	9	3	4

2

a

```
    3 8 6
  2 5 1 4
    9 7 7
+     2 7
```

b

```
    1 8 3
    9 6 4
  1 8 6 3
+ 2 0 9 8
```

c

```
  5 1 4 2
    8 6 3
    7 4 4
+ 1 0 8 8
```

d

```
  2 0 9 9
  1 8 4 7
  1 9 3 5
+ 1 2 0 7
```

3

a

```
 $61.29
 $13.91
+$10.94
```

b

```
 $28.18
 $14.63
+$ 9.72
```

c

```
 $ 8.47
 $60.08
+$21.55
```

d

```
 $28.47
 $29.66
+$28.67
```

4 Estimate then calculate. (E = estimate, A = answer)

a Residents were phoned at 3187 homes in Bendigo, 1394 in Ballarat and 914 in Geelong. How many residents were phoned? E = ☐ A = ☐

b A bookshop kept 3096 books in room A, 2515 in room B and 2845 in room C. How many books were in the three rooms? E = ☐ A = ☐

c Sandy spent $3245 renovating her laundry, $2188 on landscaping and $2840 on furniture. How much did she spend? E = ☐ A = ☐

See 2:23 and 2:24 (Addition to 999) and 2:25 (Writing algorithms).

 • *AUSTRALIAN SIGNPOST MATHS NSW 4* • ISBN 9780655709053

Addition to 999 999

Check answers by rounding to 100 000s.

400 000
+ 400 000

At the last count Jock's two sheep stations had 374 295 and 439 015 sheep. How many sheep did he have altogether?

```
  1 1   1 1
  3 7 4 2 9 5
+ 4 3 9 0 1 5
  8 1 3 3 1 0
```

Altogether Jock had 813310 sheep.

374 thousands
295 ones
374 295

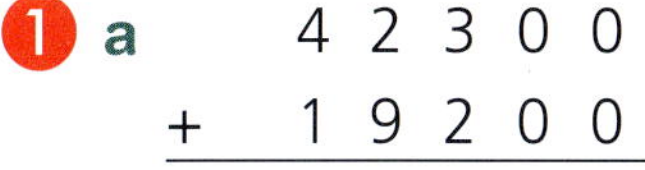

1

a 42 300 + 19 200	b 35 321 + 11 800	c 56 684 + 9 066	d 18 957 + 61 846
e 175 800 + 94 250	f 405 312 + 6 918	g 125 094 + 609 887	h 354 500 + 267 600

2

a 35 256 + 9 184 + 4 215	b 8 645 + 26 314 + 83 021	c 43 400 + 48 915 + 8 335	d 75 340 + 10 659 + 10 936
e 340 000 + 75 900 + 471 550	f 87 366 + 135 344 + 218 900	g 9 560 + 28 537 + 696 315	h 650 000 + 97 000 + 165 000

3

a 386 915 + 9 084 + 16 121 + 103 514	b 55 950 + 4 831 + 130 090 + 7 346	c 246 176 + 164 308 + 127 351 + 263 867

Use rounding to check your answers.

4

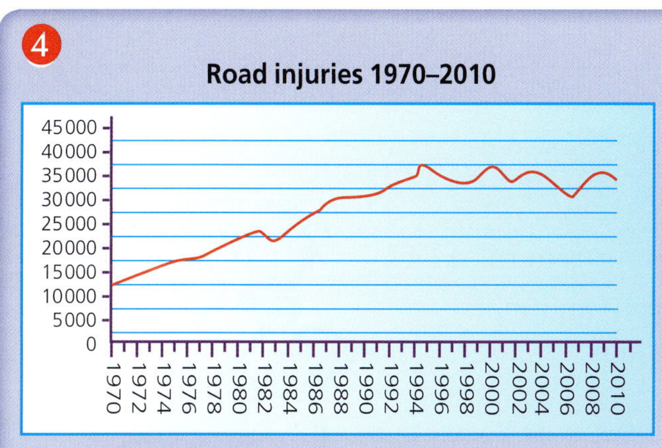

- This graph shows the number of road injuries in each year. (It could be drawn as a line of dots.)
- Find an approximation for the total number of injuries that occurred from:

a 1971 to 1980 ☐

b 1991 to 2000 ☐

c 2001 to 2010 ☐

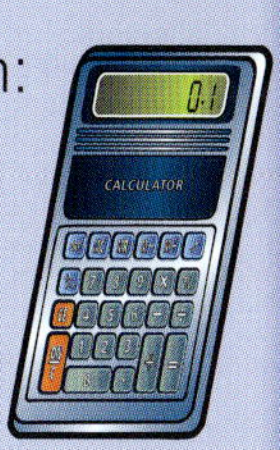

See 2:23 and 2:24 (Addition to 999) and 2:25 (Writing algorithms).

Subtraction of money

Trade a ten-cent coin for 2 five-cent coins.
Trade $1 for 10 ten-cent coins.

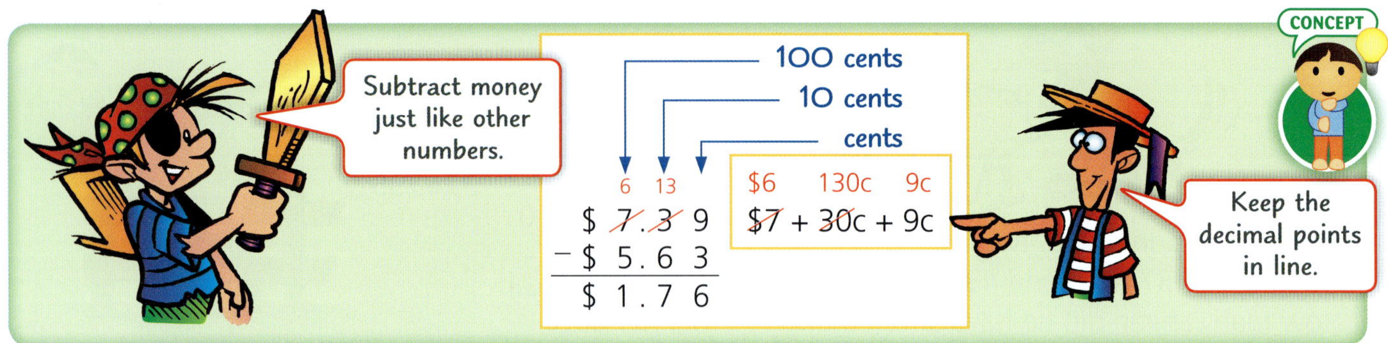

1

a \$6.52 − \$1.30	**b** \$8.79 − \$3.62	**c** \$9.85 − \$3.51	**d** \$7.82 − \$5.43	**e** \$6.24 − \$2.07
f \$4.47 − \$2.63	**g** \$5.38 − \$2.61	**h** \$7.50 − \$1.42	**i** \$3.54 − \$0.20	**j** \$7.55 − \$3.47
k \$8.57 − \$6.87	**l** \$9.57 − \$6.99	**m** \$6.50 − \$2.61	**n** \$7.90 − \$2.45	**o** \$3.52 − \$1.48

2 Write each as an algorithm or use a mental strategy to find your answer.

a \$3.35 – \$1.24 ______ **b** \$8.98 – \$4.00 ______

c \$8.56 – \$3.21 ______ **d** \$4.54 – \$4.49 ______

e \$7.00 – \$1.50 ______ **f** \$3.50 – \$1.99 ______

3 I started with \$8.50. What do I have left if I buy:

a a book for \$7.45? ______ **b** an icy pole for \$2.30? ______

c a drink for \$3.05? ______ **d** a keyring for \$7.30? ______

e a pen for \$4.95? ______ **f** marbles for \$3.55? ______

First to \$5

FUN SPOT

- Each player begins the game with \$10 and takes turns to roll a dice.
- The number shown on each dice is multiplied by 10 and that number of cents is subtracted from the player's total.
- The game continues until one player reaches \$5.

See 2:32 and 2:33 (Subtraction with trading to 999) and 2:34 (Subtraction with 2 trades to 999).

Subtraction with trading to 9999

1 thousand can be traded for 10 hundreds.

CONCEPT

2216 people started in a *Town To Surf* race, but 865 people dropped out before the finish. How many people finished the race?

- We can show 2216 with place-value blocks.
- Trade 1 hundred for 10 tens.
- Trade 1 thousand for 10 hundreds.
- Now we can subtract 865 by taking away 8 hundreds, 6 tens and 5 ones.

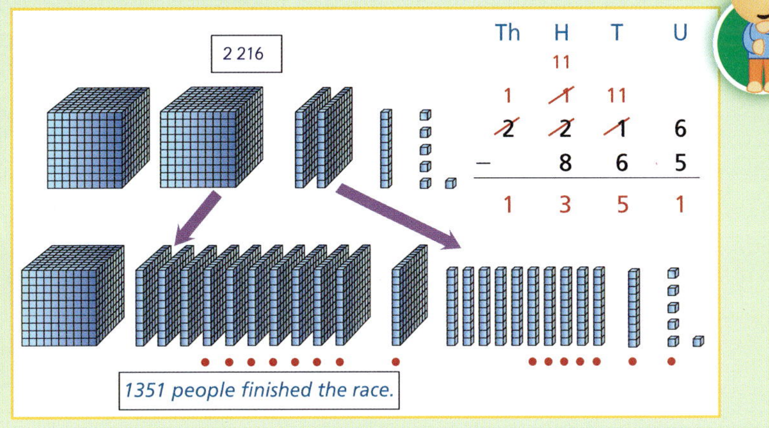

1

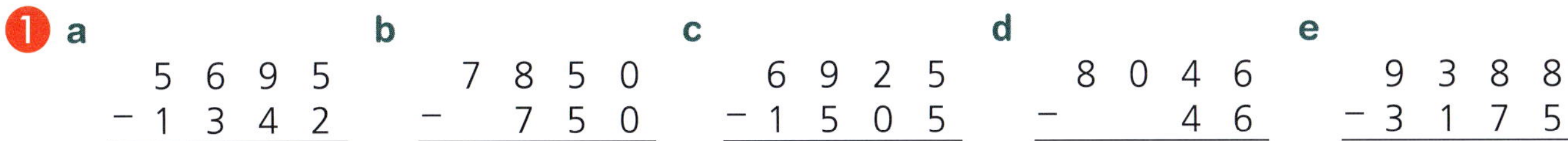

	a	b	c	d	e
	5695	7850	6925	8046	9388
−	1342	750	1505	46	3175

	f	g	h	i	j
	6450	2392	7500	6432	5299
−	380	1950	2180	129	3475

2

	a	b	c	d	e
	4381	2186	4506	7860	9945
−	1605	993	3800	870	6877

	f	g	h	i	j
	2315	6105	9031	7637	5455
−	1946	3827	7429	888	1966

3 **a** Stephanie used her phone 9690 times last year. If 7815 were related to her business, how many were not business calls?

b 3495 calls were on her mobile phone. How many were not on her mobile phone?

c During June her business received $8475 and paid out $4816. How much money did her business make in June?

4 Tran bought 8095 bricks to pave part of his backyard. He used only 7186 bricks. How many were not used?

See 2:32 and 2:33 (Subtraction with trading to 999) and 2:34 (Subtraction with 2 trades to 999).

 • *AUSTRALIAN SIGNPOST MATHS NSW 4* • ISBN 9780655709053

Four-digit subtraction from 1000s

1 thousand can be traded for 10 hundreds.

We received 6000 books from the printers.
We have sold 3721. How many do we have left?

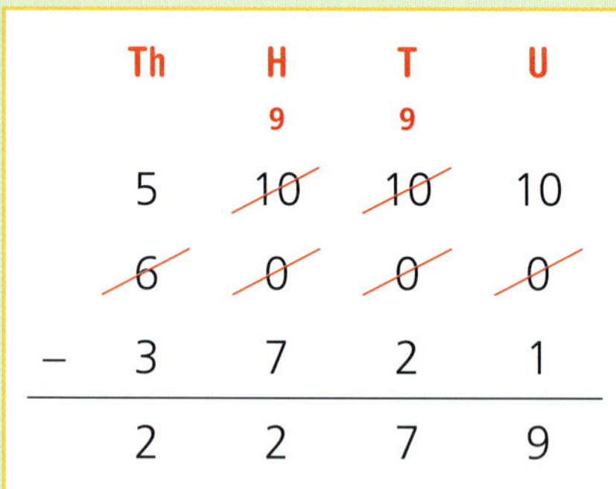

	Th	H	T	U
		9	9	
	5	~~10~~	~~10~~	10
	~~6~~	~~0~~	~~0~~	~~0~~
−	3	7	2	1
	2	2	7	9

6000 has a zero in the units, tens and hundreds columns.

CONCEPT

We trade 1 thousand for 10 hundreds, then trade 1 hundred for 10 tens, then trade 1 ten for 10 ones, and then subtract.

2279 books are left.

1

a $\begin{array}{r} 1000 \\ -\ 436 \\ \hline \end{array}$
b $\begin{array}{r} 2000 \\ -\ 301 \\ \hline \end{array}$
c $\begin{array}{r} 1000 \\ -\ 897 \\ \hline \end{array}$
d $\begin{array}{r} 3000 \\ -\ 725 \\ \hline \end{array}$

e $\begin{array}{r} 7000 \\ -\ 1832 \\ \hline \end{array}$
f $\begin{array}{r} 4000 \\ -\ 2860 \\ \hline \end{array}$
g $\begin{array}{r} 5000 \\ -\ 3900 \\ \hline \end{array}$
h $\begin{array}{r} 9000 \\ -\ 4427 \\ \hline \end{array}$

2

a $\begin{array}{r} 8000 \\ -\ 3450 \\ \hline \end{array}$
b $\begin{array}{r} 6000 \\ -\ 2988 \\ \hline \end{array}$
c $\begin{array}{r} 2000 \\ -\ 1225 \\ \hline \end{array}$
d $\begin{array}{r} 7000 \\ -\ 5355 \\ \hline \end{array}$

e $\begin{array}{r} 7000 \\ -\ 4186 \\ \hline \end{array}$
f $\begin{array}{r} 4000 \\ -\ 2695 \\ \hline \end{array}$
g $\begin{array}{r} 9000 \\ -\ 8972 \\ \hline \end{array}$
h $\begin{array}{r} 8000 \\ -\ 1367 \\ \hline \end{array}$

3

a The longest river in the world is the Nile in North Africa (6690 km). Australia's longest river system is the Murray–Darling which is 3370 km. How much shorter is this than the Nile?

b How much deeper is the Indian Ocean (7125 m at the Java Trench) than the Arctic Ocean (5450 m at the Eurasia Basin)?

c Mount Everest, the highest mountain on Earth, has an altitude of 8850 m. We needed to use a supply of oxygen as we climbed the last 5192 m of our ascent to the top. At what altitude did we begin to use oxygen?

d Tom McSeveny was born on 24 March 1916. How old was he on 24 March 2004?

e John Rivers was born on 27 March 1913. How old was he on 27 March 2004?

● Use estimation to check your answers.

See 2:32 and 2:33 (Subtraction with trading to 999) and 2:34 (Subtraction with 2 trades to 999).

 • *AUSTRALIAN SIGNPOST MATHS NSW 4* • ISBN 9780655709053

Subtraction to 999 999

100 thousand can be traded for 10 ten-thousands.

CONCEPT

986 270 people left a country during a war, and 146 523 did not return. How many returned?

HTh	TTh	Th	H	T	U
		15			
	7	~~5~~	12	6	10
9	~~8~~	~~6~~	~~2~~	~~7~~	~~0~~
− 1	4	6	5	2	3
8	3	9	7	4	7

$^{1}2$ means 12.

Another setting out:

$$\begin{array}{r} 9\ {}^{7}\not{8}\ {}^{15}\not{6}\ {}^{1}2\ {}^{6}\not{7}\ {}^{1}0 \\ -\ 1\ 4\ 6\ 5\ 2\ 3 \\ \hline 8\ 3\ 9\ 7\ 4\ 7 \end{array}$$

839 747 returned.

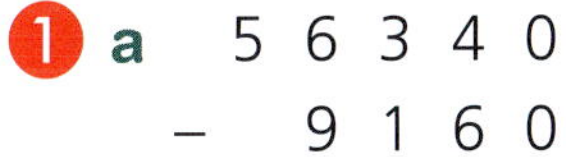

1

a $56340 - 9160$

b $87115 - 33485$

c $64009 - 21333$

d $32457 - 8098$

e $96000 - 81000$

f $89693 - 65355$

g $65250 - 9346$

h $22760 - 897$

2

a $193583 - 27638$

b $345350 - 18181$

c $560499 - 20716$

d $783615 - 9999$

e $620650 - 136177$

f $750000 - 385000$

g $684326 - 232895$

Ask: Does the answer make sense?

3

a Mr Rich wanted to buy a house advertised for sale at \$895 000. He offered \$819 900 and the offer was accepted. How much less than the advertised price did he pay?

b Mr Rich earned \$555 360 last year but had to pay \$257 285 in tax. How much did he have left?

c The house Mr Rich bought was on 12 hectares of land. 45 000 m^2 of the land was covered with trees. How many square metres were not covered by trees? (1 ha = 10 000 m^2)

d On this land, Mr Rich grew apple trees. This year he produced 112 000 apples. He sold 85 000 apples. How many were not sold?

e In February 2012 there were 842 300 part-time workers in Victoria. If 626 800 of the workers were in Melbourne, how many were outside of Melbourne?

See 2:32 and 2:33 (Subtraction with trading to 999) and 2:34 (Subtraction with 2 trades to 999).

The calendar

A leap year happens once in every four years.

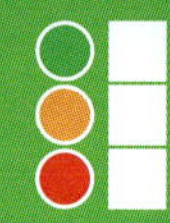

February						
Sun	Mon	Tues	Wed	Thur	Fri	Sat
		1	2	3	4	5
6	7	8	9	10	11	12
13	14	15	16	17	18	19
20	21	22	23	24	25	26
27	28	29				

Study the calendar then answer these questions.

1 a On what day of the week is the 18th?
b Write the date of the first Thursday.
c Write the date of the last Friday.
d How many Saturdays are in February?
e How many Tuesdays are there?
f On what day does February begin?
g How many days are in February on this calendar?
h How many days are in February in most years?

7 days in a week
2 weeks in a fortnight
52 weeks in a year
365 days in a year
366 days in a leap year (one year in four)
12 months in a year

2 Write the date for:
a the first Wednesday
b the first Sunday
c the last Saturday
d the second Monday

3 Write the day of:
a 10th February
b 4th February
c 19th February
d 21st February

4 Write the dates for:
a the first weekend
b the second weekend
c the third weekend
d all the Wednesdays

INVESTIGATION

Research
Last year, what was the highest temperature in:
- February?
- July?

ACTIVITY

On this timeline, show events that happen on Saturday.

7 o'clock — midday — 10 o'clock

See 3:19 (Time).

 AUSTRALIAN SIGNPOST MATHS NSW 4 • ISBN 9780655709053

The calendar

Page xxiii of the dictionary shows another way to know the days in each month.

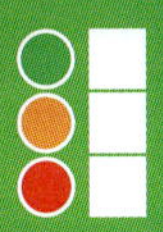

Thirty days has September, April, June and November.
All the rest have thirty-one, except for February alone,
Which has twenty-eight days clear,
and twenty-nine days each leap year.

There are 12 months in a year.

Here is a jingle to help you to remember how many days there are in each month.

A calendar shows the way a year is broken up into months, weeks and days.

January

S	M	T	W	T	F	S
		1	2	3	4	5
6	7	8	9	10	11	12
13	14	15	16	17	18	19
20	21	22	23	24	25	26
27	28	29	30	31		

February

S	M	T	W	T	F	S
					1	2
3	4	5	6	7	8	9
10	11	12	13	14	15	16
17	18	19	20	21	22	23
24	25	26	27	28		

March

S	M	T	W	T	F	S
31					1	2
3	4	5	6	7	8	9
10	11	12	13	14	15	16
17	18	19	20	21	22	23
24	25	26	27	28	29	30

April

S	M	T	W	T	F	S
	1	2	3	4	5	6
7	8	9	10	11	12	13
14	15	16	17	18	19	20
21	22	23	24	25	26	27
28	29	30				

May

S	M	T	W	T	F	S
			1	2	3	4
5	6	7	8	9	10	11
12	13	14	15	16	17	18
19	20	21	22	23	24	25
26	27	28	29	30	31	

June

S	M	T	W	T	F	S
30						1
2	3	4	5	6	7	8
9	10	11	12	13	14	15
16	17	18	19	20	21	22
23	24	25	26	27	28	29

July

S	M	T	W	T	F	S
	1	2	3	4	5	6
7	8	9	10	11	12	13
14	15	16	17	18	19	20
21	22	23	24	25	26	27
28	29	30	31			

August

S	M	T	W	T	F	S
				1	2	3
4	5	6	7	8	9	10
11	12	13	14	15	16	17
18	19	20	21	22	23	24
25	26	27	28	29	30	31

September

S	M	T	W	T	F	S
1	2	3	4	5	6	7
8	9	10	11	12	13	14
15	16	17	18	19	20	21
22	23	24	25	26	27	28
29	30					

October

S	M	T	W	T	F	S
		1	2	3	4	5
6	7	8	9	10	11	12
13	14	15	16	17	18	19
20	21	22	23	24	25	26
27	28	29	30	31		

November

S	M	T	W	T	F	S
					1	2
3	4	5	6	7	8	9
10	11	12	13	14	15	16
17	18	19	20	21	22	23
24	25	26	27	28	29	30

December

S	M	T	W	T	F	S
1	2	3	4	5	6	7
8	9	10	11	12	13	14
15	16	17	18	19	20	21
22	23	24	25	26	27	28
29	30	31				

1. Which month comes before:
   - a February? ☐ b November? ☐ c June? ☐ d October? ☐
2. How many days are in:
   - a April? ☐ b August? ☐ c December? ☐ d March? ☐
3. Look carefully at the month of May. Write the date of:
   - a the first Sunday ☐ b the first Wednesday ☐
4. Look at the month of September. What is the date:
   - a one week after 12th? ☐ b two days before 27th? ☐
5. What day is:
   - a 13th September? ☐ b 21st June? ☐ c 2nd February? ☐
   - d 31st May? ☐ e 29th August? ☐ f 3rd January? ☐
6. How many weeks and days is it from 12 July to:
   - a 25 July? ☐ b 23 August? ☐
   - c 2 October? ☐ d 25 December? ☐
7. How many weeks and days before the 13 April was:
   - a 1 January? ☐ b 26 January? ☐

See 3:19 (Time).

 • *AUSTRALIAN SIGNPOST MATHS NSW 4* • ISBN 9780655709053

Timelines

You need a line showing time and space to record what happened.

Overseas trip arrival times

1. How many foreign cities did we visit? ☐
2. Counting the days travelling, how long was our holiday? ☐ days

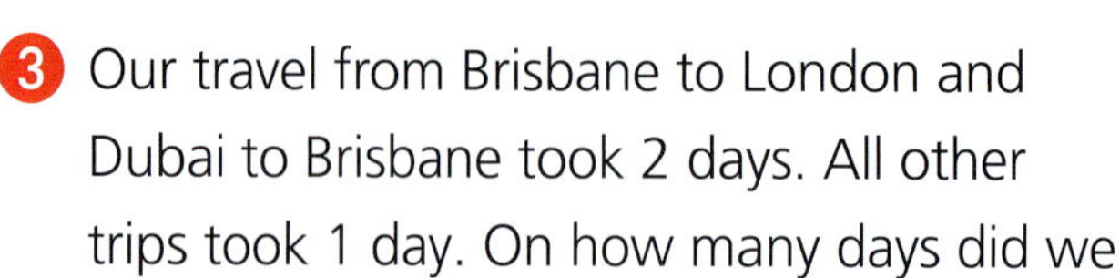

3. Our travel from Brisbane to London and Dubai to Brisbane took 2 days. All other trips took 1 day. On how many days did we travel? ☐
4. Which city did we visit on:
   - **a** 15 June? ☐ **b** 28 June? ☐
   - **c** 5 July? ☐ **d** 20 June? ☐
5. Not counting the days when we travelled, how many days did we spend in:
   - **a** Rome? ☐ **b** Istanbul? ☐
   - **c** Amman? ☐ **d** Athens? ☐
6. Where were we on:
   - **a** 12 June? ☐ **b** 18 June? ☐
   - **c** 30 June? ☐ **d** 6 July? ☐
7. We left Brisbane at 10 am on 9 June and arrived in London at 6:30 pm on 10 June. How long did it take us to travel to London? ☐
8. Make a timeline for one school day, from the time you wake up until the time you go to bed.

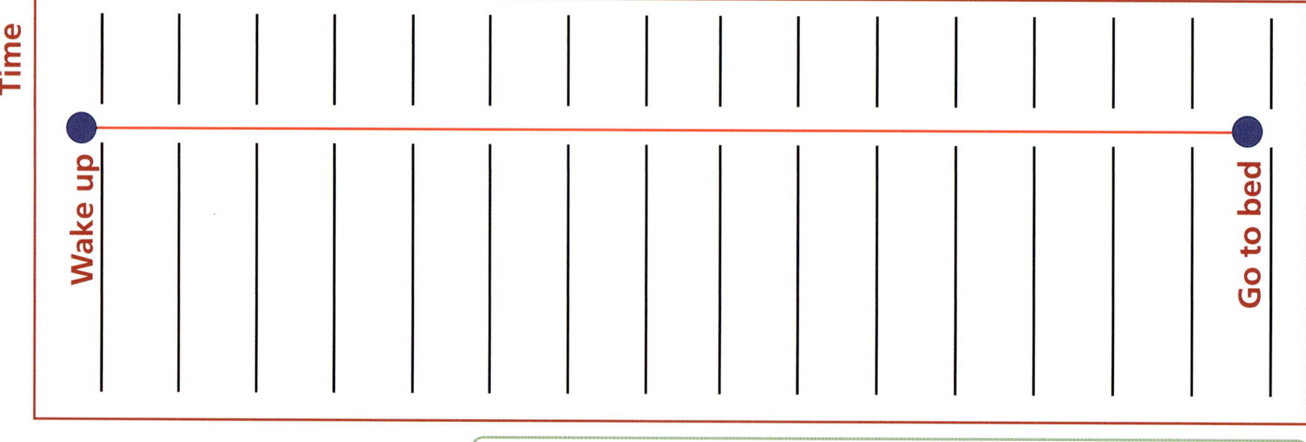

How did you make your timeline? ☐

See 3:29 (Using am and pm time).

 • *AUSTRALIAN SIGNPOST MATHS NSW 4* • ISBN 9780655709053

Comparing decimal measurements

15·45 **s** means …

15 and forty-five hundredths **seconds**.

9·31 **s** means …

9 and thirty-one hundredths **seconds**.

1 **Yes** or **No**?

a The fastest time for a race is the smallest time.

b 31·14 s is faster than 31·65 s.

c 9·65 s is slower than 8·1 s.

2 Match these race times to the number line to show their order.

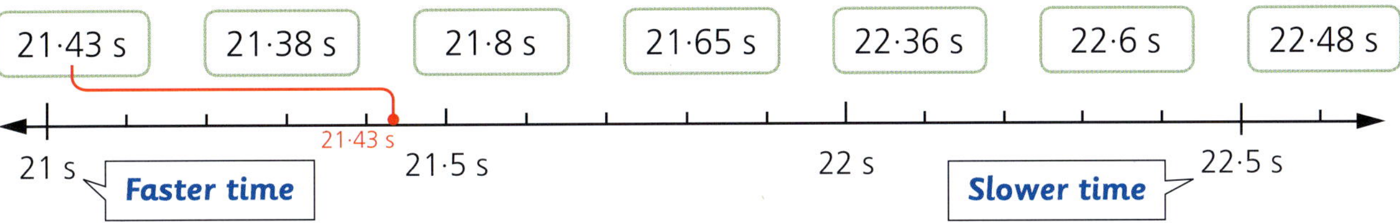

3 Circle the faster time (smallest decimal) in each pair.

a	b	c	d
4·75 s 4·70 s	31·46 s 30·40 s	39·74 s 40·06 s	59·60 s 59·50 s

e	f	g	h
29·56 s 29·83 s	19·14 s 26·99 s	36·43 s 27·86 s	19·63 s 19·62 s

A stopwatch allows accurate measurement of time intervals.

4 Examine and operate various types of stopwatches.
Discuss the following:

- Give an example of time being measured to the nearest **hundredth** of a second.
- What is the greatest length of time that can be measured on a stopwatch?
- Why does a timekeeper of a 100 m race watch for the smoke instead of listening for the sound of the gun?

- How accurately can you measure time?
Compare and discuss your results.
With a partner, find how long it takes to hop ten metres.

See 3:31 (The stopwatch).

 • *AUSTRALIAN SIGNPOST MATHS NSW 4* • ISBN 9780655709053

Temperature

Hottest time of year: December, January, February
Coldest time of year: June, July, August

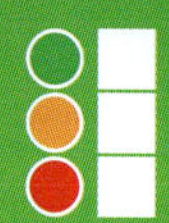

To read temperature we use the Celsius temperature scale.

0°C is the freezing point of water.
100°C is the boiling point of water.

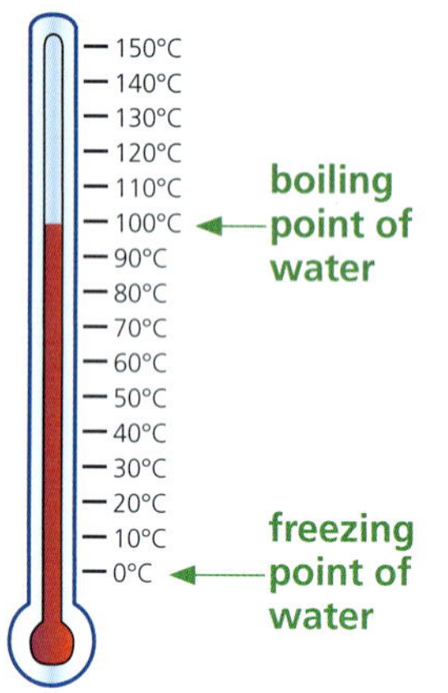

1 Draw lines to make each statement true.

The boiling point of water •	• is cool to warm weather.
35°C to 45°C •	• is cold weather.
25°C to 35°C •	• is 100°C.
15°C to 25°C •	• is 0°C.
5°C to 15°C •	• is warm to hot weather.
The freezing point of water •	• is very hot weather.

2 What temperature is shown on each thermometer?

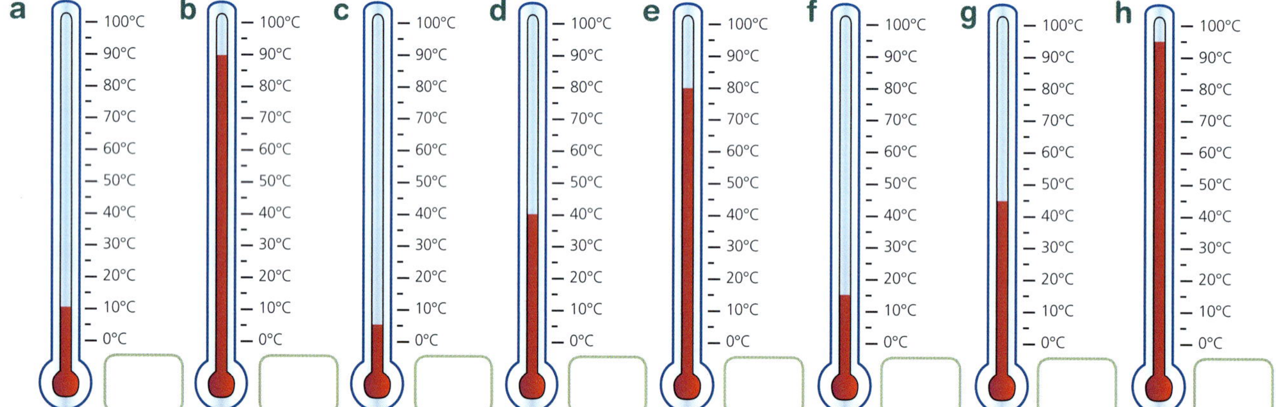

3 Each thermometer above is measuring the temperature of water.

a Which three thermometers show the water is hot?

b Which three thermometers show the water is cold?

c Which two thermometers show it is warm?

Temperature chart

Normal human body temperature is between 36·5°C and 37·5°C.

- Fill a container with warm water.
- Place a thermometer in the water and record the temperature every five minutes.
- Graph the results.
- Discuss why the temperature dropped quickly at the beginning of the experiment.

See 3:11 (Using measurement scales), 3:38 (Personal benchmarks) and *Extra Support 18* (Recording temperature).

Recording temperature

35 36 37 38 39 40

36.5° is halfway between 36° and 37° Celsius.

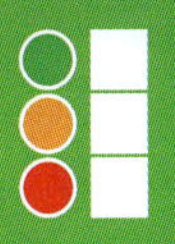

ACTIVITY

- When reading a thermometer use the nearest graduation mark.

- Read aloud these temperatures.
  - 42°C • 27°C • 19°C • 63°C • 100°C • 37°C • 84°C • 34°C
  - 16°C • 0°C • 96°C • 21°C • 39°C • 72°C • 55°C • 25°C

1 Write these measurements of temperature in short form.

a twenty-five degrees Celsius		**b** zero degrees Celsius	
c eighteen degrees Celsius		**d** fifty-eight degrees Celsius	
e eighty-six degrees Celsius		**f** thirty-seven degrees Celsius	
g forty-one degrees Celsius		**h** seventy-three degrees Celsius	

2 On each thermometer, colour the mercury to match the given temperature.

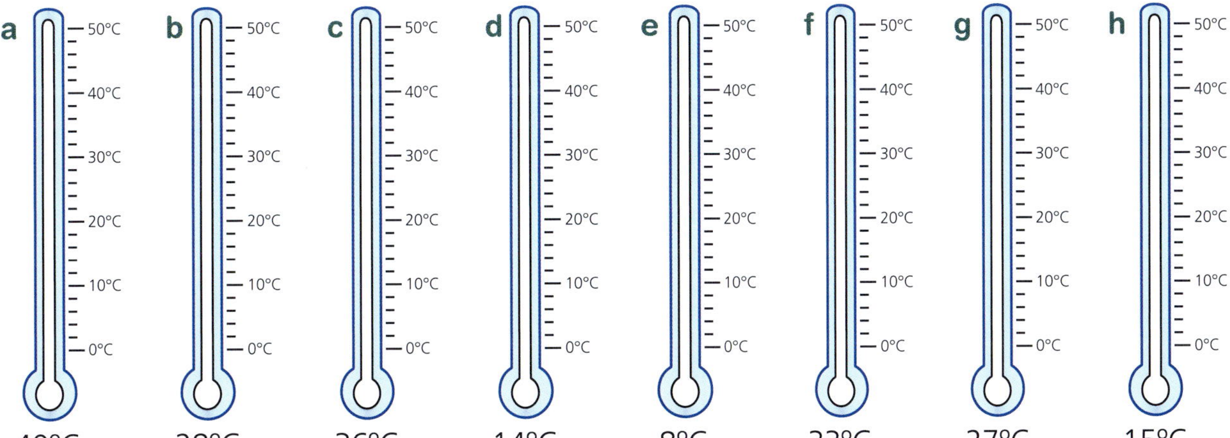

3 Draw lines to match to the most suitable temperature.

a a cold glass of milk	40°C	**f** a very cold day	100°C
b a very hot day	96°C	**g** water boiling	17°C
c a warm day	70°C	**h** body temperature	67°C
d a bowl of hot soup	26°C	**i** a cup of coffee	9°C
e a pot of very hot tea	2°C	**j** a cool day	37°C

See 3:11 (Using measurement scales), 3:38 (Personal benchmarks) and *Extra Support 17* (Temperature).

 • *AUSTRALIAN SIGNPOST MATHS NSW 4* • ISBN 9780655709053

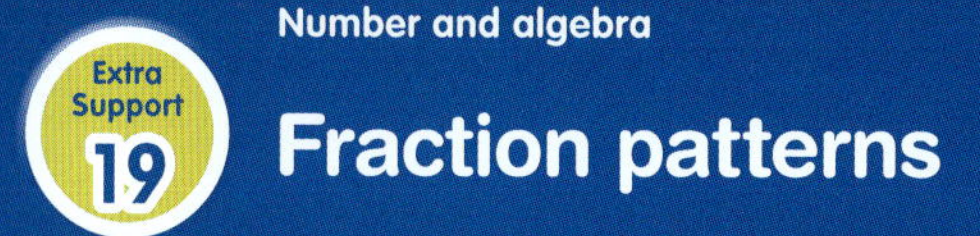

Fraction patterns

These belong on a number line that shows fractions.

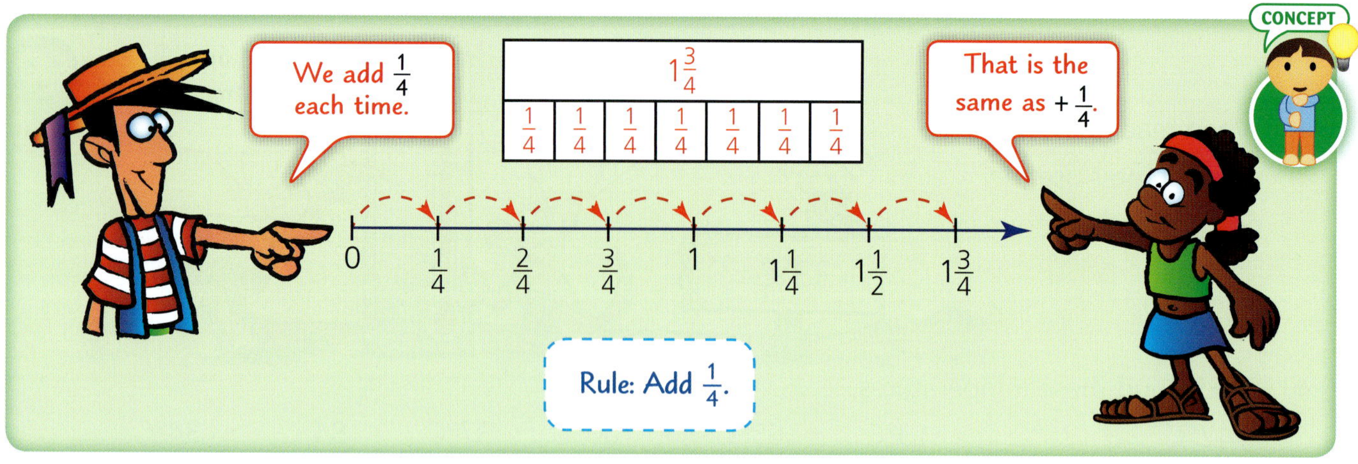

1 Complete each number line and write the rule.

a 0, ☐, 1, ☐, 2

Rule: ☐

b 0, ☐, ☐, ☐, 1

Rule: ☐

c 0, $\frac{1}{3}$, ☐, 1, $1\frac{1}{3}$, ☐, ☐, ☐, ☐, 3, ☐

Rule: ☐

d 0, ☐, ☐, ☐, ☐, ☐, ☐, ☐, 1, $1\frac{1}{8}$, $1\frac{2}{8}$

Rule: ☐

e 0, $\frac{1}{5}$, ☐, $\frac{3}{5}$, $\frac{4}{5}$, ☐, $1\frac{1}{5}$, ☐, ☐, ☐, ☐

Rule: ☐

f 0, ☐, ☐, ☐, ☐, ☐, ☐, ☐, $1\frac{2}{6}$, $1\frac{3}{6}$, $1\frac{4}{6}$

Rule: ☐

Be careful!

See 1:07 and 1:08 (Fractions beyond 1), and 1:13 (Equivalent fractions).

Answers

1:01

1 a

2 a 3 b 4 c 4 d 3

3 a 1040 b 7018 c 5179 d 9007

4 a four thousand and twenty-three
b nine thousand and thirty

5 a 6246, 6426, 6624 b 8345, 8453, 8543

6 a 8402, 8204, 8042 b 8302, 8203, 2083

7 yes

8 a 8542 b 8524

1:02

1 a 10 b 10 c 10 d 100
e 100 f 1000

2 a A b D c F d H

3 a E b A and B c E and F d A and B
e 10 times as big

1:03

1 a 3700 b 4200 c 1400 d 9300
e 6500 f 6700 g 9000 h 5900

2 a 32 000 b 83 000 c 11 000 d 57 000
e 23 000 f 52 000 g 47 000 h 69 000

3 a 50 000 b 80 000 c 30 000 d 90 000
e 90 000 f 30 000 g 70 000 h 70 000

4 a 52 967, 52 849, 52 621, 53 297, 53 346 will be circled.
b 79 621, 81 119, 75 000, 83 713, 76 014 will be circled.

5 a true b false c false d true
e true

6

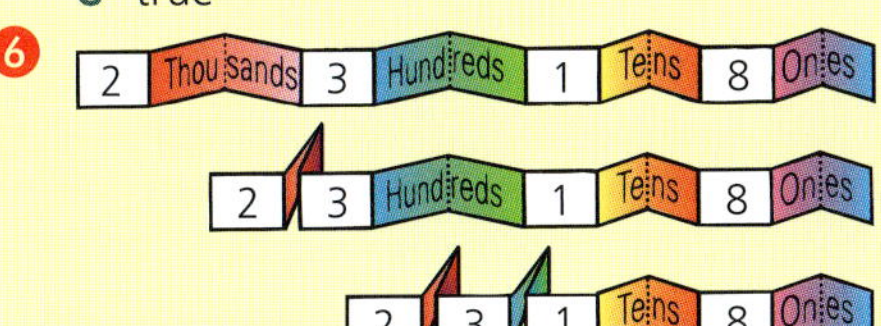

1:04

1 a

Thousands					
H	T	O	H	T	O
	9	5	0	0	0

90 000 + 5000
95 thousands
950 hundreds
50 000 + 45 000
(Answers will vary).

b

Thousands					
H	T	O	H	T	O
	4	8	0	0	0

40 000 + 8000
48 thousands
480 hundreds
30 000 + 18 000
(Answers will vary).

2 a 20 thousands and 22 thousands
b 20 thousands and 38 thousands
c 20 thousands and 17 thousands

3 a 5000, 15 000 b 3000, 13 000
c 8000, 18 000 d 3000, 13 000
e 2500, 52 500 f 1300, 41 300

4 a 22 679 b 22 697 c 97 262

1:05

1 a $\frac{1}{12}$ b $\frac{2}{3}$ c $\frac{2}{6}$ d $\frac{3}{12}$ e $\frac{7}{12}$
f $\frac{5}{12}$ g $\frac{3}{6}$ h $\frac{11}{12}$

2 a $\frac{11}{12}$ b $\frac{1}{3}$ c $\frac{4}{6}$ d $\frac{9}{12}$ e $\frac{5}{12}$
f $\frac{7}{12}$ g $\frac{3}{6}$ h $\frac{1}{12}$

3 a b c d
e f g h

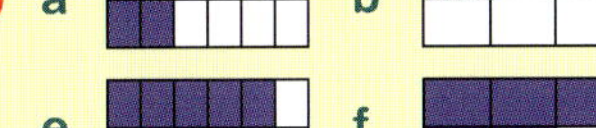

4 a $\frac{5}{6}$ b $\frac{3}{12}$ c $\frac{5}{12}$ d $\frac{11}{12}$ e $\frac{2}{6}$ f $\frac{9}{12}$

5 a $\frac{1}{6}$ b $\frac{9}{12}$ c $\frac{7}{12}$ d $\frac{1}{12}$ e $\frac{4}{6}$ f $\frac{3}{12}$

1:06

1 a $\frac{1}{2}$ will be circled. b $\frac{1}{4}$ will be circled.

2

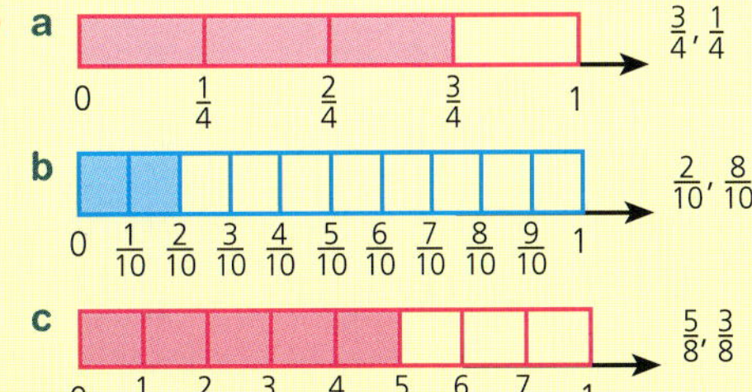

d

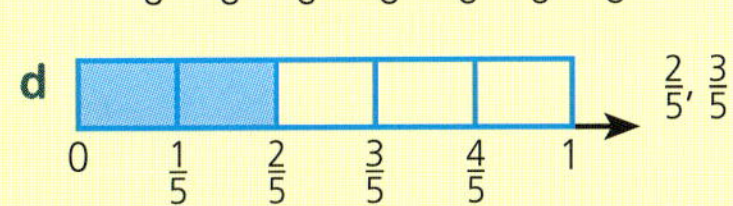

a and **c** will be circled.

3 a true b false c true
d true e false f true

Investigation: Answers will vary. Each half is half of a different quantity, so cannot be the same.

1:07

1 a $2\frac{1}{2}$ b $3\frac{1}{2}$, $\frac{7}{2}$, 7 halves

c $4\frac{1}{2}$, $\frac{9}{2}$, 9 halves d $1\frac{1}{4}$, $\frac{5}{4}$, 5 quarters

e $2\frac{2}{4}$, $\frac{10}{4}$, 10 quarters f $3\frac{3}{4}$, $\frac{15}{4}$, 15 quarters

g $2\frac{2}{3}$, $\frac{8}{3}$, 8 thirds h $1\frac{2}{6}$, $\frac{8}{6}$, 8 sixths

i $2\frac{1}{5}$, $\frac{11}{5}$, 11 fifths

2 0, $\frac{1}{4}$, $\frac{2}{4}$, $\frac{3}{4}$, $\frac{4}{4}$, $\frac{5}{4}$, $\frac{6}{4}$, $\frac{7}{4}$, $\frac{8}{4}$ (continues below)

0, $\frac{1}{4}$, $\frac{2}{4}$, $\frac{3}{4}$, 1, $1\frac{1}{4}$, $1\frac{2}{4}$, $1\frac{3}{4}$, 2

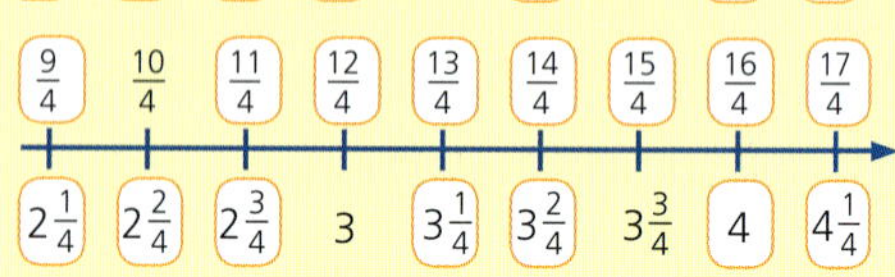

3 a $\frac{3}{2}$ b $\frac{11}{5}$ c $\frac{14}{4}$ d $\frac{9}{5}$

e $\frac{11}{4}$ f $\frac{13}{4}$ g $\frac{14}{3}$ h $\frac{21}{8}$

4 a $1\frac{3}{4}$ b $1\frac{4}{5}$ c $2\frac{3}{4}$ d $2\frac{1}{5}$

e $1\frac{3}{5}$ f $3\frac{1}{4}$ g $2\frac{4}{5}$ h $4\frac{1}{4}$

1:08

1 a 3, $3\frac{1}{3}$, $3\frac{2}{3}$, 4 b five thirds, six thirds (or 2)

2 a 1 b $1\frac{1}{2}$ c 2 d $2\frac{1}{2}$

3 a $\frac{3}{2}$ or $1\frac{1}{2}$ b $\frac{7}{2}$ or $3\frac{1}{2}$ c $\frac{17}{2}$ or $8\frac{1}{2}$

d $\frac{11}{4}$ or $2\frac{3}{4}$ e $\frac{17}{4}$ or $4\frac{1}{4}$ f $\frac{31}{4}$ or $7\frac{3}{4}$

g $\frac{33}{2}$ or $16\frac{1}{2}$

4 a $1\frac{2}{5}$ b $2\frac{1}{2}$ c $2\frac{3}{5}$ d $2\frac{1}{4}$

e $1\frac{5}{8}$ f $2\frac{2}{5}$ g $7\frac{1}{2}$ h $3\frac{2}{5}$

5 a $\frac{6}{5}$ b $\frac{11}{2}$ c $\frac{17}{5}$ d $\frac{19}{3}$

e $\frac{11}{8}$ f $\frac{17}{6}$ g $\frac{24}{5}$ h $\frac{17}{10}$

1:09

1

Thousands					
H	T	O	H	T	O
	2	6	3	2	4
1	1	6	8	0	0
5	1	3	0	4	7
9	2	6	0	1	1

2 a 34 528 b 67 934 c 58 462

d 92 748 e 82 359 f 48 673

g 359 187 h 927 235 i 715 728

3 Answers will vary.

1:10

1 a 49 768 b 37 281 c 345 022 d 978 411

2 a 26 301 b 69 309 c 692 997

3 a 28 747 b 50 378 c 839 625 d 417 713

4 a 526 493 b 895 651

5 a 8000 b 1000 c 600 000 d 80

e 900 f 400 000

1:11

1 a 400 000 b 900 000 c 200 000 d 400 000

e 800 000 f 300 000 g 700 000 h 300 000

i 200 000

2 a 70 000 b 40 000 c 80 000 d 50 000

e 60 000 f 20 000 g 90 000 h 60 000

i 30 000

3 a 347 291, 369 204, 383 978

b 834 820, 836 736, 863 846

c 380 672, 387 462, 389 245

4 a 50 000 b 80 000 c 900 d 0

e 10 000 f 600 000

Activity: Answers will vary.

1:12

1 a $\frac{2}{10}$ b $\frac{2}{5}$ c $\frac{8}{10}$ d $\frac{3}{5}$

e $\frac{1}{2}$ f $\frac{4}{10}$ g $\frac{5}{10}$ h 1

2 a $\frac{1}{10}$ b $\frac{1}{2}$ c $\frac{3}{5}$ d $\frac{4}{5}$

3 0, $\frac{1}{4}$, $\frac{2}{4}$, $\frac{3}{4}$, 1 or $\frac{4}{4}$

0, $\frac{1}{8}$, $\frac{2}{8}$, $\frac{3}{8}$, $\frac{4}{8}$, $\frac{5}{8}$, $\frac{6}{8}$, $\frac{7}{8}$, 1 or $\frac{8}{8}$

4 a $\frac{2}{8}$ b $\frac{2}{4}$ or $\frac{1}{2}$ c $\frac{1}{2}$ or $\frac{4}{8}$ d $\frac{2}{4}$ or $\frac{4}{8}$

e $\frac{3}{4}$ f $\frac{6}{8}$ g $\frac{1}{4}$ h $\frac{2}{2}$ or $\frac{4}{4}$ (or 1)

5 a true b true c false d yes

6 a 1 b 1 c 1 d 2

1:13

1 a $\frac{1}{2}$ or $\frac{4}{8}$ b $\frac{1}{2}$ or $\frac{2}{4}$ c $\frac{3}{4}$

d 1 or $\frac{2}{2}$ or $\frac{8}{8}$ e $\frac{2}{2}$ or $\frac{4}{4}$ or $\frac{8}{8}$ f $\frac{2}{4}$ or $\frac{4}{8}$

2 a $\frac{1}{3}$ b $\frac{2}{3}$ c 1 or $\frac{2}{2}$ or $\frac{3}{3}$

d 1 or $\frac{2}{2}$ or $\frac{6}{6}$ e $\frac{2}{6}$ f $\frac{4}{6}$

3 a T b T c T d F e T f T

4 a T b T c T d F e F f T

5 a $\frac{4}{3}$, $\frac{5}{3}$, $\frac{6}{3}$, $\frac{7}{3}$ or $1\frac{1}{3}$, $1\frac{2}{3}$, 2, $2\frac{1}{3}$

b $\frac{4}{4}$, $\frac{5}{4}$, $\frac{6}{4}$, $\frac{7}{4}$, $\frac{8}{4}$ or 1, $1\frac{1}{4}$, $1\frac{2}{4}$ (or $1\frac{1}{2}$), $1\frac{3}{4}$, 2

 AUSTRALIAN SIGNPOST MATHS NSW 4 • ISBN 9780655709053

c $\frac{4}{6}, \frac{5}{6}, \frac{6}{6}, \frac{7}{6}, \frac{8}{6}, \frac{9}{6}$ or $\frac{4}{6}, \frac{5}{6}, 1, 1\frac{1}{6}, 1\frac{2}{6}, 1\frac{3}{6}$ (or $1\frac{1}{2}$)

d $\frac{4}{8}, \frac{5}{8}, \frac{6}{8}, \frac{7}{8}, \frac{8}{8}, \frac{9}{8}, \frac{10}{8}$

or $\frac{4}{8}, \frac{5}{8}, \frac{6}{8}, \frac{7}{8}, 1, 1\frac{1}{8}, 1\frac{2}{8}$ (or $1\frac{1}{4}$)

6 three quarters, four quarters, five quarters, six quarters.

1:14

1 **a** **b** **c** **d**

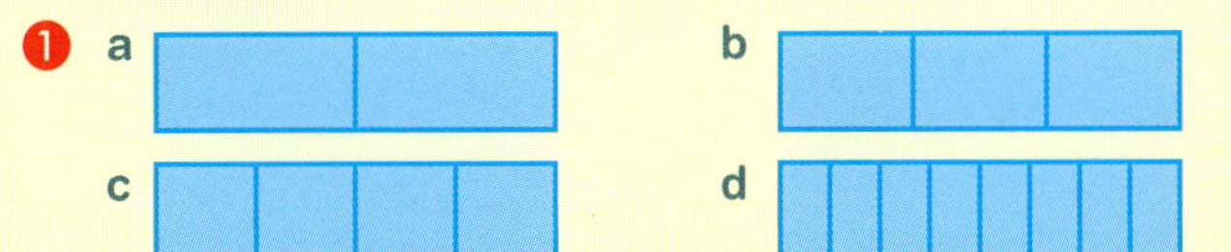

These fractions are equal to 1 whole.

2 **a** **b** **c**

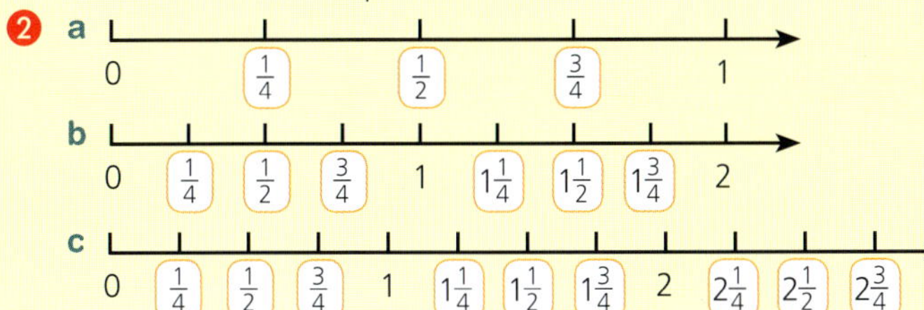

3 **a** **b** **c**

No. Each half is not the same size.

d **e** **f**

No. Each quarter is not the same size.

4 **a** 5 m **b** 7 m **c** 4 m **d** 2 m **e** 1 m

1:15

1 **a** $\frac{3}{10}$ **b** $\frac{5}{10}$ **c** $\frac{9}{10}$ **d** $\frac{7}{10}$ **e** $\frac{6}{10}$

2 **a** 0·2 **b** 0·5 **c** 0·1 **d** 0·9 **e** 0·8 **f** 0·3
g 0·7 **h** 1 **i** 0 **j** 0·4 **k** 0·6

3 **a** $\frac{3}{5}$ **b** $\frac{4}{5}$ **c** $\frac{5}{5}$

4 **a** $\frac{5}{5}$ **b** $\frac{1}{5}$ **c** $\frac{2}{5}$ **d** $\frac{4}{5}$ **e** $\frac{3}{5}$ **f** $\frac{5}{5}$

5 **a** $\frac{4}{10}$ **b** $\frac{8}{10}$ **c** $\frac{6}{10}$ **d** $\frac{2}{10}$

1:16

1 **a** 2·9 **b** 1·5

2 **a** 0·1 **b** 0·3 **c** 0·5 **d** 0·4 **e** 0·2
f 0·8 **g** 0·9 **h** 0·7 **i** 1

3 **a** 1·1 **b** 1·6 **c** 1·2 **d** 2·3 **e** 2·4
f 2·9 **g** 3·5 **h** 3·8 **i** 3·7

4 **a** $\frac{1}{2}$ or $\frac{5}{10}$ **b** $\frac{7}{10}$ **c** $\frac{1}{5}$ or $\frac{2}{10}$
d $1\frac{2}{5}$ or $1\frac{4}{10}$ **e** $3\frac{1}{10}$ **f** $2\frac{4}{5}$ or $2\frac{8}{10}$

g $6\frac{9}{10}$ **h** $5\frac{3}{10}$ **i** $7\frac{3}{5}$ or $7\frac{6}{10}$
j $2\frac{5}{10}$ **k** $5\frac{2}{5}$ or $5\frac{4}{10}$ **l** $6\frac{7}{10}$
m $\frac{9}{10}$ **n** $1\frac{9}{10}$ **o** $2\frac{9}{10}$

5 **a** 4·1 **b** 8·3 **c** 5·2

1:17

1 **a** 0·7 **b** 0·5 **c** 0·6 **d** 0·1
e 0·8 **f** 0·9 **g** 0·2 **h** 0·4
i 1·1 **j** 1·3 **k** 1·9 **l** 1·8

2 **a** $\frac{5}{10}$ – 0·5, $\frac{1}{10}$ – 0·1, $\frac{6}{10}$ – 0·6
b $\frac{8}{10}$ – 0·8, $\frac{4}{10}$ – 0·4, $\frac{9}{10}$ – 0·9
c

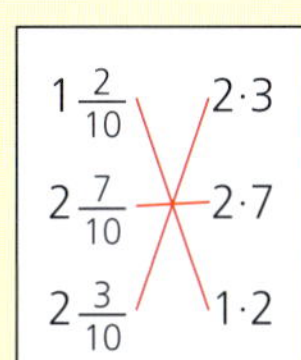

3 **a** 0·9 **b** 0·7 **c** 0·6 **d** 0·2
e 0·8 **f** 0·3 **g** 0·5 **h** 1 or 1·0
i 0·1 **j** 0·8 **k** 0·5 **l** 1·9 **m** 1·3 **n** 1·0

4 0, $\frac{1}{10}$, $\frac{2}{10}$, $\frac{3}{10}$, $\frac{4}{10}$, $\frac{5}{10}$, $\frac{6}{10}$, $\frac{7}{10}$, $\frac{8}{10}$, $\frac{9}{10}$, 1, $1\frac{1}{10}$, $1\frac{2}{10}$, $1\frac{3}{10}$
0, 0·1, 0·2, 0·3, 0·4, 0·5, 0·6, 0·7, 0·8, 0·9, 1·0, 1·1, 1·2, 1·3

5 **a** 0·7 **b** 0·6 **c** 0·5 **d** 0·9

1:18

1 100

2 **a** 16 out of 100 $\frac{16}{100}$ 0·16
b 27 out of 100 $\frac{27}{100}$ 0·27
c 18 out of 100 $\frac{18}{100}$ 0·18
d 45 out of 100 $\frac{45}{100}$ 0·45

3 0·39

4 **a** 0·36, $\frac{36}{100}$ **b** 0·79, $\frac{79}{100}$
c 0·57, $\frac{57}{100}$ **d** 0·85, $\frac{85}{100}$
e 0·27, $\frac{27}{100}$ **f** 0·18, $\frac{18}{100}$
g 0·62, $\frac{62}{100}$ **h** 0·44, $\frac{44}{100}$

1:19

1

		hundreds	tens	ones	.	tenths	hundredths	
a	$\frac{4}{10}$			0	·	4		
b	$\frac{90}{100}$			0	·	9		or 0·90
c	$\frac{20}{100}$			0	·	2		or 0·20
d	$\frac{8}{10}$			0	·	8		
e	$\frac{52}{100}$			0	·	5	2	
f	$\frac{37}{100}$			0	·	3	7	

2

		hundreds	tens	ones	.	tenths	hundredths	
a	$1\frac{6}{10}$			1	·	6		
b	$6\frac{30}{100}$			6	·	3		or 6·30
c	$58\frac{63}{100}$		5	8	·	6	3	
d	$124\frac{2}{10}$	1	2	4	·	2		
e	$84\frac{78}{100}$		8	4	·	7	8	
f	$705\frac{49}{100}$	7	0	5	·	4	9	

3 a 1·5 b 2·4 c 6·2 d 8·4

4 a 4 tenths and 6 hundredths or 46 hundredths
b 7 tenths and 3 hundredths or 73 hundredths

1:20

1 a 0·6 b 0·05 c 0·87 d 0·48

2 a C b A c C d A

3

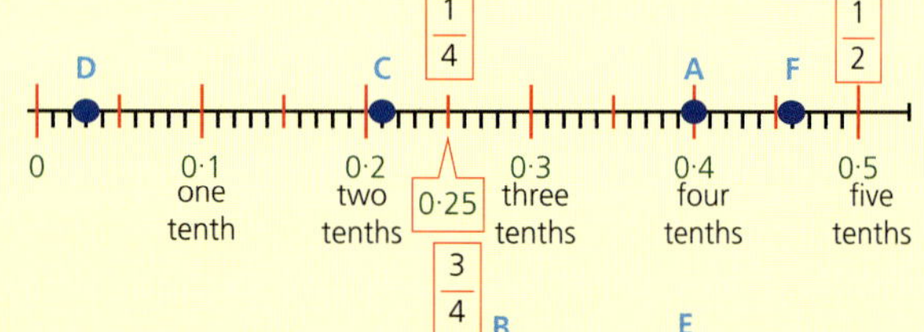

3/4
B
E
0·5
0·6 six tenths
0·7 seven tenths
0·75
0·8 eight tenths
0·9 nine tenths
1

4 a 0·5 b 0·9 c 0·3 d 1·21 e 2·3
f 2·4 g 0·3 h 0·7 i 1·5 j $\frac{1}{4}$
k 1·8 l $\frac{1}{2}$ m 0·55

5 a 0·28 b 0·85 c 0·49

1:21

1 a 0·7 b 0·3 c 0·2 d 9·2 e 8·4
f 10·9 g 0·49 h 0·28 i 0·37 j 384·4
k 458·25 l 30·5 m 703·07 n $0.95 o $52.09

2

0 0·1 0·2 0·3 0·4 0·5

0·5 0·6 0·7 0·8 0·9 1

3 a yes b yes c yes d yes

1:22

1

	ones		tenths	hundredths
a	2	·	5	9
b	6	·	7	3
c	9	·	4	1
d	5	·	2	6
e	8	·	4	8
f	7	·	1	3
g	6	·	7	9

2 a 12·56 b 35·72 c 38·37
d 17·29 e 52·19 f 46·30 or 46·3
g 92·07 h 8·06

3 a 2 hundredths or 0·02 b 4 tenths or 0·4
c 3 or 3 ones or 3 units d 8 hundredths or 0·08
e 1 or 1 one or 1 unit f 5 tenths or 0·5
g 2 or 2 ones or 2 units h 2 hundredths or 0·02
i 6 tenths or 0·6 j 1 hundredth or 0·01

1:23

Header: No

1 a 19·75 b 40·91 c 67·82 d 30·06
e 52·14 f 27·43

2 a 8 tenths and 6 hundredths
b 0 tenths and 9 hundredths
c 6 tenths and 0 hundredths

3 a 629·37 b 463·09 c 731·6 d 957·42
e 5·6 f 10·3 g 2·8 h 7.9

4 a 60 or 6 tens b 9 or 9 units
c 800 or 8 hundreds d 4 tenths or 0·4
e 2 hundredths or 0·02 f 3 tenths or 0·3
g 10 or 1 ten h 50 or 5 tens
i 8 tenths or 0·8 j 9 hundredths or 0·09
k 6 tenths or 0·6 l 5 hundredths or 0·05

2:01

1 a 5, 6, 7, 8, 9, 10, 11
b 10, 12, 14, 16, 18, 20, 22
c 15, 18, 21, 24, 27, 30, 33
d 20, 24, 28, 32, 36, 40, 44
e 25, 30, 35, 40, 45, 50, 55
f 30, 36, 42, 48, 54, 60, 66
g 35, 42, 49, 56, 63, 70, 77
h 40, 48, 56, 64, 72, 80, 88
i 45, 54, 63, 72, 81, 90, 99
j 50, 60, 70, 80, 90, 100, 110

2 a 12, 13 b 24, 26 c 36, 39 d 48, 52
e 60, 65 f 72, 78 g 84, 91 h 96, 104
i 108, 117 j 120, 130

3. a The last digits 2, 4, 6, 8 and 0 repeat.
   b The last digits 0, 4, 8, 2 and 6 repeat.
   c The last digits 5 and 0 repeat.
   d The last digits 0, 6, 2, 8 and 4 repeat.
   e The last digits 0, 8, 6, 4 and 2 repeat.
   f The last digit decreases by 1 for each term, i.e. 5, 4, 3, 2, 1, 0, 9. (Once it reaches 0 it goes back to 9.)
   g The last digit is always 0.
4. Answers will vary.

2:02

Header: 15

1.

×	0	1	2	3	4	5	6	7	8	9	10
1	0	1	2	3	4	5	6	7	8	9	10
2	0	2	4	6	8	10	12	14	16	18	20
3	0	3	6	9	12	15	18	21	24	27	30
5	0	5	10	15	20	25	30	35	40	45	50
10	0	10	20	30	40	50	60	70	80	90	100

2. a

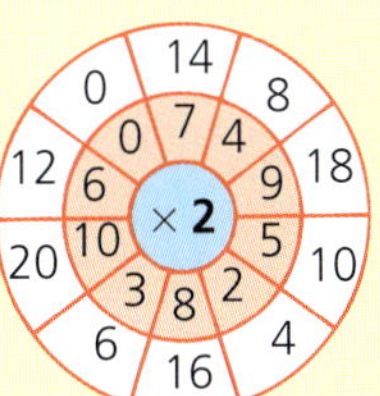

b

c

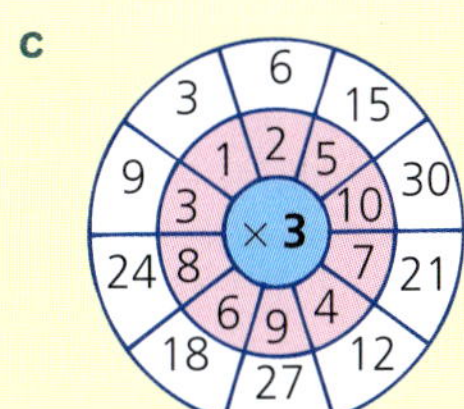

3. a 4 b 30 c 70 d 10 e 12 f 8 g 60 h 14

2:03

1. a 2, 4 b 14, 28 c 20, 40 d 16, 32
2. a 24 b 36 c 16 d 28 e 32
3.

×	0	1	2	3	4	5	6	7	8	9	10
2	0	2	4	6	8	10	12	14	16	18	20
4	0	4	8	12	16	20	24	28	32	36	40

4. a 3 × 4 = 12 b 5 × 4 = 20
   c 10 × 4 = 40 d 11 × 4 = 44
5. a

b

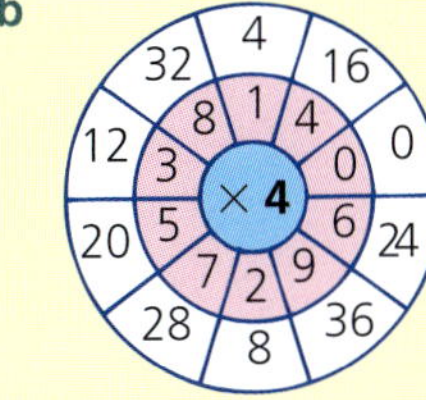

2:04

a

× 4	
0 × 4	4
1 × 4	12
2 × 4	0
3 × 4	20
4 × 4	8
5 × 4	16
6 × 4	36
7 × 4	24
8 × 4	40
9 × 4	28
10 × 4	32

b

× 4	
3 × 4	0
0 × 4	12
5 × 4	4
1 × 4	28
7 × 4	20
2 × 4	32
8 × 4	40
4 × 4	8
6 × 4	36
10 × 4	24
9 × 4	16

c

×	
6 × 10	0
3 × 1	10
4 × 0	2
5 × 2	3
2 × 1	60
7 × 2	12
4 × 10	10
6 × 2	80
10 × 1	14
9 × 2	40
8 × 10	18

d

× 5	
1 × 5	15
2 × 5	25
3 × 5	20
4 × 5	5
5 × 5	10
6 × 5	40
7 × 5	30
8 × 5	0
9 × 5	50
10 × 5	35
0 × 5	45

e

× 5	
1 × 5	50
6 × 5	10
10 × 5	5
5 × 5	40
8 × 5	30
0 × 5	45
2 × 5	25
9 × 5	35
3 × 5	20
7 × 5	0
4 × 5	15

f

×	
7 × 10	15
6 × 5	32
3 × 5	8
8 × 4	70
4 × 2	30
7 × 4	25
5 × 5	24
6 × 4	28
1 × 5	5
7 × 2	36
9 × 4	14

2:05

Header: 8 tens and 5 ones 85

1. a 98 b 93 c 97 d 38 e $69 f $38 g $88 h $78
2. a 69 b 75 c 76 d 69 e 76 f 78 g 69 h 88
   i $87 j $88 k $77 l $99

2:06

1. a 23 b 35 c 32 d 37 e 1 f 26 g 33 h 10
   i $4 j $30 k $67 l $44
2. a 88 candles b 69 lollies
3. a $79 b 27
4. a 47 – 35 = 12 b 56 – 34 = 22 c 74 – 61 = 13

2:07

1. a 41 b 90 c 73 d 84 e 43 f 82
   g 90 h 95 i 92 j 90 k 51 l 84
2. a $71 b $62 c $66 d $62
3. a 61 b 84 c 55

2:08

1. a 94 b 90 c 97 d 74 e 99 f 86
   g 85 h 92 i $93 j $71 k $76 l $71
2. a 30 emus b 83 kiwis c 54 metres d 40 birds

2:09

Header:

68 78

38 48

69 79

❶ a 55

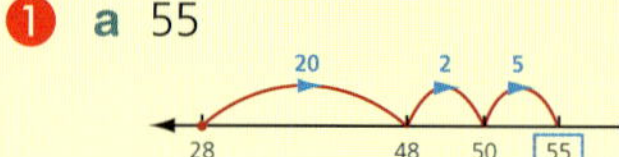

b 83 (49, +30 → 79, +1 → 80, +3 → 83)

c 84 (15, +60 → 75, +5 → 80, +4 → 84)

d 84 (57, +20 → 77, +3 → 80, +4 → 84)

e 84 (46, +30 → 76, +4 → 80, +4 → 84)

f 83 (49, +30 → 79, +1 → 80, +3 → 83)

❷ a 58 (29, +20 → 49, +1 → 50, +8 → 58)

b 71 (48, +20 → 68, +2 → 70, +1 → 71)

c 87 (69, +10 → 79, +1 → 80, +7 → 87)

d 81 (45, +30 → 75, +5 → 80, +1 → 81)

e 82 f 76 g 92 h 75

2:10

Header:

32 22

62 52

21 11

❶ a 57 (57, 60, 62, 72; jumps 3, 2, 10)

b 13

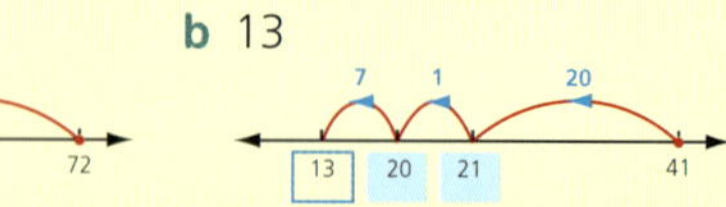

c 27

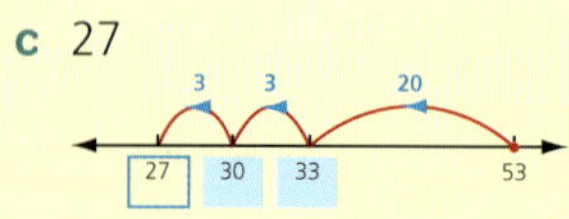

d 44

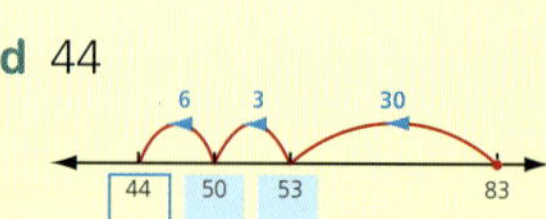

e 17

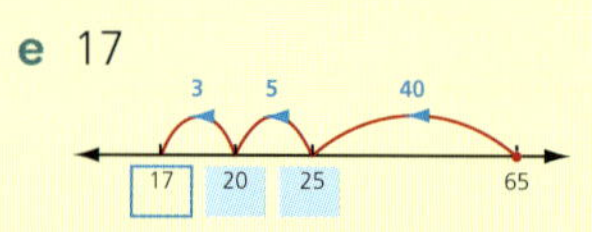

f 57

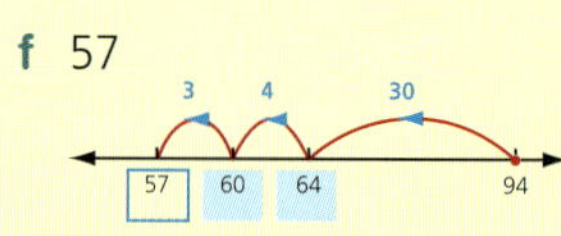

❷ a 35

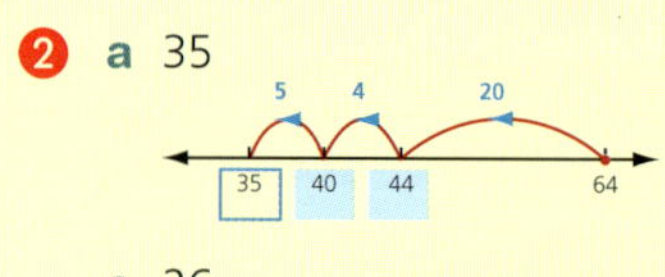

b 27

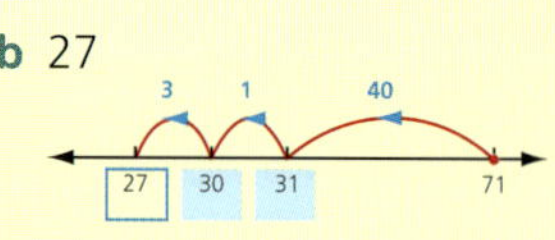

c 26

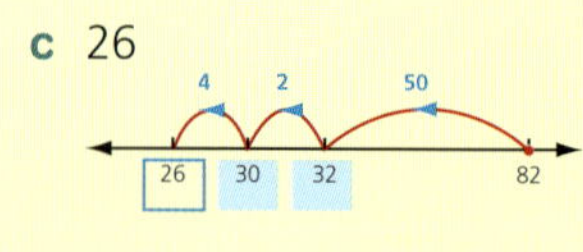

d 39 (39, 40, 47, 77; jumps 1, 7, 30)

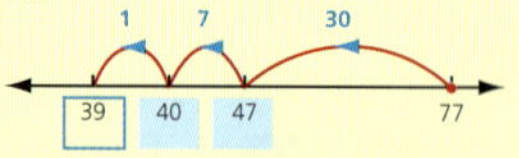

e 36 f 16 g 18 h 38

i 66 j 49

2:11

❶ a 8 b 16 c 24 d 32 e 40 f 48 g 56
h 64 i 72 j 40, 80 k 4, 8 l 8, 16 m 12, 24
n 24, 48 o 20, 40

❷ a 24 b 48 c 40 d 32 e 56 f 64 g 8 h 72
i 16 j 0 k 80 l 88

❸

×	0	1	2	3	4	5	6	7	8	9	10
8	0	8	16	24	32	40	48	56	64	72	80

×	5	3	7	4	2	9	10	1	8	6	0
2	10	6	14	8	4	18	20	2	16	12	0
4	20	12	28	16	8	36	40	4	32	24	0
8	40	24	56	32	16	72	80	8	64	48	0
3	15	9	21	12	6	27	30	3	24	18	0

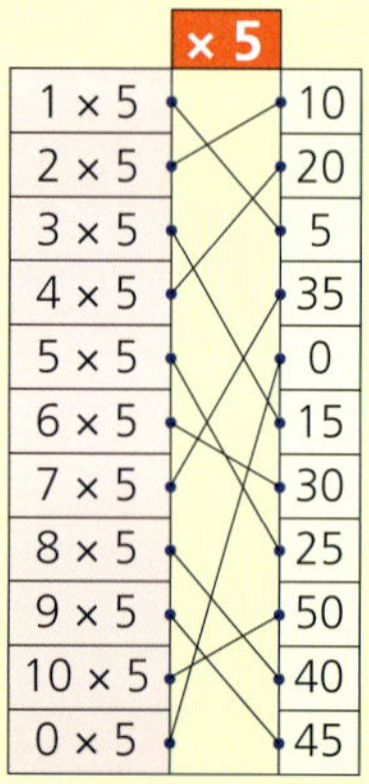

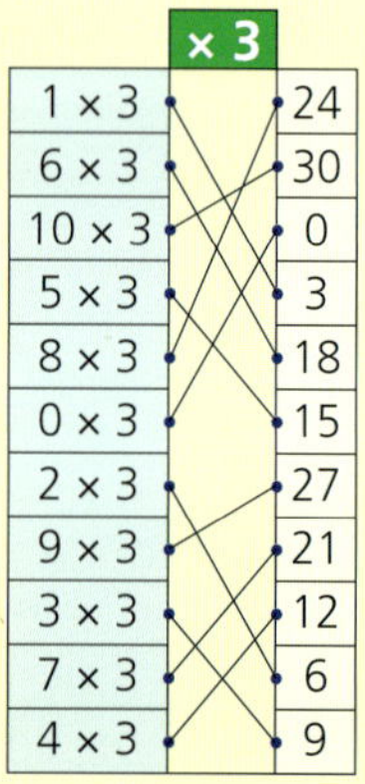

2:12

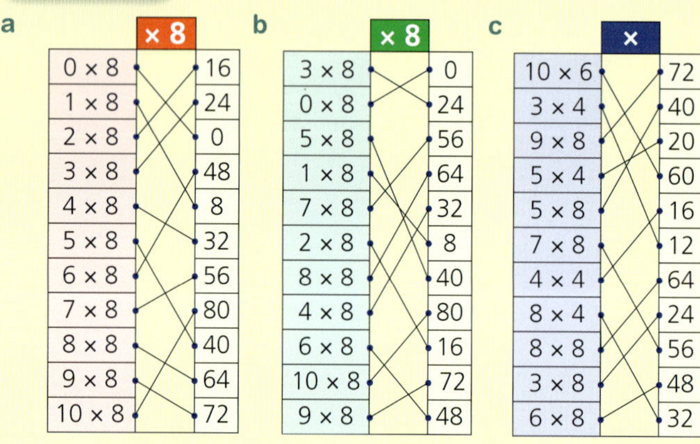

d × 5

1 × 5	10
2 × 5	20
3 × 5	5
4 × 5	35
5 × 5	0
6 × 5	15
7 × 5	30
8 × 5	25
9 × 5	50
10 × 5	40
0 × 5	45

e × 3

1 × 3	24
6 × 3	30
10 × 3	0
5 × 3	3
8 × 3	18
0 × 3	15
2 × 3	27
9 × 3	21
3 × 3	12
7 × 3	6
4 × 3	9

f × 4

7 × 4	24
6 × 4	28
3 × 4	32
8 × 4	16
4 × 4	32
8 × 4	20
5 × 4	12
6 × 4	36
1 × 4	28
7 × 4	4
9 × 4	24

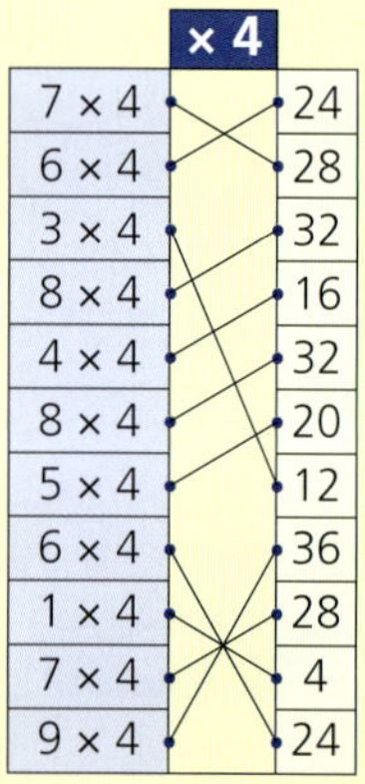

2:13

❶ a 62 b 74 c 81 d 103 e 73 f 76 g 96 h 82
i 84

❷ a 76 b 79 c 92 d 82 e $91 f $80

Investigation: Adding 3 odd numbers gives an odd number.

2:14

❶ a 61 + 88 = 149,149 b 94 + 53 = 147,147

❷ a 118 b 138 c 157 d 106 e 159 f 128
g 155 h 127 i 129

❸ Question 1 a 60 + 90 = 150 b 90 + 50 =140

Question 2 a 60 + 60 = 120 b 90 + 50 = 140
c 90 + 70 = 160 d 60 + 40 = 100
e 70 + 90 = 160 f 40 + 90 = 130
g 90 + 60 = 150 h 60 + 60 = 120
i 70 + 60 = 130

2:15

1 a 49 b 64 c 83 d 91 e 51 f 37

2 a 77 b 45 c 87 d 91

2:16

1 a 6 b 12 c 18 d 24 e 30 f 36
g 42 h 48 i 54 j 30, 60 k 3, 6 l 6, 12
m 9, 18 n 18, 16 o 15, 30

2 a 18 b 36 c 30 d 24 e 42 f 48
g 6 h 54 i 12 j 0 k 60 l 66

3

×	0	1	2	3	4	5	6	7	8	9	10
3	0	3	6	9	12	15	18	21	24	27	30
6	0	6	12	18	24	30	36	42	48	54	60

×	5	3	7	4	2	9	10	1	8	6	0
3	15	9	21	12	6	27	30	3	24	18	0
6	30	18	42	24	12	54	60	6	48	36	0

2:17

a

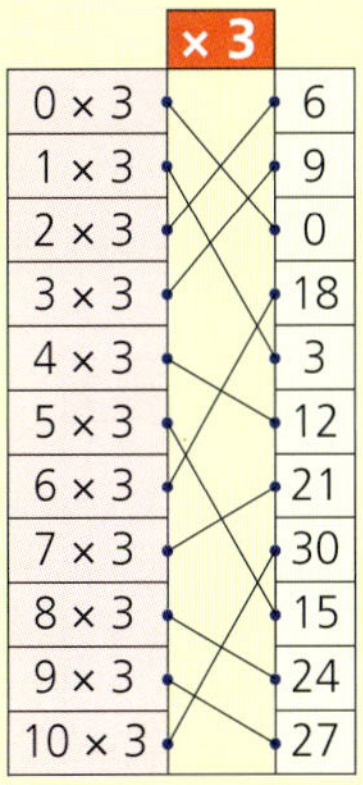

× 3	
0 × 3	6
1 × 3	9
2 × 3	0
3 × 3	18
4 × 3	3
5 × 3	12
6 × 3	21
7 × 3	30
8 × 3	15
9 × 3	24
10 × 3	27

b

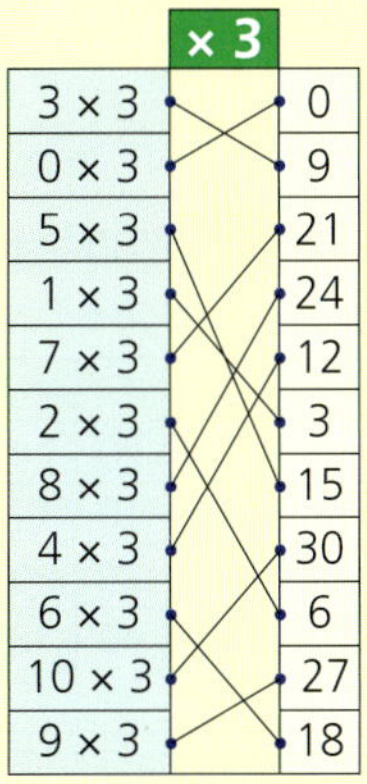

× 3	
3 × 3	0
0 × 3	9
5 × 3	21
1 × 3	24
7 × 3	12
2 × 3	3
8 × 3	15
4 × 3	30
6 × 3	6
10 × 3	27
9 × 3	18

c

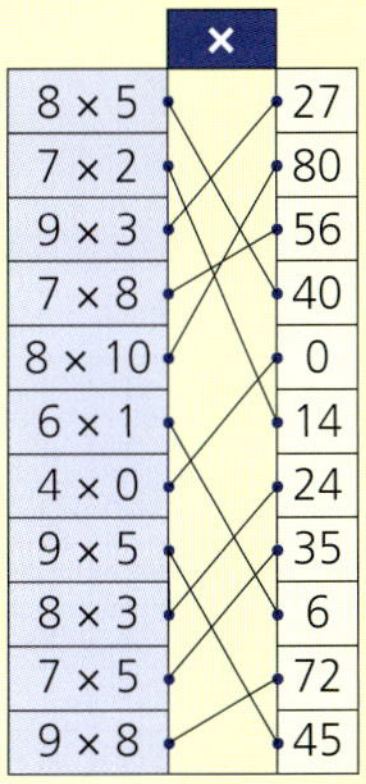

×	
8 × 5	27
7 × 2	80
9 × 3	56
7 × 8	40
8 × 10	0
6 × 1	14
4 × 0	24
9 × 5	35
8 × 3	6
7 × 5	72
9 × 8	45

d

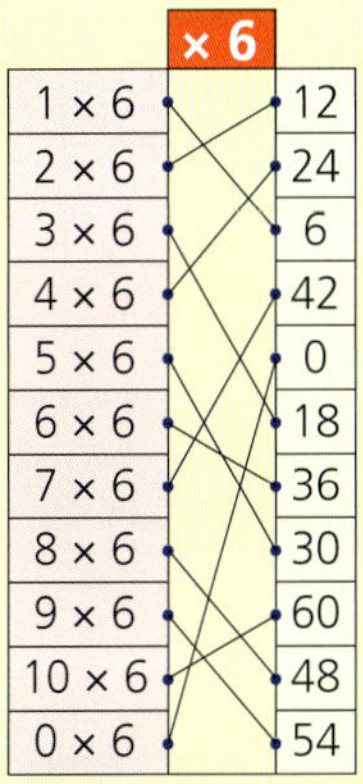

× 6	
1 × 6	12
2 × 6	24
3 × 6	6
4 × 6	42
5 × 6	0
6 × 6	18
7 × 6	36
8 × 6	30
9 × 6	60
10 × 6	48
0 × 6	54

e

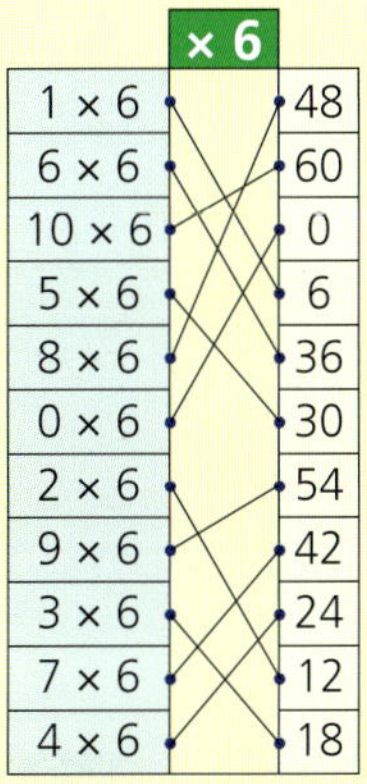

× 6	
1 × 6	48
6 × 6	60
10 × 6	0
5 × 6	6
8 × 6	36
0 × 6	30
2 × 6	54
9 × 6	42
3 × 6	24
7 × 6	12
4 × 6	18

f

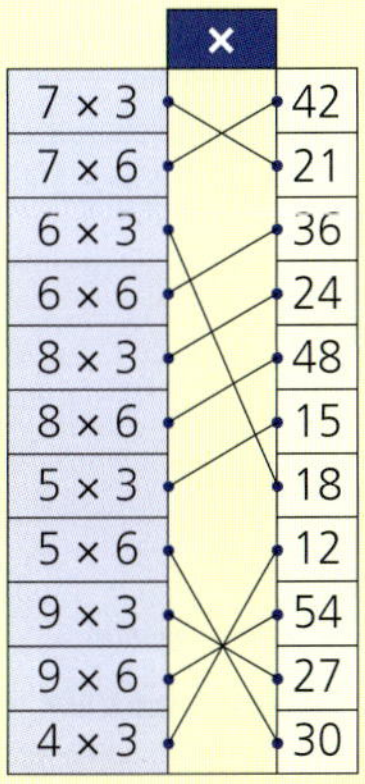

×	
7 × 3	42
7 × 6	21
6 × 3	36
6 × 6	24
8 × 3	48
8 × 6	15
5 × 3	18
5 × 6	12
9 × 3	54
9 × 6	27
4 × 3	30

2:18

1 a 26 b 36 c 37 d 44 e 19 f 18
g 73 h 47 i 38 j 18

2 a 26 b $45 c 33 d 57 cm

2:19

1 a

tens	ones
4	10
~~5~~	~~0~~

b

tens	ones
6	10
~~7~~	~~0~~

c

tens	ones
3	10
~~4~~	~~0~~

d

tens	ones
8	10
~~9~~	~~0~~

2 a 52 b 46 c 83 d $24 e $9 f $35
g 18 h 7 i 16 j 31 k $14 l $13
m $45 n $48

3 $62

2:20

1 a 6 b 7 c 8 d 7 e 18 f 16
g 19 h 15 i 16 j 19 k 38 l 44
m 28 n 29 o 19 p 55 q $26 r $18
s $37

2:21

1 a 9 b 18 c 27 d 36 e 45 f 54
g 63 h 72 i 81 j 90
In each case, total of the digits is 9.

2 a 90 b 81 c 72 d 63 e 54 f 45
g 36 h 27 i 18 j 9

3 a 45 b 81 c 63 d 72 e 45 f 9
g 27 h 54 i 18

3

×	0	1	2	3	4	5	6	7	8	9	10
3	0	3	6	9	12	15	18	21	24	27	30
9	0	9	18	27	36	45	54	63	72	81	90

×	5	3	7	4	2	9	10	1	8	6	0
3	15	9	21	12	6	27	30	3	24	18	0
9	45	27	63	36	18	81	90	9	72	54	0

2:22

a

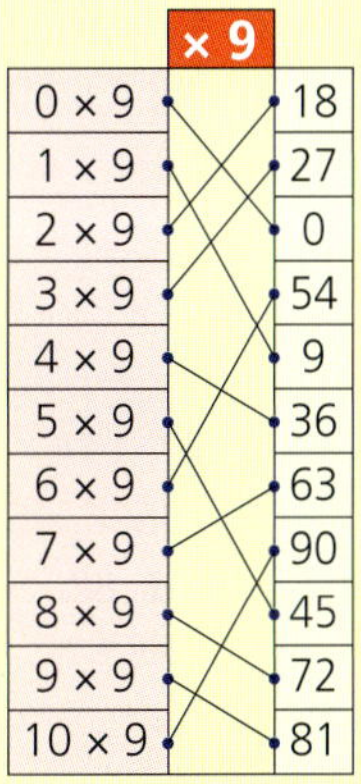

× 9	
0 × 9	18
1 × 9	27
2 × 9	0
3 × 9	54
4 × 9	9
5 × 9	36
6 × 9	63
7 × 9	90
8 × 9	45
9 × 9	72
10 × 9	81

b

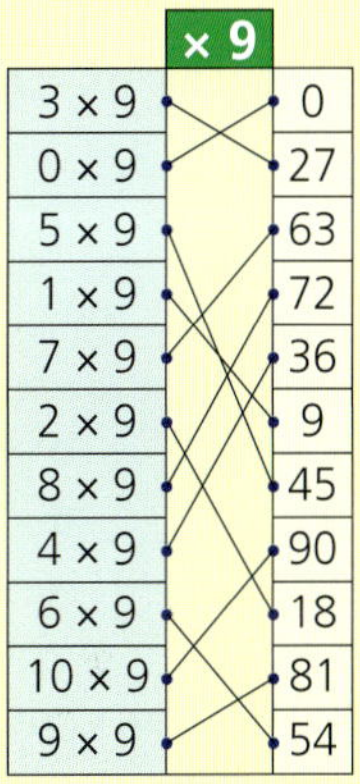

× 9	
3 × 9	0
0 × 9	27
5 × 9	63
1 × 9	72
7 × 9	36
2 × 9	9
8 × 9	45
4 × 9	90
6 × 9	18
10 × 9	81
9 × 9	54

c

×	
8 × 4	27
7 × 5	72
9 × 3	56
7 × 8	32
8 × 9	16
6 × 9	35
4 × 4	24
9 × 5	63
8 × 3	54
7 × 9	48
6 × 8	45

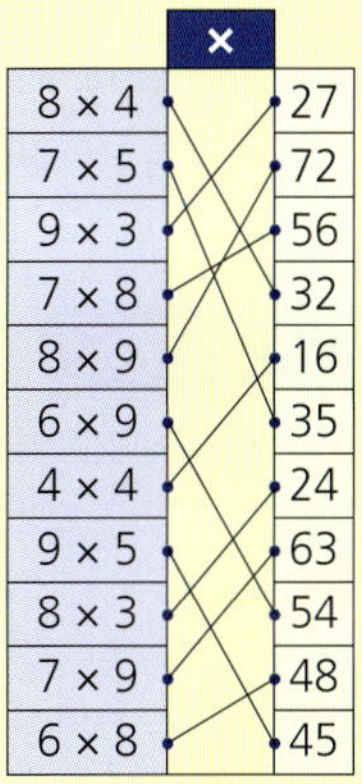

d

× 9	
6 × 9	9
1 × 9	90
3 × 9	54
10 × 9	18
5 × 9	0
7 × 9	27
2 × 9	63
8 × 9	45
4 × 9	81
9 × 9	72
0 × 9	36

e

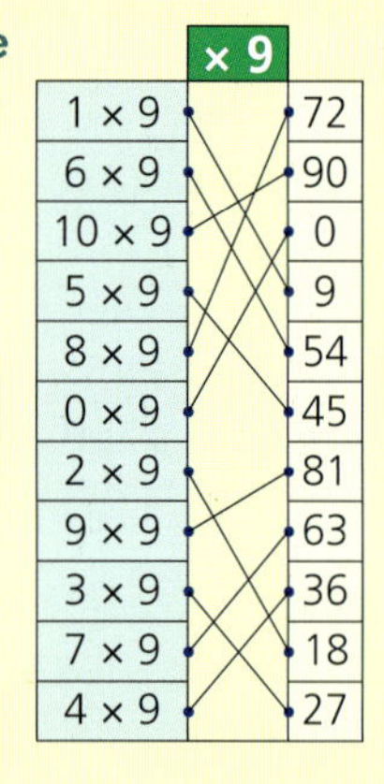

f

×	
7 × 2	42
7 × 6	14
6 × 3	30
6 × 5	8
8 × 1	72
8 × 9	20
5 × 4	18
5 × 10	36
9 × 0	54
9 × 6	0
4 × 9	50

2:23

1 **a** 154 **b** 117 **c** 108 **d** 283 **e** 790 **f** 388 **g** 516 **h** 510 **i** 428 **j** 331 **k** 514 **l** 733

2 660

2:24

1 **a** 328 **b** 601 **c** 815 **d** 713 **e** 561 **f** 456 **g** 342 **h** 463 **i** 570 **j** 293

2 **a** 365 **b** 605 **c** 628 **d** 779 **e** 414 **f** 819

2:25

Header: 800

1 **a** 334 **b** 662 **c** 361 **d** 432 **e** 615 **f** 531 **g** 792 **h** 657 **i** 727 **j** 762 **k** 321 **l** 731 **m** 805 **n** 640 **o** 962

2 **a** 432 minutes **b** 374 people **c** 377 bags **d** 921 m²

2:26

1 **a** 8 **b** 13 **c** 14 **d** 24 **e** 1 **f** 125 **g** 96 **h** 30 **i** 10

2 **a** Add 2 **b** Add 4 **c** Subtract 2 **d** Multiply by 2 **e** Divide by 3 **f** Multiply by 5 **g** Subtract 1 **h** Add 7 **i** Divide by 2

3 **a** 7, 14, 21 **b** 21, 16, 11 **c** 4, 16, 64 **d** 44, 22, 11 **e** 34, 45, 56 **f** 38, 29, 20 **g** 12, 24, 48 **h** 9, 3, 1

4 **a** 4, 8, 12, 16, … Add 4 **b** 5, 9, 13, 17, … Add 4

2:27

1 **a** 40, 35, 30, 25 **b** 137, 147, 157, 167 **c** 995, 1095, 1195, 1295 **d** 1696, 2696, 3696, 4696

2 **a** 77 **b** 99 **c** 400 **d** 88 **e** 1543 **f** 500 **g** $3\frac{1}{2}$ **h** 2

3 **a** 40, 100, 120 **b** 499, 509, 529 **c** 2, $2\frac{1}{2}$ **d** 40, 56

4 **a**

5 L — 5000 mL
4 L — 4000 mL
3 L — 3000 mL
2 L — 2000 mL
1 L — **1000 mL**

Volume of water = 4 L or 4000 mL.

b

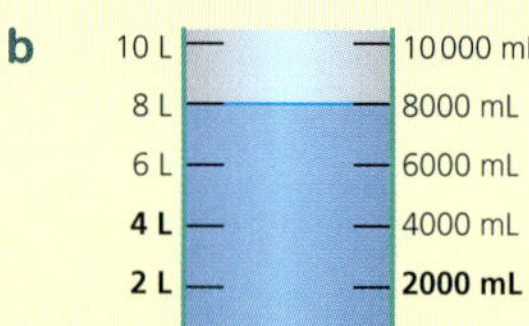

Volume of water = 8 L or 8000 mL.

5 **a** 4 kg, 5 kg **b** 4000 g, 5000 g **c** 8 km, 9 km **d** 8000 m, 9000 m **e** 8 kg, 10 kg **f** 8000 g, 10 000 g or 10 kg

2:28

1 **a** 21 **b** 21 **c** 28 **d** 28 **e** 35 **f** 35 **g** 42 **h** 42 **i** 56 **j** 56 **k** 63 **l** 70

2 **a** 0 **b** 0 **c** 7 **d** 7 **e** 14 **f** 14 **g** 21 **h** 21 **i** 40 **j** 72 **k** 48 **l** 64

3 **a** 28 **b** 42 **c** 56 **d** 49 **e** 70 **f** 63 **g** 42 **h** 63

×	0	1	2	3	4	5	6	7	8	9	10
4	0	4	8	12	16	20	24	28	32	36	40
2	0	2	4	6	8	10	12	14	16	18	20
5	0	5	10	15	20	25	30	35	40	45	50
8	0	8	16	24	32	40	48	56	64	72	80
1	0	1	2	3	4	5	6	7	8	9	10
6	0	6	12	18	24	30	36	42	48	54	60
3	0	3	6	9	12	15	18	21	24	27	30
0	0	0	0	0	0	0	0	0	0	0	0
9	0	9	18	27	36	45	54	63	72	81	90
10	0	10	20	30	40	50	60	70	80	90	100
7	0	7	14	21	28	35	42	49	56	63	70

4

×	0	1	2	3	4	5	6	7	8	9	10
7	0	7	14	21	28	35	42	49	56	63	70

×	5	3	7	4	2	9	10	1	8	6	0
7	35	21	49	28	14	63	70	7	56	42	0

2:29

a

× 7	
0 × 7	14
1 × 7	21
2 × 7	0
3 × 7	42
4 × 7	7
5 × 7	28
6 × 7	49
7 × 7	70
8 × 7	35
9 × 7	56
10 × 7	63

b

× 7	
3 × 7	0
0 × 7	21
5 × 7	49
1 × 7	56
7 × 7	28
2 × 7	7
8 × 7	35
4 × 7	70
6 × 7	14
10 × 7	63
9 × 7	42

c

×	
9 × 4	21
6 × 7	72
7 × 3	32
4 × 8	36
8 × 9	28
7 × 7	42
4 × 7	56
9 × 5	63
8 × 7	49
7 × 9	24
6 × 4	45

d

× 7	
6 × 7	7
1 × 7	70
3 × 7	42
10 × 7	14
5 × 7	0
7 × 7	21
2 × 7	49
8 × 7	35
4 × 7	63
9 × 7	56
0 × 7	28

e

× 7	
1 × 7	56
6 × 7	70
10 × 7	0
5 × 7	7
8 × 7	42
0 × 7	35
2 × 7	63
9 × 7	49
3 × 7	28
7 × 7	14
4 × 7	21

f

×	
7 × 8	42
7 × 6	56
3 × 7	30
6 × 5	70
10 × 7	72
8 × 9	20
5 × 4	21
5 × 7	36
9 × 7	54
9 × 6	63
4 × 9	35

2:30

1 a

×7	5	3	0	7	1	6	9	4	8	2
	35	21	0	49	7	42	63	28	56	14

b

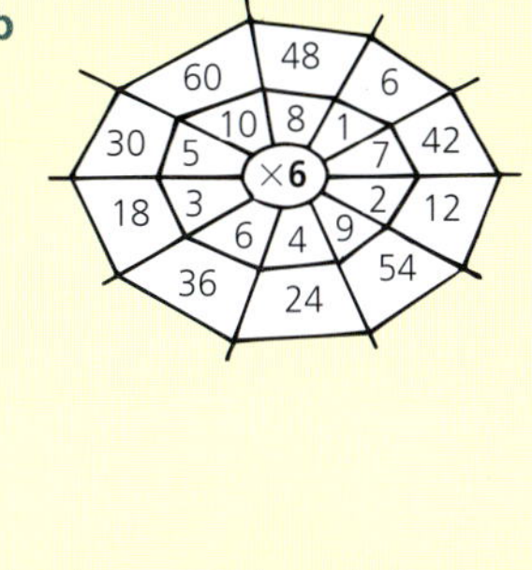

c

×9	8	7	10	0	6	3	9	4	5	1
	72	63	90	0	54	27	81	36	45	9

2 a 28 b 28 c 45 d 90 e 90 f 27
g 54 h 54 i 36 j 72 k 63 l 81
m 27 n 49 o 72 p 63 q 45 r 36

3 a 12 b 30 c 18 d 12 e 30 f 18
g 6 h 24

4 a 42 b 0 c 21 d 45 e 36 f 48

5

×	5	3	7	4	2	9	10	1	8	6	0
3	15	9	21	12	6	27	30	3	24	18	0
9	45	27	63	36	18	81	90	9	72	54	0

2:31

Header: 200

1 a 2 hundreds 4 tens 5 ones
b 6 hundreds 4 tens 5 ones
c 131 d 733 e 533 f 331
g 674 h 934 i 682 j 743
k 362 l 129 m 123 n 443
o 178 p 429 q 70 r 205

2:32

1 a 528 b 315 c 229 d 421 e 264
f 108 g 836 h 908 i 711 j 315
k 248 l 628 m 727 n 55 o 105
p 608 q 6 r 734 s 16

2:33

1 a 464 b 255 c 194 d 691 e 376
f 255 g 594 h 40 i 311 j 291
k 312 l 638 m 625 n 80 o 193
p 206 q 434 r 491

2:34

1 a 258 b 179 c 34 d 646 e 274
f 63 g 489 h 589 i 138 j 177
k 659 l 567 m 29 n 99 o 87
p 28 q 457 r 417 s 228

2:35

1 a 81 b 88 c 1200
2 a 269 b 709 c 239
3 a 544 b 795 c 852
4 a 401 b 386 c 652
5 a 539 b 897 c 977
d 985 e 788 f 878
6 a 294 b 456 c 416

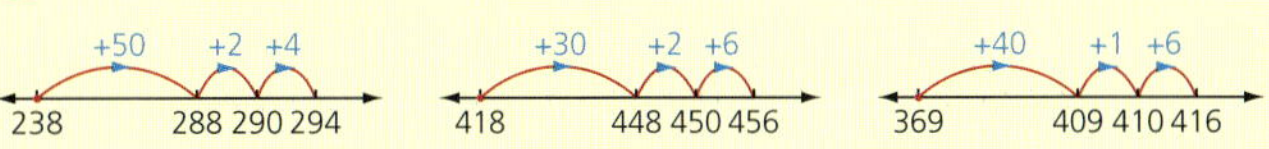

7 a 711 b 908 c 823

8 Strategies will vary.
a 399 b 99 c 431
d 84 e 1700 f 583

2:36

1 a 289 b 522 c 635 d 423 e 780 f 372
g 641 h 682 i 526
2 a 808 b 208 c 911 d 515 e 815 f 511
g 917 h 807 i 728
3 a 734 b 212 c 569 d 326 e 685 f 178
g 445 h 538 i 333
4 a 724 b 121 c 608 d 536 e 174 f 813
g 512 h 236 i 844

2:37

1 a 73 b 162 c 839 d 545 e 398
f 107 g 294 h 47
2 a 66 b 101 c 126 d 32
3 a 113 points b 419 albums c 253 books

2:38

1 a 63 b 252 c 829 d 231 e 215
f 63 g 79 h 307 i 254 j 329
k 551 l 344
2 a $703 b $826 c $144 d $676

2:39

1. a 3   b 2   c 4
2. a 3 groups, 15 ÷ 5 = 3   b 6 groups, 30 ÷ 5 = 6
   c 5 groups, 15 ÷ 3 = 5   d 6 groups, 36 ÷ 6 = 6
   e 10 groups, 30 ÷ 3 = 10   f 9 groups, 36 ÷ 4 = 9
   g 6 groups, 24 ÷ 4 = 6   h 8 groups, 48 ÷ 6 = 8
   i 4 groups, 36 ÷ 9 = 4   j 3 groups, 24 ÷ 8 = 3
   k 6 groups, 48 ÷ 8 = 6
3. a 7, 42 ÷ 6 = 7   b 7, 35 ÷ 5 = 7
   c 8, 32 ÷ 4 = 8

2:40

1. a 6   b 2   c 9   d 1
2. a 6   b 3   c 12   d 8   e 4   f 2
3. a 3   b 3   c 18   d 5   e 4   f 2
4. a 20 ÷ 4 = 5, 5   b 16 ÷ 8 = 2, 2
   c 20 ÷ 2 = 10, 10

2:41

Header: 32 ÷ 8 = 4 or 32 ÷ 4 = 8

1. a 4, 2   b 10, 2   c 9, 3
2. a 12, 4   b 16, 8   c 28, 4   d 27, 3   e 30, 5   f 15, 3
3. a 3, 4   b 8, 5   c 10, 9   d 6, 10   e 7, 8   f 5, 9
4. a 2, 2   b 6, 6   c 7, 7   d 6, 6   e 10, 10   f 3, 3
5. a 10   b 8   c 7
6. $34. Answers will vary.

2:42

1. a 24 ÷ 3 = 8, 24 ÷ 8 = 3   b 36 ÷ 4 = 9, 36 ÷ 9 = 4
   c 30 ÷ 6 = 5, 30 ÷ 5 = 6
2. a 2   b 2   c 7   d 5   e 3   f 2
   g 2   h 5   i 2
3. a 8   b 7   c 6   d 8   e 1   f 9
   g 6   h 7   i 4   j 9   k 9   l 5
4. a

18			
	÷ 2	=	9
	÷ 3	=	6
	÷ 6	=	3
	÷ 9	=	2

b

24			
	÷ 3	=	8
	÷ 4	=	6
	÷ 6	=	4
	÷ 8	=	3

c

30			
	÷ 3	=	10
	÷ 5	=	6
	÷ 6	=	5
	÷ 10	=	3

2:43

1. 83, 109, 111, 125, 127, and 3005 will be coloured red. 100, 118, 120, 130, and 6112 will be blue.
2. These numbers cannot be arranged in pairs.
3. 38, 66, 50, 74, 14, 92, 36, 100, 482, 764, 3106, 988, and 24 000 will be circled.
   75, 87, 29, 53, 41, 35, 2221, and 3825 will be underlined.

4. a 78   b 65   c 94   d 99
5. a 20, 18, 184, 28, 48, 162, 32, 112, 188
   even + even = even
   b 2, 0, 28, 12, 66, 356, 18, 190, 598
   even – even = even

2:44

1. a 14, 14, 97, 100, 34, 160, 88, 108, 100
   odd + odd = even
   b 6, 6, 6, 10, 14, 2, 22, 58, 12
   odd – odd = even
   c 24, 48, 8, 32, 40, 36, 24, 40, 16
   even × even = even
   d 24, 1, 40, 10, 6, 5, 3, 3, 6
2.

Number Types	+	–	×	÷
Even and Even	even	even	even	odd and even
Odd and Odd	even	even	odd	odd
Odd and Even	odd	odd	odd	

3. There will be crosses next to:
   6248 + 396 = 6645,   6107 ÷ 31 = 196
   283 × 654 = 28 353,   7319 + 2997 = 10 313
   173 × 881 = 152 416,   366 × 47 = 17 201
   2817 – 199 = 2617 and 68 019 ÷ 79 = 862

2:45

1. a 5   b 4   c 2   d 9   e 7
   f 1   g 4   h 6   i 8   j 9
   k 6   l 5   m 8   n 4   o 2
   p 9   q 3   r 6   s 5   t 9
   u 5   v 5   w 8   x 7
2. a 4   b 1   c 3   d 3   e 2
   f 3   g 8   h 3   i 5   j 4
   k 6   l 3   m 8   n 8   o 3
3. 2 → 6, 3, 18, 2, 20, 5, 50, 10, 80, 10 → 2

2:46

1. a

× 2	
3 × 2	8
4 × 2	6
7 × 2	12
6 × 2	14
8 × 2	18
9 × 2	16
5 × 2	20
10 × 2	10

÷ 2	
8 ÷ 2	6
6 ÷ 2	9
12 ÷ 2	10
14 ÷ 2	4
18 ÷ 2	3
16 ÷ 2	7
20 ÷ 2	5
10 ÷ 2	8

b

× 4	
3 × 4	16
4 × 4	28
7 × 4	12
6 × 4	32
8 × 4	24
9 × 4	20
5 × 4	40
10 × 4	36

÷ 4	
16 ÷ 4	7
28 ÷ 4	3
12 ÷ 4	6
32 ÷ 4	4
24 ÷ 4	8
20 ÷ 4	10
40 ÷ 4	9
36 ÷ 4	5

c

× 8	
3 × 8	32
4 × 8	24
7 × 8	56
6 × 8	48
8 × 8	64
9 × 8	72
5 × 8	80
10 × 8	40

÷ 8	
32 ÷ 8	7
24 ÷ 8	6
56 ÷ 8	4
48 ÷ 8	9
64 ÷ 8	3
72 ÷ 8	10
80 ÷ 8	5
40 ÷ 8	8

d

×	
3 × 4	28
4 × 8	32
7 × 4	12
6 × 8	64
8 × 8	48
9 × 4	80
5 × 8	40
10 × 8	36

÷	
28 ÷ 4	3
32 ÷ 8	4
12 ÷ 4	8
64 ÷ 8	10
48 ÷ 8	7
80 ÷ 8	9
40 ÷ 8	6
36 ÷ 4	5

e

×	
3 × 8	8
4 × 2	24
7 × 8	56
6 × 8	48
8 × 8	18
9 × 2	64
5 × 8	80
10 × 8	40

÷ 8	
8 ÷ 2	3
24 ÷ 8	8
56 ÷ 8	4
48 ÷ 8	9
18 ÷ 2	6
64 ÷ 8	7
80 ÷ 8	5
40 ÷ 8	10

f

×	
9 × 2	28
7 × 4	48
6 × 8	18
4 × 4	24
3 × 8	16
11 × 2	64
10 × 4	22
8 × 8	40

÷	
28 ÷ 4	6
48 ÷ 8	3
18 ÷ 2	7
24 ÷ 8	11
16 ÷ 4	9
64 ÷ 8	10
22 ÷ 2	4
40 ÷ 4	8

2:47

1. **a** 9 **b** 7 **c** 4 **d** 8 **e** 8 **f** 6
2. **a** 72 **b** 48 **c** 96 **d** 84 **e** 123
3. **a** 80 **b** 70 **c** 90 **d** 900 **e** 700 **f** 1000
4. **a** 56 **b** 96 **c** 90 **d** 168 **e** 195 **f** 231
5. **a** 160 **b** 210 **c** 320 **d** 420 **e** 180 **f** 280
6. **a** 1400 **b** 1600 **c** 3500 **d** 1800 **e** 5400 **f** 7200
7. **a** 16 **b** 37 **c** 40 **d** 20 **e** 101 **f** 30

2:48

1. about 40
2. 6 × 7 = 42 and 7 × 6 = 42
3. 42 ÷ 6 = 7 and 42 ÷ 7 = 6
4. 8 (children)
5. 18
6. **a** 200, 100, 50, 25, $12\frac{1}{2}$ **b** 80, 40, 20, 10, 5
   c 128, 64, 32, 16, 8, 4, 2, 1, $\frac{1}{2}$, $\frac{1}{4}$
   d 6, 12, 24, 48, 96, 192
   e 18, 36, 72, 144, 288, 576
7. **a** 48, 96, 192 **b** 36, 72, 144 **c** 126, 252, 504
8. 9 ways (5 using one layer and 4 using two)
9. **a** 414 (For **9a** and **b** you should have made an
   b 213 estimate and shown working.)

Investigation: true

2:49

1. **a**

×3	
3 × 3	12
4 × 3	9
7 × 3	18
6 × 3	21
8 × 3	27
9 × 3	24
5 × 3	30
10 × 3	15

÷3	
12 ÷ 3	6
9 ÷ 3	9
18 ÷ 3	10
21 ÷ 3	4
27 ÷ 3	3
24 ÷ 3	7
30 ÷ 3	5
15 ÷ 3	8

b

×6	
3 × 6	24
4 × 6	42
7 × 6	18
6 × 6	48
8 × 6	36
9 × 6	30
5 × 6	60
10 × 6	54

÷6	
24 ÷ 6	7
42 ÷ 6	3
18 ÷ 6	6
48 ÷ 6	4
36 ÷ 6	8
30 ÷ 6	10
60 ÷ 6	9
54 ÷ 6	5

c

×9	
5 × 9	90
10 × 9	45
4 × 9	72
8 × 9	36
3 × 9	54
6 × 9	27
7 × 9	81
9 × 9	63

÷9	
90 ÷ 9	4
45 ÷ 9	8
72 ÷ 9	10
36 ÷ 9	3
54 ÷ 9	5
27 ÷ 9	9
81 ÷ 9	7
63 ÷ 9	6

d

×6	
6 × 6	54
5 × 6	30
9 × 6	36
3 × 6	42
7 × 6	18
8 × 6	12
4 × 6	48
2 × 6	24

÷6	
54 ÷ 6	6
30 ÷ 6	5
36 ÷ 6	7
42 ÷ 6	2
18 ÷ 6	9
12 ÷ 6	4
48 ÷ 6	3
24 ÷ 6	8

e

×9	
8 × 9	72
3 × 9	27
5 × 9	45
7 × 9	63
9 × 9	54
6 × 9	81
4 × 9	18
2 × 9	36

÷9	
72 ÷ 9	3
27 ÷ 9	9
45 ÷ 9	8
63 ÷ 9	6
54 ÷ 9	7
81 ÷ 9	5
18 ÷ 9	4
36 ÷ 9	2

f

×	
3 × 5	80
8 × 10	25
5 × 5	15
4 × 10	45
9 × 5	40
6 × 10	20
7 × 5	60
2 × 10	35

÷	
80 ÷ 10	5
25 ÷ 5	9
15 ÷ 5	8
45 ÷ 5	6
40 ÷ 10	3
20 ÷ 10	7
60 ÷ 10	4
35 ÷ 5	2

2:50

1. **a** 10, 6 **b** 5, 8 **c** 6, 9 **d** 9, 8
   e 7, 6 **f** 4, 9
2. **a** 6 **b** 3 **c** 5 **d** 2 **e** 6
   f 8 **g** 1 **h** 6 **i** 7 **j** 8
   k 4 **l** 9
3. **a** 8 **b** 5 **c** 5 **d** 4 **e** 10
   f 6 **g** 5 **h** 10 **i** 3 **j** 8
   k 8 **l** 6 **m** 9 **n** 10 **o** 7
   p 6 **q** 9 **r** 8 **s** 9 **t** 9
   u 9 **v** 6 **w** 2 **x** 6

2:51

Header: 20c, 20c, 20c, 10c
10c, 10c, 10c, 20c, 20c

1. **a** $50, $5, $2 **b** $50, $1, 50c
   c $20, $2, $1 **d** $50, $10, 20c, 10c
   e $100, $50, $20, $10, $5, $2, $1, 50c, 10c
   f $50, $20, $20, $5, $1, 50c, 20c, 20c, 5c
   g $100, $20, $10, $2, $1, 50c, 20c, 10c
   h $100, $50, $10, $5, 50c, 20c, 5c
   i $50, $10, $5, 20c, 10c, 5c
   j $100, $50, $2, $1, 20c, 10c, 5c
   k $100, $100, $50, $20, $5, 20c, 20c
   l $100, $100, $10, $2, 50c, 20c, 10c
   m $100, $5, $2, 20c, 5c
   n $100, $100, $100, $100, $20, $2, 20c
   o $100, $100, $100, $1, 50c, 10c, 5c

Fun Spot: Answers will vary.

2:52

1. **a** 85c **b** $0.85 **c** $1.50 **d** $6.90
   e $3.25 **f** $9.45 **g** $8.90 **h** $4.50
   i $7.45 **j** $5.05 **k** $0.60 **l** $8.75
   m $7.15 **n** $4.90 **o** $0.40 **p** $8.75
   q $3.55 **r** $8.05
2. **a** $11.75 **b** $19.80 **c** $60 **d** $17.20
3.

	Total	Total rounded	Count on to give change	change
a	$11.66	$11.65	5c $11.70 30c $12 $8 $20 $30	$38.35
b	$20.33	$20.35	5c $20.40 60c $21 $9 $30 $20	$29.65
c	$21.59	$21.60	40c $22 $8 $30 $20	$28.40
d	$10.02	$10.00	$10	$10.00
e	$2.77	$2.75	25c $3 $7 $10 $10	$17.25
f	$30.51	$30.50	50c $31 $9 $40 $60	$69.50
g	$53.68	$53.70	30c $54 $6 $60 $40	$46.30

2:53

1. **a** 50c, $1, $2, $20, $20 = $43.50
   b 10c, 20c, 50c, $1, $2, $5 = $8.80
   c 10c, 20c, $1, $20, $20 = $41.30
   d $2, $5, $20, $20, $50 = $97

e $36.50 … $37 … $39 … $40 … $50

10c 50c $2 $1 $10

= $13.60

f $67.40 … $67.50 … $68 … $70 … $90 … $100

20c 10c 50c $2 $20 $10

= $32.80

2 Answers may vary.
a 50c, $1, $2, $10; change = $13.50
b 20c, 10c, 50c, $20, $20; change = $40.80
c 20c, 50c, $1, $20, $10; change = $31.70

3 Answers will vary.
a 5c, $2, $1, $5 b 5c, 50c, 50c, $2, $5
c 5c, $1, $1, $1, $2, $2, $1

2:54

1 a 560 b 910 c 330 d 6200
e 29 170 f 441 880 g 7800 h 1500
i 4800 j 91 300 k 405 400 l 750 000
m 79 000 n 98 000 o 80 000
p 300 000 q 5 835 000 r 60 000 000

2 a 46 b 42 c 326 d 947

3 a 42 b 93 c 58 d 30

4 a 67 b 37 c 19 d 35

5 a 287 b 2874 c 28 748

2:55

Header: 10

1 a 66 b 20 c 83 d 670
e 8537 f 2200 g 78 h 480
i 414 j 333 k 536 l 500
m 19 n 31 o 80 p 300
q 104 r 700

2 a 93 b 62 c 257 d 49 354

3 a 27 b 24 c 653 d 9635

4 a 83 b 92 c 73 d 956

5 a 218 b 2185 c 21 854

2:56

1 a 21 b 45 c 35 d 126
e 145 f 39

2 a 68 b 162 c 167 d 37
e 56 f 108

3 a 16 b 52 c 68 d 126
e 25 f 27 g 26 h 27
i 25

2:57

1 a 7 b 9 c 5 d 0
e 10 f 20 g 15 h 9

2 a 2 b 4 c 7 d 3
e 9 f 0 g 4 h 5
i 0 j 6 k 5 l 2
m 11 n 10 o 29

3 a 7 b 15 c 9 d 3
e 5 f 9

4 a 887 + 100 – 4 = 983 b 416 + 50 – 1 = 465
c 1076 + 100 – 3 = 1173 d 476 + 90 – 1 = 565

5 a 3 b 7 c 6 d 9
e 5 f 3 g 10 h 5
i 8 j 6 k 7 l 7
m 16 n 12 o 40 p 8
q 6 r 3

6 a 2 b 10 c 5 d 2
e 4 f 6 g 4 h 5
i 3

2:58

1 a 83 b 54 c 693 d 116
e 472 f 123, 664, 464

2 a 24 b 27 c 227 d 77
e 266 f 218, 403, 269

2:59

1 a 61 b 72 c 93 d 392 e 284 f 685

2 a 356 – 100 = 256, 256 – 20 = 236,
236 – 7 = 229
b 562 – 100 = 462, 462 – 30 = 432,
432 – 4 = 428
c 472 – 100 = 372, 372 – 40 = 332,
332 – 5 = 327

3 a We add 5 to both. 56 – 30 = 26
b We add 3 to both. 65 – 40 = 25
c We add 2 to both. 73 – 40 = 33
d We subtract 2 from both. 379 – 200 = 179
e We add 3 to both. 565 – 400 = 165
f We subtract 4 from both. 464 – 300 = 164
g We add 4 to both numbers. 535 – 500 = 35
h We subtract 4 from both. 667 – 400 = 267

4 a (– 2 and + 2), 21 + 40 = 61
b (+1 and – 1,) 70 + 31 = 101
c (+ 2 and – 2), 60 + 41 = 101
d (+ 2 and – 2), 160 + 23 = 183
e (– 2 and + 2), 243 + 40 = 283
f (+ 1 and – 1), 460 + 33 = 493
g (– 4 and + 4), 343 + 100 = 443
h (– 5 and + 5), 456 + 200 = 656

3:01

Header: 20 minutes

1 a 14 to 12 b 18 past 11 c 20 to 2 d 29 to 1
e 7 to 3 f 25 past 7 g 10 past 11 h 25 to 2
i 5 past 9 j 19 past 6

2 a   b c 
d e 

3 a 13 past 9 b 26 past 4 c 3 to 12
d 24 past 3 e 7 to 6 f 13 to 1
g half past 11 h 21 to 4 i 10 o'clock

4 a 18 past 6 b 21 past 9 c 26 past 9
d 18 to 7 e 19 to 5 f 9 to 2
g 13 past 11 h 10 to 8 i 2 to 2

3:02

1 a 12:20, 20 past 12 b 4:05, 5 past 4
c 10:25, 25 past 10 d 25 to 5
e 20 to 3 f 25 past 8
g quarter to 4 h 5 past 5
i 2:35, 25 to 3 j 11:45, quarter to 12
k 8:50, 10 to 9 l 3:55, 5 to 4
m 4:40, 20 to 5 n 10 past 6
o 25 to 1 p 10 to 12
q 5 past 7 r 5 to 10

Activity:

 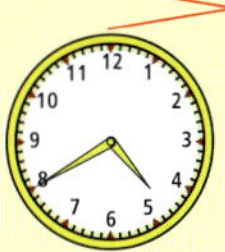  

3:03

1 a 11:16, 16 past 11 b 7:24, 24 past 7
c 4:32, 28 to 5 d 5:08, 8 past 5
e 3:47, 13 to 4 f 12:32, 28 to 1
g 9:29, 29 past 9 h 6:53, 7 to 7
i 10:04, 4 past 10 j 8:58, 2 to 9
k 8 to 3 l 2 to 5
m 19 past 9 n 9 past 7
o 22 to 12

2 a 3:15 b 2:46 c 7:27 d 9:02
e 11:40 f 4:38 g 12:23 h 5:19
i 6:54

3 a 47 b 19 c 28 d 6
e 44 f 2

3:04

1 a 26 past 7 b 6 to 7 c 19 past 12
d 2 past 10 e 18 to 12

2 a 13 to 7 b 23 past 7 c 2 past 8
d 16 past 12 e 1 to 5

3 21 min, 35 min, 7 min, 1:46 (or 14 to 2), 23 min

4 53 minutes

5 45 min, 8:20

3:05

1 a 18 cm b 12 cm c 10 cm d 14 cm
e 16 cm f 6 cm g 8 cm h 12 cm
i 12 cm j c, b, a

2 a 126 cm b 173 cm

3 a 2 m 38 cm b 2 m 13 cm

3:06

1 a 45 mm b 52 mm c 29 mm d 73 mm
e 82 mm f 16 mm

2 a 19 mm b 47 mm c 61 mm d 36 mm
e 55 mm f 72 mm

3 a 2 cm 5 mm b 6 cm 8 mm c 5 cm 1 mm
d 9 cm 2 mm e 4 cm 3 mm f 8 cm 7 mm

Activity: Answers will vary.

3:07

1 a 36 mm b 22 mm c 17 mm d 59 mm e 48 mm

2 a 38 mm b 63 mm c 19 mm d 75 mm e 58 mm
f 41 mm

3 a 32 mm b 81 mm c 19 mm d 74 mm e 28 mm
f 46 mm g 55 mm h 37 mm i 100 mm

4 a 3 cm 8 mm b 1 cm 9 mm c 4 cm 7 mm
d 8 cm 2 mm e 5 cm 1 mm f 2 cm 5 mm
g 6 cm 4 mm h 9 cm 3 mm i 7 cm 6 mm

5 a 12 cm or 120 mm b 14 cm or 140 mm
c 12 cm or 120 mm

3:08

1 Answers will vary.

2 a 4 square centimetres b 18 square centimetres
c 20 square centimetres d 6 square centimetres
e 12 square centimetres (2 rows of 6 = 2 × 6) f 10 square centimetres (2 rows of 5 = 2 × 5)

3 a, d, f, e, b, c

4 a 9 square centimetres b 12 square centimetres
c 18 square centimetres

3:09

Concept: 24 or 25

1 a A = 15 square centimetres, P = 16 cm
b A = 18 square centimetres, P = 18 cm
c A = 8 square centimetres, P = 12 cm
d A = 24 square centimetres, P = 22 cm

3:10

1–**2** Answers will vary.

3 A = 16 square centimetres B = 15 square centimetres
C = 18 square centimetres

4 C, A, B

5–6 Answers will vary.

3:11

1 a 2 cm, 22 mm b 4 cm, 37 mm c 2 cm, 17 mm
d 3 cm, 33 mm e 1 cm, 8 mm f 5 cm, 46 mm
g 0 cm, 3 mm
h A measurement of 0 cm means that the length is closer to 0 than to the next highest division on the scale.

2 a 8 kg b 15 kg c 1 kg d 11 kg
e 3 kg f 12 kg

3:12

1 Answers will vary.

2 10

3–4 Answers will vary.

3:13

1–2 Answers will vary.

3 a A) 500 mL B) 750 mL C) 250 mL
D) 1000 mL E) 250 mL
b C, E, A, B, D
c
1000
750 mL
500
mL

4 a mL b mL c L d L
e mL f mL

3:14

1 a 1 L b 7 L c 5 L d 3 L
e 6 L f 4 L g 2 L h 8 L

2 a 2000 mL b 7000mL c 3000 mL d 5000 mL
e 8000 mL f 4000 mL g 6500 mL h 9500 mL

3 a mL b L c mL d mL
e L f L g mL h L

4 a 400 mL b 200 mL c 700 mL

5 a 5 b 4 c 2 d 10

6 a 10 b 8 c 6 d 4

3:15

Header: 6 litres 6000 millilitres

1 a 1500 mL b 1250 mL c 1750 mL d 1600 mL

2 a 1300 mL b 1490 mL c 1875 mL d 1625 mL
e 1750 mL f 2500 mL

3 a 1 L 600 mL b 1 L 900 mL c 1 L 350 mL
d 1 L 250 mL e 1 L 425 mL f 2 L 750 mL

4 a L b mL c mL d mL e mL
f L g mL h mL

5 a 2 L b 1·5 L c 2·5 L d 0·5 L

3:16

1–2 Answers will vary.

3 a 60 g b 100 g c 40 kg
d 30 g e 9 kg f 70 g

4 a g b g c kg d kg e g

5 a 700 g b 500 g c 250 kg

3:17

1 a 60 g b 1 kg c 350 g
d 1700 g e 1300 g f 3 kg
g 5 kg 300 g h 14 kg 100 g

2 a g b g c kg d g e g

3 a 1500 (g) b 5900 (g)

4 a 1 (kg) b 4 (kg) c 6 (kg) d 8 (kg)

3:18

Concept: 20 past 7, 7:20, 22 past 1 or 1:22, 14 to 6 or 5:46, 23 to 11 or 10:37

1 a 10 past 11, 11:10 b 20 to 12, 11:40
c 18 past 12, 12:18 d 27 to 5, 4:33
e 22 to 4, 3:38 f 7 to 8, 7:53

3:19

1 a  b  c 
d  e 

2 a 10 to 10 b 19 past 4
c a quarter to 8 (or 15 to 8) d 28 past 8
e 5 to 3

3 a 9, the time is 9 to 7 b 22, the time is 22 to 5
c 17, the time is 17 to 1 d 3, the time is 3 to 9
e 11, the time is 11 to 2

4 a 49 b 42 c 2 d 21 e 11
f 7 g 3 h 5 i 2

5 a 3, 1 b 1095 c 36 d 2 e 5
f 156 g 4

6 23 min, 35 min

3:20

1 a 5:14 pm b 3:32 am c 7:23 pm d 4:43 am
e 10:09 pm

2 a after midday b before midday c before midday
d before midday e after midday

3 a 8 min b 25 min c 31 min
d 47 min e 56 min f 41 min

 • *AUSTRALIAN SIGNPOST MATHS NSW 4* • ISBN 9780655709053

4 a 6 min b 18 min c 24 min
d 39 min e 43 min f 57 min

5 a 9 min b 13 min c 27 min
d 34 min e 45 min f 51 min

3:21

1 A: 8 mm or 0·8 cm, B: 21 mm or 2·1 cm, C: 46 mm or 4·6 cm, D: 73 mm or 7·3 cm, E: 87 mm or 8·7 cm

2 a 6·5 cm b 2·3 cm c 9·1 cm d 4·2 cm
e 3·4 cm f 8·7 cm g 11·2 cm h 13·9 cm

3 a 1·56 m b 3·41 m c 8·19 m d 2·53 m
e 5·94 m f 4·73 m g 13·21m h 34·72 m

4 a 142 cm b 365 cm c 973 cm d 281 cm
e 218 cm f 464 cm g 607 cm h 1052 cm

Activity: Answers will vary.

3:22

Header: The perimeter is 82 cm.

1 a 256 cm b 316 cm c 540 cm d 781 cm

2 a 3·63 m b 4·25 m c 8·47 m d 5·87 m

3 a 1 m 19 cm b 8 m 53 cm c 5 m 82 cm
d 6 m 97 cm e 9 m 35 cm f 3 m 74 cm

4 a 2 cm 7 mm b 3 cm 6 mm c 5 cm 1 mm
d 1 cm 9 mm e 4 cm 2 mm f 8 cm 5 mm

5 a 3·6 cm b 6·9 cm c 12·8 cm

6 a 54 mm b 69 mm c 11 mm
d 87 mm e 43 mm f 20 mm

7 a m b cm c m d mm
e cm f m g mm h mm

3:23

1

Millimetres	cm and mm	cm as a decimal	Rounded to the nearest cm
39 mm	3 cm 9 mm	3·9 cm	4 cm
63 mm	6 cm 3 mm	6·3 cm	6 cm
56 mm	5 cm 6 mm	5·6 cm	6 cm
72 mm	7 cm 2 mm	7·2 cm	7 cm
81 mm	8 cm 1 mm	8·1 cm	8 cm
45 mm	4 cm 5 mm	4·5 cm	5 cm
94 mm	9 cm 4 mm	9·4 cm	9 cm

2 Answers will vary.

3 a 35 mm b 29 mm c 46 mm d 13 mm
e 62 mm f 38 mm g 81 mm h 56 mm

4 **A:** 140 mm **B:** 122 mm **C:** 96 mm, A has the longest perimeter.

Activity: Answers will vary.

3:24

1–4 Answers will vary.

5 a square metres b square metres
c square centimetres d square metres
e square centimetres f square centimetres
g square centimetres h square metres

6 a 16 square metres b 16 square metres
c They are equal.

7 Answers will vary. Perimeter describes the length of a shape's edge. Area describes the size of a shape's surface.

3:25

1 a 8 square centimetres, 4 square centimetres
b 18 square centimetres, 9 square centimetres
c 12 square centimetres, 6 square centimetres

2 a 6 square centimetres, 3 square centimetres
b 15 square centimetres, 7·5 square centimetres (or $7\frac{1}{2}$)
c 4 square centimetres, 2 square centimetres
d 14 square centimetres, 7 square centimetres

3:26

1 a 16 square centimetres, 8 square centimetres
b 12 square centimetres, 6 square centimetres
c 8 square centimetres, 4 square centimetres

2 a 2 square centimetres
b 2 square centimetres
c 8 square centimetres

Activity: The area is 16 square centimetres. The new area when rearranged as a rectangle is the same.

3:27

1 a 100 g b 600 g c 1 kg d 500 g e 3 kg
f 1300 g g 10 kg h 956 g i 875 g

2 a 3 kg b 7 kg c 2 kg d 5 kg e 9 kg
f 4 kg

3 a 2000 g b 1200 g c 3000 g d 1600 g
e 5000 g f 1450 g g 1980 g h 1500 g
i 7000 g

4 a 500 g b 750 g c 250 g d 1500 g
e 1750 g f 1250 g g 2500 g h 3500 g

5 C, A, B, D

3:28

1 a 1 kg b 450 g c 3 kg
d 1 kg 560 g e 2 kg 125 g

2 a 3000 g b 5000 g c 9000 g d 7000 g
e 4000 g f 6000 g

3 a 1 kg b 8 kg c 2 kg d 4 kg e 6 kg
f 5 kg

4 a 0·1 kg b 0·3 kg c 0·9 kg d 0·5 kg e 0·7 kg
f 1·4 kg

5 a 500 g b 200 g c 800 g d 600 g

6 a 1 kg 500 g b 4 kg 250 g c 3 kg 500 g
d 2 kg 250 g

Activity: Answers will vary.

3:29

Mulga line timetable		am or pm
Arriving		
Ironbark	6:10	am
Christmas Ck	7:25	am
Mt Gordon	7:50	am
Richmond	8:45	am
Wandong	10:05	am
Carbor	11:40	am
Black Hill	12:30	pm
Mulga	1:15	pm

1 a 6:10 am b 8:45 am c 11:40 am d 7:50 am
e 10:05 am f 1:15 pm
2 a Richmond b Christmas Ck c Black Hill
d Ironbark e Mulga f Wandong
3 a 8:10 am b 1:40 pm c 3:15 pm d 12:05 pm
e 2:30 pm f 10:45 am
4 a 12:00 pm or noon b 8:15 am c 11:10 am
d 12:45 pm e 5:40 am f 9:35 am
5 a Black Hill b Mulga c Richmond
d Wandong e Carbor f Mt Gordon
6

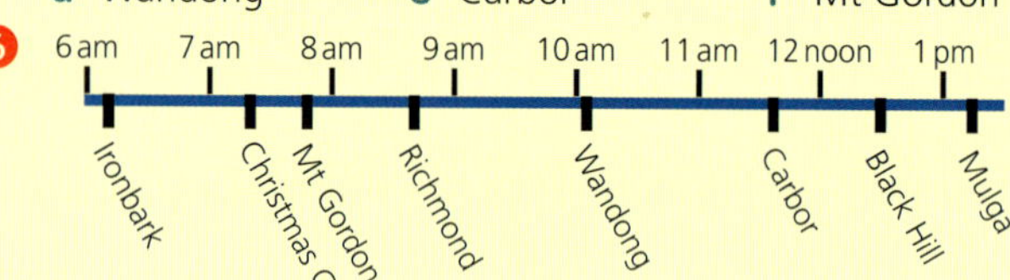

3:30

1 A 7:23:15 B 11:03:25 C 1:33:30 D 4:40:55
a A 15 B 25 C 30 D 55
b A 45 B 35 C 30 D 5
c C and D
2–4 Answers will vary.

3:31

1 Answers will vary.
2 a 01:29·15 b 04:39·19 c 16:15·38
d 00:28·35 e 02:21·00
3 a 1 minute and 31 seconds b 4 minutes and 58 seconds

3:32

Header: 7 mm
1 a 16 mm b 24 mm c 32 mm d 8 mm
e 16 mm f 8 mm
2 a 36 mm b 32 mm c 69 mm d 64 mm
e 8 mm f 48 mm g 53 mm
3 a 40 mm b 4 mm c 11 mm
d 61 mm e 32 mm f 33 mm
g 24 mm h 28 mm i 16 mm

3:33

1 a 5600 mm b 5 m 600 mm
2 a 3520 mm b 3 m 520 mm
3 a 1650 mm b 3 m 345 mm
4 a true b false c true d false e true

3:34

1 a 3 km b 7 km c 6 km
d 5 km e 10 km f 9 km
2 a 5100 m b 1400 m

3:35

1 18 m, House width is about 12 m.
The width of the truck is about 6 m.
2 20°C (20 degrees Celsius)
3 725 mL
4 1450 g (or 1 kg 450 g)
5 a 18 min b 48 min
6 7 days
7 a 2 kg 500 g (or 2·5 kg) b 3 kg 365 g
8 1545 mm (1 m 545 mm)
9 a 16 (laps) b 1050 m (21 laps)

3:36

Concept: 10 and 8, 11 and 9
1 a 100 and 97, 101 and 98, 102 and 99
b 1000 and 998, 1001 and 999
2 8
3 a 2900 (mL) b 2 L 900 mL c 2920 g (or 2 kg 920 g)
4 82 min or 1h 22 min
5 a 603 m b 750 m c 503 m
6 362 square centimetres
7 a 175 cm or 1 m 75 cm b 155 cm or 1 m 55 cm
8 1000 square centimetres

3:37

1 a 10 cubic centimetres b 30 cubic centimetres
c 40 cubic centimetres
2 a 90 cubic centimetres b 70 cubic centimetres
c 126 cubic centimetres d 72 cubic centimetres
e 36 cubic centimetres
3–4 Answers will vary.

3:38

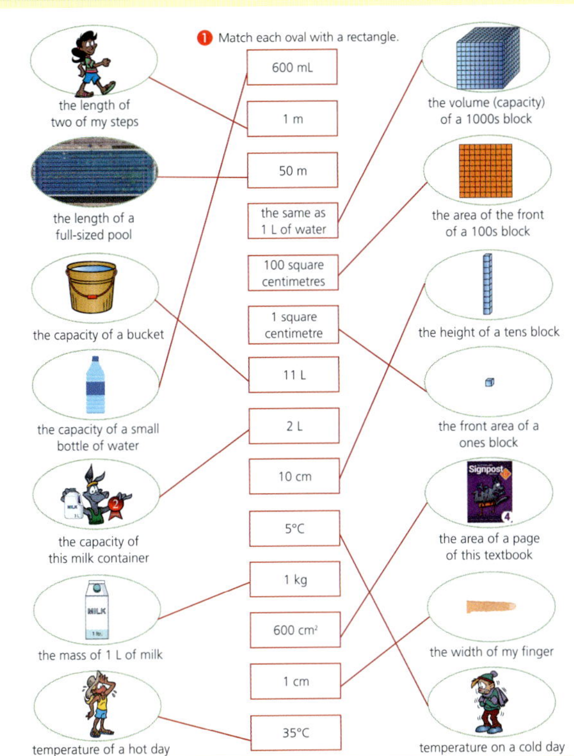

4:01

1. a C, E, F, I, J b B, E, G c A, D, H
2. E
3. a 1 b 2 c 1 d 0 e 1 f 1 g 0 h 0 i 1

4:02

1. a yes b no c no
2. a C and E b B, D and E c B and E d 4, 4 e 3, 3 f yes
3. a A and D b B c C d yes
4. Answers may vary. Diagrams may look like this:

a b c

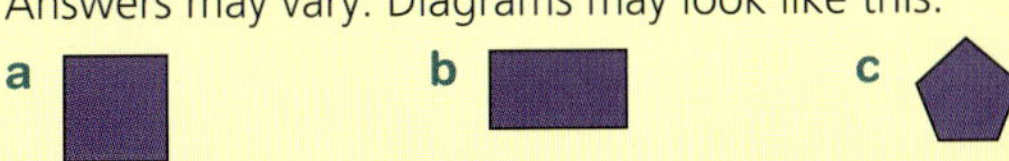

d e f

5. a B b C c A d A

4:03

1.

My angle (right angle)	Smaller	Same as my angle	Larger
	E, C, G, I	A, F, D	B, H

2. a A b C c E d G

3.

Half of a right angle	Smaller	The same	Larger
	C, E	G, I	A, B, D, F, H

4. a b

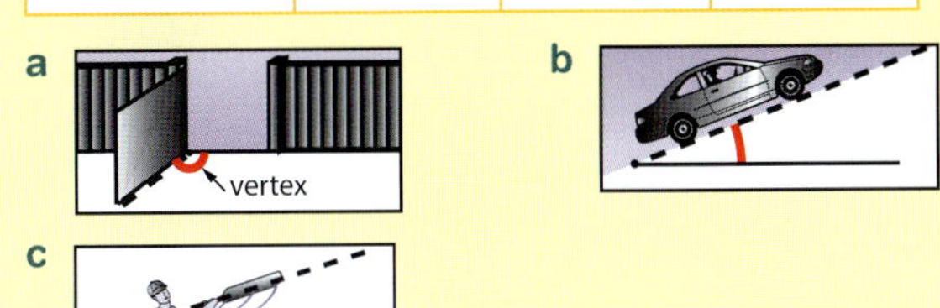

c

Activity: Answers will vary.

4:04

Header: yes

1. The prisms will be coloured red, the cylinders blue and the pyramids green.
2. a A, B, D, E b C, F
   c A, D, E. The prisms will be coloured red.
   d C. The cylinder will be coloured blue. e D
3. a A b D (or B) c E (or A) d B

Investigation: Answers will vary, e.g. a box.

4:05

Concept: A is a square pyramid. B is a hexagonal prism.

1. a D, E, G, H b A, B, C, F c A, D, F
   d A, E (also D, F) e C, G f B
2. a pyramid (square pyramid)
   b prism (rectangular prism)
   c pyramid (triangular pyramid)
   d cube or prism (square prism)
   e prism (triangular prism)

4:06

1. a A (prism) b B (pyramid) c A (prism) d B (pyramid)
2. a prism b pyramid c prism

4:07

1.

	Name of the object	Number of faces	Number of corners	Number of edges
A	triangular prism	5	6	9
B	triangular pyramid	4	4	6
C	cube	6	8	12
D	square pyramid	5	5	8
E	rectangular prism	6	8	12
F	pentagonal pyramid	6	6	10

2 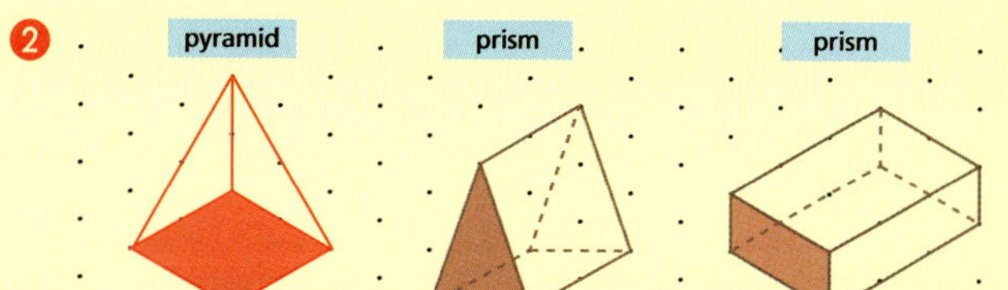

Activity: Answers will vary.

4:08

Header: 1, 3, 2

1 **a** A **b** C **c** C **d** A **e** D

2 **a**  **b** **c** Answers will vary.

3 A right angle is a quarter of a full turn. It is a square corner.

4 D, C, A, B will be drawn in this order.

Activity: Answers will vary.

4:09

1 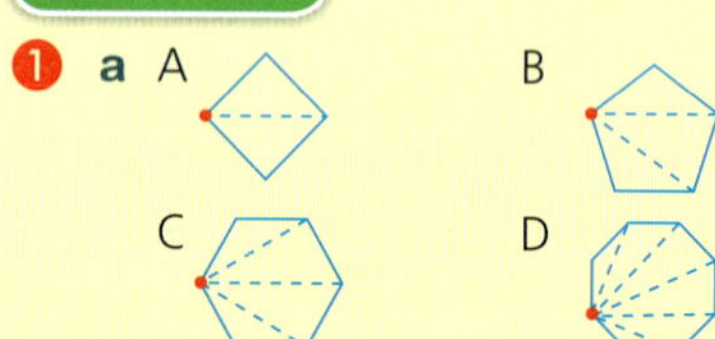

Answers may vary.

2 **a** a half turn clockwise **b** a quarter turn clockwise
c two quarter turns (or a half turn) anticlockwise

3 **a** 4 **b** 4 **c** 2

4 **a** 3 **b** 12

Activity: Answers may vary.

4:10

1 **a** A B

C D

A: 2 triangles B: 3 triangles
C: 4 triangles D: 6 tringles

There are two fewer triangles than there are sides for each shape.

b A B
4, 4 5, 5
C D
6, 6 8, 8

2

Regular shape	Number of sides	Number of angles	Number of lines of symmetry
square	4	4	4
pentagon	5	5	5
hexagon	6	6	6
octagon	8	8	8

4:11

1 **a** 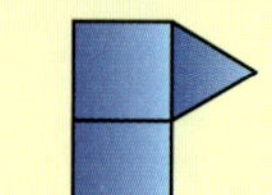 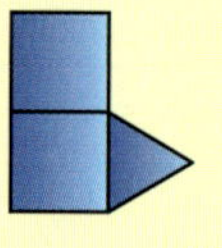 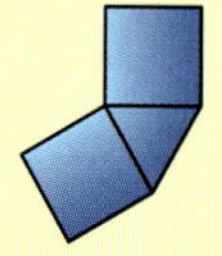

b 2

2 **a** A and D **b** E and H **c** B and F
d G and I **e** B and C **f** E and H

4:12

1 **a** Warn St **b** March St or Munn St **c** Joseph St
d Meg St **e** school **f** hospital
g police station **h** traffic lights

2 **a** school **b** police station **c** hospital

3 At the intersection of March St and Munn St.

4 **a** 2 km by road **b** 7 km by road

Activity: Answers may vary.

4:13

Answers will vary.

4:14

A cylinder, cone and sphere will be drawn.

1

Shape	Number of surfaces	Number of corners	Number of edges
cylinder	3	0	2
cone	2	1	1
sphere	1	0	0

2–4 Answers will vary.

5 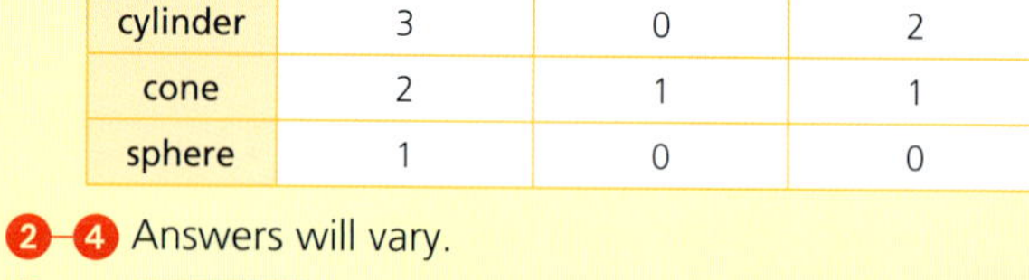
A pyramid **B** sphere **C** cylinder

D 
cone

a C **b** A, D (also B, but B has no base)

4:15

Header: circle, rectangle, triangle, square

1 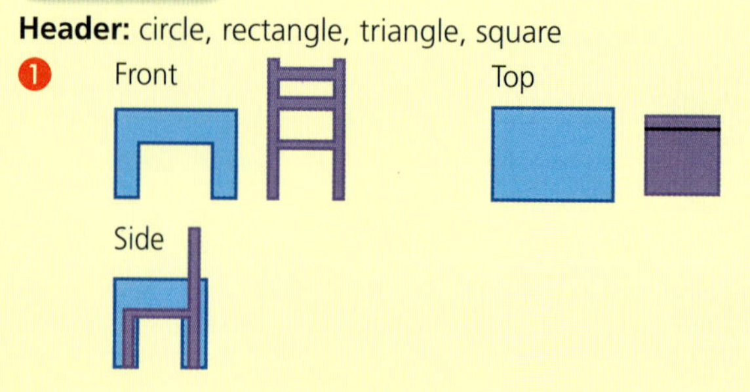

2 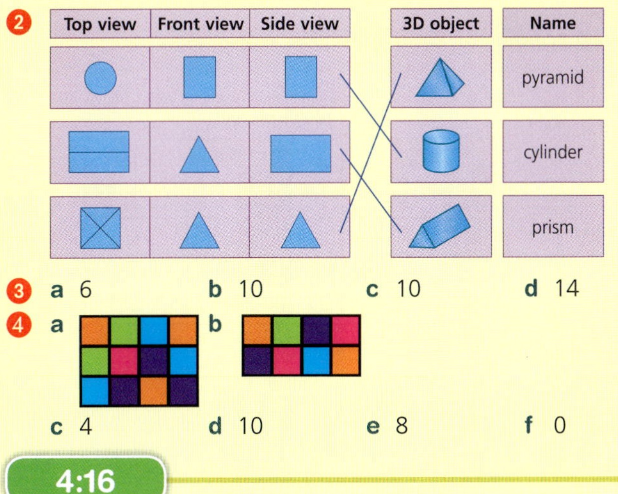

3 a 6 b 10 c 10 d 14

4 a b

c 4 d 10 e 8 f 0

4:16

1 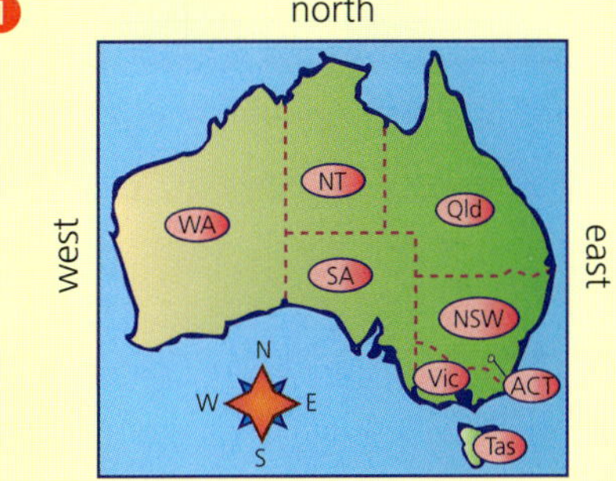

2 a Western Australia b Northern Territory
c South Australia

3 Queensland and New South Wales

4 a Jake's Grave b Bart's Cave c Queen Hill
d Land's End e Bart's Cave f Queen Hill
g Black Rock

5 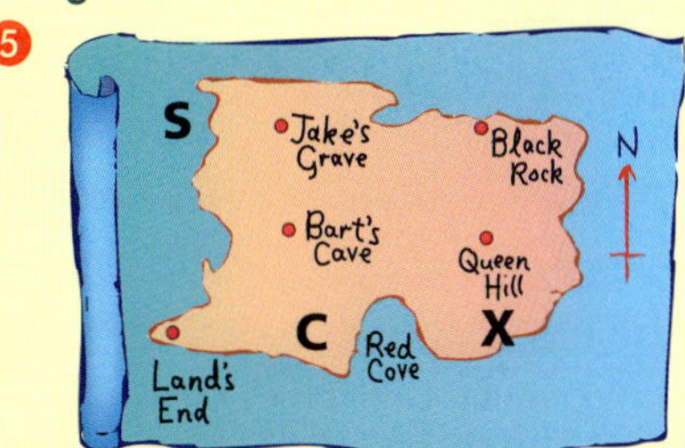

4:17

1 a prism (rectangular) b pyramid (triangular)
c prism (triangular) d pyramid (square or rectangular)
e sphere f cone g cube h cylinder

2 a museum b pool c park d station

3 a A b G c D d A

4 Move 2 units south-east and 1 unit north-east.

4:18

1 a cherries b carrot c apple
d banana e pear f strawberry
g left, middle h right, middle i left, bottom
j left, top k right, top l right, bottom

2 a Ruby b Rex c Tom d Chris
e Sophie f Ethan g Georgia h Oscar

3 a 2, A b 4, C c 2, B d 2, D e 1, B
f 1, A g 5, A h 1, C i 5, D j 5, C
k 3, B l 5, B m 3, A n 4, A

4:19

1 a Mildura b Lakes Entrance c Griffith
d Warrnambool e Horsham f Echuca

2 a column 4, 2nd row b column 4, 3rd row
c column 3, 2nd row d column 3, 2nd row
e column 1, 1st row f column 5, 3rd row
g column 3, 3rd row h column 2, 4th row
i column 4, 1st row and column 5, 1st row
j Echuca k Albury l Mildura

3

4:20

Answers will vary.

1 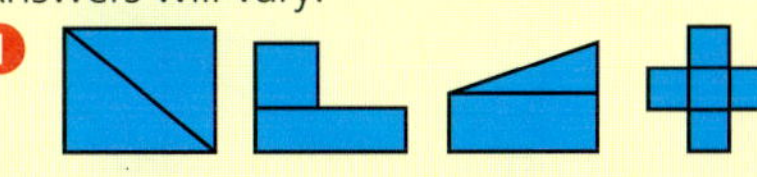

2  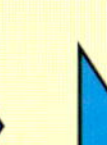  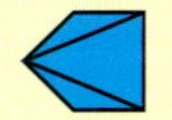 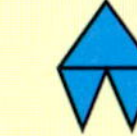

3 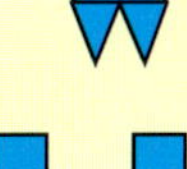 or 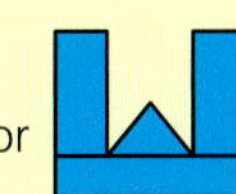

4 All the shapes except the 2nd and 3rd shape in Question 1 will be circled.

Activity: Answers will vary.

4:21

1 a A, B, G, H b C, D, J, K c E, F, I, L

2 a D, C, A b D, G, E c J, H, F
d K, B, L e K, C, G f G, F, L

3 a obtuse b right c acute
d obtuse e obtuse f acute
g acute h right

4 a B and E b B and C, or A and E
c A and D

4:22

1 a acute b straight c right d reflex
e revolution f obtuse g reflex h acute

❷

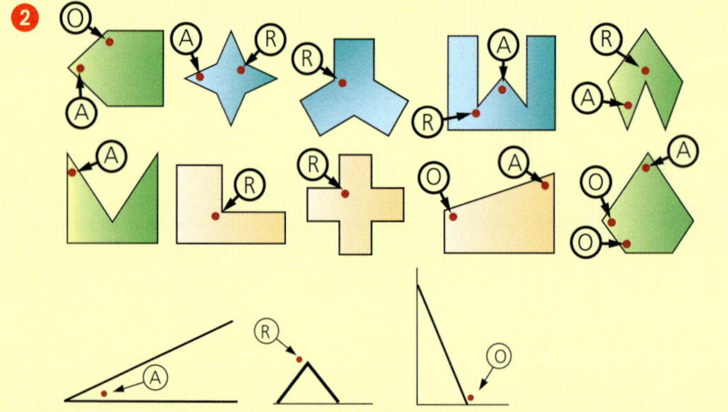

4:23

❶ **a** E, F, G, N, A, J, L, P **b** H, O, D, M **c** B, C, K, I

❷ **a** Triangles are used to make rigid shapes in the structure, making it strong.

b O, D, M **c** P, N, F **d** L, E, G

e Answers will vary, e.g. rows of bricks, train lines.

❸ **a** ABI IKP KLC CJB

b AHGO FHPM DEML DNOJ AJLP EFGN

❹ **a** Yes, if the base is a square; no, if otherwise.

b H, O, F and N

Activity: Answers may vary, e.g. use a spirit level.

4:24

❶

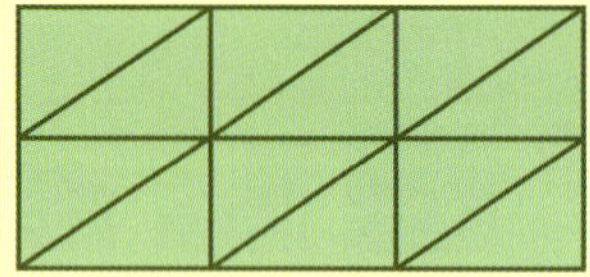

a G **b** H

❷ **a** K **b** L **c** K **d** M

❸ **a** yes

b

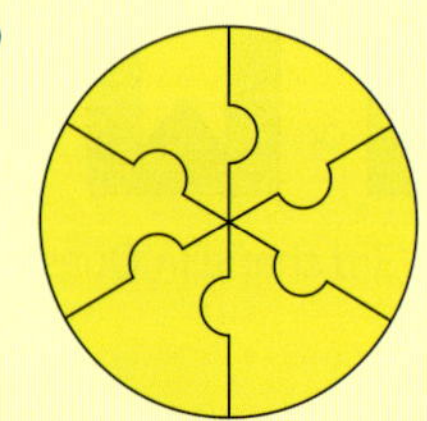

❹–❺ Answers will vary.

4:25

Header: Yes

❶ **a** D, E, F, G, H

b

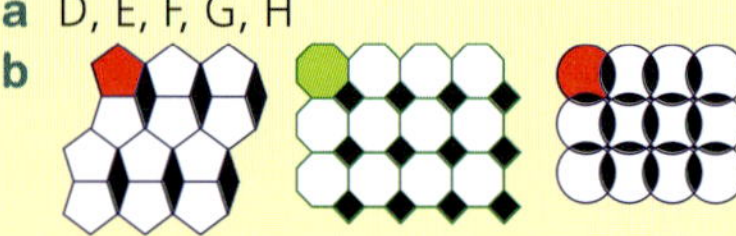

❷ **a** Answers may vary.

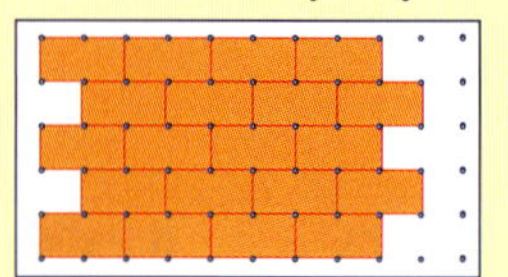

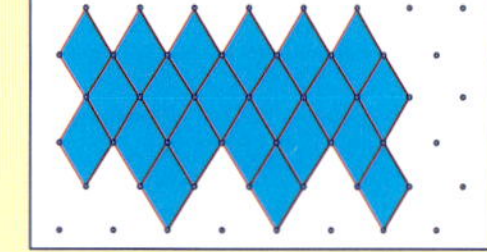

Ten more tiles will be drawn on each.

b yes

4:26

❶ & ❸

× 4 and × 5 tables facts

O	A	B	C	D	E	F	G	H
1	× 4 tables				× 5 tables			
2	1	4	✓		1	5		L
3	2	8			2	10		✓
4	3	12			3	15		
5	4	16			4	20		
6	5	20			5	25		
7	6	24	M	✓	6	30		
8	7	28			7	35		
9	8	32			8	40		
10	9	36			9	45	✓	
11	10	40			10	50		
12	11	44			11	55		
13	12	48			12	60		
14	✓	Test results		K		Test results		
15	Susan	8	11		Susan	10	12	
16	Alan	7	10		Alan	12	12	

❷ **a** 28 **b** 15 **c** 10 **d** 10 **e** 8

❹ **a** 5 **b** 12 **c** Yong **d** F5 **e** A1

4:27

❶ yes, yes

❷ Two models, with two views each, will be drawn.

5:01

❶

Buttons			
	Red	Blue	Green
Large	5	8	6
Small	7	9	11

❷

Buttons		
Red	Blue	Green
12	17	17

❸

Buttons	
Large	19
Small	27

❹ Graphs may vary.

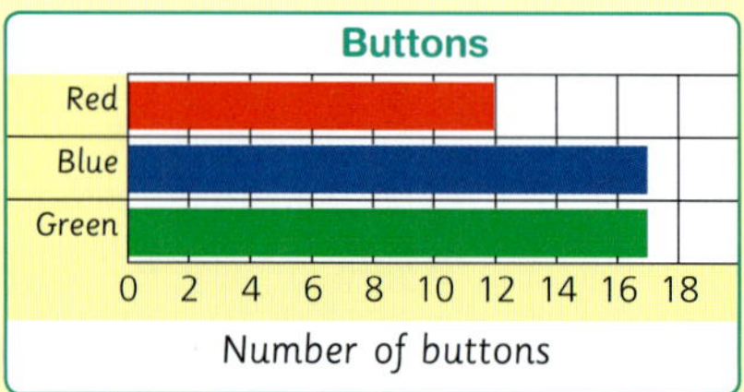

❺ Answers will vary.

❻

Number of times thrown					
⚀	⚁	⚂	⚃	⚄	⚅
4	4	4	3	3	3

 • *AUSTRALIAN SIGNPOST MATHS NSW 4* • ISBN 9780655709053

5:02

1. **a** red **b** yes **c** no **d** 3 **e** 3
2. red, blue, yellow
   a red **b** yellow **c** red **d** impossible **e** 4
   f 3 **g** 1
3. Answers may vary.
4. Answers may vary.

Activity: 25

5:03

1. E A B D C
2. **a** Alf and Emma **b** Alan and Mia
   c Rachel and Aria **d** yes
3. **a** impossible **b** not likely **c** certain
   d very likely **e** certain

5:04

1. **a** 13 **b** Saturday **c** Thursday
   d 20 **e** 97
   f Answers may vary; possibly because the family was at home more because there was no school or work.
2. 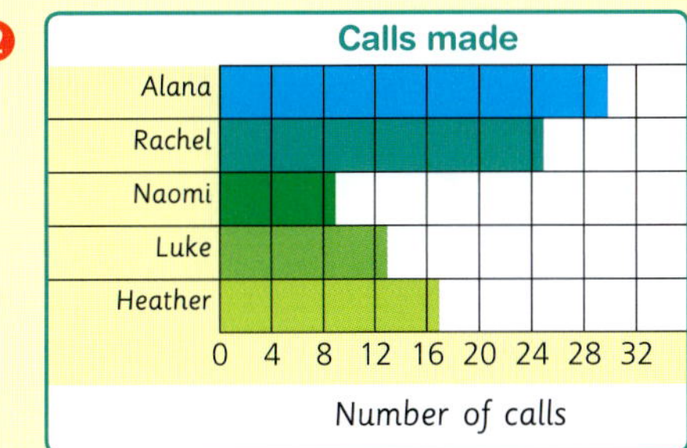

3. 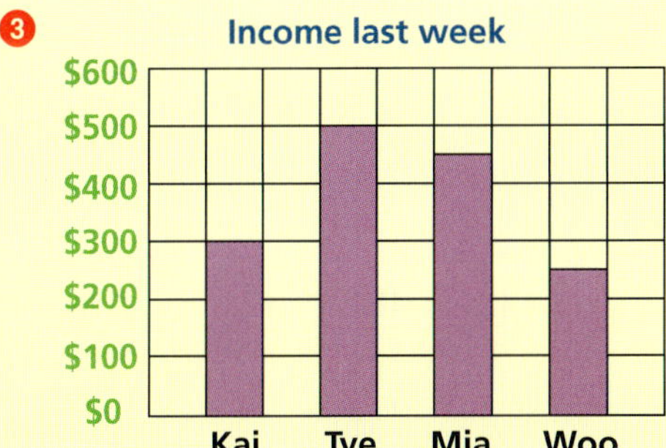

4. 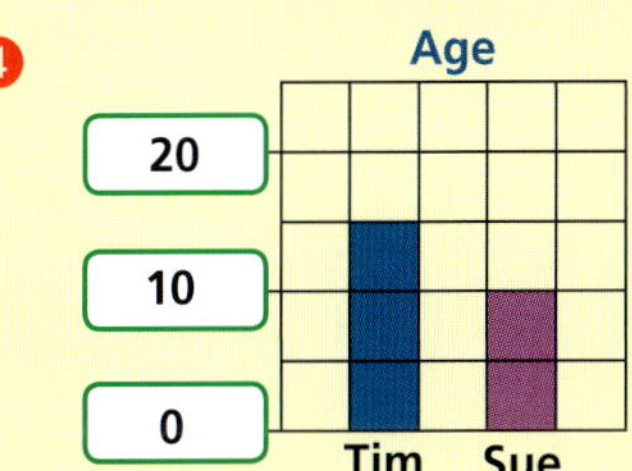

5:05

1. **a i** 16 **ii** 6 **iii** 0
   b 14 **c** 32 **d** 132 **e** class discussion
2. **a** tennis **b** 36 **c** 32 **d** 116

5:06

1. **a** unlikely **b** impossible **c** very likely
   d certain **e** impossible **f** even chance
2. **a** two yellow **b** two blue **c** a blue and a yellow
3. **a** B and E **b** C and F **c** A and D
4. **a** no **b** 2 heads, 2 tails or a head and a tail

Investigation: head and tail are equally likely

5:07

1. **a** 20 **b i** $\frac{9}{20}$ **ii** $\frac{11}{20}$
2. even chance
3. **a** likely **b** unlikely **c** impossible
   d very unlikely **e** very unlikely
4. **a** Jack, Emma, Luke
   Emma can win with (1, 5), (2, 4), (3, 3), (4, 1), and (5, 1).
   Luke can win with (1, 1), (1, 3), (2, 2) and (3, 1).
   b Jack

5:08

1. **a**

Sport	Tally	Total
Tennis	卌 卌 卌 卌 卌 卌 卌 卌 卌	45
Athletics	卌 卌 卌 卌 卌 卌 卌	35
Swimming	卌 卌 卌 卌 卌 卌 卌 卌 III	43
Hockey	卌 卌 卌 卌 卌 III	28
Basketball	卌 卌 卌 卌 卌 卌 卌 III	38
Cricket	卌 卌 卌 卌 卌 卌 卌 卌 II	42
Football	卌 卌 卌 卌 卌 卌 卌 卌 卌 I	46
Other	卌 卌 卌 卌 IIII	24

   b football **c** 8 **d** 80
   e squash, netball, baseball, T-ball etc. (Two will be named.)

5:09

Answers will vary.

5:10

1. **a–g** Answers will vary.
   h Yes, the more trials, the more accurate the result.
   i A, B, C, D, E

5:11

1. **a** E **b** D **c** C **d** A **e** B
2. E, A, C, B, D
3. **a** D, C, B, A, E **b** B, D, C, E, A **c** E, D, A, B, C
4. Answers will vary.

5:12

1

Abbie's survey

Children in families

Category	Tally	Number
1 child	𝍸 I	6
2 children	𝍸 𝍸	10
3 children	𝍸 II	7
4 children	III	3
5 children	II	2
6 children		0
more than 6	I	1

This data should be entered into a spreadsheet and a horizontal column graph should be created.

2 A survey should be conducted and the table completed.

5:13

1 **a** 30 **b** Tuesday **c** 100 **d** 100
e Answers will vary. The shop may have been closed on Thursday. **f** 10

2 **a** car **b** 100 **c** Approximately 200 students
d no
e

Key: 🧍 = 10 students	
Bus	🧍 🧍 🧍
Walk	🧍 🧍 🧍 🧍 🧍 🧍
Car	🧍 🧍 🧍 🧍 🧍 🧍 🧍
Bike	🧍 🧍 🧍 🧍

f Answers will vary. It is quicker to draw and count the number of students.

3 Answers will vary.

5:14

1 **a** unlikely **b** equally likely
c likely **d** yes

2 Answers will vary.
a 5 is most likely of the possible outcomes.
b Answers will vary. Each time a counter is drawn there is an even chance of drawing red, so in ten draws there should be about 5 red.
c–d Answers will vary.

4 **a** E **b** E **c** E

5:15

Answers will vary.

5:16

1 **a** heads
b No, the results will vary each time the experiment is completed. There is an even chance that heads or tails will be tossed on each throw.

2 **a** 5 **b** Answers will vary.
c They are equally likely. **d** yes
e The more often an experiment is completed, the more likely the percentages will reflect the expected pattern.

3 **a** 1 head and 1 tail
b–e Answers will vary.
f 2 heads and 2 tails have the same chance of occurring. 1 head and 1 tail is likely to occur twice as often as 2 heads or 2 tails.

ES 1

1 **a**

+	
2 + 6	1
4 + 6	7
0 + 1	8
5 + 7	9
5 + 6	10
0 + 7	11
4 + 5	12
7 + 10	15
8 + 7	17
10 + 10	18
9 + 9	20

b

+	
2 + 3	4
4 + 3	5
2 + 2	7
5 + 4	9
8 + 5	8
8 + 0	10
7 + 5	11
1 + 9	12
10 + 5	13
6 + 5	15
10 + 9	19

c

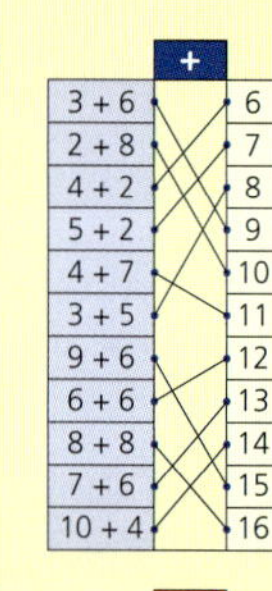

d

+	
3 + 4	5
6 + 2	6
4 + 5	7
3 + 2	8
2 + 4	9
8 + 4	10
4 + 9	11
5 + 5	12
4 + 7	13
7 + 8	14
5 + 9	15

e

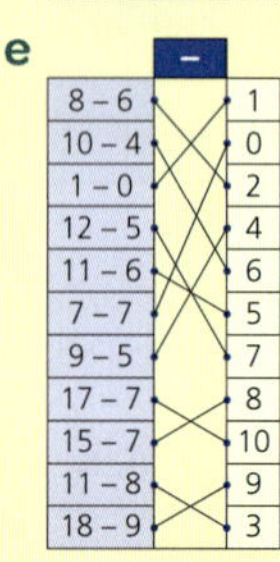

f

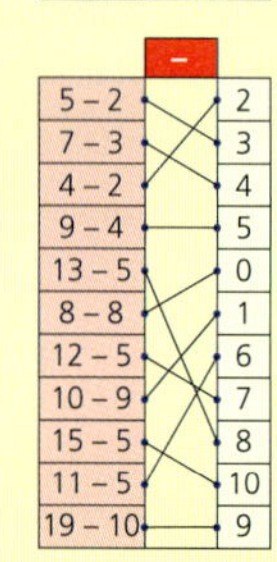

g

−	
6 − 4	0
5 − 2	1
10 − 9	2
7 − 7	3
9 − 3	4
7 − 3	5
10 − 3	6
14 − 5	7
9 − 4	8
18 − 8	9
10 − 2	10

h

−	
6 − 5	0
9 − 9	1
6 − 3	2
8 − 6	3
8 − 4	4
16 − 9	5
9 − 4	6
16 − 7	7
17 − 7	8
10 − 4	9
17 − 9	10

ES 2

1 **a** 7 + 5 = 7 + 3 + 2 = 12 **b** 12 **c** 26 **d** 27
e 21 **f** 27 **g** 22 **h** 21 **i** 24 **j** 23
k 26 **l** 25 **m** 28 **n** 23 **o** 23

2 **a** 29 + 5 = 29 + 1 + 4 = 34 **b** 32 **c** 31 **d** 35
e 32 **f** 30 **g** 33 **h** 43 **i** 44 **j** 43
k 41 **l** 45 **m** 42 **n** 42 **o** 42

3 **a** 48 + 4 = 48 + 2 + 2 = 52 **b** 52 **c** 55 **d** 53
e 53 **f** 51 **g** 53 **h** 61 **i** 62 **j** 61
k 62 **l** 63 **m** 62 **n** 63 **o** 63

ES 3

Answers will vary.

ES 4

1 a flip b slide c flip d turn e slide
f flip g turn h flip i slide j turn
k a, c, f and h are symmetrical.

2

a flip

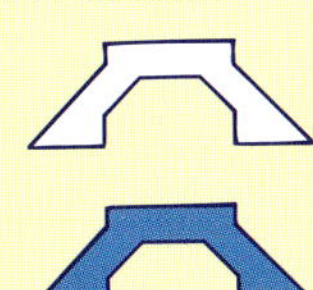

b slide

c turn

ES 5

1 a $0.78 b $1.52 c $4.73
d $5.31 e $6.69 f $8.25
g $4.70 h $8.51 i $6.43
j $7.11 k $6.08 l $6.97
m $5.40 n $6.29 o $7.14

2 a $3.79 b $5.77 c $5.68
d $8.68 e $6.49 f $8.48

3 a $9.55 b $8.20 c $8.85
d $8.70

4 a $4.88 b $8.83 c $9.37 d $9.01

ES 6

1 a 5468 b 8975 c 7588 d 3798 e 7967
f 6324 g 8600 h 7251 i 3573 j 8240

2 a 7195 b 4885 c 4343 d 8925
e 8019 f 7505 g 9281 h 4339
i 7617 j 7932

3 a $9149 b $8291 c $7909
d $6297 e $9430

ES 7

1 a 7561 b 6935 c 9818 d 7482

2 a 3904 b 5108 c 7837 d 7088

3 a $86.14 b $52.53 c $90.10 d $86.80

4 a your estimate, 5495 b your estimate, 8456
c your estimate, $8273

ES 8

Header: 800 000

1 a 61 500 b 47 121 c 65 750 d 80 803
e 270 050 f 412 230 g 734 981 h 622 100

2 a 48 655 b 117 980 c 100 650 d 96 935
e 887 450 f 441 610 g 734 412 h 912 000

3 a 515 634 b 198 217 c 801 702

4 Answers will vary.
a about 17 500 b about 35 000
c about 32 500

ES 9

1 a $5.22 b $5.17 c $6.34
d $2.39 e $4.17 f $1.84
g $2.77 h $6.08 i $3.34
j $4.08 k $1.70 l $2.58
m $3.89 n $5.45 o $2.04

2 a $2.11 b $4.98 c $5.35
d $0.05 e $5.50 f $1.51

3 a $1.05 b $6.20 c $5.45
d $1.20 e $3.55 f $4.95

ES 10

1 a 4353 b 7100 c 5420 d 8000 e 6213
f 6070 g 442 h 5320 i 6303 j 1824

2 a 2776 b 1193 c 706 d 6990 e 3068
f 369 g 2278 h 1602 i 6749 j 3489

3 a 1875 b 6195 c $3659

4 909

ES 11

1 a 564 b 1699 c 103 d 2275
e 5168 f 1140 g 1100 h 4573

2 a 4550 b 3012 c 775 d 1645
e 2814 f 1305 g 28 h 6633

3 a 3320 km b 1675 m c 3658 m
d 88 years old e 91 years old

ES 12

1 a 47 180 b 53 630 c 42 676 d 24 359
e 15 000 f 24 338 g 55 904 h 21 863

2 a 165 945 b 327 169 c 539 783 d 773 616
e 484 473 f 365 000 g 451 431

3 a $75 100 b $298 075 c 75 000 m²
d 27 000 apples e 215 500

ES 13

1 a Friday b 3rd c 25th d four
e five f Tuesday g 29 h 28

2 a 2nd b 6th c 26th d 14th

3 a Thursday b Friday c Saturday d Monday

4 a 5th and 6th b 12th and 13th
c 19th and 20th d 2nd, 9th, 16th and 23rd

ES 14

1. a January b October c May d September
2. a 30 b 31 c 31 d 31
3. a 5th b 1st
4. a 19th September b 25th September
5. a Friday b Friday c Saturday d Friday e Thursday f Thursday
6. a 1 week 6 days b 6 weeks c 11 weeks 5 days d 23 weeks 5 days
7. a 14 weeks 4 days b 11 weeks

ES 15

1. 7
2. 29 days
3. 11
4. a Paris b Istanbul c Dubai d Rome
5. a 4 b 3 c 2 d 2
6. a London b Paris c Istanbul d Dubai
7. 1 day 8 hours 30 minutes
8. Answers will vary.

ES 16

1. a Yes b Yes c Yes
2. 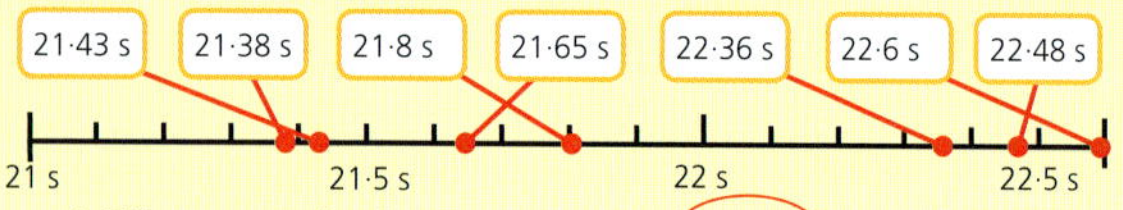

3. a 4·75, 4·70 b 31·46, 30·40 c 39·74, 40·06 d 59·60, 59·50
   e 29·56, 29·83 f 19·14, 26·99 g 36·43, 27·86 h 19·63, 19·62
4. Answers will vary.

ES 17

1. 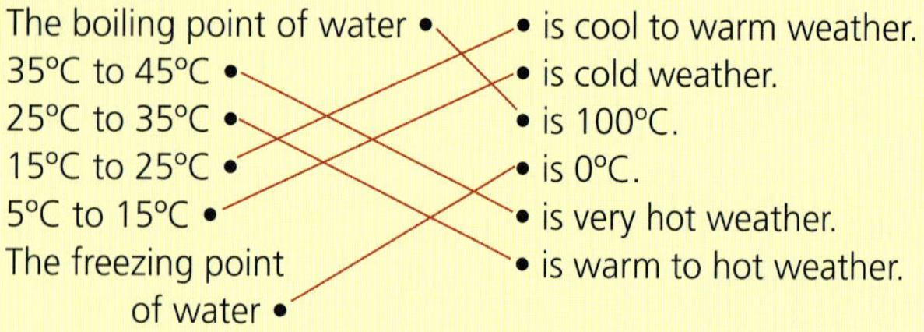

2. a 10°C b 90°C c 5°C d 40°C e 80°C f 15°C g 45°C h 95°C
3. a b, e, h b a, c, f c d, g

ES 18

1. a 25°C b 0°C c 18°C d 58°C e 86°C f 37°C g 41°C h 73°C
2. a 40°C b 28°C c 36°C d 14°C

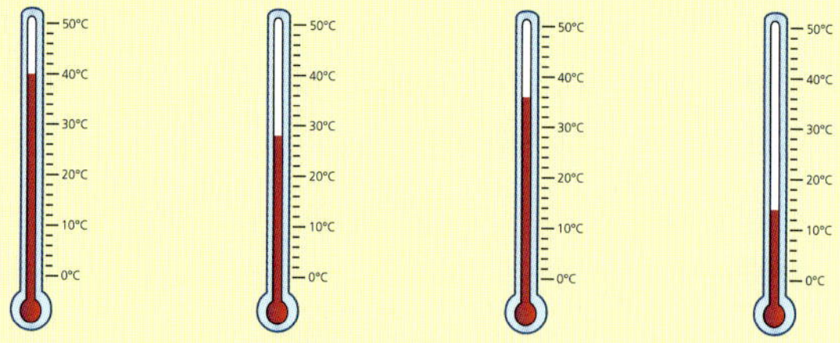

e 8°C f 33°C g 27°C h 15°C

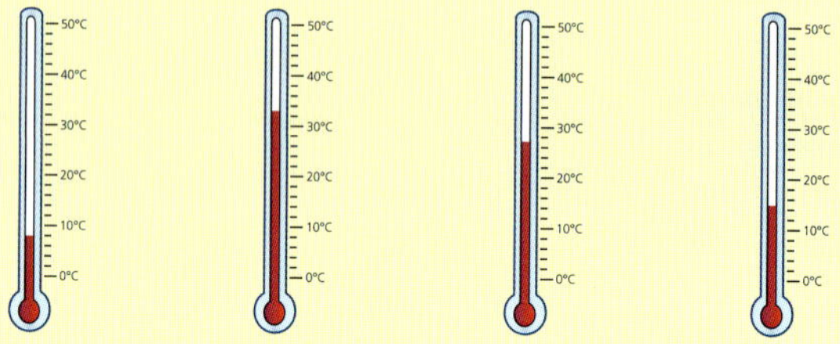

3. a 2°C b 40°C c 26°C d 70°C e 96°C f 9°C g 100°C h 37°C i 67°C j 17°C

ES 19

1. a $0, \frac{1}{2}, 1, 2$. Rule: Add $\frac{1}{2}$.
   b $0, \frac{1}{4}, \frac{2}{4}$ (or $\frac{1}{2}$), $\frac{3}{4}$, 1. Rule: Add $\frac{1}{4}$.
   c $0, \frac{1}{3}, \frac{2}{3}, 1, 1\frac{1}{3}, 1\frac{2}{3}, 2, 2\frac{1}{3}, 2\frac{2}{3}, 3, 3\frac{1}{3}$. Rule: Add $\frac{1}{3}$.
   d $0, \frac{1}{8}, \frac{2}{8}$ (or $\frac{1}{4}$), $\frac{3}{8}, \frac{4}{8}$ (or $\frac{1}{2}$), $\frac{5}{8}, \frac{6}{8}$ (or $\frac{3}{4}$), $\frac{7}{8}, 1, 1\frac{1}{8}, 1\frac{2}{8}$.
   Rule: Subtract $\frac{1}{8}$.
   e $0, \frac{1}{5}, \frac{2}{5}, \frac{3}{5}, \frac{4}{5}$, 1 (or $\frac{5}{5}$), $1\frac{1}{5}, 1\frac{2}{5}, 1\frac{3}{5}, 1\frac{4}{5}, 2$.
   Rule: Add $\frac{1}{5}$.
   f $0, \frac{1}{6}, \frac{2}{6}$ (or $\frac{1}{3}$), $\frac{3}{6}$ (or $\frac{1}{2}$), $\frac{4}{6}$ (or $\frac{2}{3}$), $\frac{5}{6}$, 1 (or $\frac{6}{6}$), $1\frac{2}{6}, 1\frac{3}{6}, 1\frac{4}{6}$.
   Rule: Subtract $\frac{1}{6}$.

 • AUSTRALIAN SIGNPOST MATHS NSW 4 • ISBN 9780655709053